Labor and the Class Idea in the United States and Canada

Why are unions weaker in the United States than in Canada, despite the two countries' socioeconomic similarities? Many view this crossborder distinction as a by-product of longstanding differences in political cultures and institutions. However, using detailed archival and statistical data, Barry Eidlin finds that this divergence is relatively recent, the result of different ruling-party responses to working-class upsurge in both countries during the Great Depression and World War II. In Canada, a hostile state response led to labor being incorporated as a class representative. In the United States, a co-optive state response led to labor being incorporated as an interest group. This embedded the "class idea" – the idea of class as a salient, legitimate political category – more deeply in Canadian policies, institutions, and practices than in the United States. Eidlin illustrates this through comparative studies of party–class relations, the effects of postwar Red Scares, and labor policy divergence. In each case, different patterns of political incorporation enabled or constrained labor's legitimacy and organizational capacity in different ways. Canadian labor's role as a class representative legitimized it and expanded its organizational capacity, while US labor's role as an interest group delegitimized it and undermined its organizational capacity. As a result, union density remained more stable in Canada, but collapsed in the United States.

Barry Eidlin is Assistant Professor of Sociology at McGill University. He is a comparative historical sociologist interested in the study of class, politics, social movements, and institutional change. His research has been published in the *American Sociological Review*, *Politics & Society*, *Sociology Compass*, and *Labor History*, among other venues. He also comments regularly in various media outlets on labor politics and policy.

Cambridge Studies in Contentious Politics

General Editor

Doug McAdam, *Stanford University and Center for Advanced Study in the Behavioral Sciences*

Editors

Mark Beissinger, *Princeton University*
Donatella della Porta, *Scuola Normale Superiore*
Jack A. Goldstone, *George Mason University*
Michael Hanagan, *Vassar College*
Holly J. McCammon, *Vanderbilt University*
David S. Meyer, *University of California, Irvine*
Sarah Soule, *Stanford University*
Suzanne Staggenborg, *University of Pittsburgh*
Sidney Tarrow, *Cornell University*
Charles Tilly (d. 2008), *Columbia University*
Elisabeth J. Wood, *Yale University*
Deborah Yashar, *Princeton University*

Books in the Series

Rina Agarwala, *Informal Labor, Formal Politics, and Dignified Discontent in India*
Ronald Aminzade, *Race, Nation, and Citizenship in Post-Colonial Africa: The Case of Tanzania*
Ronald Aminzade et al., *Silence and Voice in the Study of Contentious Politics*
Javier Auyero, *Routine Politics and Violence in Argentina: The Gray Zone of State Power*
Phillip M. Ayoub, *When States Come Out: Europe's Sexual Minorities and the Politics of Visibility*
Amrita Basu, *Violent Conjunctures in Democratic India*
W. Lance Bennett and Alexandra Segerberg, *The Logic of Connective Action: Digital Media and the Personalization of Contentious Politics*
Nancy Bermeo and Deborah J. Yashar, *Parties, Movements, and Democracy in the Developing World*
Clifford Bob, *The Global Right Wing and the Clash of World Politics*
Clifford Bob, *The Marketing of Rebellion: Insurgents, Media, and International Activism*
Charles Brockett, *Political Movements and Violence in Central America*
Marisa von Bülow, *Building Transnational Networks: Civil Society and the Politics of Trade in the Americas*
Valerie Bunce and Sharon Wolchik, *Defeating String-Nameitarian Leaders in Postcommunist Countries*
Lars-Erik Cederman, Kristian Skrede Gleditsch, and Halvard Buhaug, *Inequality, Grievances, and Civil War*

(continued after index)

Labor and the Class Idea in the United States and Canada

BARRY EIDLIN
McGill University

CAMBRIDGE
UNIVERSITY PRESS

CAMBRIDGE
UNIVERSITY PRESS

University Printing House, Cambridge CB2 8BS, United Kingdom

One Liberty Plaza, 20th Floor, New York, NY 10006, USA

477 Williamstown Road, Port Melbourne, VIC 3207, Australia

314–321, 3rd Floor, Plot 3, Splendor Forum, Jasola District Centre,
New Delhi – 110025, India

79 Anson Road, #06–04/06, Singapore 079906

Cambridge University Press is part of the University of Cambridge.

It furthers the University's mission by disseminating knowledge in the pursuit of education, learning, and research at the highest international levels of excellence.

www.cambridge.org
Information on this title: www.cambridge.org/9781107106703
DOI: 10.1017/9781316227183

© Cambridge University Press 2018

This publication is in copyright. Subject to statutory exception and to the provisions of relevant collective licensing agreements, no reproduction of any part may take place without the written permission of Cambridge University Press.

First published 2018

Printed in the United States of America by Sheridan Books, Inc.

A catalogue record for this publication is available from the British Library.

Library of Congress Cataloging-in-Publication Data
Names: Eidlin, Barry, author.
TITLE: Labor and the class idea in the United States and Canada / Barry Eidlin, McGill University, Montreal.
DESCRIPTION: Cambridge, United Kingdom ; New York, NY : Cambridge University Press, 2018. | Series: Cambridge Studies in contentious politics | Includes bibliographical references.
IDENTIFIERS: LCCN 2017048764| ISBN 9781107106703 (hardback) | ISBN 9781107514416 (paperback)
SUBJECTS: LCSH: Labor movement – United States. | Labor movement – Canada. | Labor policy – United States. | Labor policy – Canada. | Labor – United States. | Labor – Canada.
CLASSIFICATION: LCC HD8072.5 .E379 2018 | DDC 322/.20973–dc23
LC record available at https://lccn.loc.gov/2017048764

ISBN 978-1-107-10670-3 Hardback
ISBN 978-1-107-51441-6 Paperback

Cambridge University Press has no responsibility for the persistence or accuracy of URLs for external or third-party internet websites referred to in this publication and does not guarantee that any content on such websites is, or will remain, accurate or appropriate.

In memory of my parents,
Anne Eidlin (1939–2012)
and
Fred Eidlin (1942–2016)

Contents

List of Figures	page ix
List of Maps	xii
List of Tables	xiii
Acknowledgments	xiv
List of Abbreviations	xx
Introduction	1
PART I EXPLAINING UNION DENSITY DIVERGENCE	**29**
1 Structural and Individual Explanations	31
2 Policy Explanations	51
3 Working Class Power in the United States and Canada	106
Part 1 – Summing Up	153
PART II POLITICAL ARTICULATION AND THE CLASS IDEA	**157**
4 Party–Class Alliances in the United States and Canada, 1932–1948	159
5 Repression and Rebirth: Red Scares and Labor's Postwar Identity, 1946–1972	191
6 Class versus Special Interest: Labor Regimes and Density Divergence, 1911–2016	221
Conclusion	256
Appendix A: Data	272
Appendix B: Archival Sources	295

Appendix C: Permissions 296
Bibliography 297
Index 343

Figures

0.1	Union density, United States and Canada, 1911–2016	page 6
0.2	Income shares of the top 1 percent in the United States, Canada, and selected industrialized countries, 1913–2015	7
1.1	Service sector shares of total nonfarm employment in the United States and Canada, 1931–2016	33
1.2	Public sector union density in the United States and Canada, 1961–2016	34
1.3	Private sector union density in the United States and Canada, 1961–2016	35
1.4	Public sector shares of total nonfarm employment in the United States and Canada, 1961–2016	37
1.5	Percentage of all nonfarm employment in the manufacturing sector in the United States, and percentage of all US union members who work in the manufacturing sector, 1956–2016	42
1.6	Percent of the adult population who approve of unions in the United States and Canada, 1936–2016	45
2.1	Imports plus exports as a percentage of gross domestic product in Canada and the United States, and the US share of Canadian balance of international payments, 1950–2014	58
2.2	Ratio of Canadian to US private sector union density, and Canadian to US dollar exchange rate, 1961–2016	59
2.3	Private sector union density and trade policy, United States and Canada, 1961–2016	60

2.4	Number of US NLRB representation elections held and number of elections won by unions, 1936–2016	67
2.5	Number of employees eligible to vote in US NLRB representation elections, 1936–2016	68
2.6	Union win rate in US NLRB representation elections, 1936–2016	69
2.7	Number of Ontario LRB certification applications disposed of and granted, 1949–2015	70
2.8	Number of covered employees in successful Ontario LRB certification applications, 1956–2015	72
2.9	Ontario LRB union win rate, 1949–2015	73
2.10	Number of US NLRB unfair labor practice charges filed and ratio of ULPs to representation elections, 1937–2016	75
2.11	Number of Ontario LRB unfair labor practice charges filed and ratio of ULPs to certification applications, 1976–2015	76
2.12	Success rate of US private sector first contract negotiations after two fiscal years, 1996–2004	79
2.13	US union density in actual right-to-work states and non-right-to-work states, 1939–2016	88
2.14	US union density in all possible right-to-work and never-right-to-work states, 1939–2016	89
2.15	Strikers as a percentage of nonfarm employment in the United States and Canada, 1911–2016 (five-year moving average)	100
2.16	Number of person-days lost to strikes per nonfarm employee in the United States and Canada, 1911–2016 (five-year moving average)	101
2.17	Percentage-point difference between union density and strikers as a percentage of nonfarm employment in the United States and Canada, 1911–2016	103
3.1	Pooled results of highest scores of selected measures from the World Values Survey for the United States and Canada	118
3.2	Pooled results of lowest scores of selected measures from the World Values Survey for the United States and Canada	118
3.3	Pooled results to the question "How should business and industry be managed?" from the World Values Survey for the United States and Canada	119
3.4	Union density, United States and Canada, 1911–1934	123
3.5	Year-to-year percentage change in nonfarm employment in the United States and Canada, 1922–1937	124

3.6 Year-to-year percentage change in union membership in the United States and Canada, 1922–1935   124

4.1 Independent left third party (ILTP) vote shares in the United States and Canada, 1867–2009 (six-year moving average)   162

Maps

1.1 Union density by state/province in 2016 and increase in number of people employed from 1939 to 2016   *page* 40
2.1 US states' right-to-work status, 2017   83
2.2 US states' and Canadian provinces' percentage-point change in union density from 1939 to 2016, 2017 right-to-work status, and indication of increase/decrease in union density from 1939 to 2016   86

Tables

0.1	Differences in organizing logics	page 17
1.1	Voting intentions of nonunion and union employees in the United States and Canada, 1994–1995	45
1.2	Voting intentions of nonunion and union employees in the United States and Canada, 1996	46
6.1	Differences in organizing logics	223
A.1	Union density, United States and Canada, aggregate and public vs. private, 1911–2016	277
A.2	US union density organized by state (including right-to-work status), 1939–2016 (%, ordered by 2016 rank)	280
A.3	Canadian union density by region, selected years, 1941–2016 (%)	283
A.4	Service sector employment as share of nonfarm employment, United States and Canada, 1931–2016	284
A.5	Number of workers involved in strikes, United States and Canada, total, as percentage of nonagricultural workforce, and person-days idle due to strikes, 1911–2016 (selected years)	289
A.6	Comparison of US and Canadian values	291
A.7	List of sources for votes cast in Canadian federal and provincial elections, 1867–2009	293
A.8	List of Canadian left-wing third parties	294

Acknowledgments

Although it is a well-worn cliché to say that books are collaborative efforts, this in no way makes it any less true. It certainly applies in the case of this book.

The manuscript started off as my dissertation, which I wrote in the sociology department at the University of California, Berkeley. There I was fortunate to receive guidance from a brilliant group of advisors. Kim Voss was there from the start, providing a healthy mix of sharp criticism and empathic support as I worked my inchoate musings into a discernible argument, and ultimately this book manuscript. Dylan Riley exposed me to the world of comparative historical sociology in his seminar and ever since has played a central role in helping me to understand what my project is really about. Neil Fligstein was incredibly generous with his time, offering ideas and strategic advice over many a coffee. Margaret Weir and Paul Pierson both helped me grapple with central problems of political power, state institutions, and American political development.

Beyond my formal advisors, many other scholars have played important roles in shaping this project over time. Julia Adams, Maria Akchurin, Jason Beckfield, Daniel Béland, Fred Block, Chris Brooks, David Camfield, Elisabeth Clemens, Dorothy Sue Cobble, Cedric de Leon, Ivan Ermakoff, Janice Fine, Chad Goldberg, Jason Kaufman, Howard Kimeldorf, Richard Lachmann, Matthew Lange, Mara Loveman, Michael McCarthy, Erin McDonnell, Jim Naylor, Ann Orloff, Josh Pacewicz, Dan Slater, Adam Slez, Cihan Tuğal, Micah Uetricht, Nick Wilson, and Erik Olin Wright all read and commented on parts of the manuscript. Four anonymous reviewers provided detailed, constructive criticisms, which dramatically improved the quality of the manuscript.

Acknowledgments

Robin Archer, Eileen Boris, David Brady, Robert Brenner, Kate Bronfenbrenner, Peter Bruce, Nick Carnes, Tony Chen, Victor Tan Chen, Vivek Chibber, Dan Clawson, Marc Dixon, Cybelle Fox, Katy Fox-Hodess, Michael Goldfield, John A. Hall, Heather Haveman, Jeff Haydu, Chris Howell, Shannon Ikebe, Kristen Gray Jafflin, Jerome Karabel, Jasmine Kerrissey, Jennifer Klein, Brian Lande, Margaret Levi, Nelson Lichtenstein, Stephanie Luce, James Mahoney, Antonia Maioni, Damon Mayrl, Ben Moodie, Chris Rhomberg, Ian Robinson, Joel Rogers, Jake Rosenfeld, Michael Schwartz, Gay Seidman, Judy Stepan-Norris, George Strauss, Chris Tilly, Axel van den Berg, and Suzi Weissman all lent their insights and observations at critical points in the project. Sylvia Allegretto, John-Paul Ferguson, Pablo Gaston, Barry Hirsch, Felice Martinello, Suresh Naidu, Jake Rosenfeld, Adam Slez, Sara Slinn, and Jon Stiles were my heroes when it came to compiling and parsing statistical data on labor unions and political parties. Kevan Harris delivered some clutch archival data collection related to the 1932 US presidential campaign, in addition to providing a helpful sounding board. Kristi McClamroch did a fantastic job with the figures and maps, and Felix Fuchs did likewise for the cover art.

Three friends and colleagues deserve special mention. First, after several months of frustration after returning from my archival research in 2009, I had the good fortune of running into Suresh Naidu again, several years after we first met at the UC Berkeley Institute for Research on Labor and Employment (IRLE). Our long discussions while negotiating LA traffic or working in Pasadena coffee shops refreshed and refocused my thinking. They played a key role in reframing the project and moving it forward. Second, I must offer a special note of thanks to Nick Wilson. We entered the UC Berkeley PhD program together, went through the entire program together as fellow comparative historical sociologists, and finished together. For much of that time, we shared an office at IRLE. Through personal, intellectual, and academic ups and downs, Nick has been a steadfast friend, ruthless critic, and intellectual sparring partner. Third, Cedric de Leon saw promise in my work when he put an early draft of what is now Chapter 4 on a panel for the 2010 American Sociological Association meeting in Atlanta. He introduced me to the sociology of political parties and helped me develop the political articulation model that provides the theoretical framework for this book.

One of the most humbling parts of this entire project was coming to grips with just how much I had to learn about Canadian labor and politics, despite being born and raised in Canada. In order to make my way through the scholarship and develop even a modicum of expertise, I had to rely on the kindness and generosity of an amazing network of Canadian scholars of labo(u)r and politics. Even prior to beginning my graduate training, I turned to David Camfield for perceptive analysis of politics and current events. As my project developed, he was always willing to offer comments, criticisms, and reassurance. When I was first planning the Canadian portion of my research travels, I reached out to Gregor Murray and Charlotte Yates. Both were beyond helpful in sharing their own knowledge and expertise, as well as in connecting me with other Canadian scholars and providing me institutional home bases at the Inter-University Centre for Research on Globalization and Work (CRIMT)/ University of Montreal and the Labour Studies Department at McMaster University, respectively. Through Charlotte I met Rianne Mahon. She and her husband Rob Ryan opened their home in Ottawa to me as I spent the winter of 2008–2009 digging through materials at Library and Archives Canada. Although that winter was one of the coldest on record, and quite a shock after several years of balmy Bay Area winters, their warmth and hospitality more than made up for the frigid temperatures. At the same time, their knowledge of Canadian labor and politics made for fascinating dinner table discussion. Further discussions with Elaine Bernard, Thomas Collombat, Tony Giles, Sam Gindin, Mona-Josée Gagnon, Bob Hebdon, Rob Hickey, Pradeep Kumar, Felice Martinello, David McNally, Jim Naylor, Bryan Palmer, Leo Panitch, Craig Riddell, Herman Rosenfeld, Stephanie Ross, Jacques Rouillard, Chris Schenk, Sara Slinn, Charles Smith, Donald Swartz, and Don Wells expanded my thinking and sharpened my analysis. I owe a special debt of gratitude to Harry Arthurs, who inadvertently helped me come up with the title of this book and its central concept of the "class idea" as a result of a casual remark during a meeting we had in a Cabbagetown coffee shop.

While nobody would mistake what appears in the following pages as anything other than an academic study, the central problems I address emerged out of my previous life as a full-time union organizer. Most of those years were spent with Teamsters for a Democratic Union (TDU), the rank-and-file reform movement inside the Teamsters Union. In those formative years, I developed what I consider to be an extended political family, which shaped my thinking and pointed me toward the key questions to ask. Above all I must thank TDU National Organizer Ken Paff for somehow having faith that an awkward, idealistic college kid could survive in the trenches of Teamster politics, and for teaching me what it really means to be an organizer. In my early days as an intern at

Labor Notes magazine, Kim Moody, Mike Parker, and Jane Slaughter took time to teach me the labor history we don't learn in school, and why the working class matters. Mark Brenner, Steve Early, Dianne Feeley, David Finkel, Barbara Harvey, Peter Landon, David Levin, Stephanie Luce, and Charlie Post have all provided education, inspiration, and guidance for many years, and continue to do so. More broadly, I would like to thank the many labor leaders and activists, both rank and file and elected, that I have had the pleasure of meeting and working with through my work with TDU, *Labor Notes*, and the political organization Solidarity. While anyone can point to the many reasons to be pessimistic about the future of labor and class politics in the United States and Canada, it is these people that continue to provide a source of hope.

In addition to help from individuals, many organizations and institutions have played essential roles in seeing this book through to completion. I am deeply grateful to the critical feedback I received from participants in seminars sponsored by the Center for Culture, Organizations, and Politics, and the Labor Transformations Working Group at UC Berkeley; the Politics, Culture, and Society Brown Bag at the University of Wisconsin–Madison; the Political Parties Working Group and Comparative Historical Workshop at Northwestern University; CRIMT at the University of Montreal; the Center for the Study of Work, Labor, and Democracy at the University of California, Santa Barbara (UCSB); and the students in Matthew Lange's Winter 2017 Comparative Historical Methods graduate seminar at McGill.

The UC Berkeley sociology department provided an enriching intellectual environment and rigorous training to help me grow as a scholar. The Institutes for Research on Labor and Employment (IRLE) at both UC Berkeley and UCLA connected me to vibrant communities of labor researchers, while also providing me with institutional homes. Special thanks go to UC Berkeley IRLE research librarians Terry Huwe and Janice Kimball for helping me track down obscure research materials. After graduating from Berkeley, I had the good fortune of benefiting from two postdoctoral fellowships, the first at the University of Wisconsin–Madison and the second at the Rutgers School of Management and Labor Relations. Each offered me a stimulating setting to pursue my research, including this book. My colleagues at McGill University have gone above and beyond what one could expect in making me feel welcome and supported.

Comparative historical research is only possible with the help of dedicated, competent archivists and librarians. In the course of my research I benefited from the patience and expertise of library professionals at the Confédération des syndicats nationaux (Confederation of National Trade Unions, CSN) in Montreal, Quebec; the Kheel Center Archives at the Martin P. Catherwood Library at Cornell University in Ithaca, New York; the George Meany Memorial Archives in Silver Spring, Maryland; the Hagley Museum in Wilmington, Delaware; Library and Archives Canada in Ottawa, Ontario; the National Archives in College Park, Maryland; the Walter P. Reuther Library at Wayne State University in Detroit, Michigan; and the Special Collections at Georgetown University in Washington, DC.

I have based some portions of this book on previously published articles. Chapter 4 includes material from "Why Is There No Labor Party in the United States? Political Articulation and the Canadian Comparison, 1932–1948," published in the *American Sociological Review* (June 2016), as well as "Continuity or Change? Rethinking Left Party Formation in Canada," which appeared as chapter 2 in *Building Blocs: How Parties Organize Society*, edited by Cedric de Leon, Manali Desai, and Cihan Tuğal (Stanford, CA: Stanford University Press, 2015). Chapters 1, 2, 3, and 6 include material from "Class vs. Special Interest: Labor, Power, and Politics in the United States and Canada in the Twentieth Century," published in *Politics & Society* (June 2015). Parts of the concluding chapter appeared in *Jacobin* under the title "Labor's Legitimacy Crisis Under Trump" (July 5, 2017).

Financial support for this book came from the Association for Canadian Studies in the United States (ACSUS), the Canadian Embassy in Washington, the National Science Foundation (a Graduate Research Fellowship, Doctoral Dissertation Improvement Grant #0902276, and an ASA-NSF Postdoctoral Fellowship, Grant #0956546), Oberlin College, the UC Berkeley Canadian Studies Program, the UC Berkeley Institute of International Studies, the UC Berkeley Department of Sociology, the UC Berkeley Graduate Division, and the University of California Labor and Employment Research Fund.

It was Lew Bateman at Cambridge University Press who first agreed to work with me on this book manuscript, but it was Robert Dreesen who got it across the finish line. I offer my thanks to both of them, as well as to Meera Seth for helpful assistance along the path to publication and to Dawn Wade for her skilful copyediting.

An essential part of keeping the mental focus and stamina necessary to see this book to completion was making sure that my body did not slip into decrepitude and disrepair. My method of choice has been the sport of weightlifting. I must thank my coaches for keeping me on the right track for all these years: Pierre Augé in Ottawa; Skipp Benzing and Keysha McClenton Benzing in Madison; John Margolis in Montreal; Dini Wong in Berkeley; and especially Eric LeClair and Michael Keating in Los Angeles, who have been with me in one way or another throughout the entire process.

Anne Quismorio came into my life just as I was beginning to embark on this research project. As such, she has seen it unfold from its early stages. Although the vagaries of research, teaching, and the academic job market have required us to live apart for long stretches of time, she has been a source of strength and support throughout. I couldn't ask for more in a spouse and life partner.

I attribute any remaining typos in this manuscript to Popper, our tabby, who stayed up many a late night with me as I wrote. He may have gotten in the way, but he made the process more bearable.

Finally, I must thank my family for all the help and support they have provided me. Thanks to Eric and Renae for offering a haven just a few blocks away when I lived in Berkeley, and to Alena and Steve for their welcoming home back in Ontario. And thanks to both couples for their wonderful additions to the family, Elsie, Clay, Ryo, and Aya.

My parents both played outsized roles in helping me get this book done, even though neither lived long enough to see the final product. My mother, Anne, never stopped believing in me, urging me on with cries of *ganbatte*, Japanese for "you can do it!" As for my father, Fred, I can't imagine how this project would have been possible without him. A political scientist himself, he always taught me to ask the tough questions. "It's not that simple" was his frequent refrain as I was growing up and trying to make sense of the world. While I like to think that I have carved my own path with this book, it bears both of their indelible marks. I dedicate it to their memory.

Abbreviations

AAA	Agricultural Adjustment Act
ACCL	All-Canadian Congress of Labour
ACF	American Commonwealth Federation
ACWA	Amalgamated Clothing Workers of America
AES	Agricultural Extension Service
AFBF	American Farm Bureau Federation
AFL	American Federation of Labor
AFL-CIO	American Federation of Labor-Congress of Industrial Organizations
AFSCME	American Federation of State, County, and Municipal Employees
ALP	American Labor Party
ASU	Alabama Sharecroppers' Union
BSCP	Brotherhood of Sleeping Car Porters
CAA	Christian American Association
CAUT	Canadian Association of University Teachers
CAW	Canadian Auto Workers
CAWIU	Cannery and Agricultural Workers Industrial Union
CBRE	Canadian Brotherhood of Railway Employees
CCF	Cooperative Commonwealth Federation
CCL	Canadian Congress of Labour
CEP	Communications, Energy, and Paperworkers Union
CEQ	Centrale de l'enseignement du Québec (Congress of Quebec Teachers)
CFL	Canadian Federation of Labour
CIO	Congress of Industrial Organizations

List of Abbreviations

CIR	Center for Individual Rights
CIRB	Canada Industrial Relations Board
CIW	Coalition of Immokalee Workers
CLC	Canadian Labour Congress
CMA	Canadian Manufacturers Association
CPUSA	Communist Party, USA
CPC	Communist Party of Canada
CSN	Confédération des syndicats nationaux (Confederation of National Trade Unions)
CSQ	Centrale des syndicats du Québec (Congress of Quebec Unions)
CTCC	Confédération des travailleurs catholiques du Canada (Canadian Catholic Confederation of Labour)
CtW	Change to Win Federation
CWA	Communications Workers of America
DOL	United States Department of Labor
EFCA	Employee Free Choice Act
EPIC	End Poverty in California
FBI	Federal Bureau of Investigation
FCA	First Contract Arbitration
FE	Farm Equipment Workers
FERA	Federal Emergency Relief Agency
FHA	Farmers' Holiday Association
FLPF	Farmer–Labor Political Federation
FLSA	Fair Labor Standards Act
FMCS	Federal Mediation and Conciliation Service
FTA	US-Canada Free Trade Agreement
FTQ	Fédération des travailleurs et travailleuses du Québec (Quebec Federation of Labour)
GDP	Gross Domestic Product
GM	General Motors
HEW	United States Department of Health, Education, and Welfare
IBT	International Brotherhood of Teamsters
IDIA	Industrial Disputes Investigation Act
IFLWU	International Fur and Leather Workers Union
ILGWU	International Ladies' Garment Workers Union
ILTP	Independent Left Third Party
IRDIA	Industrial Relations and Disputes Investigation Act
IWW	Industrial Workers of the World

JIC	Joint Industrial Council
KOL	Knights of Labor
LMRA	Labor-Management Relations Act (Taft-Hartley Act)
LMRDA	Labor-Management Reporting and Disclosure Act (Landrum-Griffin Act)
LNPL	Labor's Non-Partisan League
LSR	League for Social Reconstruction
NAFTA	North American Free Trade Agreement
NAM	National Association of Manufacturers
NDP	New Democratic Party
NDWA	National Domestic Workers Alliance
NFU	National Farmers Union
NIRA	National Industrial Recovery Act
NLB	National Labor Board
NLRA	National Labor Relations Act (Wagner Act)
NLRB	National Labor Relations Board
NLRB-GC	National Labor Relations Board General Counsel
NPA	National Progressives of America
NPL	Nonpartisan League
NRTWF	National Right to Work Foundation
NYTWA	New York Taxi Workers Alliance
OECD	Organisation for Economic Cooperation and Development
OLRB	Ontario Labor Relations Board
PATCO	Professional Air Traffic Controllers Organization
PSSRA	Public Service Staff Relations Act
PSSRB	Public Service Staff Relations Board
RCMP	Royal Canadian Mounted Police
RNMP	Royal Northwest Mounted Police
ROC	Restaurant Opportunities Center
RTW	Right to Work
SDS	Students for a Democratic Society
SEIU	Service Employees International Union
SGGA	Saskatchewan Grain Growers' Association
STFU	Southern Tenant Farmers Union
SWOC	Steel Workers Organizing Committee
TDU	Teamsters for a Democratic Union
TLC	Trades and Labour Congress of Canada
UAW	United Auto Workers
UE	United Electrical Workers Union

UFC(SS)	United Farmers of Canada (Saskatchewan Section)
UFCW	United Food and Commercial Workers
ULP	Unfair Labor Practice
UMMSWA	United Mine, Mill, and Smelter Workers of America
UMWA	United Mine Workers of America
USCC	United States Chamber of Commerce
USCS	United States Conciliation Service
USWA	United Steel Workers of America
VW	Volkswagen
WCL	World Confederation of Labour
WRPS	Worker Representation and Participation Survey
WU	Workers United
WUL	Workers' Unity League
WVS	World Values Survey

Introduction

On February 14, 2014, workers at a Volkswagen (VW) auto assembly plant in Chattanooga, Tennessee, voted 712 to 626 against joining the United Auto Workers (UAW) union. The defeat was the latest in a series of failed attempts by the UAW to organize foreign-owned "transplants" in the US South, going back decades (Minchin 2017; Silvia 2016). It was a particularly stinging rebuke for then-UAW President Bob King, who had staked his legacy on the transplants. "If we don't organize these transnationals, I don't think there's a long-term future for the UAW," he warned in 2011 (Thomas 2011).

This time was supposed to be different. The UAW had secured an agreement from Volkswagen management to remain neutral in the election campaign. In previous organizing drives at other manufacturers, management had waged fierce campaigns to convince workers not to unionize. Without the employer trying to influence the outcome, UAW leaders thought that workers would be much more likely to join the union (Brooks 2016; Greenhouse 2014). But those leaders were wrong – the UAW lost.

Anti-union observers quickly cheered the result, suggesting that it showed just how obsolete and unpopular unions are today. "If UAW union officials cannot win when the odds are so stacked in their favor, perhaps they should re-evaluate the product they are selling to workers," opined National Right to Work Foundation President Mark Mix (Woodall 2014). For their part, UAW officials blamed a campaign of outside interference led by Tennessee's political establishment, including Governor Bill Haslam and US Senator Bob Corker. They threatened to withhold state subsidies if workers unionized, and intimated that Volkswagen would only guarantee new production if workers rejected the UAW.

The politicians were helped by Washington-based anti-union groups like Mix's organization and the Grover Norquist–backed Center for Worker Freedom. These groups funded sophisticated media outreach and backed anti-union workers in the plant. Their campaign linked the UAW to the Obama administration – unpopular in Republican-dominated Tennessee – and blamed it for the disappearance of US manufacturing jobs. Additionally, despite VW upper management's neutrality pledge, lower-level managers actively supported the anti-union campaign (DePillis 2014; Elk 2014).

Analysts more sympathetic to the union recognized that outside interference contributed to the drive's defeat, but they also criticized the UAW's own strategy. They highlighted provisions in the neutrality agreement with VW that hampered the UAW's ability to organize – including a ban on union house visits, a key tactic that organizers use to build union support and inoculate against management attacks. UAW organizers also made little effort to build community support. Instead, they relied on VW management's willingness to "partner" with the union. As King said in response to the anti-union campaign in Chattanooga,

> Our philosophy is, we want to work in partnership with companies to succeed ... With every company that we work with, we're concerned about competitiveness ... [W]e are showing that companies that succeed by this cooperation can have higher wages and benefits because of the joint success ... What I hope the American public understands is that those people who attack this are attacking labor-management cooperation. They don't believe in workers and management working together (quoted in DePillis 2014).

Such rhetoric may have softened management opposition, but it left the union vulnerable to charges that it was too soft on management – that "the UAW has already sold us out," as anti-union VW worker Mike Jarvis put it (quoted in Pare 2014).

UAW leaders appealed the election results with the National Labor Relations Board (NLRB), citing the outside interference from state politicians and Washington think tanks as improper. But they withdrew their appeal just as hearings were about to get underway, amid concerns that those charged with interfering would obstruct the legal process and drag out the appeal for years, defeating the union through endless delay. Instead, they cut their losses. "The UAW is ready to put February's tainted election in the rearview mirror and instead focus on advocating for new jobs and economic investment in Chattanooga," King said (quoted in Becker and Woodall 2014).

The city of Winnipeg, Manitoba, lies about 1,400 miles, or 2,200 kilometers, northwest of Chattanooga, across the US–Canada border from North Dakota. In early 2015, a group of workers at a branch of the iconic Tim Hortons coffee chain in the city's Wolseley neighborhood connected with a union called Workers United (WU), and started talking about unionizing their workplace. They were concerned about low wages, unpredictable scheduling, and management favoritism.

Management soon caught on. They responded by organizing a mandatory meeting of all thirty-five branch workers, also known as a "captive audience meeting." While franchise owner Kamta Roy Singh was at the front of the room, he told those assembled that Tim Hortons' head office had instructed him to hold the meeting. In it, he leveled a series of threats against the workers, including that he would shut down the location if they unionized. After the meeting, the general manager took aside one of the workers and fired her for talking to a union representative.

In response, WU filed an Unfair Labour Practice charge with the Manitoba Labour Relations Board and reached out to allies at the Manitoba Federation of Labour, the Winnipeg Labour Council, and the University of Winnipeg Students' Association. Together, they launched a public campaign to get the fired worker reinstated. Management quickly caved under the pressure and reinstated the worker within weeks.

In June 2015, the Manitoba Labour Relations Board issued a ruling that found franchisee Singh guilty of several labor law violations. As a remedy, the board issued a consent order granting WU "discretionary certification," meaning that the board automatically recognized them as the workers' union. Additionally, the board awarded the previously fired worker $1,500 to compensate for emotional stress. The ruling made the Wolseley restaurant one of only a handful of unionized Tim Hortons locations across Canada (Kirbyson 2015; Nesbitt 2015; Workers United Canada Council 2015).

After nine months of tough negotiations, WU managed to negotiate a first contract with Singh. The win at the Wolseley Tim Hortons sparked interest among other food service workers in Winnipeg. WU has since gone on to unionize workers at two KFC/Taco Bell restaurants in the city, as well as a second Tim Hortons location (Fowlie 2017; Kostuch Media 2016; 2017).

Both stories offer insights into the challenges that workers and unions face in the United States and Canada today. On the US side, the UAW's failure in Chattanooga shows just how dire organized labor's situation is. Organizing a union has never been easy, but the obstacles that US workers face today are truly formidable. Staunch employer opposition is a given, meaning that workers who try to organize a union often put their livelihoods on the line (Bronfenbrenner 2009). Even in cases where employers agree to remain neutral, as with VW, other employers and politicians may step in to lead the anti-union charge – especially in the South, a region of the United States where unions have never established a strong foothold.

Once workers have mustered the courage to confront their employer and start on a unionization campaign, they face a thicket of legal regulations that, while originally intended to facilitate unionization, now create opportunities for employers to thwart workers' organizing efforts (Friedman 2015; Rogers 1990). As with the UAW's election appeals in Chattanooga, many workers and unions decide to cut their losses and move on when faced with these legal obstacles.

Even as legal hurdles and employer hostility to unionizing persist, unions themselves have struggled to respond to the challenge. Some, like the UAW, have sought to dodge the anti-union onslaught by pitching a message of "cooperation" with management, even as management seeks to avoid unions entirely. Others have plowed resources into developing innovative organizing strategies (Bronfenbrenner and Hickey 2004). The latter have produced some results, but not enough to turn the tide.

As a result, US unions are in crisis. Today, barely one in ten workers holds a union card. In the private sector, that number is barely one in twenty. This is down from one in three workers overall in the 1950s, and is the lowest level seen since the early days of the Great Depression (Carter et al. 2006; Hirsch and Macpherson 2011).

On the Canadian side, the situation is challenging, but not quite as bleak. As the Tim Hortons campaign shows, Canadian workers seeking to unionize often face stiff employer resistance, just like their US counterparts. And, as in the United States, they also have to navigate bureaucratic legal procedures to exercise their labor rights. Although some Canadian unions are committed to organizing, the overall level of commitment is uneven (Kumar and Schenk 2006).

The main difference between Canada and the United States is that in Canada, the labor laws still work. Employers like Kamta Singh may threaten and fire workers for trying to organize, but they pay the price for breaking the law. In Singh's case, that meant being forced to compensate the fired worker and bargain with the union. By comparison, when the UAW appealed the Chattanooga election, those they charged with illegal interference openly vowed to flout any subpoenas and gum up the proceedings. "Everyone understands that after a clear defeat, the UAW is trying to create a sideshow, so we have filed a motion to revoke these baseless subpoenas," said Senator Corker's chief of staff. "Neither Senator Corker nor his staff will attend the hearing" (quoted in Williams 2014). There was little that either the state or the union could do to stop them (Brooks 2016).

This is not to say that the situation for labor is great in Canada. The thirty-five Tim Hortons workers in Winnipeg may have won their union, but only after a tough fight. Meanwhile, the chain as a whole remains mostly nonunion, as does most of the Canadian service sector (Doorey 2013). The community and labor mobilization in defense of the workers' organizing campaign was an important gesture of solidarity, but such mobilization is nowhere near the scale necessary to get unions back on track.

Compared to the United States though, Canadian unions are in much better shape. Overall union density – the percentage of nonagricultural workers who are union members – currently stands at 28.4 percent in Canada, nearly three times higher than in the United States (Hirsch and Macpherson 2011; Statistics Canada 2016). Canadian unions have taken some hits, but they have managed to hold steady.

Why is this? As much as Canadians insist on their "not-Americanness," and as much as Americans remain unaware of their neighbor to the north, the two countries have much in common (Lipset 1989). Yet when it comes to unions and the broader climate for worker organizing, the differences are vast.

But US and Canadian union density rates have not always been so different. Figure 0.1 shows how union density changed in the United States and Canada between 1911 and 2016. We see that prior to the 1960s, union density looked remarkably similar in both countries. Indeed, it was often higher in the United States than in Canada. It was only in the mid-1960s that union density diverged, declining in the United States and stabilizing in Canada.

Why then, after tracking each other for decades, did union density diverge in the United States and Canada starting in the mid-1960s? That is the question at the heart of this book.

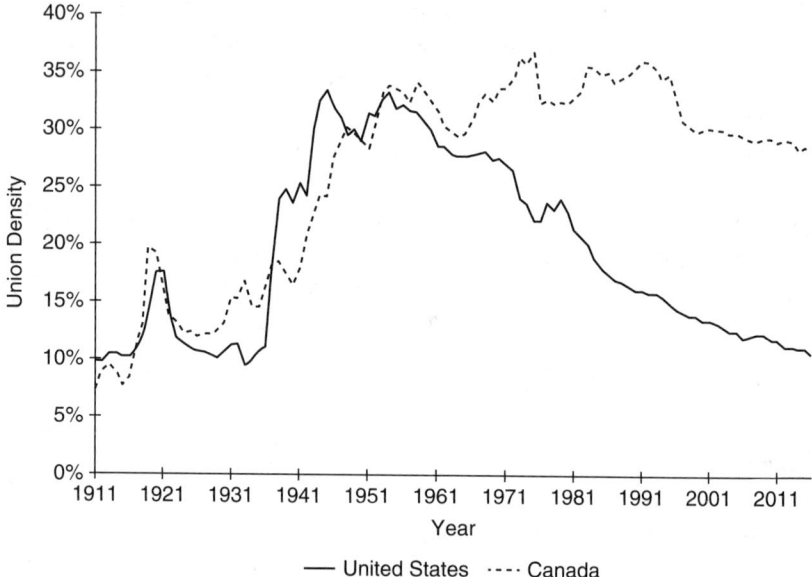

FIGURE 0.1 Union density, United States and Canada, 1911–2016
Source: See Appendix A

WHY UNIONS (STILL) MATTER

But first we should ask a more basic question: why does it matter that US unions are in worse shape than Canada's? In an era when unions everywhere seem to be in decline and many dismiss the very idea of trade unions as antiquated, focusing attention on the state of organized labor may seem hopelessly out of date. Why bother with what looks like a dying institution?

At a fundamental level, unions matter because they powerfully influence workers' everyday lives. On average, unionized workers earn more and are more likely to have adequate health insurance, pension coverage, paid leave, and other benefits than their nonunionized counterparts doing similar work (Buchmueller, DiNardo, and Valletta 2002; Budd and Na 2000; Fang and Verma 2002; Freeman and Medoff 1984; Murray 2004). This is particularly the case in countries like the United States and Canada, where many social benefits are provided through employers rather than the government, and collective bargaining is largely done at the firm level. This means that contracts negotiated between employers and the unions representing their workers apply only to those specific firms and workplaces, which ties the negotiated wages, benefits, and work rules closely to those specific firms and workplaces.

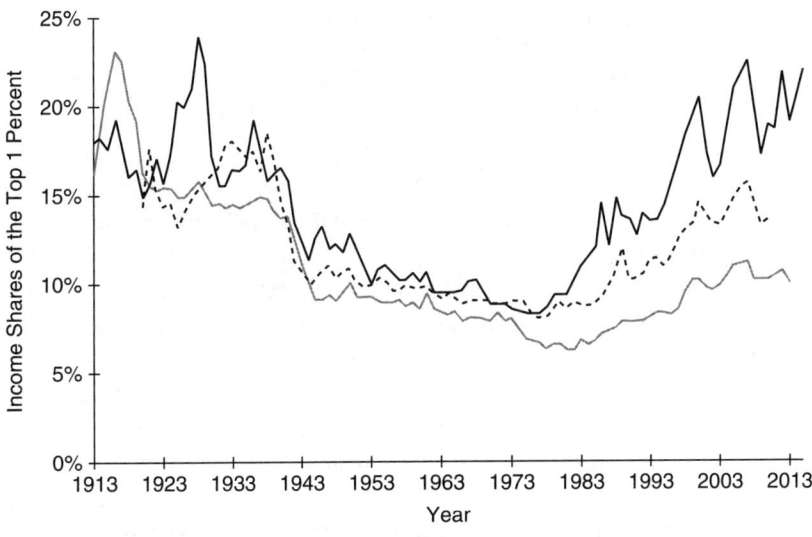

FIGURE 0.2 Income shares of the top 1 percent in the United States, Canada, and selected industrialized countries, 1913–2015
Source: World Wealth and Income Database, http://www.wid.world

But union density has important implications even for those who are not union members. Unions play a key role in reducing economic inequality throughout entire societies. Inequality has been on the rise across the industrialized world for the past three decades, but the magnitude of that growth has differed considerably across countries. Using data from the World Wealth and Income Database compiled by Piketty and his collaborators, Figure 0.2 shows that inequality in both the United States and Canada, defined as the share of total income accruing to the top 1 percent of earners, has been above the average for available industrialized countries. However, the increase has been dramatically higher in the United States. The share of income going to the top 1 percent in the United States grew by 125 percent between 1980 and 2015 (from 8.18 percent to 18.39 percent), as compared to 52 percent in Canada (from 8.06 percent to 12.22 percent in 2010) and 58 percent for available industrialized countries (from 6.43 percent to 10.16 percent in 2013).[1]

---

[1] Industrialized countries for which data are available include Australia, Canada, Denmark, Finland, France, Germany, Ireland, Italy, Japan, Korea, Netherlands, New Zealand, Norway, Portugal, Spain, Sweden, Switzerland, the United Kingdom, and the United States.

Much of that difference can be attributed to differences in union strength. Existing research shows that higher unionization rates are associated with lower levels of economic inequality (Alderson and Nielsen 2002; Alderson, Beckfield, and Nielsen 2005; Atkinson 2003; Western and Rosenfeld 2011). This is due to unions' ability to "decommodify" labor: they can limit the degree to which workers' wages and working conditions are set by brute market forces, in the same way that the price of commodities such as oil or corn are set (Esping-Andersen 1990). Given sufficient union density, this effect extends beyond unionized workplaces, such that unions can set standards for wages and working conditions throughout the labor market.

As union density declines, so too does unions' wage-setting capacity. Thus, Western and Rosenfeld (2011) find that union density decline accounts for roughly one-third of the increasing gap in US income inequality between the top and bottom quintiles among males over the past forty years, similar to the effect of growing gaps in educational attainment in the same time period. Using different methodologies, Card et al.'s (2004) comparative study of the United States, United Kingdom, and Canada shows that unions continue to play a key role in reducing inequality for male workers, and that differences in union density explain a large portion of cross-country differences in male wage inequality. And in a study of twenty advanced economies from the early 1980s to 2010, International Monetary Fund economists found that "a 10 percentage point decline in union density is associated with a 5 percent increase in the top 10 percent income share" (Jaumotte and Osorio Buitron 2015: 17).

Stronger unions also have a stronger political voice, meaning they can fight for more redistributive social policies and regulations to check employers' power (Rosenfeld 2014). Globally, this power is often exerted through relations that unions have with labor-based or socialist political parties. While party and union interests are not always perfectly aligned, and party-union relations can be strained, unions that are numerically stronger can generally exert greater political power. Existing research comparing US and Canadian social policy highlights the role that stronger unions and their links to a labor-based political party, the New Democratic Party (NDP), play in explaining Canada's more extensive set of protective policies, including its universal public health-care system, more generous unemployment insurance and pensions, and more equitable education and community planning policies (Chen 2015; Maioni 1998; McCarthy 2017; Zuberi 2006). Union strength thus has important consequences for the shape of the political and policy landscape more broadly.

Beyond questions of dollars and cents and particular policies, stronger unions make for a stronger democracy. It is workers, often organized into unions, who have pushed to expand democratic rights and notions of "social citizenship," usually by creating disruption and social instability to which political elites had to respond (Ahmed 2013; Marshall 1992; Rueschemeyer, Stephens, and Stephens 1992). And as one of the only types of membership organizations run not only *for* working-class people, but *by* them, unions offer workers the opportunity to develop the confidence, leadership, and organizational skills necessary to be politically active (Levi et al. 2009). In this sense, they can serve as "schools for democracy" that incorporate working-class voices into the existing political system (Lipset, Trow, and Coleman 1956; Sinyai 2006). Research shows that there is a lack of working-class political representation in the United States, and that this skews the political landscape in favor of the wealthy and powerful (Carnes 2013). Unions can provide a fertile training ground for working-class political leaders, and where they are stronger, we find more working-class political representation (Carnes 2015).

Beyond "regular politics," some unions have been vehicles for pushing a more transformative political vision (Ahlquist and Levi 2013; Gourevitch 2014; Stepan-Norris and Zeitlin 2003). Union decline in the United States has thus narrowed the scope of political debate, as well as the range of actors contributing to that debate. By contrast, while it is important to acknowledge the real limits of labor's political power in Canada (Ross and Savage 2012), the combination of a stronger labor movement and a labor-based political party (the NDP) has created an organizational infrastructure for developing working-class leaders and keeping unions in closer dialogue with social movements and a broader left politics (Bernard 1994; Schenk and Bernard 1992).

In the workplace, unions don't just mean higher pay and benefits for workers. They also allow workers to make their voice heard on the job (Freeman and Medoff 1984). They can offer recourse and respite from the pettiness and arbitrary treatment that far too many workers experience far too often at the hands of management. This is why workers often cite the need for dignity and respect on the job even more than pay or benefits as their primary motivation to unionize (Bronfenbrenner et al. 1998; Forrest 2000).

Unions provide voice by creating mechanisms at work for exercising and defending many of the basic rights we take for granted as citizens in a democracy, such as freedom of speech, freedom of assembly, due process and equal protection under the law, and more. Without unions, workers have to check these rights at the door when they show up to work every day (Anderson 2017; Edwards 1979; Jacoby 1985). While these rights do exist in some nonunion workplaces, they are there at management's discretion and are subject to change without notice (Edelman 1990). To be sure, just as the reality of political democracy often falls far short of its promise, the same can be said of efforts to build workplace democracy. But whereas citizens in a democracy are at least theoretically given opportunities to have a say in politics and society, union decline has meant that many workers have no means of implementing, let alone improving, mechanisms for articulating and defending their rights at work (Hyman 2016; Summers 1979).

Far from being an arcane statistic tracking the decline of an antiquated institution, then, union density shapes broader social trends affecting inequality and democracy. Understanding why union density changes, and why it varies across countries, helps explain a lot about the shape of politics and social policy in those countries.

EXPLAINING US–CANADA UNION DIVERGENCE

Unions are still crucial social institutions. But the question remains: why did union density diverge in the United States and Canada? Many others have sought to answer this question. Common explanations point to cross-border differences in the structure of employment, worker and employer attitudes toward unions, labor policies, political institutions, national values, internal union cultures, and the structure of racial divisions.

As I will show in Part I, these explanations are incomplete. The argument I advance in this book is that US–Canada union density divergence was the outcome of political struggles organized by parties – a process of *political articulation* (De Leon, Desai, and Tuğal 2015). Specifically, it resulted from different ruling party responses to worker and farmer unrest during the Great Depression and World War II. My core argument is that in Canada, the outcome of these struggles embedded what I call "the class idea" more deeply in policies, institutions, and practices than in the United States, where class interests were reduced to "special interests." By this I mean that in Canada, politics and policy recognized class divisions – and the power imbalances underlying them – more than in the United States. There, politics and policy delegitimized class divisions, concealing structural power imbalances behind a pluralist idea of formally equal interest groups, each negotiating deals to maximize their narrow self-interest. The class idea broadened Canadian labor's legitimate scope of action, while the pluralist idea narrowed that of US labor. This allowed Canadian labor to remain stronger than its US counterpart as the postwar settlement between labor and capital unraveled beginning in the 1970s, leading to union density divergence.

Paradoxically, US labor's long-term decline resulted from what was initially a more *pro-labor* ruling party response to worker and farmer unrest, while Canadian labor's comparative long-term strength resulted from a more *hostile* ruling party response. These different ruling party responses resulted in different processes of working-class "political incorporation" in both countries. By this I mean the process whereby workers and their organizations switched from being a problem for the state to address through ad hoc legal and police repression, to being a constituency for state actors to address and mobilize via formalized channels, particularly specialized laws, political bargaining, and administrative policies (Collier and Collier 1991).[2]

In the United States, the Democratic Party under President Franklin D. Roosevelt's leadership adopted a *co-optive* response to worker and farmer upsurge, successfully incorporating organized labor as an *interest group* within the New Deal coalition. This led to important short-term gains for labor, including increased union membership and improved job-based social benefits. But Democrats' co-optive response also accentuated *intra*-working-class divisions, which weakened the basis for independent Left parties, eliminating political threats from the Democrats' left flank and undermining the organizational platform for class politics.

By contrast, the ruling Liberal and Conservative parties in Canada adopted a *coercive* response to worker and farmer upsurge. This left labor politically excluded for nearly a decade longer than their US counterparts. But while this meant that US unions were winning concessions within the New Deal framework while Canadian unions

---

[2] Note that this conception of "political incorporation" differs from how it is often used, which is to refer to the moment when workers win the right to vote. This happened quite early in both the US and Canada, over the course of the nineteenth century. But as I discuss below, in neither country were workers initially incorporated *as workers*. This only happened later, in the 1930s and '40s. Also, political incorporation differs from political articulation in referring to the entry of new actors into the political arena, as opposed to the reconfiguration of existing actors. Incorporation can happen as part of an articulation process, as in this case.

were not, it also left room for a class-based political party, the Cooperative Commonwealth Federation (CCF), to develop in Canada. The ruling Liberals only acceded to labor's demands for legal recognition under duress in the mid-1940s, as wartime labor unrest and the growing electoral threat of the CCF forced their hand. As a result, labor was politically incorporated not as an interest group, but as a *class representative*, seen as pushing not only for the rights of dues-paying union members but of *the working class itself*. Canadian ruling parties' hardline response mitigated intra-class divisions and pushed labor to ally with the CCF (later the NDP). This institutionalized a political threat to the left of the ruling parties and legitimized class as a political organizing principle in Canada. Meanwhile, in the United States, a similar threat was absorbed into the coalition of an already-existing party, the Democrats, but as a special interest group like any other.

These key cross-border differences in the 1930s and '40s led to differences in the structure of both countries' labor relations regimes, the organizational structure and culture of labor unions, and state regulation of labor–capital relations. Each of these weakened US labor while reinforcing Canadian labor, leading to the divergence in union density starting in the 1960s.

In terms of labor regimes, US labor policy and institutions were polarized along partisan lines, with representation allotted by party affiliation. This made it easier for workers' class interests to appear as the narrow interests of a Democratic Party interest group. By contrast, Canada's tripartite system, with representation for labor, employers, and the state, recognized the legitimacy of competing class interests – and the role of the state in regulating conflict between them. As a result, the US labor regime was less institutionalized and more politically contingent – and thus more susceptible to erosion over time – than the Canadian regime.

The consequences of this difference were massive and would play out in the decades to come. Organizationally, the collapse of a political Left independent of the Democrats in the United States meant that postwar Red scares had a more devastating impact on unions (and the Left as a whole) there than they did in Canada. A combination of strategic missteps related to the Communist Party's "Popular Front" strategy and anti-Communist attacks backed up by policies such as the Taft-Hartley Act drove a wedge between labor and the Left in the United States. Deprived of left allies externally, and purged of left activists and organizers internally, US labor became increasingly reliant on fighting for influence inside a broad and unstable New Deal coalition, weighed down by a racist, reactionary Southern bloc.

As the coalition came under stress amidst the upsurge of the 1960s, US labor found itself largely alienated from the nascent social movements of the period, and focused on defending its own narrowly constructed privileges, particularly around the defense industry. As the economic boom of the 1960s gave way to the crisis of the 1970s, labor's isolation from those movements gave bite to the charge that it was a narrow "special interest." This left it vulnerable to an aggressive employer offensive, with little recourse from its ostensible allies in the Democratic Party, who were distancing themselves from labor by that point.

By contrast, the link between Canadian labor and the Left, while strained by Cold War anti-communism, was not severed. A significant layer of left-wing leaders and organizers remained within the union ranks, thanks especially to unions' decision to recognize the CCF as the "political arm of labor." Labor reasserted its political independence in the early 1960s by helping to found the NDP, a more explicitly labor-based party that replaced the CCF. That party used its leverage both in opposition and in some provincial governments to defend and improve labor laws at the federal and provincial levels. Meanwhile, as the New Left emerged in the 1960s, it did so partly within the structures of the NDP. This created a fraught but very real connection between labor and the New Left that was absent in the United States. It helped ensure that the social movements of the 1960s found a more hospitable reception in the Canadian unions than did their US counterparts, infusing unions with a movement tinge. As the state and employers intensified attacks on labor in the 1970s, Canadian labor was better able to countermobilize in defense of its postwar gains.

In terms of state regulation of labor–capital relations, the US labor regime's system of "industrial pluralism" explicitly downplayed the state's role in regulating labor–capital relations and did little to buttress labor's institutional legitimacy. Instead, it emphasized the idea of a voluntary, contractually determined relationship between labor and capital. As management began to reassert its self-perceived "right to manage" in the 1960s, state intervention on behalf of workers was noticeably absent. Management's squeeze provoked worker push-back on shop floors across the United States, but this was not interpreted as a crisis in industrial relations. Rather, it was viewed as a crisis of individual worker alienation in a postindustrial society – a case of the "blue collar blues." As such, the wave of industrial unrest of the late 1960s and early 1970s failed to coalesce into a more coordinated countermobilization. This left room for employers to intensify their attack on labor, aided by the state's laissez-faire approach. Politically weakened and organizationally moribund, US labor's slow decline since the 1950s accelerated into a rout by the late 1970s.

By contrast, the Canadian labor regime's class representative structure gave labor more institutional legitimacy than its US counterpart. It also gave the state more leeway to intervene in industrial disputes in the name of imposing industrial peace. This not only led to more frequent and aggressive state intervention in labor disputes than in the United States, but it also had a galvanizing effect on Canadian labor. Because the Canadian state intervened more often in workplace battles, it gave labor a bigger, more unified target for its ire than the scores of individual employers that US workers were confronting. State intervention via imposed settlements and back-to-work legislation sparked massive mobilization on the part of Canadian labor, which engaged in an unprecedented wave of strikes in the late 1960s and 1970s. This provoked a crisis in Canada's system of industrial relations, to which politicians felt they had to respond. The proposed reforms to the industrial relations system placed tighter constraints on labor's scope of action, particularly around strikes. But in affirming the importance of preserving collective bargaining relationships and shoring up labor's institutional legitimacy, they provided a framework for maintaining labor's organizational strength. While union membership growth stalled in the ensuing decades, it did not shrink nearly as much as in the United States.

THE CLASS IDEA AND THE ORGANIZATION OF INTERESTS

At its core, the argument outlined above involves an analysis of the political organization of interests and, more specifically, the organization of *class* interests. Most theories of interest groups and voluntary organizations tend to view all such groups as governed by similar logics and interests (Moe 1980; Olson 1965). This may be helpful for constructing broad and diverse comparisons, but it comes at an analytical price. As Claus Offe and Helmut Wiesenthal explain,

[D]ifferences in the position of a group in the class structure ... not only lead to differences in power that the organizations can acquire, but also lead to differences in the *associational practices*, or logics of collective action, by which organizations of capital and labor try to improve their respective position vis-à-vis each other; these differences tend to be obscured by the "interest group" paradigm and the underlying notion of a unitary and utilitarian logic of collective action that covers all associations (1980: 76).

Simply put, there is something different about working-class organizations. Offe and Wiesenthal focus on the negative aspect of this difference, namely the steeper information and coordination costs that working-class organizations face under capitalism. But there is also a positive aspect. We know this implicitly from the research studying differences among welfare states, as it specifically identifies Left-party strength as a critical factor. It does not, for example, point to density of social movement or other voluntary organizations.

What is it about working-class organizations that makes them stand out? Rueschemeyer et al. (1992) argue that by virtue of its structural position as a socially dominated and economically exploited group under capitalism, the working class has the most to gain from the expansion of democracy, understood as broad political inclusion. Put more bluntly, the working class has an objective interest in not being exploited. In pursuing that interest, it is more likely to pursue policies and strategies that seek to reduce social inequality and improve life quality for broad sectors of society. Thus, in seeking to realize its particular class interests, it is likely to achieve more general social benefits (Chibber 2017).

The problem with this formulation, of course, is that it is impossible to speak of "the working class" as an undifferentiated, unified actor. Collective actors such as classes do not simply exist; they are formed and re-formed through social struggles (for a review, see Eidlin 2014). Moreover, to the extent that we can ascribe interests to classes, the mere fact that such a class interest exists in no way guarantees that members of that class will either be aware of it or mobilize in pursuit of it. Interests must be *organized*. In particular, it is parties and unions that do the work of organizing interests when it comes to creating something identifiable as "the working class."

The process of interest organization is subject to internal challenges and external constraints. Looking first at internal challenges, organizations must, among other tasks: 1) define group interests; 2) create awareness of those interests; 3) develop a shared understanding of those interests; and 4) mobilize to pursue their interests. Without trivializing the real costs involved, Offe and Wiesenthal note that organizations of the powerful can accomplish these tasks using fairly instrumental calculations:

The powerful are fewer in number, are less likely to be divided among themselves, have a clearer view of what they want to defend, and have larger resources for organized action, all of which imply that they are likely to succeed in recreating the initial situation [their dominance] (1980: 78).

But for organizations of the relatively powerless, the organization of interests must go beyond a purely instrumental cost-benefit analysis:

> [T]hose in the inferior power position can increase their potential for change only by overcoming the comparatively higher costs of collective action by *changing the standards according to which these costs* are *subjectively estimated* within their own collectivity. Only to the extent that associations of the relatively powerless succeed in the formation of a collective identity, according to the standards of which these costs of organization are subjectively deflated, can they hope to change the original power relation (Offe and Wiesenthal 1980: 78).

These collective identities are not infinitely variable, nor are they infinitely malleable. They are subject to structural constraints, most importantly actors' ability to provide for their material existence. While collective identities can subjectively deflate the costs of collective action, they cannot make those costs disappear entirely (Chibber 2017).[3] They are also constrained by preexisting political cultures and institutional arrangements, which create particular, historically determined "repertoires of contention" from which actors can draw (McAdam, Tarrow, and Tilly 2001).

Furthermore, processes of collective identity formation are shaped by the universe of organizations within which they operate, and the logic governing relationships between these organizations. A central part of my argument is that these environmental-level organizing logics play a critical role in the organization of interests. They do so by "naturalizing" the connections linking sets of actors and organizations – who belongs, who is an ally, who is an enemy – as well as the sets of strategies and actions available to actors and organizations. According to this approach, repertoires of contention and scopes of action will vary depending on the different organizing ideas structuring the environment in question.

The question then arises: where do these different organizing ideas come from? While many social and cultural factors matter, I focus on the decisive role that political conflict organized by parties, unions, and

---

[3] This is not to say that it is impossible to deflate the subjective costs of collective action to the point that individuals will prioritize the group identity over their material existence. There are plenty of examples of people literally "dying for the cause." The point is that threats to actors' material existence will impose limits on the types of collective identities that emerge and prove effective and, by extension, the structure and functioning of the organizations mobilizing those collective identities. The type of collective identity and organization that will motivate people to come to a protest is different from that which will get them to go on strike and lose days or weeks of pay, which is in turn different from that which will get them to face down rows of heavily armed soldiers.

The Class Idea and the Organization of Interests

TABLE 0.1 *Differences in organizing logics*

Organizing Logic	Class Idea	Pluralist Idea
Group role – Labor	Class representative	Interest group
Group role – Capital	Class representative	Interest group/ individual employers
Group role – State	Mediator	Adjudicator
Rights	Collective	Individual
Bargaining	Group-based	Contract-based
Interests	Class/general	Special/particular
Institutionalization	High	Low
Politicization	Low	High

employers – a process of "political articulation" – plays in shaping these organizing ideas (De Leon et al. 2015).

Returning to the question of explaining union density divergence in the United States and Canada, the key difference driving divergence in both countries was that US labor was incorporated as an *interest group* over the course of the 1930s and '40s, whereas Canadian labor was incorporated as a *class representative*. While the difference may seem semantic, the two identities tie into two different organizing ideas, which I call the "class idea" and the "pluralist idea." These organizing ideas tied class organizations to different logics for staking group claims and bargaining with other groups, including parties and state agencies. In turn, this shaped labor's strategies around politics and policy in the postwar period, while also affecting the degree to which labor's political gains were institutionalized. The key differences are summarized in Table 0.1.

What the table outlines is how, by virtue of being classified as an "interest group," US labor was embedded within an environmental logic governed by a "pluralist idea." The pluralist idea is organized around a conception of groups as made up of individuals, each with individual rights and particular interests. Interest group bargaining is tied to contract-based rights, whereby groups are free to negotiate with each other, subject only to their respective abilities to extract concessions and/or reach agreement. Importantly, within the logic of the pluralist idea there is little room for labor to stake claims to represent a more universal, general interest. Instead, labor is framed as a "special" interest, one whose claims carry equal weight to any number of other organized interests trying to make claims on the state. Based on this organizing logic, it is possible to see how political and policy gains would remain tenuous, weakly institutionalized, and constantly subject to challenge from rival groups.

In contrast, by virtue of being incorporated as a class representative, Canadian labor was embedded within an environmental logic governed by a class idea. Although not nearly as extensive as corporatist schemes of codetermination in parts of Europe, class as an organizing idea is much more evident in Canadian politics and policy than in the United States. The class idea is organized around a conception of society made up of a set of groups, each of which should be entitled to representation and consideration from the state. While claims based on individual rights are common, indeed the norm, there is also separate recognition of collective rights. While collective bargaining with employers is based on contractual rights, negotiations with the state are more embedded in a discourse of social rights. Because of this, there is greater room within the class idea for labor to represent a general interest beyond its particular membership. Based on this organizing logic, it is possible to see how political and policy gains would become more strongly institutionalized and less subject to challenge from rival groups than in the United States.

CLASS, POLITICS, AND AMERICAN EXCEPTIONALISM

Explaining why union density diverged in the United States and Canada pushes us to revisit – and rethink – the complex relationship between class and politics in the North American context. While the concepts themselves may seem vague and abstract, class and politics have very real and powerful consequences for people's everyday lives. They play a big role in determining how healthy we are, what we do and how much time we spend at work, how much time we have to ourselves outside of work, what kind of education we can provide our children, what kinds of neighborhoods we live in, and more.

The fact that politics plays a key role in shaping our everyday lives may be uncontroversial, but the importance of class has been less accepted, particularly in the United States. Although class issues and rhetoric came to the fore with a vengeance in the 2016 presidential election, the idea of the United States as a classless society continues to be a powerful part of the national mythology. According to the story, which reached its apogee in the decades following World War II, Americans live in a society where they are born equal, where anyone with the proper work ethic and motivation can get ahead. While there may be some who are richer than others, this is largely the result of individual achievement, not social distinctions. Class differences, in this view, are un-American, something that the settlers who colonized the United States rejected in declaring their independence from the British (Bell 1960; Lipset 1963).[4]

To the extent that class plays a role in this story, there is only one class worth mentioning: the "middle class." It is by definition a vague and all-encompassing term, embracing everyone from janitors and autoworkers to lawyers and business owners. It is an identity closely associated with another powerful national idea, namely the "American Dream." The middle class is made up of those who either have achieved, or can reasonably expect to achieve, the American Dream. This dream, in turn, is generally associated with gaining access to a distinct but evolving set of benchmarks related to consumption and economic stability. Central to achieving this dream is the stable middle-class job, which provides a family-supporting wage, health benefits, and a pension. It also enables the purchase of certain telltale middle-class consumer goods, such as a TV, a car, and a private home (Cullen 2003; Hochschild 1995).

This story of a classless society diverges sharply from reality. Research shows that class divisions exist in the United States and that they have grown in recent decades. It shows that intergenerational class mobility, meaning the likelihood that someone might achieve a class position higher (or lower) than their parents, is shrinking, and is already less than mobility levels in many other capitalist democracies. Furthermore, it shows that class divisions are taking a toll on Americans' health, their educational opportunities, and even their overall levels of happiness (Beller and Hout 2006; Case and Deaton 2017; Gamoran 2001; Hout 2003; Neckerman and Torche 2007; Olafsdottir 2007; Pappas et al. 1993; Wilkinson and Pickett 2009). As for stable middle-class jobs, it shows that these are disappearing as the labor market polarizes between a small group of protected, highly paid jobs and a growing number of low-wage, low-benefit, low-security jobs (Autor and Dorn 2013; Kalleberg 2011; Wright and Dwyer 2003).

In the face of this evidence of growing class inequality, the myth of the United States as a classless or broadly middle-class society has taken a beating. The confident narrative of the postwar period has shifted to

---

[4] This idea of a classless society also has purchase in Canada, as most famously described and criticized by John Porter (1965).

one of concern among liberals and even some conservatives about a "shrinking," "disappearing," or "hollowed out" middle class (Madland 2015; Ornstein 2007; Reich 2015; Temin 2017; YG Network 2014). Still, this narrative of concern itself shows how resilient the idea of the United States as a middle-class meritocracy remains. It frames the growing class inequality of recent decades as something alien to American social life, not an enduring feature of it.

That is why politicians will routinely speak of "standing up for the middle class" or "defending the American Dream," but aside from democratic socialist Senator Bernie Sanders, it is rare to hear mainstream American politicians speak of "the working class" (Sanders 2016). Even US labor union leaders, heads of organizations that are by definition working class, will rarely utter the term. They will speak of defending "the middle class," "working families," or "workers' rights," but seldom "the working class."

The one time when it is appropriate to use the term "working class" in US politics is during election season. But even then, it gets used in two very limited ways. First, in analyses of voting behavior, pollsters, reporters, and strategists use it as shorthand to identify a specific demographic: blue-collar, non-college-educated white men – even though this is only a fraction of what constitutes the actual US working class today (Edsall 2012; Levison 2013; Zweig 2017). Second, it refers to cultural styles associated with that demographic by the politicians trying to appeal to them. A candidate can have "blue collar" or "working-class appeal" by invoking their scrappy hometown roots, as former Vice President Joe Biden does with his frequent talk of growing up in Scranton, Pennsylvania. It can also involve a fondness for certain activities, like playing football, drinking beer, or driving a pickup truck. Personal traits like being white and male, as well as having a gruff, forthright speaking style certainly help (Reeve 2012). This understanding of class as a kind of cultural performance is what allows someone as unlikely as billionaire real estate magnate-turned-President Donald Trump to say that "I consider myself in a certain way to be a blue-collar worker" (Bump 2017; Edelman 2016).

Talking substantively about the working class in American politics is difficult because it conflicts with the idea of the classless society (Merelman 1991). After all, in a country ostensibly without classes, engaging in class politics, i.e. mobilizing politically around class identities or class demands, appears as a divisive act. It seems to create cleavages and conflicts where none existed before. Politicians will routinely accuse opponents advocating even mildly redistributive policies of engaging in "class warfare" (Page and Jacobs 2009).[5] The epithet is used not simply to characterize the opponent's policy, but to delegitimize it. Class politics is considered out of bounds of legitimate US political discourse. Even at times when it has resonated, as with the Trump and Sanders presidential candidacies in 2016, it was precisely their class-based political appeals that marked them as outsiders who were shaking up the political establishment.

Why is this? What makes the myth of the classless society so persistent, and why are class politics considered out of bounds in the United States? For many, these characteristics are core tenets of "American exceptionalism," the idea that the US is somehow unique and different from other countries (Ceaser 2012; Lipset 1996; Madsen 1998).[6] The concept is slippery, used by proponents and critics alike to refer to everything from US military dominance and foreign policy; to cultural traits like religiosity, civic associationism, and philanthropy; to policy questions like the size of government, criminal justice, and politics and social policy.

Focusing on this last element, the United States does in fact stand apart from other advanced industrialized countries. It has a smaller public welfare state, meaning that it has fewer and less generous state-funded social programs (Esping-Andersen 1990; Flora and Heidenheimer 1981; Huber and Stephens 2001; McCarthy 2017).[7] It also has higher rates of social and economic inequality (Alderson and Nielsen 2002; Alderson et al. 2005; Atkinson 2003). Fewer US workers are members of unions (Visser 2006), and it is the only industrialized country without a mass socialist or labor-based political party (Archer 2007; Lipset and Marks 2000; Sombart 1976).

---

[5] The fact that, as Page and Jacobs show, most Americans do not view redistributive policies as a form of class warfare does not change the fact that such attacks resonate with US political culture. Indeed, the very fact that Page and Jacobs had to write a book debunking the idea that Americans view redistributive policies as un-American shows how pervasive the perceived cultural taboo on class politics remains.

[6] Whether this uniqueness is seen as a good or bad thing depends heavily on one's political orientation. To some toward the right of the political spectrum, it can be a sign of America's unique, God-given greatness. To others on the Left, it is evidence of America's false promise to many of its citizens. And still others, like Lipset himself, prefer to see it as a "double-edged sword" (Lipset 1996).

[7] The relative difference in welfare state size shrinks considerably when we consider the "private welfare state" in the United States, which is far larger than that of any other country (Gottschalk 2000; Hacker 2002). However, this configuration of public- and private-provided social benefits is in itself a feature unique to the United States.

According to the exceptionalist narrative, these characteristically American features derive from values and traditions that trace back to the nation's founding. As Lipset argues,

> Born out of revolution, the United States is a country organized around an ideology which includes a set of dogmas about the nature of a good society. Americanism ... is an "ism" or ideology in the same way that communism or fascism or liberalism are isms ... [T]he nation's ideology can be described in five words: liberty, egalitarianism, individualism, populism, and laissez-faire ... The American Revolution sharply weakened the *noblesse oblige*, hierarchically rooted, organic community values which had been linked to Tory sentiments, and enormously strengthened the individualistic, egalitarian, and anti-statist ones which had been present in the settler and religious background of the colonies ... America has been dominated by pure bourgeois, middle-class individualistic values (Lipset 1996: 31–32).

Therefore, according to this approach, the myth of the classless society is programmed into the cultural DNA of the country. Americans tolerate higher levels of inequality because they believe that everyone has an equal shot at success. They reject the kind of expansive welfare state seen in other countries out of concern with individual liberty. They join unions less because their laissez-faire individualism is incompatible with the collectivist logic that underlies trade unionism. And they don't support a socialist or labor party because such a party's ideology conflicts directly with the Americanist ideology that underpins their entire values system. To engage in class politics then, to mobilize collectively around an idea that implies structural and unequal social divisions, is to violate the American creed.

This book takes a different view. While not denying the current outlier status of the US relative to other advanced industrialized countries, it offers a different account of how we got here. The exceptionalist cultural DNA narrative is compelling, especially as it appears to describe the current-day political terrain. However, as is often the case when we create stories about the past based on our knowledge of the present, the cultural account is too neat and tidy. It ignores too much inconvenient evidence, and dismisses too many paths not taken.

In highlighting some of those alternate paths, this book offers a more convincing account of the origins of modern-day American exceptionalism. It is one wherein American exceptionalism, to the extent we can speak of it, was made, not born. And in many crucial respects, it was made relatively recently, around the middle of the last century to be precise. When it comes to understanding class politics in the United States, it is in fact more useful to look back to the crucible of the Great

Depression and World War II than to the purported legacy of the American Revolution. US working-class politics and organization certainly had their own peculiarities prior to that, but they looked far less exceptional then than they did in the years afterward. This book is about figuring out what changed.

THE CANADIAN COMPARISON

The very idea of exceptionalism implies comparison. Something can only be exceptional in relation to an imagined normal – an exception to the rule. Thus, any examination of what makes the United States different requires a comparative reference point. As already referenced above, the United States is usually viewed as exceptional in relation to other so-called advanced industrialized countries. This generally includes the countries of Western Europe, Great Britain, Japan, and former British settler colonies, such as Australia, Canada, and New Zealand. It is by comparison to these other countries that the United States appears as an outlier, in terms of the size and shape of its welfare state, its levels of inequality, its weak labor unions, and its lack of class-based political organization.

But while such broad-level comparisons are useful for establishing overall patterns of similarity and difference, they are less useful for developing explanations. The problem is that there is so much variation across the countries that make up the reference group that it is impossible to identify any specific causal factors with any degree of confidence.[8]

Paired country comparisons offer a means of more carefully identifying salient differences and the causal processes behind them. Initially, scholars studying American exceptionalism made either implicit or explicit paired comparisons with European countries, such as France (Tocqueville 2004) or Germany (Sombart 1976). These comparisons highlighted the contrast between societies with or without feudal pasts. But beginning in the mid-twentieth century, scholars such as Lipset and Louis Hartz (Hartz 1955; 1964) began to expand their comparative inquiry to understand variation

---

[8] This heterogeneity across countries has led some scholars to question the degree to which it is in fact possible to speak solely of an American exceptionalism (Zolberg 1986). Depending on the criteria under examination, it is possible to develop accounts of a British exceptionalism, a German exceptionalism, a French exceptionalism, a Swedish exceptionalism, and so on. While keeping this reference group heterogeneity in mind, the US stands out so distinctly along the criteria I have identified (welfare states, inequality, unions, and parties), that for the purposes of this analysis it is appropriate to speak specifically of American exceptionalism.

among what Hartz referred to as "fragment societies." This was his term for "new" societies that were founded by social fragments of the old European societies, often minoritarian groups at odds with the dominant social classes.

Cut off from the motherland and removed from the social struggles driving historical development there, these fragments became the whole of the new societies. Deprived of ideological challengers, these now-dominant fragment groups "[lost] the stimulus toward change that the whole provides" (Hartz 1964: 3). Instead they became immobilized, confined within the ideological framework that characterized the cast-off founding groups. So for example, using Hartz's terms, Latin America became a "feudal" fragment, the United States became a "liberal bourgeois" fragment, and Australia became a "radical" fragment. According to this theory, the United States' status as a "liberal" fragment meant that it was frozen in the political tradition of eighteenth-century Lockean liberalism, deprived of challenges either from a truly conservative, feudal right, or its complement, a truly radical, socialist Left.

Aside from the United States, there was another liberal fragment: Canada, or at least English Canada. Like the United States, English Canada also lacked a feudal past, and therefore – according to fragment theory – strongly resembled the United States as a liberal society. While differences between the two were considered subtle at most, their existence was explained by the relative "impurity" of the Canadian liberal fragment. Compared to the "pure" Lockean liberalism of the United States, Canadian liberalism was tainted by a "Tory tinge" (Horowitz 1968; McRae 1964).

For Hartz, the differences between the United States and Canada were relatively insignificant, as he was primarily interested in developing his fragment theory of national development. To this end, the important thing was to outline and emphasize the differences *between* different fragments, rather than the differences *within* the same fragment. But whereas Hartz downplayed the differences between the two countries, Lipset saw an opportunity in the Canadian comparison to develop a deeper understanding of American exceptionalism, the liberal tradition, and cross-national differences more broadly. As he put it,

> Knowledge of Canada or the United States is the best way to gain insight into the other North American country. Nations can be understood only in comparative perspective. And the more similar the units being compared, the more possible it should be to isolate the factors responsible for differences between them. Looking intensively at Canada and the United States sheds light on both of them (Lipset 1989: xiii).

It was precisely *because* Canada was so similar to the United States that the comparison was worthwhile. Based on this insight, Lipset returned time and time again to the US–Canada comparison in his prolific writings. He was not alone in this regard. Several other scholars have pursued this cross-national comparison, creating a vibrant literature in the process (Card and Freeman 1994; Kaufman 2009; Maioni 1998; Orloff 1993).

Building on this body of work, I too have chosen to compare the United States with Canada. Despite strong economic, social, and cultural similarities, the two countries differ sharply when it comes to class politics. Most noticeably, unlike the United States, Canada has a mass-based labor party, the NDP. As shown in Figure 0.1, nearly three times more Canadian workers belong to unions than in the United States. Canada also has a more expansive public welfare state (Chen 2015; Maioni 1998; McCarthy 2017; Zuberi 2006) and lower levels of economic inequality (Atkinson 2003; Foster and Wolfson 2009). Moreover, while the two countries have continued to grow more economically and culturally integrated since Lipset began his comparative inquiries, their political differences have persisted, if not increased (Kaufman 2009).

Although this study grapples with many of the same political differences that Lipset did in his examinations of the United States and Canada, it differs when it comes to explaining them. Lipset traces those differences back to differences in national values systems, which in turn developed out of the conditions surrounding the outcome of the American Revolution:

> Americans do not know but Canadians cannot forget that two nations, not one, came out of the American Revolution. The United States is the country of the revolution, Canada of the counterrevolution. These very different formative events set indelible marks on the two nations ... The effort to create a form of rule derived from the people, and stressing individualism made America "exceptional" ... The desire to build free institutions within a strong monarchical state made Canada distinctive, different from its mother country but also from its sibling across the border (Lipset 1989: 1).

Lipset's explanation rests on the assertion of an abiding and long-standing political *difference* between the two countries. Again, as with the narrative about American exceptionalism described above, this assertion of long-standing cross-national difference seems plausible, especially given the sharpness of the current-day differences.

But against Lipset and others, my research found a different story. Rather than being the product of long-standing cultural differences, I found that what we now recognize as significant differences in US and Canadian class politics are the product of a relatively recent political *divergence*. And again, the political tumult of the Great Depression and World War II is key to understanding how and why that divergence occurred.

SOURCES

Much of the core evidence for this book involves primary materials gathered from eight archives in the United States and Canada over the course of 2008 and 2009. These archival collections comprised a wide array of personal and professional materials from key labor, business, and state actors and organizations in both countries. Materials included personal correspondence, office memoranda, speech transcripts, diaries, legislative hearings, case transcripts, official government commission reports and proceedings, pamphlets and other mobilizing and educational materials, contemporary news accounts, and more. I include a list of archival sources in Appendix B.

I use a variety of statistical data to trace broad trajectories of social, economic, and organizational processes over the course of the twentieth century. Much of this statistical data is used to evaluate the validity of competing explanations for diverging union density that comprises the first section of the study. More detailed information on statistical data is included in Appendix A.

Given that the empirics of this comparative case study cover two countries over the better part of a century, I also rely on a wide range of secondary materials to elaborate my account of US–Canada political differences. There is a rich existing historiography examining twentieth-century labor and politics in both countries, particularly for the critical period in the 1930s and '40s, and a bevy of high-quality studies of the 1970s have been published in recent years. This allows for a careful evaluation of competing historical interpretations. In developing my argument, I use the primary and statistical data to offer a fresh reinterpretation of existing accounts.

OVERVIEW

To explain how the class idea became more embedded in Canadian politics, policies, and organizational practices relative to the United States, this book proceeds in two steps, each of which comprises its own section.

Part I examines in detail the existing set of competing explanations for US–Canada union density divergence. Chapter 1 evaluates structural and individual factors, Chapter 2 evaluates policy differences, and Chapter 3 examines differences in working-class power, which includes differences in political institutions, national characteristics, internal union characteristics, and the structure of racial divisions.

Having examined the strengths and limitations of existing explanations, Part II proceeds to elaborate an alternative explanation for union density divergence – the political articulation thesis. This section is organized around three central questions that are essential to explaining US–Canada union density divergence, and to which existing accounts do not have adequate answers. Each of these questions comprises its own chapter. First, in Chapter 4, I take on the question of why party systems changed in both countries. More specifically, I examine why US labor abandoned efforts to form an independent political party in favor of an alliance with the Democratic Party at the very same moment that Canadian workers forged an alliance with farmers to establish an independent Left party, the CCF.

In Chapter 5, I examine the diverging relationships between labor and the Left that developed in the United States and Canada in the postwar decades. I seek to explain why, despite similar past histories of left repression and rebirth, did Cold War anti-communism have a more devastating impact in the United States than in Canada?

In Chapter 6, I examine the formation and development of US and Canadian labor regimes, the set of policies and practices governing labor–management relations in both countries. Here the central question involves explaining why the US labor regime eroded over time, while the Canadian regime remained more resilient.

In each of these chapters, I focus the inquiry on the consequences deriving from different processes of political incorporation: US labor's political incorporation as an interest group, compared to Canadian labor's political incorporation as a class representative. Finally, I conclude the study by bringing the analysis up to the present day, examining the challenges that labor has faced in both countries in an age dominated by free market orthodoxy, and offering some considerations and conjectures about the future of class politics in the United States and Canada.

PART I

EXPLAINING UNION DENSITY DIVERGENCE

1

Structural and Individual Explanations

> If you went to a factory in the 1970s, you would have seen assembly lines of people. Such workers were much more amenable to the idea of "class consciousness." Go to a factory today and you might you get a few people monitoring robots and other whizzy bits of machinery. Add to the mix globalisation, which makes it harder for unions to regulate work, the rise of a more flexible service sector, and government policies ... and the loss of union clout seems inevitable.
>
> "Why Trade Unions Are Declining"
> (*The Economist* 2015)

> Labor union membership is an outdated concept for most working Americans. It is a relic of Depression-era labor-management relations.
>
> J. Justin Wilson, Center for Union Facts
> (quoted in Greenhouse 2010: B5)

Much of today's conventional wisdom sees US union decline as the result of structural changes in the economy, particularly the shift from manufacturing to service employment, and geographic employment shifts from union strongholds in the Northeast and Midwest to the largely union-free South and Southwest (Bluestone and Harrison 1982; Craver 2005; Dickens and Leonard 1985; Hildebrand 1979; Juris and Roomkin 1980; *New York Times* 2008). Another common view is that unions have declined either because workers no longer believe they are necessary, or employers have become more aggressively anti-union (Bronfenbrenner 1994, 2009; Fantasia and Voss 2004; Farber 1990; Jacoby 1991; Kleiner 2001; Weiler 1983).

Comparing the United States with Canada provides a useful way of evaluating these common explanations. In this chapter, we will first focus on structural explanations for union decline, comparing differences in the timing and extent of sectoral and geographic employment shifts. We will also consider the argument that Canada's larger and more heavily unionized public sector conceals a pattern of union density convergence in the private sector. Then, we will compare shifts in attitudes toward unions in both countries among workers and employers to gauge the power of individual explanations.

STRUCTURAL EXPLANATIONS

The Service Sector Shift

If union decline were the result of the shift from heavily unionized manufacturing jobs toward less-unionized, more difficult to organize service sector jobs, we would expect to see relatively higher levels of manufacturing employment in Canada compared to the United States over time, particularly since the mid-1960s.

That is not what we see. Figure 1.1 shows that the share of service sector employment[1] grew at almost the same rate in both countries. While service sector employment has a slightly smaller share in Canada, the gap is nowhere near large enough to account for the union density gap.[2]

The Public Sector Confounder

Supporters of the service sector shift hypothesis argue that the divergence in aggregate union density is an artifact of Canada's larger and more heavily unionized public sector, which conceals a trend of union density convergence in the private sector (Jones 1992; Troy 1990, 1992, 2000).

---

[1] For a discussion of the criteria used to distinguish between manufacturing and service sector employment, see Appendix A.

[2] Troy (1992) argues that the apparent divergence between US and Canadian union density rates is actually an artifact of Canada's slower shift to service sector employment. If that were the case, we would expect the lag effect to wear off at some point. But that has not happened. While private sector union density has declined in both countries, the decline has been far more dramatic in the United States than in Canada (see Figure 1.3). There has been no convergence.

An additional counter from Troy is that "intrusive" labor policies in Canada, paired with more protectionist trade and currency exchange policies, shielded Canadian private sector unions from the full brunt of shifts in the global labor market. But to the extent that this is true, it simply begs the question as to why Canadian policies were more pro-labor than those in the United States. See Chapter 6 for more on this.

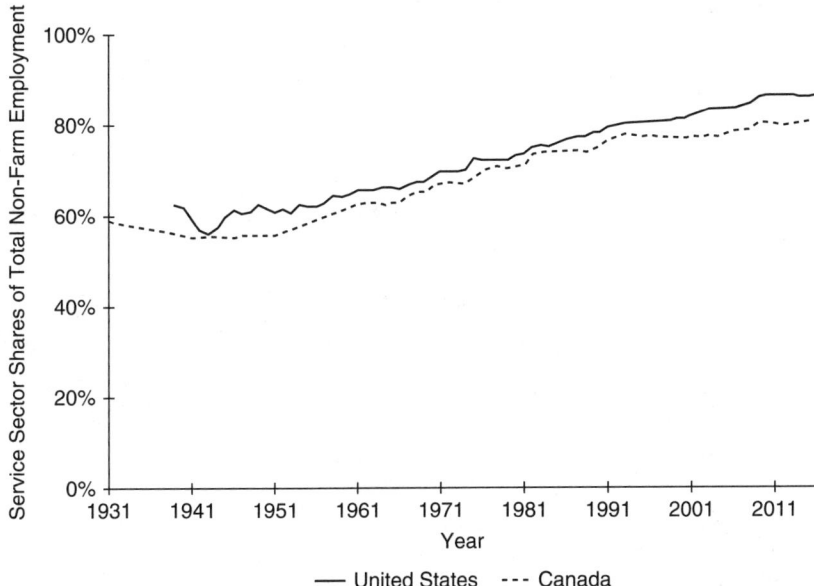

FIGURE 1.1 Service sector shares of total nonfarm employment in the United States and Canada, 1931–2016
Source: See Appendix A

A central assumption of this approach is that the dynamics affecting the growth of public and private sector unionism are so fundamentally different that they should be examined as separate union movements. Likewise, a key corollary of this approach is that, while state policies may play a role in determining union density in the public sector, such interventions are ultimately fruitless in the private sector.

Again, if the public sector confounder explanation is correct, we would first expect to find that public sector employment is in fact a larger proportion of overall employment in Canada than in the United States. Second, we would expect not only that Canadian public sector density should be higher than US public sector density, but also that the gap between public and private sector density should be larger than in the United States.

What do the data show? There are serious limitations to the available historical data disaggregating public and private sector union density, as well as difficulties with defining what constitutes public or private sector employment. I discuss these limitations in Appendix A.[3] That said, these

---

[3] The main problem is that Canadian public sector data is only available beginning in 1960. But given that public sector unionism was not a significant portion of union membership

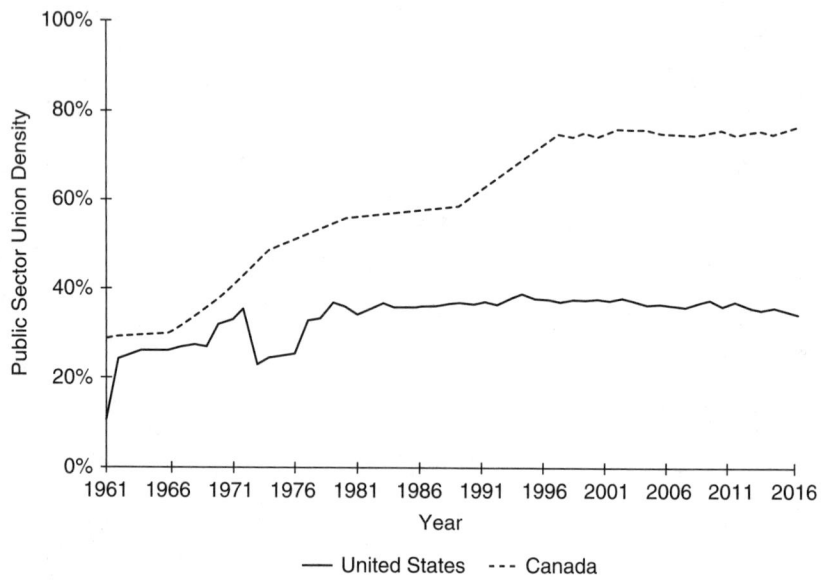

FIGURE 1.2 Public sector union density in the United States and Canada, 1961–2016
Source: See Appendix A

calculations remain the best estimates of disaggregated public and private sector unionization over time in the United States and Canada.

Figures 1.2 and 1.3 report union density statistics for the United States and Canada, disaggregated into public and private sector membership between 1961 and 2016. Looking first at public sector density, we see significant growth in both countries from the early 1960s through the mid-1970s. US public sector density fell behind somewhat in this period, but still grew at a healthy pace. The divergence occurred in the mid-1970s. At this point, US public sector density peaked at 40 percent, then flatlined in the high 30 percent range. Meanwhile, in Canada, public sector density continued its upward trajectory, reaching the mid-70 percent range by the mid-1990s, then stabilizing in that range for the remainder of the period.[4]

---

until the 1960s, and that the US–Canada divergence only began in 1964, this lack of historical data is less problematic than it might initially seem. There is also the problem of how to define employment in the Transportation, Communications, and Utilities (TCU) sector, which I discuss in detail in Appendix A.

[4] Given that public sector union density calculates the number of union members as a percentage of total public sector employment, as opposed to total number of union-eligible public sector employees, many scholars agree that Canadian public sector union density is approaching saturation levels (Rose 1984).

Structural Explanations

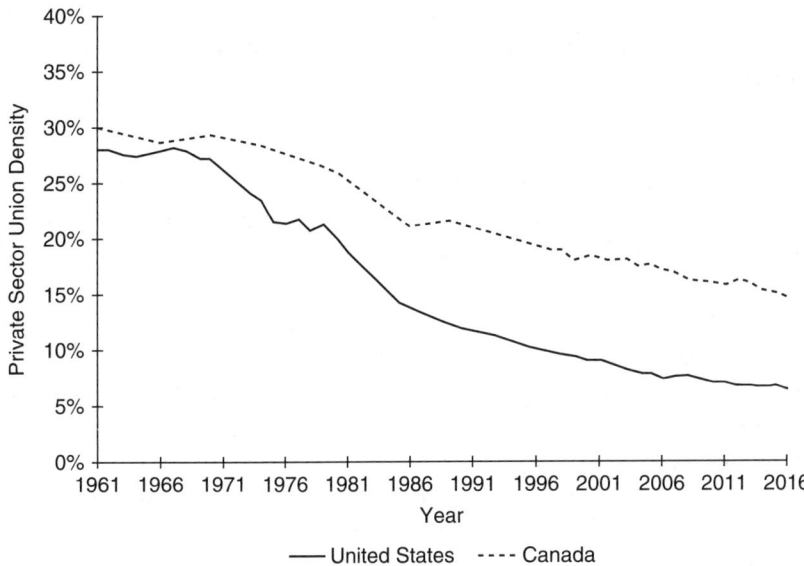

FIGURE 1.3 Private sector union density in the United States and Canada, 1961–2016
Source: See Appendix A

Over the entire 1961–2016 period, Canadian public sector union density rates went from being virtually identical to those in the United States in 1961, to being 122 percent higher in 2016.

Looking next at the private sector, we see that union density did decline in both countries. However, the trajectories of decline were quite different. In the United States, private sector union density experienced a large and continuous decline over the entire time period, dropping from 27.9 percent in 1961 to a mere 6.4 percent in 2016. Private sector union density in Canada declined significantly over the entire time period as well, dropping by half, from 30 percent in 1961 to 14.6 percent in 2016. However, the Canadian pattern was much less linear than in the United States. Private sector density was relatively stable through the 1960s into the 1970s, then dropped sharply between 1974 and 1986, from 28.3 percent to 21.0 percent. Canadian density leveled off through the end of the 1990s, then declined again by about four percentage points over the course of the 2000s and has been relatively stable since 2010. The bulk of Canadian private sector union density decline in Canada was concentrated in the late 1970s and early 1980s.

Over the entire 1961–2016 period, Canadian private sector union density rates went from being virtually identical to those in the United States in 1961, to being 128 percent higher in 2016.

Overall, the data show that public sector union growth starting in the 1960s mitigated private sector union density decline in both countries. But public sector growth in Canada *did not* mask a pattern of density decline and *convergence* in the private sector. Rather, there was density divergence in both sectors.

Indeed, what is striking about the US–Canada density divergence is how proportionally uniform it is across the public and private sectors. As of 2016, public sector density stands at 34.4 percent in the United States compared to 76.3 percent in Canada, or more than double. Similarly, private sector density currently stands at 6.4 percent in the United States compared to 14.6 percent in Canada, again more than double. These ratios have been relatively constant since the mid-1990s.

But what about the *size* of the public sector? Might Canada's larger public sector artificially insulate a greater proportion of the labor market from market forces that would otherwise drive down unionization rates, as they have in the United States (Troy 1992, 2000)?

Empirically, it is true that public sector employment as a percentage of total employment has been consistently higher in Canada relative to the United States over the past fifty years, as Figure 1.4 shows. Given that this is the sector that has experienced the greatest growth in union density in both countries, and is by far the most heavily unionized sector, the fact that Canada's public sector has been between one and a half to two times larger than that of the United States has certainly increased the relative difference in aggregate union density levels.

However, the fact that the Canadian public sector is proportionally larger than that of the United States still leaves important questions unanswered. At a basic level, there is the issue that the difference in public sector size between the two countries has remained fairly constant, even as union density rates have diverged. Also, even though the compositional effect may partially explain the divergence in aggregate union density, it does not explain why public sector union density in Canada has grown so much more than in the United States.

But beyond questions of simple arithmetic, the issue of the different sizes of the United States and Canadian public sectors raises the deeper question of *why* the Canadian public sector is bigger than that of the United States. Unlike the distinction between, say, the transportation and manufacturing sectors, which is definitional, the distinction between the public and private sectors is inherently a *political* decision. Governments decide which social and economic tasks are best organized and executed via private market mechanisms, and which tasks, for reasons of social

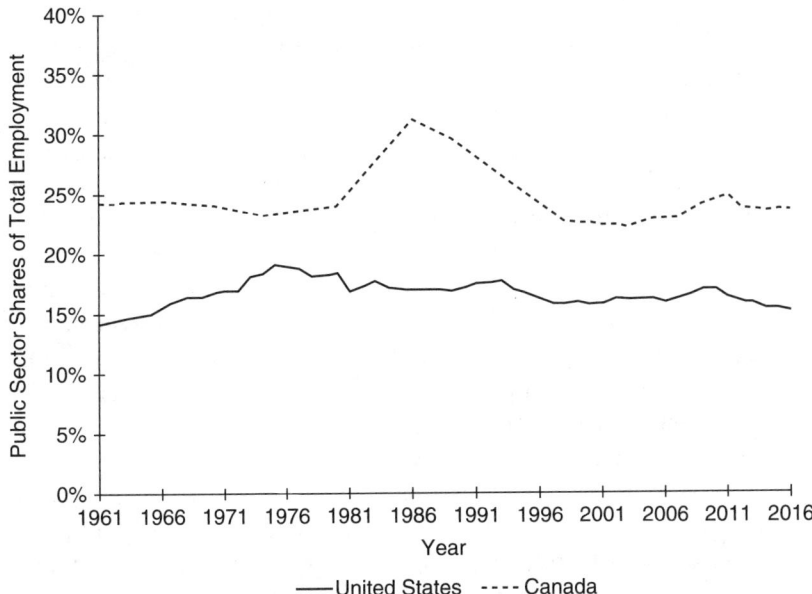

FIGURE 1.4 Public sector shares of total nonfarm employment in the United States and Canada, 1961–2016
Source: See Appendix A

necessity, equity concerns, market inefficiencies, or other factors, require the greater insulation from market forces that the public sector provides.

In other words, Canada's comparatively larger public sector is not simply a given, but is rather a product of policy decisions.[5] The starkest example of this would be the difference between the US health-care system, which is largely private, and the Canadian health-care system, which is largely public (Maioni 1998). Instead of helping to explain diverging union density rates, then, the difference in public sector sizes is part of what needs to be explained.

The broader question though is why we insist on making such a hard and fast distinction between public and private sector unionism in the first place (McAlevey 2016). At an institutional level, the distinction makes sense because public and private sector unions operate in different contexts. The laws governing union certification and collective bargaining for public and private sector unions are different. With a few notable exceptions, the laws governing public sector unions are considered to be more

---

[5] I thank Stephanie Ross for this insight.

favorable toward unions, and public sector employers today are generally less likely to resist unionization attempts (Freeman 1988). Due to these institutional differences, many analysts choose to separate the two sectors.

Labor economists distinguish between public and private sector unions because of their different relations to markets. Private sector unions are more subject to market forces, whereas public sector unions are more insulated from them. Given that the central tenet of the structural shift hypothesis is that market forces, not government policies, ultimately shape the trajectories of national labor movements, it makes sense that proponents of this argument would focus their analysis on the portion of the labor movement most subject to those market forces. As a result, their primary interest in public sector unions lies in demonstrating that their growth has masked underlying patterns of union decline in the private sector. The implicit assumption is that it is the private sector unions that truly matter.

However, there are downsides to discounting the importance of public sector unionism. At the most basic level, discounting the strength of public sector unionism involves discounting a large segment of the overall labor market, currently anywhere from 15 to 25 percent of overall employment. Public sector employers are now among the largest employers in many communities across both the United States and Canada, and many of the largest labor unions in both countries primarily represent public sector workers. To say that these employers, workers, and unions simply don't factor into the shape of the overall economy or labor market is dubious at best (McCartin 2006).

Furthermore, while public and private sector unions may operate in different legal environments when it comes to their specific duties as collective bargaining agents, they operate in similar political and organizational environments. Many unions on both sides of the border organize in both the public and private sectors, and gains in the public sector can leverage gains in the private sector. For example, unions often act in the political realm on behalf of both public and private sector workers, and can mobilize for government policies that improve the wages and working conditions of workers in all sectors. Additionally, given that public sector jobs are present in every community, having a large public sector union membership means that more people are more likely to know or have regular interactions with union workers, which in turn increases the "normalcy" of union membership. This can have an effect on overall attitudes toward unions (Godard 2003: 464, n. 7).

Moreover, the symbolic power of public and private sector unions is intimately linked. To illustrate this, we need only think of the negative example in the United States of President Reagan's dismantling of the Professional Air Traffic Controllers Organization (PATCO) air traffic controllers' union in 1981. Despite the fact that PATCO was a public sector union, its defeat is now seen as a symbolic marker for the beginning of a new, more hostile era for labor unions as a whole, in both the public and private sectors (Fantasia and Voss 2004: 66–68; Farber and Western 2002; McCartin 2006). More recently, we saw public and private sector unions join together to fight efforts by governors in Wisconsin and Ohio to implement legislation aimed at restricting public sector unions' ability to function. Both public and private sector union members saw this legislation not only as an attack on public sector workers, but on unions as a whole. And likewise, the mass demonstrations organized in response to these legislative initiatives were viewed as a defense of labor unions in general, not public sector workers in particular.

So even though Canada and the United States may differ in the size of their public sectors, this difference does not adequately explain union density divergence. Not only does it not account for why Canadian public sector union density grew much larger than in the United States, but using the relative size difference to explain density divergence ignores the political questions involved in determining the size of the public sector in the first place. Furthermore, viewing public sector unionization solely as a mitigating factor covering up declining private sector unionism overlooks the independent importance of public sector unionism as a phenomenon, and the close political and organizational links between public and private sector unionism.

Shifts in Geographic Distribution

The geographic distribution argument holds that union density declined in the United States as a result of employment shifting from higher-density states in the Northeast and Midwest to lower-density states in the Southeast and Southwest (Bluestone and Harrison 1982: 165). By contrast, the more even distribution of union density rates across provinces in Canada meant that whatever shifts in aggregate employment occurred had little effect on aggregate union density rates there.

Map 1.1 overlays 2016 union density and changes in employment between 1939 and 2016 by state/province. It shows that US interstate union density is currently more dispersed than Canadian interprovincial density. This is consistent with historical patterns. US ranges have varied from a low of 20.3 percentage points separating the highest-density and

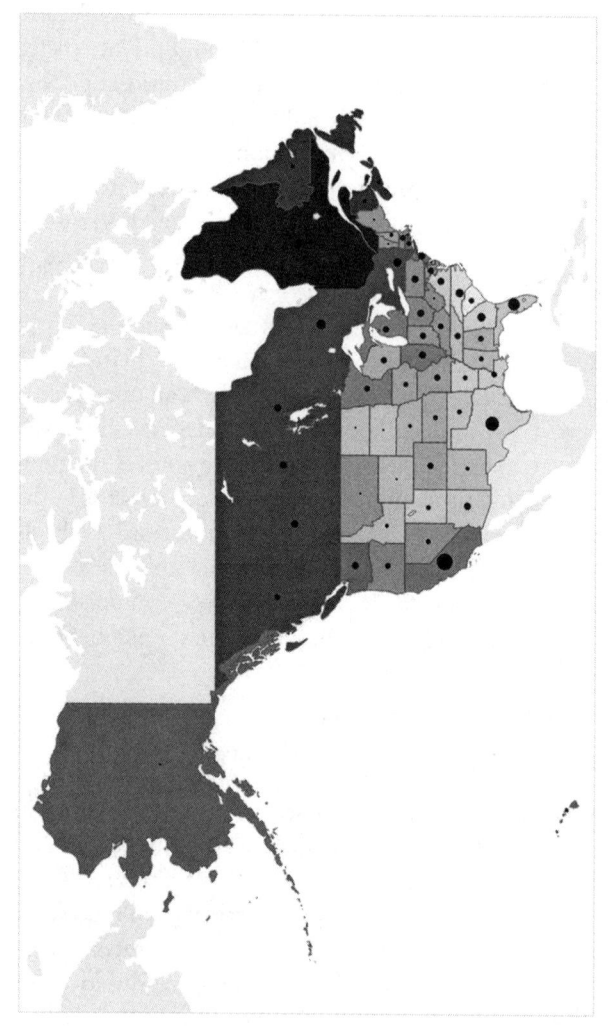

MAP 1.1 Union density by state/province in 2016 and increase in number of people employed from 1939 to 2016

lowest-density states in 2012, to a high of 45.8 percentage points in 1953. By contrast, Canadian ranges have varied from a low of 8.6 percentage points in 1987 and 1988 to a high of 25 percentage points in 1955. In other words, Canadian interprovincial union density dispersion at its peak barely surpassed US interstate union density dispersion at its lowest point.[6]

Furthermore, these density differences in the United States are geographically clustered. As of 2016, nine out of the ten lowest-density states are in the South or Southwest, whereas eight of the ten highest-density states are Northeastern or West Coast states,[7] and the other two are Midwestern states. Twenty of the twenty-one lowest-density states are located in the Southeast, Southwest, or Mountain/Great Plains regions,[8] whereas fourteen of the fifteen highest-density states are located in the Northeast, Midwest, or West Coast. So to the extent that employment did shift from the higher-density to lower-density regions, this could have caused aggregate union density rates to decline.

At first glance, the map does not show a clear pattern of larger overall employment growth in lower-density states. Many low-density states in the US South did add large numbers of jobs, but so too did some high-density states, particularly in the West.[9] While four of the ten lowest-density states (Georgia, North Carolina, Texas, and Virginia) are among the ten highest employment-growth states, so too are three of the ten highest-density states (California, New York, and New Jersey). Similarly, eight of the twenty lowest-density states are among the twenty highest-employment-growth states, as are eight of the twenty highest-density states.

However, shifts in aggregate employment only tell part of the story. We must also consider the types of jobs that have moved. In addition to being clustered geographically, union membership in the United States is

---

[6] For tables showing detailed historical state- and provincial-level union density data, see Appendix A, Tables A.2 and A.3.
[7] Here, "West Coast" states include Alaska and Hawaii.
[8] The one exception is Wisconsin, where union density has collapsed since Governor Scott Walker took office in 2011, declining from 13.5 percent to 8.2 percent. Walker's Act 10 for the public sector and right-to-work law for the private sector are likely contributing factors.
[9] It is true that lower-density states generally experienced higher *rates* of employment growth. However, the map displays the absolute change in the number of people employed, as opposed to percentage change by state, because our main interest here is to determine factors affecting aggregate union density at the national level, not to determine which states have experienced the largest proportional growth in employment. Since union density is calculated by dividing the number of union members by the number of nonagricultural workers, larger states that add more workers to their employment rolls by definition increase the size of the overall denominator (nonagricultural workers) more than do smaller states, even if percentage-wise, the smaller states may have experienced higher rates of employment growth.

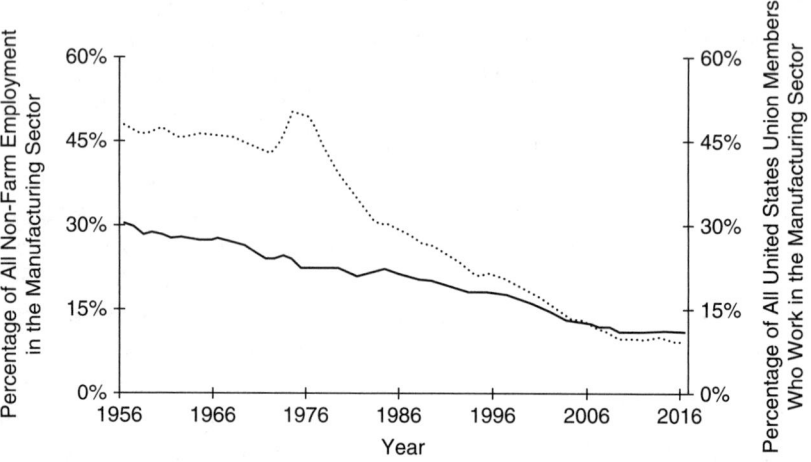

— Percentage of All Non-Farm Employment in the Manufacturing Sector
····· Percentage of All United States Union Members Who Work in the Manufacturing Sector

FIGURE 1.5 Percentage of all nonfarm employment in the manufacturing sector in the United States, and percentage of all US union members who work in the manufacturing sector, 1956–2016

Sources: Total non-farm and manufacturing employment, 1956–1983: BLS Current Employment Survey. Manufacturing union membership, 1956–1978: Historical Statistics of the United States, Table Ba4832-4844. Union membership, by industry: 1956–1978. Non-farm employment and total union membership, 1973–2016: US Current Population Survey, via www.unionstats.com. Manufacturing employment and manufacturing union membership, 1983–2016: US Current Population Survey, via www.unionstats.com.

also clustered by industry. For much of the twentieth century, the manufacturing sector was labor's stronghold. As Figure 1.5 shows, as late as the mid-1970s, half of all US union members were in the manufacturing sector, even as only a quarter of all jobs were. Only around the year 2000 did the number of manufacturing sector union members as a proportion of all union members begin to equal the number of manufacturing sector jobs as a proportion of all jobs. If manufacturing jobs in particular were moving from high-density to low-density states, then that could have had a disproportionate effect on union density overall.[10]

[10] In Canada, a similar pattern as in Figure 1.5 prevails, except that number of manufacturing sector union members as a proportion of all Canadian union members only reached 42.6 percent at its peak in 1965, and reached parity with the number of manufacturing sector jobs as a proportion of all jobs by 1990.

Available measures of value added, or net output, do suggest that manufacturing activity – and by extension employment – shifted toward the low-density South in the decades following World War II. Between 1947 and 2003, the South's share of national value added in manufacturing rose from 13.2 to 30.7 percent. Between 1947 and 1989, the rate of growth of real value added in manufacturing in the US South was more than double the rate for the country as a whole (Moody 2007). Additionally, a systematic analysis by Farber (1985) showed that employment shifts from the heavily unionized North Central and Northeast to the South from 1953 to 1978 accounted for 16 percent of the decline in union membership over that time period.

Taken together, these findings suggest that geographic employment shifts were a contributing factor to union decline, though not likely the central culprit. Also, the geographic shift argument takes as given the wide inter-state dispersion of union density rates, when this dispersion is part of what must be explained. Why is union density so uneven across the United States, and why is it so geographically clustered?

Overall, the geographic shift hypothesis hints at part of *what* happened to cause US–Canada union density divergence, but does not explain *why* it happened.

While variants of the structural shift hypothesis may seem plausible at first glance, upon closer inspection they only provide partial answers to the question of why US and Canadian union density rates diverged. While US employment did shift from more highly unionized goods-producing jobs to less unionized service sector jobs, Canada underwent a similar shift without suffering a decline in unionization rates. Recent decades have been difficult for private sector unions in both countries, but less so in Canada, where union density remains more than twice as high as in the United States. The growth of public sector unionism has been an important mitigating factor for labor movements in both countries, offsetting declines in the private sector. However, this growth of public sector unionization does not explain the aggregate divergence in US–Canada union density, as both public and private sector density rates diverged, and cross-border ratios for public and private density are very similar. As for differences in the geographic distribution of employment shifts, this does appear to be a key difference between the United States and Canada, and a potential contributing factor to diverging union density. However, what remains to be explained is *why* interstate union density rates are so much more dispersed in the United States than are interprovincial rates in Canada.

INDIVIDUAL DIFFERENCES

If structural explanations for union density divergence are insufficient, what about individual explanations? Did US and Canadian union density diverge because US workers did not want to be unionized as much as their Canadian counterparts? Or was it because US employers were much more hostile toward unions than they were in Canada?

Shifts in Unionization Preferences

The preference shift argument holds that union density has diverged in the United States and Canada because US workers' desire to join or remain in unions has declined relative to their northern counterparts.

To evaluate the argument, we can turn to available individual survey data. From the 1940s through to the present, the Gallup organization included questions in its poll in both the United States and Canada that sought to gauge respondents' attitudes toward labor unions.[11] Figure 1.6 reports the percentage of respondents who indicated general approval of labor unions in both countries.

The first thing to notice is that in both countries, approval of labor unions is much higher than rates of union membership. Approval rates always exceed disapproval rates in both countries, and in the United States are almost always an absolute majority. Second, approval rates are relatively similar in both countries over time, with rates in Canada actually somewhat *lower* than in the United States. Third, although union approval rates declined in the United States, they also did in Canada. Unlike union density rates, which diverged sharply, union approval rates in both countries largely followed a similar trajectory.

Of course, general attitudes toward unions are an imperfect measure of individual workers' actual propensities to join a union. More

---

[11] In Canada, there were three different questions posed. For 1950 to 1958 and 1976 to 2001, the question asked was "Generally speaking, do you think that labour unions have been a good thing or a bad thing for Canada?" Between 1961 and 1975, the question asked was "In general do you approve or disapprove of labour unions?" The Canadian Gallup Poll ended in 2001, and the Angus Reid Strategies Group took over responsibility for asking questions regarding union approval. In 2007, the Angus Reid poll asked the question "Do you agree or disagree with the following statements? Labour unions are a necessary and important entity in our society." For the United States, the question asked was "In general, do you approve or disapprove of labor unions?" The 2013 data point for Canada is from a Harris/Decima survey conducted for the Canadian Association of University Teachers (CAUT). The question asked then was "Generally speaking, do you think unions make a positive or negative contribution to our society?"

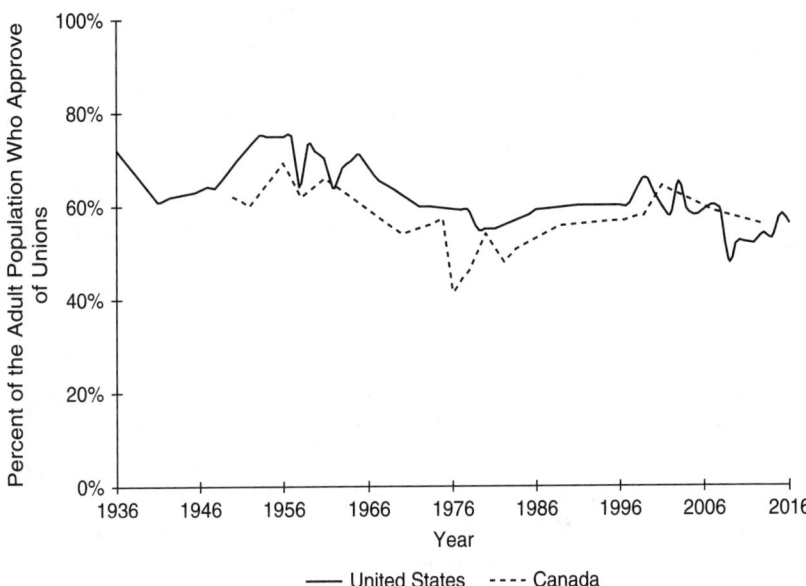

FIGURE 1.6 Percent of the adult population who approve of unions in the United States and Canada, 1936–2016
Sources: US: Gallup poll, various years, www.gallup.com/file/poll/149282/Labor_Union_Approval_110831.pdf. Canada: Canadian Institute of Public Opinion, The Gallup Report, various years, finding aid at http://data2.archives.ca/pdf/pdf001/p000000715.pdf. For 2007, Canadian data is from Angus Reid Strategies poll. For 2013, Canadian data is from a Harris/Decima survey conducted for the Canadian Association of University Teachers (CAUT).

TABLE 1.1 *Voting intentions of nonunion and union employees in the United States and Canada, 1994–1995*

	United States		Canada	
	Nonunion	Union	Nonunion	Union
Vote for/retain union	35.50%	90.94%	36.64%	80.09%
Vote against union	64.50%	9.06%	63.36%	19.91%

Source: WRPS. Percentages exclude "don't know/no response" responses.

direct measures of union support are only available for recent decades. Table 1.1 reports results collected in the mid-1990s as part of the Worker Representation and Participation Survey (WRPS), developed by Richard Freeman and Joel Rogers (Freeman and Rogers

1998).[12] According to this survey, 36 percent of nonunionized workers in the United States said that they would vote in favor of union representation if given the opportunity, while 91 percent of unionized workers said that they would vote to keep the union at their workplace. In Canada, 37 percent of nonunionized workers said that they would vote in favor of union representation, while 80 percent of unionized workers said that they would vote to keep their union. At the time that the surveys were administered, union density rates stood at 35 percent in Canada and 15 percent in the United States.

Similarly, Seymour Martin Lipset and Noah Meltz designed a survey to measure US and Canadian workers' demand for union representation, which was conducted in 1996. While their results for Canada largely match those of Freeman and Rogers, they found significantly higher numbers of nonunionized US workers who would vote in favor of union representation if given the opportunity.[13] As reported in Table 1.2, 48 percent of nonunionized workers in the United States said that they would

TABLE 1.2 *Voting intentions of nonunion and union employees in the United States and Canada, 1996*

	United States		Canada	
	Nonunion	Union	Nonunion	Union
Vote for/retain union	48.2%	90.5%	33.0%	85.8%
Vote against union	51.8%	9.5%	66.7%	14.2%

Source: Lipset and Meltz, Survey on Attitudes toward Work and Unions. Percentages exclude "don't know/no response" responses.

---

[12] The first wave of the US WRPS survey was conducted September–October 1994. The Canadian WRPS survey was conducted in November 1995. Workers not represented by a union were asked "If you were asked today whether employees like you should be represented by a union, would you be for or against forming one?" Workers already represented by a union were asked "If you had to decide today whether to keep the union or employee organization at your workplace, would you choose to keep it or get rid of it?"

[13] It is unclear why there is such a discrepancy between the two surveys specifically on the question of nonunion US workers' demand for union representation. This is especially puzzling because 1) the responses to the other questions line up much more closely; and 2) the questions in the Lipset-Meltz survey were in many cases borrowed from the WRPS survey to ensure comparability (Campolieti, Gomez, and Gunderson 2007b: 52).

vote in favor of union representation, while 91 percent of unionized workers said that they would vote to keep the union at their workplace. In Canada, 33 percent of nonunionized workers said that they would vote in favor of union representation, while 86 percent of unionized workers said that they would vote to keep their union.

While the WRPS and Lipset-Meltz surveys only provide snapshots taken in the mid-1990s, they do cast doubt on the idea that union decline is a reflection of workers' preference not to be in a union. On the contrary, these surveys suggest that there is what economists would call "frustrated demand" for unions. Given actual union density rates at the time of the surveys of 15 percent in the United States and 35 percent in Canada, this suggests that 29–39 percent of US workers and 16–17 percent of Canadian workers would have liked to be union members, but were not.

Having time series data with responses to these questions would offer more reliable evidence with which to evaluate the preference shift argument. But combining the cross-sectional data we do have with the Gallup data showing relatively similar and declining levels of approval for unions over time in the United States and Canada suggests that it is unlikely that union density divergence is the result of diverging individual preferences for union representation.

Employer Hostility

The employer hostility argument holds that US employers are exceptionally hostile toward unions, and as such have fought workers' unionization efforts much harder than their Canadian counterparts.

Two forms of evidence exist to evaluate this claim. First, there are surveys of US and Canadian employers (Saporta and Lincoln 1995; Wright 1990). While these are easily quantifiable and comparable, they are cross-sectional analyses and do not measure changes in employer attitudes over time. Second, there are historical accounts of US employer behavior that we can compare with accounts of Canadian employer behavior (Jacoby 1991; Pentland 1968; Taras 1997; Yarmie 2003). While such accounts are less systematic than the survey data, they do allow for an examination of employer attitudes and behaviors over time.

Looking first at the survey data, Saporta and Lincoln (1995) analyzed responses given by managerial employees to questions about workplace relations as part of the Comparative Project on Class Structure and Class

Consciousness (Wright 1990).[14] Saporta and Lincoln's analysis found no significant different difference between US and Canadian managers' responses to any of the questions (1995: 557–558). These findings held even when analyzing the ostensibly more anti-union US South and more ostensibly pro-union Canadian province of Quebec separately (561–563). They did find that US workers were generally more hostile to employers than Canadian workers (560).

Similarly, Lipset and Meltz' survey (2004) asked questions specifically to respondents who identified themselves as managers. Their findings indicated more *pro*-union sentiments among US managers as compared to Canadian managers. Fully 68 percent of US managers expressed general approval of unions, compared to 57 percent of Canadian managers. When asked more specific questions about how they would react to a union organizing drive in their workplace, 59 percent of US managers stated that they would either welcome the union or do nothing to stop it. By comparison, only 37 percent of Canadian managers reported that they would act in similar ways. At the other end of the spectrum, 7 percent of US managers stated that they would resort to strong measures such as threats in order to fight the union's campaign, as opposed to 12 percent of Canadian managers.

Overall, the existing survey data suggest that, at an attitudinal level, US and Canadian employers are not that different from each other as individuals.[15] Depending on which findings we consult, Canadian employers even appear to be *more* hostile toward unions than their US counterparts. However, around the time that both the Wright and the Lipset and Meltz surveys were administered, union density had

---

[14] Managers were asked to rate how strongly they agreed or disagreed with the following four statements:

1. Imagine that workers in a major industry are out on strike over working conditions and wages. Which of the following outcomes would you like to see occur?
   a. Workers win
   b. Make some concessions
   c. Make major concessions
   d. Go back to work without winning
2. During a strike, management should be prohibited by law from hiring workers to take the place of strikers.
3. Striking workers are generally justified in physically preventing strike-breakers from entering the place of work.
4. Corporations benefits owners at the expense of workers and customers.

[15] At least they were not that different twenty years ago when the surveys were administered, which is around thirty years after US–Canada union density divergence began.

already sharply diverged in both countries, standing at 30.9 percent in Canada as opposed to 14.1 percent in the United States by 1997 (19.0 percent vs. 9.7 percent in the private sector). It is thus unlikely that individual employer attitudes are driving union density divergence.

While the survey data show that US and Canadian employers had similar attitudes in the 1990s, has this long been the case? There are very few historical comparative studies of US and Canadian employer behavior that can help us with this question. One of the most detailed is Yarmie's (2003) cross-border comparison of employers in Washington state and British Columbia around the turn of the twentieth century. He finds that in many respects, Canadian employers matched their US counterparts both in their vociferous opposition to unions and in their dedication to asserting their "right to manage" (587). Not only did Vancouver employers engage in anti-union "open-shop" campaigns similar to those in Seattle, but their employer organizations coordinated with each other, often organizing across borders (574–587).

Yarmie's findings are not new. Amidst the working-class upheaval of the late 1960s, the Canadian government tasked two of the country's most prominent industrial relations scholars, H. Clare Pentland and Stuart M. Jamieson, with producing reports analyzing the historical trajectory of labor relations in Canada.[16] Both authors found important similarities between levels of employer aggression in the United States and Canada. Pentland wrote that

[Canadian E]mployers ... shared the general hostility of employers everywhere to unionism, and especially to the upstart unionism of noncraft workers. Much that employers did in the [Canadian] west seems a reflection of the campaigns against noncraft unionism that were being carried on at the same time in Britain and the United States: there was, for instance, a great flourishing of labour injunctions. And, as elsewhere, the intensity of employer feeling was certainly raised by the socialist proclivities of the unions involved. But, in addition to this, there was a special ruthlessness of western employers, perhaps appropriate to stark relationships in a land without traditions (Pentland 1968: 93).

Furthermore, Pentland found that Canadian employer hostility did not wane as the twentieth century progressed. In surveying the state of post-World War II labor relations, he concluded that "the prime fact about employer attitudes in this period [1948–1967] ... is that they exhibit much the same character at the end of the period as in 1945: hard-line, conservative, authoritarian, and suspicious of unions" (1968: 370–371).

---

[16] We will return to these government-commissioned studies in Chapter 6.

Echoing Pentland, Jamieson concurred that

> Employers in Canada are and have been no less hostile to unions than were their United States counterparts. Indeed, the record seems to indicate that they were even more hostile in some respects. Suspicion and hostility towards "alien," "Yankee-dominated" unions provided, until fairly recently, a special rationale in some circles for intransigent opposition to organized labour. And, particularly among the larger concerns in primary and manufacturing industries, employers in Canada succeeded far longer than in the United States in refusing to recognize and bargain collectively with unions (Jamieson 1968: 51).

To the extent that there were differences between US and Canadian employers with regard to unions, they had more to do with economic policy than ideology. A more state-directed, tariff-protected form of economic development in Canada meant that Canadian employers were more likely than their US counterparts to acquiesce to government intervention in their business affairs. At the same time, the need to maintain political support for the tariff created an incentive for employers to hold back on all-out, scorched-earth anti-union campaigns (Yarmie 2003: 578).

Yarmie's study examines employer behavior in the late nineteenth and early twentieth centuries, and Pentland and Jamieson's studies were completed in the late 1960s. But according to proponents of the employer hostility argument, it was in the 1970s that levels of employer aggressiveness increased dramatically in the United States (Freeman and Medoff 1984; Goldfield 1989a). These studies cannot capture that change. However, the types of employer aggression cited in studies about the more recent period are focused primarily on employers' aggressive use of labor laws to delay and prevent worker attempts to unionize. We will address this form of employer aggression via use of labor laws in the following chapter.

While not conclusive, the existing survey and historical evidence suggests that employers in Canada and the United States have been united in their staunch opposition to unions. To the extent that we see cross-border variation, it is related to differences in policies and institutions that enable or constrain US and Canadian employers' ability to act on their mutual anti-union animus. Our next chapter will examine the substance of these policy differences in detail.

2

Policy Explanations

On February 13, 2016, the United States labor movement dodged a bullet. That day, news broke that Supreme Court Justice Antonin Scalia had been found dead in his bed at a remote hunting ranch in Shafter, Texas. Court watchers quickly recognized that his death meant a reprieve from what some considered a virtual death sentence for labor unions (Garden 2016).

The case in question was *Friedrichs v. California Teachers Association.*[1] It pitted a group of California teachers backed by anti-union organizations like the Center for Individual Rights (CIR) and the National Right to Work Foundation (NRTWF) against their union. It sought to exempt the teachers from any requirement to contribute toward the cost of negotiating and enforcing union contracts that covered their workplaces.

A ruling in favor of the plaintiffs would have overturned a nearly forty-year-old precedent known as *Abood v. Detroit Board of Education.*[2] That decision had established the "fair share" or "agency fee" requirement for members who objected to joining the union (Lithwick 2016). Because unions are legally obligated to represent all workers covered by their contracts, regardless of their membership status, abolishing the "fair share fee" requirement would have created what economists call a "free rider" problem: it would have given workers an incentive to enjoy their union-negotiated benefits without paying for them. These so-called right-to-work laws covering private sector workers have been passed in twenty-eight of fifty states, but *Friedrichs* would have extended such provisions to public sector workers in twenty-three states and the District of Columbia.

---

[1] *Friedrichs v. California Teachers Association*, 578 US ___ (2016)
[2] *Abood v. Detroit Board of Education*, 431 US 209 (1977)

Union supporters worried that an unfavorable decision in the case would be a huge financial blow that would decimate public sector unions' membership and cripple their ability to function (Marvit 2015).

Anticipating an adverse ruling, unions readied their plans for a post-*Friedrichs* world of dwindling membership and resources (California Teachers Association 2014; Epps 2016). But Scalia's death put an end to the imminent threat, as a deadlocked court meant that *Abood* would stay in place for the time being. Nevertheless, the arguments during *Friedrichs*, as well as previous Supreme Court decisions, made clear that unions' legal footing had eroded considerably since *Abood*. The Court's 2014 *Harris v. Quinn* decision, involving home health-care workers in Illinois, stopped short of invalidating "fair share" fees for all public sector workers, but it invited broader challenges to *Abood*.[3] Writing for the majority, Justice Samuel Alito declared that supporting the state's and the union's argument for fair share fees "would approve an unprecedented violation of the bedrock principle that, except perhaps in the rarest of circumstances, no person in this country may be compelled to subsidize speech by a third party that he or she does not wish to support." The *Friedrichs* plaintiffs explicitly based their argument on the contention that fair share fees constituted such compelled speech – a potential violation of the First Amendment (Center for Individual Rights 2016).

In January 2015, around the time that *Friedrichs* was making its way to the US Supreme Court, the Supreme Court of Canada issued its own set of rulings affecting workers, unions, and employers. The three decisions, dubbed the "New Labour Trilogy,"[4] reversed a set of nearly thirty-year-old precedents fittingly known as the "Labour Trilogy."[5] In the New Labour Trilogy decisions, the justices determined that the rights to join a union, engage in meaningful collective bargaining, and go on strike were constitutionally protected under the Canadian Charter of Rights and Freedoms. They declared that "collective bargaining is a necessary precondition to the meaningful exercise of the constitutional guarantee of freedom of association" (6), that "the right to strike is an essential part of

---

[3] *Harris v. Quinn*, 134 S. Ct. 2618 (2014).
[4] *Mounted Police Association of Ontario v. Canada (A.G.)*, 2015 SCC 1, *Meredith v. Canada (A.G.)*, 2015 SCC 2, and *Saskatchewan Federation of Labour v. Saskatchewan*, 2015 SCC 4.
[5] *Reference re Public Service Employee Relations Act (Alta.)*, [1987] 1 S.C.R. 313 ("*Alberta Reference*"), *PSAC v. Canada*, [1987] 1 S.C.R. 424, and *RWDSU v. Saskatchewan*, [1987] 1 S.C.R. 460.

a meaningful collective bargaining process" (248), and that "the ability to strike ... is an affirmation of the dignity and autonomy of employees in their working lives" (249).

The New Labour Trilogy was no fluke. The previous year, the court issued a decision in *United Food and Commercial Workers (UFCW) Local 503 v. Wal-Mart Canada.*[6] The case involved workers at a Walmart store in Jonquière, Québec, who were among the first Walmart workers in North America to join a union. The Walmart workers alleged that, rather than negotiate with their union, the company instead shut down the store in 2005 and laid off all the workers. Because they alleged that the store closing was not due to economic considerations, but rather to avoid the union, they charged that Walmart had violated the law.

In their 5–2 decision, the Supreme Court of Canada agreed with the workers and their union that Walmart had broken the law. The majority decision asserted that "the true function of the Labour Code is to foster the exercise of the right of association. Its purpose in circumscribing the employer's powers is *not merely to strike a balance* or maintain the status quo during the negotiation of a collective agreement, but is more precisely to facilitate certification and ensure that the parties bargain in good faith" (325, emphasis added).

Comparing the two courts' recent rulings says a lot about the current state of US and Canadian labor law. Whereas the US Court defined union activity as an infringement on individuals' constitutional right to freedom of speech, the Canadian Court defined it as an integral part of individuals' constitutional right to freedom of association. As a result, the US Court endorsed policies that undermined unions' ability to function, while the Canadian Court sanctioned policies that both strengthened unions and imposed limits on employer and government power.

Beyond the attitudes of the two Supreme Courts in these cases, many have argued that broader differences in labor laws explain the difference in US and Canadian union density. They contend that US labor laws have hamstrung unions' ability to organize new members, while doing little to prevent employers from quashing workers' efforts to unionize (Getman 2016). By contrast, they maintain that stronger Canadian labor laws have better protected workers' right to unionize there (Card and Freeman 1994; Riddell 1993).

In this chapter, we assess whether this argument holds water. Doing so will require a deep dive into the thicket of macroeconomic and labor

---

[6] *United Food and Commercial Workers, Local 503 v. Wal-Mart Canada Corp.*, 2014 SCC 45.

policies that, taken together, constitute the legal regimes governing labor relations in the United States and Canada. While we will consider different policies separately, this is purely for analytical clarity. No single policy is solely responsible for shaping union density trajectories. Rather, it is the labor law regimes as a whole that strengthen or weaken unions.

I recognize that such a deep dive requires a measure of dry analysis that may try the patience of some readers. To spoil the ending, I conclude from an historical analysis of labor relations policy in both countries that, while *current* differences in labor law end up protecting Canadian workers and their unions more than their US counterparts, this was not always the case. US law was previously considered more *pro-labor* than Canadian law. Moreover, many of the key provisions that scholars identify as contributing to higher Canadian union density were only implemented a decade or more *after* US and Canadian union density began to diverge. What remains to be explained is why the US labor law regime eroded over time, while the Canadian labor law regime strengthened. If you are prepared to accept this conclusion and move on, then feel free to skip this chapter. If, however, you would like to see the evidence for yourself, then I invite you to dive in with me.

HOW COULD LABOR POLICIES AFFECT UNION DENSITY?

At a basic level, it is worth recalling that since union density is a percentage, it can change due to changes in the numerator (union members) or the denominator (nonagricultural workers). Different policies can affect the growth patterns of both.

Looking first at policies that could affect the denominator, the first thing to note is that labor policy in both the United States and Canada is designed so that unions must "run to stand still." That is because existing law in both countries establishes union representation at the firm or workplace level. This means that, to become union members, workers must either create a union in a previously nonunion workplace or get hired on in a workplace where a past generation of workers at that firm previously took such action. Absent this, new jobs in both countries are "born" nonunion and must be made into union jobs.[7]

---

[7] This differs from corporatist models prevalent in many parts of Europe, where collective bargaining agreements are negotiated at the sectoral level between peak associations of workers and employers. The terms of those agreements apply to all employers in a given sector.

As such, the jobs that disappear due to normal ebbs and flows in the business cycle come from a mix of already-unionized or nonunionized firms, but new jobs come from the existing mix of union and nonunion firms, *plus* newborn firms that are by definition nonunion. Unless unions constantly organize new workers to make up for the members they lose at unionized firms that close or downsize, or employment at already-unionized firms outpaces employment growth in new and existing non-union firms, union density will decline. This dynamic cannot explain US–Canada union density divergence, since it affects union growth in both countries, but it will factor into the discussion in Chapter 3 when we discuss differences in unions' internal characteristics.

Other broad state policies can shape the labor market in ways that can affect union density. In particular, some have argued that the cheaper Canadian dollar and protectionist trade agreements, particularly the 1965 Canada–United States Automotive Products Trade Agreement (Auto Pact), sheltered heavily unionized manufacturing industries in Canada (Troy 2000: 709–710).

If exchange rates explained density divergence, we would expect to see the density gap widen as the Canadian dollar weakened against the US dollar. If trade policy had an impact, we would expect to see changes in the trajectory of Canadian union density as trade policy shifted from the more protectionist policy of the 1960s to a more deregulated "free trade" policy starting in the late 1980s and early 1990s. Specifically, we would expect to see union density divergence after implementation of the Auto Pact in 1965, and convergence after implementation of the US–Canada Free Trade Agreement (FTA) in 1988, followed by the North American Free Trade Agreement (NAFTA) in 1994.

Turning to policies that could affect the numerator, policies can affect union density by making it easier or harder for workers to join and/or remain in unions, and/or by making it easier or harder for employers to resist workers' attempts to unionize.

Scholars have identified four areas of labor policy that are of particular importance in explaining union density trajectories in both countries:

1) Rules governing the *certification process*, meaning the process that workers use to join or leave a union.
2) Rules governing the negotiation and implementation of a *first collective bargaining agreement*, as the collective bargaining-focused model of union representation in both the United States and Canada means that union membership has few concrete benefits

for workers until they are spelled out in a contract negotiated with company management.[8]

3) Rules governing *union security*, meaning policies to ensure unions' institutional stability, most notably so-called right-to-work laws.
4) Rules governing unions' permitted *scope of activity*, particularly around striking.

Some policies potentially affect both the union density numerator and denominator. This is most notably the case for right-to-work laws, as discussed in the chapter introduction (Davis and Huston 1995; Hogler, Shulman, and Weiler 2004; Moore 1998). While the *Friedrichs* case did not impose right-to-work provisions across the entire US public sector, a new case, *Janus v. AFSCME*, may end up doing that (Marvit 2017). Some conservative Republicans have also proposed a law that would expand right-to-work laws to the entire country, although it is unlikely to pass (Eidelson 2017c).

Given the free rider problem that right-to-work laws create, critics charge that they decrease the likelihood that workers will join a union while imposing additional costs on unions that are legally required to represent non-dues payers. This could lead to a decline in the union density numerator as union membership declines. At the same time, proponents of these laws argue that they promote job growth, which could increase the number of nonunion jobs in the union density denominator.

In our analysis of geographic employment shifts in the previous chapter, we saw that high-density and low-density states are regionally clustered in the United States, and that the dispersion between US state union density rates is higher than between Canadian provincial rates. While lower-density states experienced higher *rates* of employment growth over the past seventy years than higher-density states, there was no clear relation between union density and the absolute growth in employment: many of the lowest-density states added large numbers of jobs, but so too did many of the highest-density states. What remained to be explained,

---

[8] Some unions in the US have developed forms of union membership and activity that are not centered around collective bargaining and contract enforcement. These "nonmajority unions" exist in workplaces where achieving traditional representation is either extremely difficult or illegal, particularly among public employees in states where collective bargaining for state employees is prohibited. While they often deploy innovative tactics and provide useful potential models for union revitalization, such unions only form a minute proportion of overall union membership (Freeman 2004).

however, was the question of why there is such a wide dispersion between high-density and low-density states.

As we will see shortly, most lower-density states are also right-to-work states. If right-to-work laws are in fact holding down union membership while promoting higher rates of nonunion employment growth in certain states, this could be a driver of union density decline in the United States.

Macroeconomic Policy

Did more interventionist Canadian macroeconomic policy, in the form of a weak currency and protectionist trade policies, affect US–Canada union density divergence?

Exchange Rate Policy

If a cheaper Canadian dollar was shoring up union density by sheltering employment in Canadian export sectors, we would expect to see union density rise as the Canadian dollar falls, and vice versa.

A key fact shaping Canadian exchange rates is that Canada's economy is heavily reliant on foreign trade. Canadian exports and imports historically comprise from 35 up to 85 percent of GDP, as compared to between 8 and 30 percent of GDP for the United States (see Figure 2.1). This makes Canada particularly sensitive to shifts in the balance of payments, especially when it comes to its largest trading partner, the United States. As Figure 2.1 also shows, trade with the United States alone has comprised between 63 and 75 percent of all Canadian foreign trade since 1950.[9]

Canada has tended to pursue a policy of floating exchange rates. Canada first left the gold standard in 1914, and aside from interludes from 1939 to 1950 and 1962 to 1970 when it was pegged to the US dollar, Canada's currency has floated ever since (Helleiner 2005; 2006). Since the early 1970s the Canadian dollar has fluctuated significantly against its US counterpart. It was at parity for much of the 1970s, eroded then recovered over the course of the 1980s, depreciated in the 1990s to a low of USD$0.62 in 2002, recovered back to parity in the subsequent decade, and has declined again in recent years (Devereux 2009: 3–6).

How did these currency fluctuations correlate with changes in union density? Figure 2.2 tracks changes in the Canada–US exchange rate against the ratio of Canada–US private sector union density from 1961 to

---

[9] Prior to World War II, Great Britain served as Canada's largest trading partner.

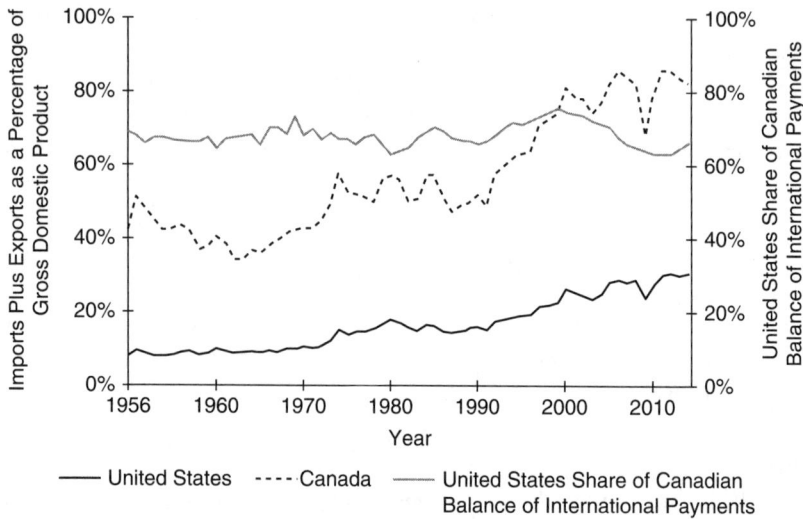

FIGURE 2.1 Imports plus exports as a percentage of gross domestic product in Canada and the United States, and the US share of Canadian balance of international payments, 1950–2014
Sources: For imports plus exports as percentage of GDP: Feenstra, Robert C., Robert Inklaar and Marcel P. Timmer. 2015. "The Next Generation of the Penn World Table," *American Economic Review*, 105(10), 3150–3182, available for download at www.ggdc.net/pwt. For US percentage of Total Canadian Balance of International Payments: 1950–1980: Statistics Canada. Table 376-0001 – Balance of international payments, current account, annual (dollars) and Table 376-0002 – Balance of international payments, capital and financial account, annual. 1981–2016: Statistics Canada. Table 376-0101 – Balance of international payments, current account and capital account annual.

2016.[10] To clarify the interpretation of the chart, as the union density gap widens between the two countries, the density ratio line rises. As the value of the Canadian dollar falls, the line rises, as the line measures the rising value of the US dollar against its Canadian counterpart. So if both lines are rising together, it shows that union density is diverging as the Canadian dollar's value is falling, as the exchange rate hypothesis would predict.

The data do show a relationship between union density shifts and exchange rates through the mid-1980s. However, as the Canadian dollar strengthened in the late 1980s, and then again in the 2000s (signified by

---

[10] We focus on private sector union density, as this is where exchange rates would have the most effect.

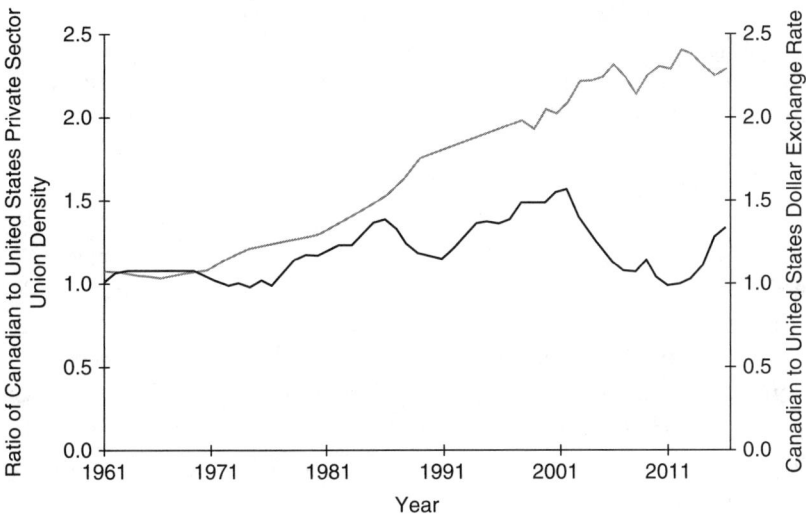

FIGURE 2.2 Ratio of Canadian to US private sector union density, and Canadian to US dollar exchange rate, 1961–2016
Source for exchange rates: Compiled by Prof. Werner Antweiler, University of British Columbia, http://fx.sauder.ubc.ca/etc/USDpages.pdf. See Appendix A for union density sources.

the falling exchange rate line), the union density gap between the United States and Canada continued to increase.

In sum, exchange rate fluctuations show little relation to US–Canada private sector union density ratios after the mid-1980s, suggesting that they cannot explain density divergence.

Trade Policy

Turning next to trade policy, the hypothesis is that the protectionist Auto Pact sheltered heavily-unionized Canadian manufacturing from market forces relative to US manufacturing. Additionally, the hypothesis predicts that the turn to more liberalized trade policy in Canada with the 1988 FTA and 1994 NAFTA would erode union density as "natural" market forces were allowed to have their effect.

The 1965 Auto Pact was in some ways a precursor to the liberalizing free trade agreements that followed it a few decades later in that it laid ground rules that allowed for greater cross-national integration of the auto industry. But from the Canadian perspective, it was also a protectionist measure in that its rules guaranteed a certain amount of Canadian-based production (Anastakis 2005; Johnson 1993). By extension, this would also implicitly guarantee a certain degree of union membership, as a large portion of the jobs in the Canadian auto industry were unionized. For this reason, the Auto Pact enjoyed strong labor support (Anastakis 2004). By contrast, the FTA and NAFTA contained little in the way of job and union protections, and were bitterly resisted by Canadian unions. They saw these free trade agreements as enabling the importation of US-style labor rights, which by the late 1980s were noticeably weaker than in Canada.

Is there any relationship between the implementation of these trade agreements and changes in union density rates? Figure 2.3 reproduces Figure 1.3, charting private sector union density trends in the United States and Canada, with vertical lines marking the implementation of the three trade pacts.[11]

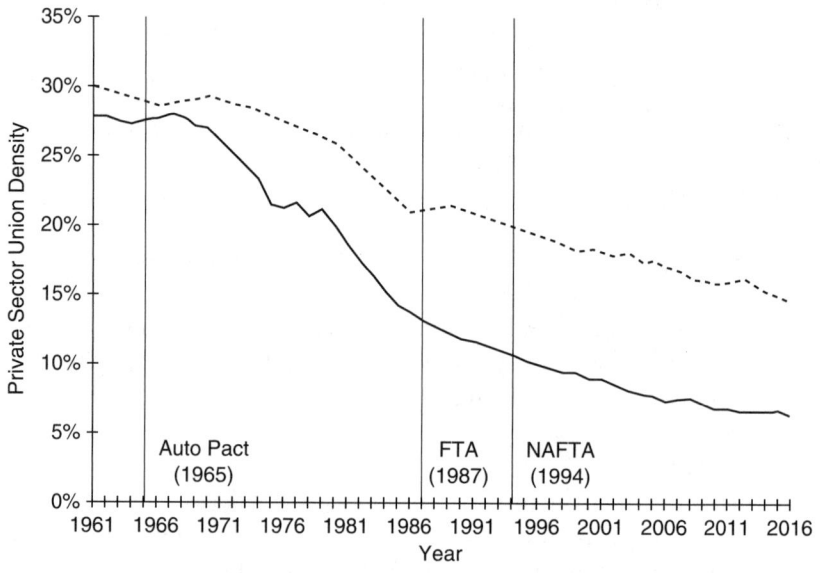

FIGURE 2.3 Private sector union density and trade policy, United States and Canada, 1961–2016
Source: See Appendix A

---

[11] We focus on private sector density trends, as this is where we would most likely expect to see a trade policy effect.

The data show a weak relation between the Auto Pact and union density growth, as private sector density declined in both countries, albeit at different rates. Interestingly, Canadian private sector union density declined more under the Auto Pact than it has under the FTA or NAFTA, dropping by 7.6 percentage points (from 28.6 to 21.0 percent) in the twenty-three years when the Auto Pact was ostensibly shielding unions, as compared to only 4.5 percentage points (from 19 to 14.5 percent) in the twenty-three years since the adoption of NAFTA.[12]

In sum, the evidence suggests that trade policy cannot explain union density divergence. While Canadian private sector density did decline after the adoption of NAFTA, the decline was much less than what happened during the ostensibly protective Auto Pact period.

Labor Law Regimes

If macroeconomic policies cannot fully explain union density divergence, then what about the effect of labor laws? In this section, we will examine the effects of the four areas of labor law identified above: regulations governing union certification, negotiation and implementation of a first contract, union security, and unions' permitted scope of activity. In examining each of these sets of policies, we want to understand how they make it easier or harder for workers to join and stay in a union, as well as how they make it easier or harder for employers to fight union representation.

Before proceeding, we must note one key cross-border difference that complicates a systematic comparison of labor law regimes. Labor relations policy is largely determined at the federal level in the United States and at the provincial level in Canada. Only 10 percent of Canadian workers are subject to federal labor laws. As such, there is a degree of variation in labor policy across provinces. The analysis below will not explore this variation exhaustively, but will acknowledge it when relevant.

Additionally, the discussion of labor laws will focus primarily on laws governing unionization in the private sector. This is mainly because those who focus on the role of labor law in driving density divergence themselves focus almost exclusively on the private sector.[13] Also, at a practical level,

---

[12] Due to limitations in the available data, Canadian union density rates reported for the Auto Pact era are for 1966 and 1986; for the NAFTA era, 1997 and 2016.

[13] The assumption in this literature is that laws governing public sector unionization are more favorable toward workers and as such do not constitute a problem worth addressing. Of course, efforts in recent years to curtail public sector collective bargaining in Indiana, Iowa, Ohio, and Wisconsin – as well as the fact that collective bargaining for

adding public sector regulations would add dozens of different jurisdictions to our analysis, making it too unwieldy. We will take up the role of public sector unions in density divergence in greater detail later on.

Union Certification

The basic framework governing union certification is similar in both countries. The Canadian certification model is explicitly based on the model established by the 1935 US National Labor Relations Act, also known as the Wagner Act (Adams 1995; Godard 2004; Taras 1997). Union certification in both countries is determined at the firm level. Workers at a given worksite who are deemed to share a "community of interest" seek certification for their group as a "bargaining unit." This is very different from the more coordinated process in many parts of Europe, where union representation is organized by sector and bargaining occurs at a national level between peak associations of unions and employers.

This decentralized system of union representation creates incentives for individual employers to resist unionization, as they fear that they will be saddled with additional labor costs for higher wages and benefits that their nonunion competitors will not share. However, in the case at hand, both countries are similar with regard to firm-level certification and bargaining (Blanchflower and Freeman 1992). Even though this gives both US and Canadian employers strong incentives to resist unionization, other policies seem to increase US employers' hostility.

There are two primary means of seeking union certification. In the United States, certification happens through a representation election process supervised by the National Labor Relations Board (NLRB). With this process, after presenting a required number of authorization cards to a NLRB representative (at least 30 percent of workers in the bargaining unit at issue), workers vote using a secret ballot either in favor of or against joining a particular union (or unions, if there are competing unions on the ballot).[14] If 50 percent plus one of those voting vote in favor

---

public sector employees remains illegal in five US states – suggest that this assumption may not be well-founded.

[14] This mandatory election process was not codified in the NLRA itself but was the result of a precedent set in *Cudahy Packing Co.*, 13 NLRB 526 (1939). Also, as the election process has become more and more dysfunctional in recent years, as outlined below, certain unions have pursued certification strategies that bypass the NLRA process entirely. With these "non-Board" strategies, unions wage a sustained, coordinated campaign to pressure an employer to recognize and bargain with the union without going through the election process.

of union representation, then the union is certified. Six of ten Canadian provinces[15] use a similar representation election process, although as we will see, the rules governing the election process in Canada differ from those in the United States.

Four Canadian provinces[16] as well as the federal jurisdiction use a second means of union certification, known as "card-check recognition."[17] With this method, workers can obtain recognition for their union by presenting to an administrative board authorization cards signed by a set percentage of the designated bargaining unit (HRSDC 2009). Once the cards are verified, the union is certified. In both cases, there are rules delimiting the scope of permitted campaign activities for employers and unions. Parties violating these rules can be charged with unfair labor practices (ULPs), which are then adjudicated by the relevant labor board.

While the difference between representation elections and card-check recognition may seem small, the effects are large. Several studies of Canadian provinces that have switched from card-check to elections show a reduction in union certification success rates (Johnson 2002; Riddell 2004; Slinn 2004).

To understand why the difference between elections and card-check has such a large effect on the likelihood of certification success, we must consider the different obstacles and opportunities that each system creates for workers and employers. We will first consider both systems as they function ideally, then as they function in practice.

With card-check, there is one main obstacle facing workers who seek to unionize: getting enough coworkers in their bargaining unit to sign union membership authorization cards. Once workers achieve that benchmark, they are certified and can begin negotiating a collective bargaining agreement with their employer. With elections, the process of gathering authorization cards is only the first obstacle in a longer process. Once workers under an election system have collected enough card signatures, they then confront a second obstacle: the representation election campaign. Mobilizing for an election campaign requires additional resources and

---

[15] Alberta, British Columbia, Newfoundland and Labrador, Nova Scotia, Ontario, and Saskatchewan.
[16] Manitoba, New Brunswick, Prince Edward Island, and Quebec.
[17] Prior to 1976, all Canadian jurisdictions used a super-majority card-check recognition process, with elections required below the super-majority threshold (elections required a majority of eligible workers, not merely voters, in order to achieve certification). Most of the provinces that now require representation elections only moved to an election-based system in the past two decades (Johnson 2004; Mayer 2007).

effort on the part of the workers who seek to unionize, as well as for the union they seek to join, compared to what is required under a card-check system. Finally, there is the actual election itself, which creates a third mobilizational hurdle for workers seeking to unionize.

On the employer side, card-check provides little opportunity for employer intervention. The decision about whether or not to unionize is framed as a decision that workers at a given worksite make among themselves. Once enough authorization cards are signed, it is the job of the labor board to determine whether the appropriate support threshold has been achieved. By contrast, the structure of the representation election process itself shifts the entire framework of the decision to unionize. Instead of being a decision made among the workers themselves, it creates a structure that explicitly sees employers as having a legitimate stake and voice in the workers' decision. Rather than simply choosing whether or not to join a union, workers are expected to choose between the union – construed as an outside force – and the employer. Within this confrontational election structure, employers become a side in a battle, and are offered the opportunity to make their views on unionization known to the workers. Unsurprisingly, their views are almost invariably negative. Furthermore, given the power imbalance inherent in the employment relationship, management's act of expressing its views can often take on a coercive character.

So even under ideal circumstances, representation elections present more obstacles to certification for workers and more opportunities for employers to intervene than does card-check. But the reality of the union certification process is far from ideal. The way that union representation elections are run transforms what nominally appears to be a textbook example of democratic process – a vigorous campaign followed by a secret ballot election – into an arduous, harrowing ordeal for workers who go through the process.

Employers exploit to the fullest their opportunities to intervene in the representation election process. They mount vigorous anti-union campaigns involving threats, harassment, intimidation, promises to change conditions of employment, and more (Bronfenbrenner 1994; Bronfenbrenner and Juravich 1995; Freeman and Kleiner 1990; Freeman and Medoff 1984; LaLonde and Meltzer 1991). Employers routinely compel workers to attend "captive audience" meetings during work hours, where they are subjected to management presentations warning them of the risks of joining a union. During these presentations, employers will often combine promises of improved behavior with threats of worksite closings or relocations. Certain workers can also be taken aside for special one-on-one meetings with supervisors, and suspected union campaign leaders are sometimes fired (Bronfenbrenner 1994).

While these types of employer coercion are illegal, the penalties are so minimal that it is cheaper for employers to violate the law and defeat the union than to comply and risk facing the union wage premium (Weiler 1983; Worster 2003). In the United States, and increasingly in parts of Canada, employers seeking to resist unionization can hire consultants and lawyers who can advise them on how to remain "union-free" while managing the legal technicalities. They are part of an entire union avoidance industry that has blossomed over the past forty years (Logan 2006).

Meanwhile, workers and union representatives remain at a distinct disadvantage in the election process. While employers are free to campaign throughout the workday, existing law in both the United States and Canada prohibits union representatives from campaigning in the workplace, and even workers themselves are only permitted to discuss union campaign issues on nonwork time in nonwork areas (Godard 2004: 27). Employers can also use their specialized legal team to file endless motions to delay election proceedings and wear down workers (Campolieti, Riddell, and Slinn 2007a; Ferguson 2008; Roomkin and Block 1981; Seeber and Cooke 1983). Research shows that these delaying tactics reduce the likelihood of union certification and are both more widespread and more effective in preventing unionization in the United States relative to Canada (Riddell 2010; Thomason 1994; Thomason and Pozzebon 1998).

However, if representation elections so clearly reduce the likelihood of union certification compared to card-check procedures, why didn't union density drop as much in Canada, especially in provinces that switched to a representation election format? Here, the key difference lies in laws regulating employer intervention in the election process. In Canadian provinces that have elections, the time between petitioning for an election and holding the election is short, usually between five and ten days (Campolieti et al. 2007a). By contrast, until recently most US representation elections have been held within fifty days of petitioning, with many elections held eight or more weeks after. This delay has given management much more time to mount an anti-union campaign and chip away at union support (Godard 2004). In April 2015, the NLRB implemented new rules governing union elections, which expedited the process considerably (National Labor Relations Board 2014). While preliminary results remain inconclusive, they suggest that the new rules have sped up the certification process, but have not led to an increase in the number of elections held, or to an increase in unions' win rate (Trottman 2016). Additionally, the expedited election rules are likely to be rolled back under the Trump administration (Richardson and Kanu 2017).

CHANGES IN UNION CERTIFICATION OVER TIME   Given the current state of labor laws in the United States and Canada, it is clear that *current* differences in the letter and application of the laws surrounding union certification have had an effect on union density rates. But how do these current-day differences explain diverging union density rates over time? Have laws governing union certification changed, and if so, how?

In fact, differences in union certification policies are a relatively recent development in US and Canadian labor law. Many of the key provisions that scholars identify as contributing to more pro-union outcomes in Canada, particularly laws regarding card-check and speedy elections, date from the 1970s (Campolieti et al. 2007a; Weiler 1983). Prior to that, laws regarding union certification were generally considered *more* restrictive in Canada than in the United States (Woods 1973: 81–83). As Woods observed in the early 1960s, "Canadian policy regarding union membership, voting quotas, and the absence of a responsibility to bargain with uncertified unions has made recognition more difficult to attain in Canada [compared to the United States]" (1962: 235–236). Whereas the US Wagner Act guaranteed bargaining unit certification with a simple majority of votes cast in a certification election, most Canadian provinces and the federal jurisdiction required the votes of a majority of *eligible voters* to certify a bargaining unit. Nonvoters were thus counted in Canada as votes against union representation (Logan 2002: 132–136). How and why then did laws change in Canada over the course of the 1970s and 1980s to facilitate union certification?

In addition to understanding why Canadian labor laws changed, we must understand what happened to labor law in the United States. There, the formal rules governing union certification have not changed much since the passage of the Taft-Hartley Act in 1947. But the interpretation and enforcement of the rules changed dramatically, to the point that they went from being an example which Canadian scholars and labor leaders admired, to being one they sought to avoid. Why did the effects of US union certification procedures change, even as the laws stayed the same?

POLICY BREAKDOWN VS. POLICY STABILITY: EVALUATION OF EMPIRICAL EVIDENCE   To understand how the application of union certification laws has changed, we can start by examining the functioning of the certification machinery in both countries over time. One central indicator of how that certification machinery is working is simply the number of certification elections run in a given year, as well as the union win rate in those elections. If the policies are promoting collective

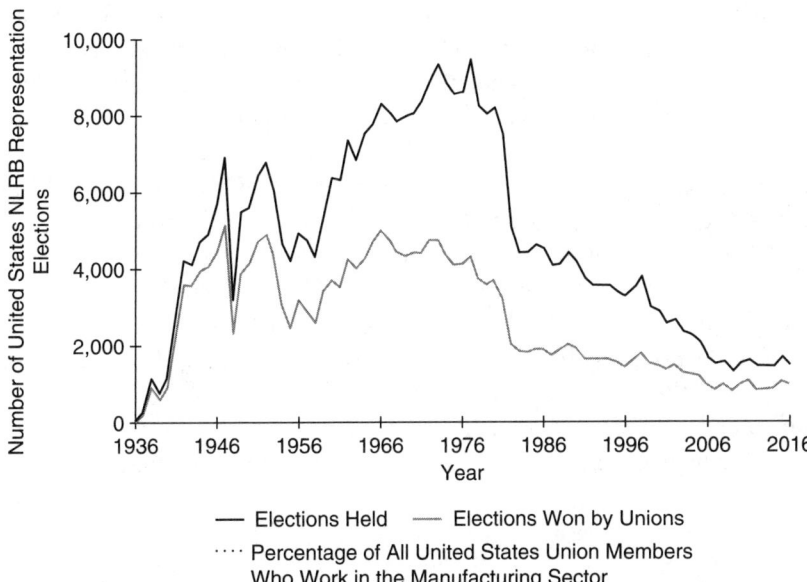

FIGURE 2.4 Number of US NLRB representation elections held and number of elections won by unions, 1936–2016
Sources: For 1936-1998: Carter, Susan B. et al. 2006. Historical Statistics of the United States Millennial Edition Online. New York: Cambridge University Press, Table Ba4946-4949. National Labor Relations Board elections and results: 1936-1998. For 1999-2009: Bureau of Labor Statistics, https://www.bls.gov/opub/mlr/cwc/national-labor-relations-board-nlrb-union-representation-elections-1997-2009.pdf. For 2010-2016: https://www.nlrb.gov/news-outreach/graphs-data (NOTE: The NLRB removed much of its detailed election data from its website in mid-2017).

bargaining, we should see increases in the number of petitions for certification as well as relatively high and stable union win rates over time.[18] By the same token, declines in the number of elections, even in the absence of policy changes, could indicate shifts in policy application.

Looking first at the United States, Figure 2.4 charts both the number of NLRB representation elections held and the number of those won by unions, from the beginning of NLRB elections in 1936 to 2016. It shows not only that the number of representation elections declined between the mid-1970s and mid-1980s, but also that this drop was virtually

---

[18] As will be discussed in greater detail below, increased organizing activity is not necessarily a function of more favorable certification policies. More favorable policies can sometimes be the result of increased organizing activity.

unprecedented, and that the number of elections has continued to decline ever since. From a peak of 9,484 elections in 1977, the number collapsed, reaching 5,116 by 1982. While the pace of decline slowed in the ensuing years, the downward trajectory continued, reaching a mere 1,496 by 2016. Despite the fact that the overall size of the US workforce has expanded dramatically since World War II, the NLRB today holds as many elections as in the waning days of the Great Depression.

The pattern holds when we look at how the number of voters eligible to participate in NLRB elections has changed. Figure 2.5 shows that, after an initial burst during World War II when millions of workers voted in NLRB elections (with most of those workers voting to become union members), the annual number of workers participating in NLRB elections fluctuated between approximately 400,000 and 800,000 workers until 1977, at which point there was also a sharp drop. Between 1977 and

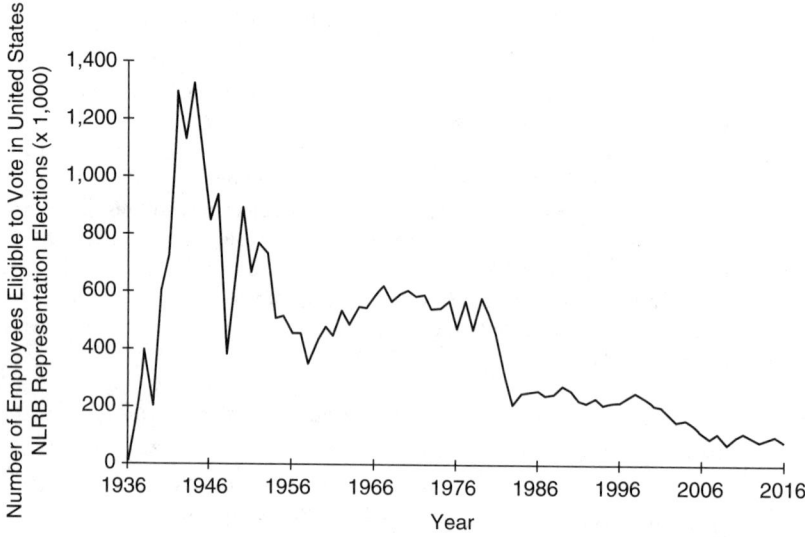

FIGURE 2.5 Number of employees eligible to vote in US NLRB representation elections, 1936–2016

Sources: For 1936-1998: Carter, Susan B. et al. 2006. Historical Statistics of the United States Millennial Edition Online. New York: Cambridge University Press, Table Ba4946-4949. National Labor Relations Board elections and results: 1936-1998. For 1999-2009: Bureau of Labor Statistics, https://www.bls.gov/opub/mlr/cwc/national-labor-relations-board-nlrb-union-representation-elections-1997-2009.pdf. For 2010–2016: https://www.nlrb.gov/news-outreach/graphs-data (NOTE: The NLRB removed much of its detailed election data from its website in mid-2017).

1982, the number of workers participating in NLRB representation elections plummeted from 570,716 to 297,764. Much of that drop, from 449,243 to 297,764, happened in a single year, between 1981 and 1982. The number of workers participating in NLRB elections continued to decline through the new millennium, reaching 86,145 by 2016, a level not seen since the early days of the Wagner Act. Again, the scale of this decline is larger than it appears, as these figures are absolute numbers, while the overall size of the workforce is much larger than it was eighty years ago.

Looking at win rates, Figure 2.6 shows that unions currently win nearly 70 percent of representation elections, having clawed their way back from a low of 40.3 percent in 1982. However, this increase is mitigated by the fact that it is an increasing percentage of a dramatically shrinking total. Not only does it leave aside the many workers who petition for elections but are never able to vote, but it also obscures the fact that, due to the

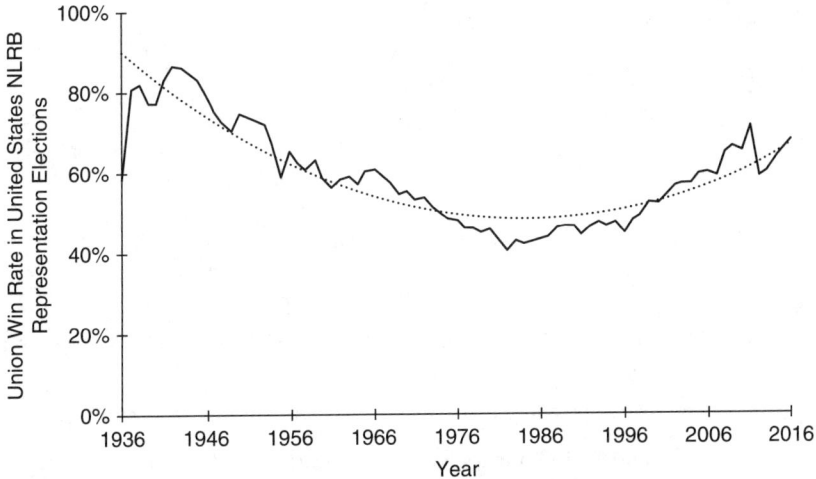

FIGURE 2.6 Union win rate in US NLRB representation elections, 1936–2016
Sources: For 1936-1998: Carter, Susan B. et al. 2006. Historical Statistics of the United States Millennial Edition Online. New York: Cambridge University Press, Table Ba4946-4949. National Labor Relations Board elections and results: 1936-1998. For 1999–2009: Bureau of Labor Statistics, https://www.bls.gov/opub/mlr/cwc/national-labor-relations-board-nlrb-union-representation-elections-1997-2009.pdf. For 2010-2016: https://www.nlrb.gov/news-outreach/graphs-data (NOTE: The NLRB removed much of its detailed election data from its website in mid-2017).

hostile climate and difficult odds, union organizers today are much more strategic in choosing which campaigns to pursue all the way to the election phase. In many cases, organizers will halt a campaign rather than risk losing an election (Bronfenbrenner 2009).

The patterns look quite different in Canada. Due to differences in data collection across provinces and difficulty in obtaining reliable time-series data for all provinces, I focus here on certifications in the province of Ontario, which comprises over one-third of the total Canadian workforce, and whose trends approximate those for the country as a whole (Martinello 1996: 32). Figure 2.7 shows the number of union certification applications disposed of and granted at the Ontario Labour Relations Board (OLRB) from its founding in 1949 to 2015.[19]

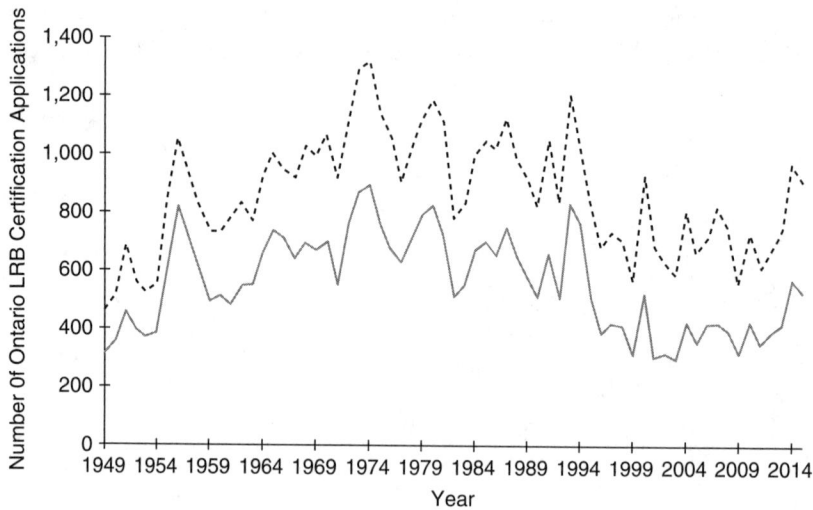

FIGURE 2.7 Number of Ontario LRB certification applications disposed of and granted, 1949–2015
Sources: For 1949-1998: Martinello, Felice. 1996. Certification and Decertification Activity in Canadian Jurisdictions. Kingston, Ontario: IRC Press/Industrial Relations Centre, Queen's University (data updated by Martinello for 1997-1998). For 1999–2015: OLRB Annual Reports, http://cirhr.library.utoronto.ca/research/special-collections/ontario-labour-relations-board-annual-reports

---

[19] This includes both elections and card-check recognitions. OLRB data are reported by fiscal year, which goes from July 1 to June 30. As such, FY2015 data includes certification applications through June 2016.

As in the United States, we see a rise in certification applications from the beginning through to a peak in 1974, at which point the number of applications began to decline. However, the rise and decline was nowhere near as drastic in Ontario as in the United States. Whereas disposal of certification applications in Ontario rose by 187 percent (from 460 to 1,320) between 1949 and 1974, representation elections in the United States increased by 723 percent (from 1,152 to 9,484) between 1938 and the peak in 1977.[20] Likewise, applications in Ontario decreased by 32 percent (from 1,320 to 899) between 1974 and 2015, whereas NLRB representation elections fell by 84 percent (from 9,484 to 1,496) between 1977 and 2016. As for certifications granted (union wins), they rose in Ontario by 183 percent between 1949 and the 1974 peak (from 315 to 894), compared to a rise of 450 percent in the United States between 1938 and its peak in 1947 (from 945 to 5,194). From there, certifications granted fell by 41 percent in Ontario (from 894 to 528) between the 1974 peak and 2015, as compared to a drop of 80 percent in the United States (from 5,194 to 1,017) between the 1947 peak and 2016.[21] Overall, fluctuations in certification applications have been more gradual and more muted in Ontario than in the United States.

Also, unlike in the United States, there was no steep and lasting drop in representation applications in Ontario in the early 1980s. While the numbers did drop in 1982 and 1983, amidst a deep recession, they rebounded to a range well within historical levels for the following decade. It was only in the mid-1990s that Ontario saw a steep drop in certification applications, a drop that persisted through the first decade of the twenty-first century, although applications have risen recently. Between 1994 and 1996, disposal of certification applications fell by 35 percent, from 1,046 to 684, and certifications granted fell by almost 50 percent, from 762 to 387. This coincided with a transition in government, from a (relatively) pro-labor NDP government led by Bob Rae to an aggressively anti-labor Conservative government led by Mike Harris. One of the first things the Harris government did upon assuming office was to replace the NDP's Bill 40, a set of labor law reforms that favored unions and collective bargaining, with its own Bill 7, which repealed Bill 40 and imposed tighter

---

[20] I exclude data from 1936 and 1937, as the constitutionality of the NLRA was still in question during that period, and thus the certification process was not fully functional during those years.
[21] For a more chronologically appropriate comparison, union wins in the US dropped by 82 percent from a 1970s peak of 4,787 election wins in 1972 to 864 wins in 2009.

restrictions on unions. Several studies have documented both the positive effects of Bill 40 and the negative effects of Bill 7 on union growth (Campolieti et al. 2007a; Martinello 2000).

The US–Ontario differences also apply to the number of workers involved in union certification procedures. Unfortunately, the worker-level data available for Ontario are not directly comparable to those in the United States, as they measure the number of eligible workers in winning certifications only, as opposed to eligible workers in all representation elections. Nevertheless, the data are instructive, as reported in Figure 2.8. Aside from a massive spike in 1962, the number of eligible workers in winning certification cases[22] was relatively stable from 1956 to 2000, fluctuating between 15,000 and 30,000. As with certification applications, the number of eligible workers dropped in 1982 and 1983, but it quickly recovered in subsequent years. That number fell dramatically between 2000 and 2015, from 31,620 to 10,147.

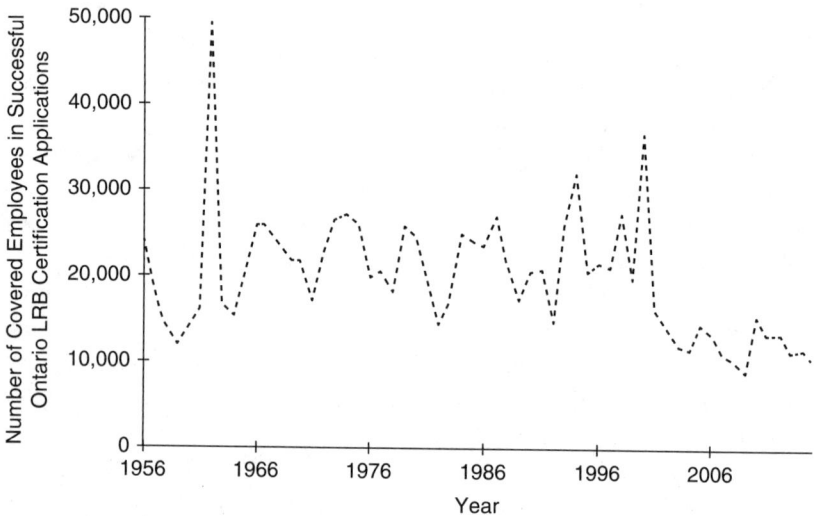

FIGURE 2.8 Number of covered employees in successful Ontario LRB certification applications, 1956–2015
Sources: For 1949–1998: Martinello, Felice. 1996. Certification and Decertification Activity in Canadian Jurisdictions. Kingston, Ontario: IRC Press/Industrial Relations Centre, Queen's University (data updated by Martinello for 1997–1998). For 1999–2015: OLRB Annual Reports, http://cirhr.library.utoronto.ca/research/special-collections/ontario-labour-relations-board-annual-reports

---

[22] This roughly translates into the number of new workers brought into unions in a given year.

How Could Labor Policies Affect Union Density? 73

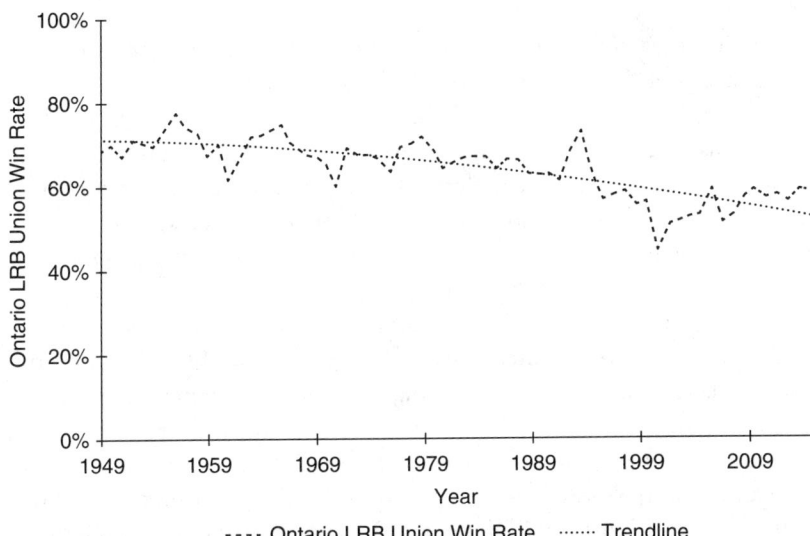

FIGURE 2.9 Ontario LRB union win rate, 1949–2015
Sources: For 1949-1998: Martinello, Felice. 1996. Certification and Decertification Activity in Canadian Jurisdictions. Kingston, Ontario: IRC Press/Industrial Relations Centre, Queen's University (data updated by Martinello for 1997–1998). For 1999–2015: OLRB Annual Reports, http://cirhr.library.utoronto.ca/research/special-collections/ontario-labour-relations-board-annual-reports

It is also important to note that the certification rate in Ontario has not fluctuated as wildly as has the union win rate in the United States. Figure 2.9 shows that the rate tended to fluctuate between 60 and 80 percent for much of the OLRB's history, up until 1995. At that point, the rate fell as low as 45 percent in 2001 and has not risen above 60 percent ever since. This drop coincided with one of the major policy changes contained in Harris' Bill 7: the implementation of mandatory representation elections.

In sum, the evidence shows that, even as formal policy regarding union certification in the United States remained unchanged, organizing activity and effectiveness fell sharply starting in the late 1970s and accelerated through the 1980s. During that same time period, organizing activity remained relatively stable in Ontario and the rest of Canada, even as formal policies changed.[23] In a seemingly ironic twist, it was the United

---

[23] While organizing activity in Ontario has declined in recent years, it has not been nearly on the same scale as US decline. It is also a much more recent decline, dating back to the mid-1990s, and is associated with key changes in labor laws that brought Ontario law closer in line to existing US policy. The discussion of recent crises in the Canadian labor movement

States, the jurisdiction with the least formal policy intervention, that saw the greatest change in policy outcomes. This suggests that something changed about the application of US certification policy.

But if policy application has changed in the United States, how and why has it changed? And furthermore, why has Canadian policy remained relatively stable, even while undergoing regular and periodic amendments? To begin to understand this, we must examine another key facet of the union certification machinery: the regulation of employer resistance.

"HERE RULES EXIST": EMPLOYER RESISTANCE AND UNION CERTIFICATION As detailed above, a key part of what makes the certification election process so challenging for workers seeking to unionize is employer resistance (Bronfenbrenner 1994, 2009; Campolieti et al. 2007a). How has this changed over time? While imperfect, one way to measure employer resistance is to examine data regarding how often employers are charged with breaking the law in the course of the union certification process. These charges, known as "unfair labor practice" charges, or ULPs, are filed with the NLRB in the United States. The board then processes the charges, collecting evidence and conducting hearings where necessary, and issues a ruling.

The measure is imperfect because ULPs can be filed against both employers and unions, and the existence of a charge does not necessarily indicate a violation of the law. Nevertheless, given that a large majority of ULPs are filed against employers, aggregate ULP data does provide a decent metric of employer behavior. As for the number of charges compared to the number of actual violations found, it is important to note that most ULP cases are settled before they receive a formal determination from the NLRB. Also, employers routinely take advantage of the ULP process to draw out the certification process and delay elections. As such, an increase in the sheer number of cases can be taken as a sign of employers using the process itself as a delaying tactic.

Figure 2.10 tracks the annual number of ULP charges filed, as well as the number of ULPs per representation election, from 1937 to 2016. The graph shows a steady rise in the absolute number of ULPs starting in the late 1950s, but accelerating in the 1970s, reaching a peak of 31,281 cases filed in 1980. While the absolute number subsequently declined, it never dropped

---

will be taken up in the concluding chapter. For the purposes of this chapter, we are focused on why Canadian organizing activity did not suffer a similar crisis as in the US in the late 1970s and 1980s.

How Could Labor Policies Affect Union Density? 75

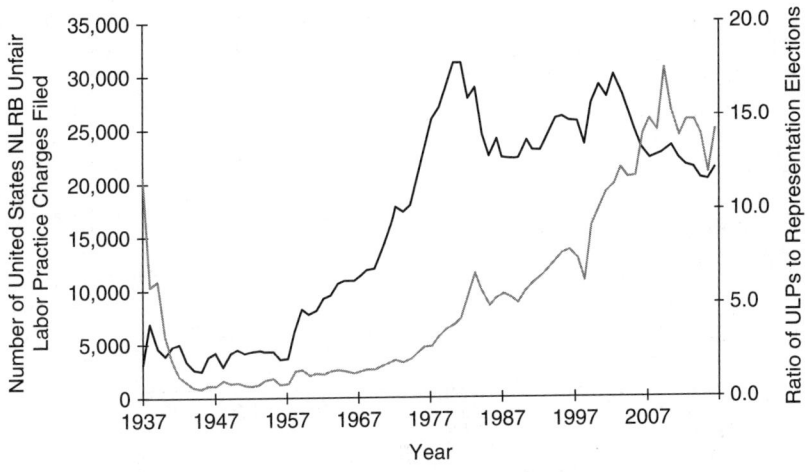

— Number of United States NLRB Unfair Labor Practice Charges Files
— Ratio of ULPs to Representation Elections

FIGURE 2.10 Number of US NLRB unfair labor practice charges filed and ratio of ULPs to representation elections, 1937–2016
Sources: For 1937–2016: Carter, Susan B. et al. 2006. Historical Statistics of the United States Millennial Edition Online. New York: Cambridge University Press, Table Ba4950-4953. Complaints of unfair practices received and remedial actions taken by the National Labor Relations Board: 1936–1998. For 1999–2016: https://www.nlrb.gov/news-outreach/graphs-data. NOTE: The NLRB removed much of its detailed data from its website in mid-2017. NOTE: I exclude 1936, since the minuscule number of elections (due to employers not recognizing the constitutionality of the NLRA) artificially inflates the ULP election ratio.

below 22,000, despite the fact that the absolute number of representation elections was declining significantly in this same time period.

If we look at changes in the ratio of ULPs per representation election over time, we see that it has grown substantially over the past thirty years, also shown in Figure 2.10 (plotted against the secondary y-axis along the right side of the chart). We see that the number of ULPs per election more than doubled between 1977 and 1984 from 2.7 to 6.6. The ratio then stayed within a range of 5 to 8 ULPs per election for most of the 1980s and '90s, then began a sharp rise again in the late 1990s, moving from 6.2 ULPs per election in 1998 to an unprecedented 17.6 ULPs per election in 2009. This suggests that, even as the number of elections has declined, as has the number of workers participating in union elections, employers have intensified their efforts to resist unionization.

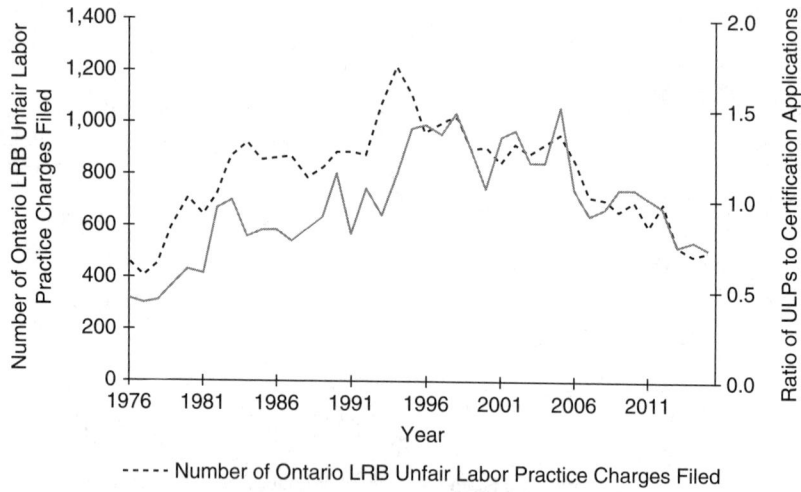

FIGURE 2.11 Number of Ontario LRB unfair labor practice charges filed and ratio of ULPs to certification applications, 1976–2015
Sources: For 1976–1998: Martinello, Felice. 1996. Certification and Decertification Activity in Canadian Jurisdictions. Kingston, Ontario: IRC Press/Industrial Relations Centre, Queen's University (data updated by Martinello for 1997–1998). For 1999–2015: OLRB Annual Reports, http://cirhr.library.utoronto.ca/research/special-collections/ontario-labour-relations-board-annual-reports

Turning again to Ontario for a representative Canadian comparison, Figure 2.11 shows that the number of ULPs filed there increased sharply between the mid-1970s and mid-1990s, nearly tripling from 406 in 1977 to 1,216 in 1994. There were especially steep increases late 1970s and early 1980s, and then again in the early 1990s. The number of ULPs filed then fell by nearly half over the next fifteen years, back down to 497 in 2015. This is a different pattern than in the United States, where ULP frequency dropped off in the 1980s after peaking in 1980, then rose again in the late 1990s.

But where the two countries truly differ is in the number of ULPs per certification attempt. Whereas US ULP ratios began their sharp upward climb in the early 1970s to reach the current level of over 14 ULPs per certification election, Canadian ULP ratios between 1976 and 2015 barely exceeded 1.5 ULPs per certification application at their peak in 2005. Even assuming a certain number of false claims, the data show that US employers are much more likely than their

Canadian counterparts to violate laws surrounding union certification, particularly since the early 1970s. Given how closely this increase in alleged employer violations coincides with the divergence in US–Canada union density rates, it does appear that it could be one of the key factors driving density divergence.[24]

However, the data on employer hostility raise the issue of why US employers became so much more aggressive when they did, and why their Canadian counterparts did not. An initial hypothesis might be that US employers harbor more anti-union animus than their Canadian counterparts. But as we saw in the previous chapter, there is little difference in individual US and Canadian employer attitudes, and Canadian employers have just as long a history of anti-union hostility as their US counterparts.

Nonetheless, even if we grant that Canadian employers have retained hostile attitudes toward unions over time, the ULP data show that they have been considerably more circumspect in acting on those hostile attitudes than US employers in recent years. The question remains as to why this is the case.

A second hypothesis could be that Canadian employers have been less likely to deploy aggressive anti-union tactics because they are less effective in the Canadian setting. However, Thomason and Pozzebon (1998) found that aggressive employer practices have in fact been very effective in reducing union support in Canadian certification campaigns. So even though aggressive tactics have shown a positive payoff for Canadian employers, they have adopted them much less than in the United States. Why?

The answer, Thomason and Pozzebon suggest, lies beyond any single policy difference. Rather, it lies in different normative frameworks established by policy regimes in both countries. They cite surveys of Canadian industrial relations executives done by Thompson (1995) in the early 1990s. A quote that succinctly captures the difference in normative frameworks comes from "a manager at a US-owned firm, which is nonunion in the US but partially organized in Canada." He explained that "we play by the rules where we operate. In the United States, there are no rules. Here rules exist, and we follow them." (Thompson 1995: 113).

---

[24] More recent studies, such as that of Bentham, suggest that employer opposition is "neither as infrequent nor as innocuous in Canada as has often been assumed" (2002: 181). While this may be true, it is certainly a relatively recent development in Canada, dating back to the 1990s. Moreover, relative to the US, even the current more elevated levels are roughly one-tenth as large as what we see in the US.

Note that this executive does not emphasize differences between the rules in both countries. Rather, he emphasizes shared understandings of the overall framework: in Canada, "rules exist." In the United States, they do not. Put differently, the fundamental difference shaping employer behavior in the United States and Canada is the *legitimacy of the framework* governing labor relations in either country. While both countries started off their respective eras of industrial legality in the 1930s and 1940s with similar frameworks of rules, those frameworks changed over time. In the United States, the framework eroded, to the point where employers can reasonably act as if "there are no rules." In Canada, the framework may have weakened, but there remains a sense among employers that "rules exist."

First Contract

Once workers successfully certify their bargaining unit, the next step is to bargain a first contract with management. Most of the material benefits of union membership in the United States and Canada only come through securing a union contract.

The rules governing first contract negotiations differ between the United States and Canada. In the United States, there is no statutory compulsion to reach a first contract agreement. Rather, union certification only requires employers to "bargain in good faith" with the union. By contrast, in seven of eleven Canadian jurisdictions, the law provides for what is called "first contract arbitration" (FCA).[25] In these jurisdictions, if the employer and union are unable to reach a first agreement after a set time period, their demands are submitted to the relevant labor board or an arbitrator, who can then settle the terms of the agreement. Provisions determining when impasse has been reached, how long boards and arbitrators can take to consider the case, how long arbitrated agreements can last, and other matters, vary between jurisdictions (Slinn and Hurd 2011).

FCA matters because the first contract negotiation process has become a major additional hurdle to union representation for workers who manage to get through the certification gauntlet, as employers delay and drag out the bargaining process. Bronfenbrenner's (2009) study of certification

---

[25] The jurisdictions are British Columbia (1973), Quebec (1978), Federal (1978), Manitoba (1982), Newfoundland and Labrador (1985), Ontario (1986), and Saskatchewan (1994). An eighth jurisdiction, Prince Edward Island, adopted FCA in 1995, but has never implemented the process (Slinn and Hurd 2011: 45).

How Could Labor Policies Affect Union Density?

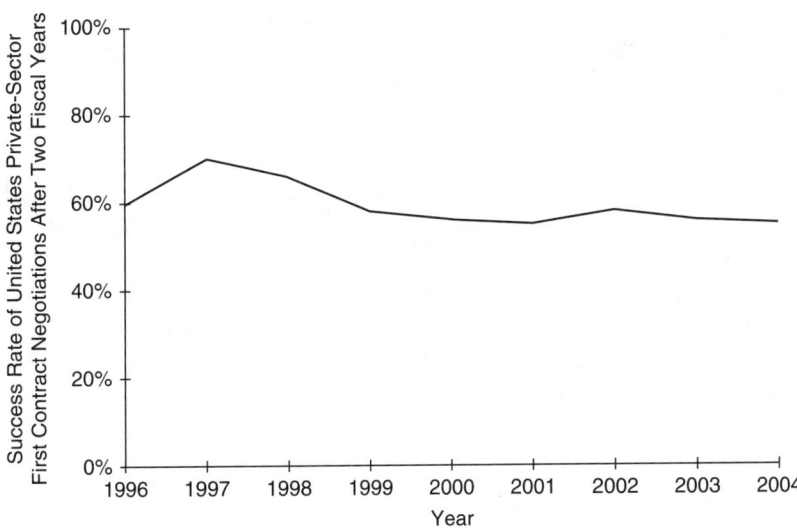

FIGURE 2.12 Success rate of US private sector first contract negotiations after two fiscal years, 1996–2004
Source: Johnson 2010: Table 1

elections between 1999 and 2003 found that only 48 percent of certified bargaining units had obtained first contracts within one year after their election, 63 percent had obtained an agreement within two years, and only after more than three years had 75 percent of units obtained a first agreement. Ferguson's (2008) study of organizing drives between 1999 and 2004 had even starker findings, with fewer than 39 percent of certified bargaining units obtaining a first contract within one year and no more than 56 percent of certified units obtaining an agreement within two years. Similarly, Johnson's (2010) tabulations of Federal Mediation and Conciliation Service (FMCS) data, reproduced as Figure 2.12, showed that the two-year success rate for bargaining units in achieving a first contract between 1996 and 2004 varied between 55 and 70 percent. Overall, these findings suggest that between one-quarter and half of all groups of US workers who manage to overcome the obstacles of the union certification process still fail to establish unions in their workplaces.

As in the case of union certification, many employer stalling tactics surrounding first contract negotiation are technically illegal. However, many employers find the potential cost of breaking the law worth the benefit of union avoidance. Even in the event of a guilty verdict, the delay involved with processing ULP charges chips away at workers' resolve. Moreover, if employers can delay contract negotiations for at least one year, the NLRA allows them to organize a drive to decertify the union, a provision that provides major incentives for employers to stall. Ferguson's (2008) study of 22,000 organizing drives between 1999 and 2004 found that employer ULPs decreased the likelihood of reaching a first contract within one year by 30 percent.

In Canada, FCA shifts the employer incentives considerably. Instead of having the potential benefit of being able to decertify the union, as in the United States, employers in Canada who delay reaching agreement with the union run the risk of having an agreement imposed upon them that could be more costly than a negotiated agreement. Reflecting on his time as a labor arbitrator in British Columbia, Weiler (1980) remarked that

> we imposed very few agreements... But when we did write agreements against an anti-union employer, we made the compensation package rather generous. We stated quite forthrightly that that was what we were doing, in order to provide a disincentive to other employers adopting the kinds of tactics which would get them before the Labour Board.

While FCA can be a powerful weapon, it is rarely used. Existing studies of FCA in Canada show that it functions more as an incentive to reach voluntary agreement than as a substantive remedy (Johnson 2010; Slinn and Hurd 2011). Most certified bargaining units in Canada are able to reach a first contract through the collective bargaining process.

FIRST CONTRACT NEGOTIATION IN HISTORICAL PERSPECTIVE

Laws governing first contract negotiation currently differ between the United States and Canada. But how has this changed over time? Historical data for first contract negotiations in the United States is much less available than for union certifications, but existing data show a significant drop in successful first contract negotiations. Weiler's (1984) compilation of first contract data for the United States showed a drop in the success rate from 86 percent in 1955 to 63 percent in 1980. The vast bulk of the drop, from 78 percent to 63 percent, happened between 1970 and 1980. Using data compiled by the US FMCS, the Dunlop Commission (1994) found that only 56 percent of certified bargaining units obtained first contracts in the years from 1986 through 1993. That figure has at best rebounded slightly and in most cases has declined since then. But even if the first contract success rate has remained relatively constant since the early 1980s, this rate is a percentage of an ever-shrinking total of certified bargaining units, as shown in Figure 2.4.

Historical data on first contracts is even less available for Canada than for the United States, but existing data show a different situation. In the early 1980s, the federal jurisdiction and Ontario had success rates of 83 and 87 percent, respectively, compared to 63 percent in the United States. Bain's (1981) study of Canadian certifications in 1978–1979 found that between 70 and 80 percent of certified bargaining units were able to negotiate first contracts. Bentham's (1999) survey of employers done in 1996 found that over 92 percent of certified bargaining units in her survey were able to negotiate first contracts (167).[26] Although these findings are far from conclusive, they do suggest that Canadian workers have generally been more successful than their US counterparts in negotiating first contracts.

Data aside, what is striking is how differently governments in both countries responded to growing evidence that certified bargaining units were increasingly having difficulty in negotiating first contracts. They began to take note of the problem in both countries in the 1960s, and more seriously in the 1970s. Legislators in both countries proposed FCA legislation to address the problem. But whereas US efforts to establish FCA failed with the defeat of the 1977 Labor Law Reform Act,[27] Canadian efforts succeeded. British Columbia led the way with its FCA law in 1973, followed by Quebec in 1977, and the federal jurisdiction in 1978. Manitoba, Newfoundland and Labrador, Ontario, and Saskatchewan all joined the fray in subsequent years.

The FCA legislation example highlights Canadian governments' greater willingness and ability to intervene actively in the collective bargaining process through legislative remedies. This more active governmental role is unrelated to greater pro-labor sympathies, as reforms were enacted by both more liberal and more conservative governments. It is also independent of labor influence on government policymakers. Indeed, both employers *and* unions bitterly resisted the implementation of FCA when it was first proposed in the early 1970s (Backhouse 1980), although labor ultimately came around to supporting it (Muthuchidambaram 1980: 394–395). Regardless, unions were clearly not the ones leading the charge for the policy.

---

[26] Bentham's number may exaggerate Canadian unions' success in negotiating first contracts, as her survey only had a 25 percent response rate (1999: 70).
[27] The 2009 Employee Free Choice Act also contained provisions for some form of first contract arbitration. However, it too was ultimately unsuccessful.

Thus, in addition to the differences in the stability of the overall labor relations framework that we saw in our examination of union certifications, the case of FCA legislation points to another cross-country difference we must explain: the greater willingness and ability of the Canadian state to intervene in the collective bargaining process.

Union Security and the "Right to Work"

As Republicans have taken over more US state legislatures and governor's mansions in recent years, a key part of their legislative agenda has been to enact innocuous-sounding laws proclaiming the "right to work" (RTW). Since 2012, such laws have been passed in Indiana, Kentucky, Michigan, Missouri, West Virginia, and Wisconsin. This could bring the total number of RTW states to twenty-eight, depending on political outcomes or judicial rulings in two states (see Map 2.1).[28]

The recent push has brought RTW laws back into the spotlight after decades of relative obscurity. Initially promoted in the early 1940s by oil company lobbyist Vance Muse and his organization, the Christian American Association (CAA), RTW laws spread rapidly, with fourteen states enacting RTW laws by the spring of 1947. While most regulations governing labor relations are set at the federal level, Section 14(b) of the NLRA, an amendment that was part of the 1947 Taft-Hartley Act, gave individual states the right to implement these right-to-work laws. By 1958, twenty states had passed RTW laws, although some subsequently repealed them.[29] After that, only a handful of states passed RTW laws prior to the recent uptick (Dixon 2009; National Right to Work Committee 2017).

Despite their name, RTW laws have nothing to do with guaranteeing a right to employment. Rather, they exempt individual workers in unionized workplaces from having to pay for the costs associated with

---

[28] The West Virginia legislature passed a right-to-work law in February 2016, and a revised version in April 2017, both over governor's vetoes, but it has been blocked from taking effect by a judicial injunction (Zuckerman 2017). The Missouri legislature passed a right-to-work law in February 2017, which was promptly signed by newly elected Governor Eric Greitens, and was slated to take effect in August 2017. However, opponents of the law gathered more than enough signatures to put the right-to-work question on the 2018 midterm election ballot. This put the law on hold, pending the results of the referendum (Ancel 2017; KY3 2017). If the West Virginia court injunction is lifted, and voters uphold the right-to-work law in Missouri, then those two states would become the twenty-seventh and twenty-eighth right-to-work states, respectively.

[29] Delaware and New Hampshire repealed RTW in 1949. Louisiana passed (1954) and repealed (1956) RTW, then passed it again in 1976. Indiana passed RTW in 1957, repealed it in 1965, and then passed it again in 2012 (Dixon 2009; National Right to Work Committee 2017).

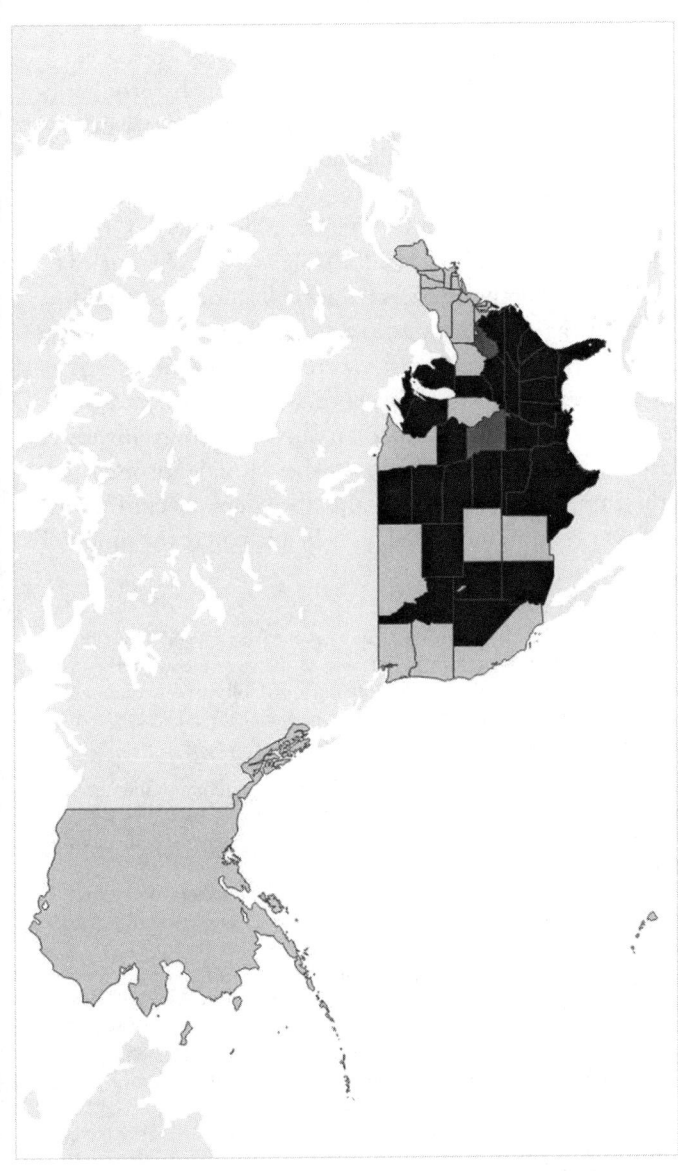

MAP 2.1 US states' right-to-work status, 2017
Sources: Reed, W. Robert. 2003. "How right-to-work laws affect wages." *Journal of Labor Research* 24(4):713–730, p. 728 n. 7, and National Right-to-Work Committee, "State Right-to-Work Timeline," https://nrtwc.org/facts-issues/state-right-to-work-timeline-2016/. Note that Missouri and West Virginia are shaded differently, as the status of their laws was still pending as this book went to press.

negotiating and enforcing their union contract. In union-speak, RTW laws mandate the "open shop," which prohibits any kind of what are known as "union security" provisions.[30] Proponents contend that RTW laws protect workers' individual liberty by preventing them from being forced to contribute to organizations with which they disagree. Meanwhile, critics charge that RTW laws hamstring unions by eroding their funding base. They argue that the laws create an incentive for workers to "free ride" on the union, taking advantage of union-negotiated wages and benefits without paying for them.

In Canada, the situation is different. Whereas twenty-six of fifty US states now mandate the open shop via RTW laws,[31] seven out of eleven Canadian jurisdictions compel universal dues collection, essentially banning the open shop (Taras and Ponak 2001a; Taras 1997).[32] The first Canadian regulations governing union security were set up in 1946 as part of the settlement of a bitter 1945 strike by Ford workers in Windsor, Ontario. The settlement developed by Canadian Supreme Court Justice Ivan Rand articulated what became known as the "Rand Formula." The judge ordered the company to agree to mandatory dues checkoff for every worker, regardless of union membership.[33] In exchange, the union

---

[30] "Union security" refers to methods of ensuring that workers who benefit from the provisions of a collective bargaining agreement contribute to the costs associated with enforcing the agreement. These provisions are negotiated into collective bargaining agreements that are circumscribed by federal and state/provincial law. The types of union security clauses that can be negotiated include

- *Closed shop:* only union members are eligible to apply for jobs, and union members must remain in good standing in order to retain the job;
- *Union shop:* members and nonmembers can apply, but nonmembers are required to join the union within a certain time after beginning work;
- *Maintenance of membership:* workers can choose whether or not to join the union. If they join, they cannot revoke their membership for the duration of the collective bargaining agreement;
- *Agency shop:* workers can choose whether or not to join the union. If they do not join, they are still required to pay "agency" or "fair share" fees, representing the portion of union membership dues devoted to contract enforcement and representation costs.
- *Open shop ("Right to work"):* no union security provision. Workers can benefit from collective bargaining agreement provisions without having to join the union or pay fair share fees.

[31] This excludes Missouri and West Virginia, which have both passed RTW laws that have yet to be enacted, as discussed in note 28.

[32] British Columbia, Federal, Manitoba, Newfoundland and Labrador, Ontario, Quebec, and Saskatchewan.

[33] "Dues checkoff" means that union membership dues are deducted at regular intervals directly from the union member's paycheck.

How Could Labor Policies Affect Union Density? 85

agreed to mandatory, government-supervised strike votes prior to engaging in strikes between contracts, a no-strike pledge for the life of the contract, and a pledge to police and discipline union members who engaged in illegal strikes. The Rand Formula quickly diffused throughout Canada, becoming the standard union security provision in Canadian collective bargaining agreements (Fudge and Tucker 2001). However, the laws forbidding the open shop are a more recent addition to the Canadian industrial relations landscape, with most only adopted in the 1970s (Taras and Ponak 2001a: 548).

The key difference then between the United States and Canada in terms of union security provisions is that there is a group of US states that prohibit all forms of union security, whereas there is a group of Canadian provinces that require at least a basic form of union security.

To evaluate the extent to which differences in union security provisions might affect US–Canada union density divergence, the first step is to evaluate the extent to which RTW laws have or have not played a role in driving US union density decline. If they do play a role, then it would follow that the lack of such laws in Canada could be a factor in explaining union density divergence.

Existing research shows mixed results (Devinatz 2011; Ellwood and Fine 1987; Farber 1984; Hogler et al. 2004; Moore and Newman 1984; 1988). The central problem in estimating the effect of RTW laws on union density is showing causality. That is, RTW laws could have a negative effect on unionization in a given state, or states that are already weakly unionized could be more likely to adopt RTW laws.

An examination of some basic descriptive statistics can help get a sense of the plausibility of the hypothesis that RTW laws negatively affect unionization rates. Map 2.2 reports data on percentage-point changes in union density by state/province from 1939 to 2016 (1941–2016 for Canada). It also includes information about which states have RTW laws.[34] A cursory examination of the map shows that there is a marked relationship between being a RTW state and shrinking union density. Eleven states out of the twenty with the heaviest union density losses are RTW states, compared with zero of the seven states that experienced net union density growth. In terms of current union density, every single one of the sixteen lowest-density states is a RTW state, as are nineteen of the

---

[34] Tables reporting the underlying data, including information on the dates in which states adopted their RTW statutes, are included in Table A.2.

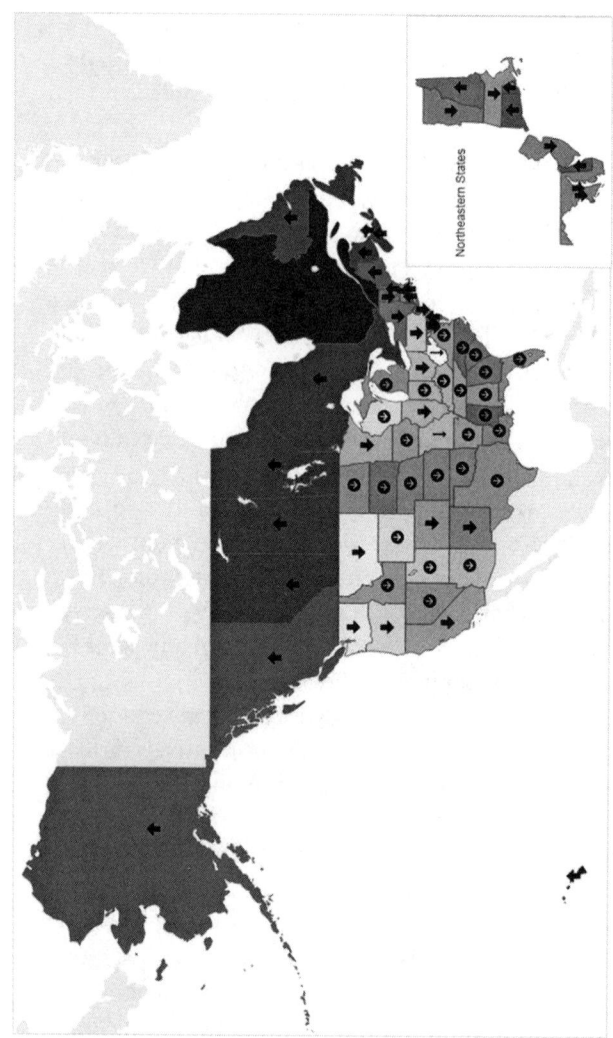

MAP 2.2 US states' and Canadian provinces' percentage-point change in union density from 1939 to 2016, 2017 right-to-work status, and indication of increase/decrease in union density from 1939 to 2016
Source: See Appendix A, Table A.2

bottom twenty-three. By contrast, only two of the fifteen highest-density states are RTW states (Nevada and Michigan).

Additionally, as mentioned when we examined the geographic shift argument earlier, employment shifts from higher-density states in the Northeast and Midwest to lower-density states in the South, particularly in the manufacturing sector, have contributed to union density decline. Since the Southern states are all RTW states, it could be that the RTW laws are keeping union density low in these states, which is in turn what has made geographic employment shifts lead to lower union density.

Given these findings, it seems that RTW laws did lower union density. However, there remains the problem of what economists call "endogeneity": RTW laws could in fact cause lower union density, but it is equally possible that lower-density states are more likely to adopt RTW laws.

To begin, Figure 2.13 shows US union density between 1939 and 2016, disaggregated by RTW and non-RTW states.[35] The trend lines show that RTW states on average have consistently lower union density than non-RTW states. Furthermore, union density in both RTW and non-RTW states has moved along roughly similar trajectories, albeit at different levels.[36]

The problem of endogeneity becomes clearer if we conduct a small thought experiment. If, instead of adding states to the RTW or non-RTW categories depending on if and when they actually enacted RTW legislation, we can group the states based on whether or not they have *ever* enacted RTW legislation and see how these two groups of states behave over the course of the entire period. Figure 2.14 reproduces Figure 2.13 using this grouping of all *possible* RTW states, as compared to states that have *never* enacted RTW legislation. Here we see that union density has been consistently lower in states that at some point adopted RTW legislation. The fact that RTW states as a whole are consistently lower-density states, both before and after enacting RTW legislation, along with the fact that both RTW and non-RTW states follow similar trajectories of growth

---

[35] States that change their RTW laws are switched over to the relevant group in the first full year after the change. So, for example, if a state adopted a RTW law in 1947, they are counted as part of the RTW group beginning in 1948.

[36] Mean union density in RTW states rose by 21 percent between 1945 and 1952 (from 15.9 percent to 19.2 percent). It then fell by 69 percent between 1963 and 2016 (from 19.5 percent to 6.0 percent). By comparison, mean union density in non-RTW states rose by 66 percent between 1939 and 1953 (from 21.4 percent to 35.5 percent). It then fell by 58 percent between 1953 and 2016 (from 35.5 percent to 14.9 percent).

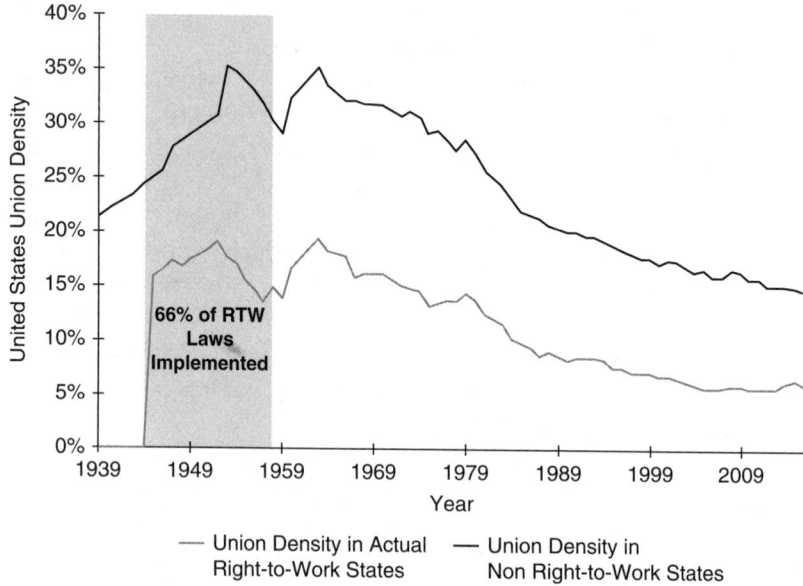

FIGURE 2.13 US union density in actual right-to-work states and non-right-to-work states, 1939–2016

Sources: Union membership: 1939–1963: Troy, Leo, and Neil Sheflin. 1985. US Union Sourcebook: Membership, Finances, Structure, Directory. West Orange, NJ: Industrial Relations Data and Information Services, Table 7.2, p. 7-4. 1964–2016: Barry T. Hirsch, David A. Macpherson, and Wayne G. Vroman, "Estimates of Union Density by State," *Monthly Labor Review*, Vol. 124, No. 7, July 2001, pp. 51–55 (up-to-date data available at www.unionstats.com). Sources, right-to-work status: Reed, W. Robert. 2003. "How right-to-work laws affect wages." *Journal of Labor Research* 24(4):713–730, p. 728 n. 7, and National Right-to-Work Committee, "State Right-to-Work Timeline," https://nrtwc.org/facts-issues/state-right-to-work-timeline-2016/. Note that since Kentucky, Missouri, and West Virginia all passed right-to-work laws in 2016 or later, and Missouri and West Virginia's laws were still pending as this book went to press, they do not show up among the "actual right-to-work" states.

and decline, suggests that other factors outside of RTW laws have affected union density rates.

This conclusion is consistent with another analysis by Farber (1984), which showed that lower union density in RTW states is an effect of preexisting factors which weaken unions in those states. Indeed, his analysis shows that unionization is significantly lower than elsewhere in the entirely RTW South, even *after* controlling for the presence of RTW laws.

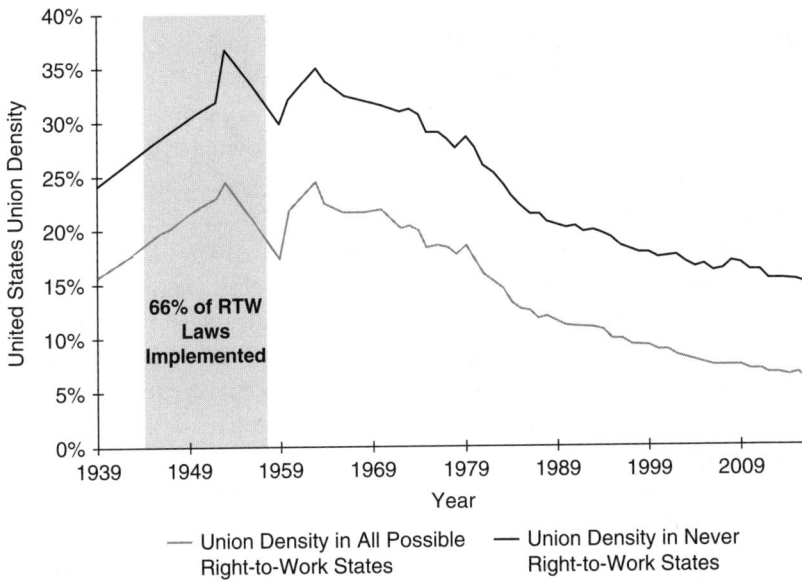

FIGURE 2.14 US union density in all possible right-to-work and never-right-to-work states, 1939–2016
Sources, union membership: Troy, Leo, and Neil Sheflin. 1985. US Union Sourcebook: Membership, Finances, Structure, Directory. West Orange, N.J.: Industrial Relations Data and Information Services, Table 7.2, p. 7-4. 1964–2016: Barry T. Hirsch, David A. Macpherson, and Wayne G. Vroman, "Estimates of Union Density by State," *Monthly Labor Review*, Vol. 124, No. 7, July 2001, pp. 51–55 (up-to-date data available at www.unionstats.com). Sources, right-to-work status: Reed, W. Robert. 2003. "How right-to-work laws affect wages." *Journal of Labor Research* 24(4):713–730, p. 728 n. 7, and National Right-to-Work Committee, "State Right-to-Work Timeline," https://nrtwc.org/facts-issues/state-right-to-work-timeline-2016/. Note that since Missouri's and West Virginia's right-to-work laws were still pending as this book went to press, and I define "possible right-to-work states" as those that have ever *enacted* a right-to-work law, they are still included among the "never right-to-work" states.

This is an important point, because it emphasizes the fact that RTW laws do not exist in isolation. Rather, they reflect a state's overall political history and climate. For example, it is no accident that the earliest adopters of RTW laws were the states of the former Confederacy, a region with a deep history of labor repression (Dixon 2008; 2010; Wiener 1979). Again, a thought experiment can help clarify this point. What could we reasonably expect to happen to union density if an existing RTW state, say

South Carolina, were to repeal its RTW law? By itself, the likely answer is that not much would change. There are many factors that contribute to South Carolina having the lowest union density in the United States, of which an RTW law is only one. To the extent that we would expect to see a change in union density in South Carolina following the hypothetical repeal of its RTW law, it would most likely be due to the popular mobilization and shift in political climate that would be necessary to repeal RTW, not the repeal of the law itself.

The recent wave of states adopting RTW laws reinforces this point. It is no coincidence that these states are Rust Belt states where unions were once powerful but have been decimated in recent decades. This new rash of state RTW laws reflects the culmination of an ongoing pattern of union decline and growing employer strength. While scholars will be watching closely in the coming years to see what happens to union density, wages, employment, and more in these new RTW states, the RTW laws will only be exacerbating a preexisting process of union decline.

In sum, the evidence shows that there is a clear relationship between low union density and RTW laws. However, it is unclear whether this is because RTW laws cause low union density, or because low-density states are more likely to adopt RTW laws. Regardless of the possible effects of RTW, the main question that remains to be explained is the persistence of strongly unequal regional distribution of unionization in the United States, with a more-unionized Northeast, Midwest, and West Coast, and a less-unionized Southeast, Great Plains, and Southwest.

RIGHT-TO-WORK AND US–CANADA UNION DENSITY DIVERGENCE
While the effect of RTW laws on union density remains inconclusive when analyzed solely within the US context, a comparison with Canada could shed explanatory light. Do differences in union security provisions play a role in driving density divergence?

Whereas RTW laws in the US forbid union security clauses, seven Canadian jurisdictions, comprising 90 percent of Canadian workers, require agency shops. Taras and Ponak (2001a; 2001b) argue that this difference is key to understanding the divergence of US and Canadian union density rates. Their analysis of collective bargaining agreements shows that nearly twice as many US contracts (22 percent versus 12 percent) have no union security clause.

Additionally, Taras and Ponak show that the gap between union membership rates and collective bargaining coverage rates is more than twice as large in US RTW states as that in any other jurisdiction

(21.2 percent, compared to 8.8 percent in non-RTW states), and that nonmandatory Canadian provinces have a higher gap than mandatory Canadian provinces (11.9 percent compared to 7.5 percent). Thus, lack of union security clauses does seem to exacerbate free-riding.

While these cross-border differences are real, they do not in themselves constitute an adequate explanation for union density divergence. As discussed above, RTW laws and lower union density may be related, but the causal relations remain murky.

What is clear is that union density in the United States is far more regionally uneven than in Canada. Additionally, it is clear that employment in the United States has shifted from higher-density states to lower-density states, at least in critical higher-density sectors like manufacturing. While these lower-density states tend to be RTW states, there appear to be other factors contributing to those states' low union density. Our explanation of US–Canada density divergence must be able to account for this regional unevenness of US union density.

Furthermore, even if we accept that RTW laws have played an important role in driving union density divergence, what remains to be explained is why US labor law was amended to allow RTW laws, whereas in Canada, not only have RTW laws failed to take hold, but as Taras and Ponak note, something like the opposite of RTW, i.e. mandatory agency shop laws, has been enacted instead.

Scope of Activity: Strike Policy

Finally, we consider policies governing unions' permitted scope of activities. Specifically, we will focus on policies regulating strike activity, the archetypal form of worker collective action, and the ultimate basis for unions' organizational power (Getman and Marshall 2000). Protecting the strike weapon mitigates the power imbalance between workers and management.

Strike policy regulates both union and employer behavior. On the union side, policies regulate when and under what conditions workers can go on strike. Once a strike is underway, policies regulate specific forms of strike activity. On the employer side, policies regulate when and under what conditions employers can lock their workers out. Once a strike or lockout is underway, policies regulate if and when employers can continue operating their businesses using replacement workers, or "scabs."

Under contemporary labor regimes, strike and lockout regulations primarily affect union density in two ways. First, they facilitate or impede either party's ability to achieve their aims at the bargaining table. If regulations are more restrictive toward unions, by making striking harder and making employers' use of replacements easier, union membership may appear less attractive to workers. In some cases, frustrated workers may vote to decertify their bargaining unit. In others, workers may be permanently replaced by scabs, who then vote to decertify the unit. Second, strike regulations can exert a demonstration effect on workers and employers, both within the affected bargaining unit as well as beyond it. Restrictions on striking can embolden employers, making them less willing to bargain with worker representatives and more willing to draw out the bargaining process. Similarly, the restrictions and difficulties that unionized workers encounter in the course of exercising their legal right to strike may convince other workers that unionization is not worth the effort, especially in cases where, as reviewed above, the certification process itself can be so onerous.

In this section, we will first examine regulations of workers' ability to strike. Second, we will examine regulations of employers' ability to replace strikers, Third, we will evaluate how these regulations have affected strike activity in the United States and Canada, and how this may have affected union density rates in both countries.

STRIKE REGULATION IN THE UNITED STATES AND CANADA   Labor laws restrict strike activity in both the United States and Canada, but those restrictions have evolved differently over time. In the United States, the right to strike has eroded to the point where it is a dead letter. In Canada, the right to strike has come to be recognized as part of Canadians' constitutionally protected freedom of assembly, although in practice, federal and provincial governments have shown a penchant for finding exceptions to that right and ordering strikers back to work.

The 1935 Wagner Act explicitly safeguarded the right to strike as a fundamental right in the United States. It stated in Section 13 that "nothing in this Act shall be construed so as to interfere with or impede or diminish in any way the right to strike."

However, the 1947 Taft-Hartley Act did diminish the right to strike.[37] Most importantly, Section 303 forbade what are known as "secondary boycotts," meaning union efforts to exert pressure on an employer by picketing a different employer with which the targeted employer has a strategic relationship, such as a key supplier or customer. Section 8(d) mandated a sixty-day written notification prior to terminating or

---

[37] Labor-Management Relations (Taft-Hartley) Act, Public Law No. 78–101, 61 Stat. 136 (1947).

modifying a collective bargaining agreement, and specified that workers who engaged in strikes inside the sixty-day period could be fired. Section 301 made unions that engaged in strikes when a no-strike clause was in place liable for a breach of contract, opening them to employer lawsuits. Section 208 gave the president the authority to intervene in and halt strikes deemed to constitute a "national emergency," and Section 305 explicitly forbade strikes by public sector employees.

The 1959 Landrum-Griffin Act[38] tightened restrictions on the right to strike, forbidding recognition strikes and "hot cargo" agreements, a specific form of secondary boycott where an employer not directly covered by the collective bargaining agreement under negotiation agrees not to handle goods or use services provided by the struck employer.

In addition to imposing restrictions on the right to strike, Taft-Hartley's right-to-work provisions enshrined into law individual workers' right *not* to engage in strike activity (McCammon 1990: 214). By guaranteeing the "right to scab" as well as the right to strike, the law reproduced the free-rider problem we saw in our analysis of union security provisions. An individual worker could refuse to participate in a strike, thus undermining the union's collective capacity, while still benefiting from union protections after the strike, without suffering any consequences. Far from creating an equivalence between workers' individual right to participate or not participate in strike activity, reframing union activity as a set of individual rights eroded the collective right to strike (McCammon 1990, 1994).

In addition to these restrictions by legislative amendment, US workers' right to strike has also been limited by legal rulings and interpretations (Klare 1977; McCammon 1990). Some of the more important rulings are listed below:[39]

- In 1939, the Supreme Court ruled in *NLRB v. Fansteel Metallurgical Corp.*[40] that sit-down strikes, where workers physically occupy their workplace premises, are illegal. This was barely two years after the Wagner Act was deemed constitutional, in the aftermath of a wave of sit-down strikes inspired by the success of General Motors workers in Flint, Michigan, who made strategic use of factory occupations to win union recognition in the winter of 1936–1937 (Bernstein 1970).

---

[38] Labor-Management Reporting and Disclosure (Landrum-Griffin) Act of 1959, Public Law No. 86–257, 73 Stat. 519 (1959) (codified as amended in sections of 29 USC).
[39] This selection of cases is far from exhaustive. More detailed analyses of legal restrictions on the right to strike can be found in (Klare 1977; McCammon 1990; Pope 2008).
[40] *NLRB v. Fansteel Metallurgical Corp.*, 306 US 240 (1939).

- Also in 1939, the Court ruled in *NLRB v. Sands Manufacturing Co.*[41] that workers had no right to strike if they were attempting a midterm modification of their contract. This restriction held even if workers believed they were simply enforcing their existing contract rights and even if their contract did not contain a no-strike clause. In the case at hand, the employer successfully fired and replaced the entire striking workforce.
- The 1957 *Textile Workers of America v. Lincoln Mills of Alabama* decision,[42] along with the "Steelworkers Trilogy" of 1960,[43] left unions vulnerable to lawsuits for breach of contract for resorting to strikes over contract grievances instead of arbitrating them.
- In 1962, the Court's decision in *Local 174, Teamsters v. Lucas Flour Co.*[44] implied a no-strike clause during the life of all collective bargaining agreements, even if such a provision was not explicitly present in the agreement. This extended Section 301 of the Taft-Hartley Act to all unions, outlawing wildcat strikes and holding union officials legally liable for policing their members' activity.
- In 1970, the Court's ruling in *Boys Market, Inc. v. Retail Clerks*[45] tightened regulation of wildcat and other mid-contract strikes. In addition to being open to lawsuits, offending unions could now be subject to labor injunctions to block the strike. This revived the use of the labor injunction, which had been a favored tool of management and the state against unions prior to its being outlawed in 1932 with the passage of the Federal Anti-Injunction (Norris-LaGuardia) Act (Silverstein 1993).
- In 1976, the Court ruled in *Hudgens v. NLRB*[46] that strikers' First Amendment right to free speech via picketing was subordinate to business owners' property rights (the ruling involved strikers who were picketing a business located in a shopping mall).

---

[41] *NLRB v. Sands Manufacturing Co.*, 306 US 332 (1939).
[42] *Textile Workers Union of America v. Lincoln Mills of Alabama*, 353 US 448 (1957).
[43] The trilogy included *United Steelworkers of America v. American Manufacturing Co.*, 353 US 564 (1960), *United Steelworkers of America v. Enterprise Wheel and Car Corp.*, 363 US 593 (1960), and *United Steelworkers of America v. Warrior and Gulf Navigation*, 363 US 574 (1960).
[44] *Local 174, Teamsters v. Lucas Flour Co.*, 369 US 95 (1962).
[45] *Boys Market, Inc. v. Retail Clerks*, 398 US 235 (1970).
[46] *Hudgens v. NLRB*, 424 US 507 (1976).

All told, legislative amendments and legal interpretations have limited the right to strike in the United States to the point where it is meaningless today (Burns 2011; Getman and Marshall 2000; Pope 2008).

In Canada, restrictions on the right to strike have followed a different path. Whereas the US Wagner Act explicitly sought to protect and promote free collective bargaining, the initial goal of Canadian labor policy was to promote industrial peace by controlling labor militancy. This principle was articulated in Order-in-Council PC 1003 (1944), which created the framework for modern labor relations in Canada. It was subsequently codified in the Rand Formula and the Industrial Relations and Disputes Investigation Act (IRDIA) of 1948 (Fudge and Tucker 2001; McInnis 2002).[47]

Given the policy goal of controlling labor militancy, many of the restrictions on striking that developed over time in the United States were incorporated into Canadian laws from the beginning. For example, the laws explicitly prohibited recognition and mid-contract strikes, leaving violators vulnerable to legal injunctions (i.e. the standard reached in the United States in 1970 with the *Boys Market* ruling). This rendered illegal not only wildcat strikes – those engaged in without official union authorization, but also sympathy strikes – those engaged in to support the efforts of another group of workers to negotiate with their employer (Wells 1995a).

In many cases, Canadian law surrounding strikes was *more* restrictive than corresponding US law. Whereas US law after Taft-Hartley required unions to specify procedures for authorizing strikes in their bylaws, and to file copies of their bylaws with the government, Canadian law mandated a government-supervised strike authorization vote. Whereas US law has evolved through legal judgments toward requiring extensive mediation or arbitration procedures prior to engaging in strikes, Canadian law required a period of compulsory government-directed conciliation. Whereas Taft-Hartley in the United States mandated a sixty-day written notification of the intent to reopen a contract or go on strike, Canadian law mandated a cooling-off period prior to going on strike if conciliation failed (Taras 1997: 300).

---

[47] As previously mentioned, jurisdiction for most regulation of labor relations passed to the provinces after World War II. However, the provinces all modeled their relevant governing legislation after the IRDIA. Thus, the relevant language governing strikes was relatively similar across the country. In a few cases, particularly British Columbia and Quebec, it was even more restrictive (Fudge and Tucker 2001).

Secondary boycotts were also declared illegal in Canada, but later than in the United States, as a result of the Ontario Court of Appeals' 1963 decision in the case of *Hersees of Woodstock Ltd. v. Goldstein*.[48] In it, the court held that "the right, if there be such a right, of the [union] to engage in secondary picketing of the [employer's] premises must give way to the [employer's] right to trade." As in the US *Hudgens* decision, property rights trumped rights of assembly and expression.

With the adoption of the Canadian Charter of Rights and Freedoms in 1982, the question of whether the Charter's guarantee of the freedom of assembly included the right to bargain collectively and picket gained greater urgency. In a series of 1987 rulings dubbed the "Labour Trilogy,"[49] the Supreme Court of Canada held that these rights were not protected by the Charter (Fudge 2010: 3–5; Panitch and Swartz 2003: 62–74). The trilogy held sway in Canadian labor relations jurisprudence until 2002, when the first cracks began to show with the Court's decision in *RWDSU v. Pepsi*.[50] Reversing *Hersees*, the Court ruled that secondary picketing was Charter-protected freedom of expression. As such, it was only illegal in cases where it involved specific "wrongful action" (Adell 2003; Dinsdale and Awrey 2003).[51]

The Court dealt a further blow to the Trilogy with its 2007 decision in *Health Services and Support v. B.C.*[52] Citing decades of critical Canadian labor historiography, the Court's ruling endorsed the idea that collective bargaining was a "fundamental freedom" protected by Section 2(d) of the Charter, which guarantees of freedom of association. But while the decision offered a full-throated defense of the right to collective bargaining, it wavered on the right to strike. Several of the very scholars upon whose research the court based its decision criticized it for affirming an industrial pluralist model of collective bargaining that had long since disappeared in reality (Adams 2008; Fudge 2010; Tucker 2008). Nonetheless, *B.C. Health Services* represented a partial expansion of the right to strike, especially when compared with the erosion of that right under US law.

---

[48] *Hersees of Woodstock Ltd. v. Goldstein* (1963), 38 D.L.R. (2d) 449 (Ont. C.A.).

[49] These cases included *Reference re Public Service Employee Relations Act (Alta.)*, [1987] 1 S.C.R. 313 ("Alberta Reference"), *PSAC v. Canada*, [1987] 1 S.C.R. 424, and *RWDSU v. Saskatchewan*, [1987] 1 S.C.R. 460.

[50] *Retail, Wholesale and Department Store Union, Local 558 v. Pepsi-Cola Canada Beverages(West)Ltd.*, [2002] 1 S.C.R. 146 [*Pepsi*].

[51] The court left open the question of what exactly constituted "wrongful action," clearing the way for further legal wrangling and interpretation.

[52] *Health Services and Support – Facilities Subsector Bargaining Assn. v. British Columbia*, [2007] 2 S.C.R. 391, 2007 SCC 27.

Most recently, as recounted in the chapter introduction, the Canadian Supreme Court decisively reversed the Labour Trilogy in 2015 with a series of decisions now known as the "New Labour Trilogy."[53] The court held that the right to strike was fully protected under Section 2(d) of the Charter, declaring that it "is an essential part of a meaningful collective bargaining process in our system of labour relations" (248).

Although the formal right to strike has expanded over time in Canada, in practice federal and provincial governments have often violated the letter and spirit of the law by using "temporary" back-to-work legislation. The result is what Panitch and Swartz (2003) have termed a regime of "permanent exceptionalism." Indeed, Canada differs sharply from the United States in its frequent, consistent use of emergency back-to-work legislation as a means of regulating class conflict (Adams 1989).

Panitch and Swartz document a sharp rise in the use of back-to-work legislation beginning in the mid-1970s, when the annual average use of such measures jumped to five, as compared to fewer than one per year prior to 1965. Since then, average annual use of back-to-work legislation hovered around four or five, then dropped down to 2.5 in the 1990s, but bounced back to over five in the 2000s (Panitch and Swartz 2006: Table 15.1). This trend has continued in recent years, with several national strikes being quashed by "emergency" back-to-work legislation (Canadian Foundation for Labour Rights 2016; Parliament of Canada n.d.). By contrast, Taft-Hartley emergency back-to-work injunctions have only been used a total of thirty-five times since the Act was passed in 1947. Of those, only two were issued in the past forty years – one in 1978 and the latest in 2002 (J. S. Gross 2004). While government injunctions have proliferated in Canada since the mid-1970s, they have virtually disappeared in the United States.

In sum, the right to strike exists in both the United States and Canada, but it has been carefully circumscribed. In the United States, legislative amendments and legal interpretations have restricted the right to strike to the point where it is a dead letter. In Canada, legal restrictions on striking were initially tighter than in the United States, but have been relaxed in recent years. This has primarily been a result of court rulings declaring striking to be part of workers' fundamental, Charter-protected freedom of assembly. But despite expanding formal protection of the right to strike,

---

[53] *Mounted Police Association of Ontario v. Canada (A.G.)*, 2015 SCC 1, *Meredith v. Canada (A.G.)*, 2015 SCC 2, and *Saskatchewan Federation of Labour v. Saskatchewan*, 2015 SCC 4.

Canada differs sharply from the United States in its reliance on "exceptional" back-to-work legislation as a means of controlling labor militancy.

REGULATION OF STRIKEBREAKERS IN THE UNITED STATES AND CANADA Another significant difference between US and Canadian strike policy has to do with rules governing employers' ability to hire replacement workers (scabs) during the course of a strike or lockout. Rules facilitating striker replacement enable employers to continue operating their business in the course of a strike, thus blunting the union's economic weapon. Conversely, rules limiting striker replacement sharpen the strike weapon, requiring the employer to bear the cost of their workers' withdrawal of labor.

While neither labor regime initially specified rules for replacement workers, US law moved toward protecting and expanding employers' right to hire replacements, while Canadian law moved to limit this right. This policy divergence became especially pronounced in the 1970s, at the very moment that union density began to diverge in both countries. The timing suggests that differences in the regulation of strikebreakers could have played a role in density divergence.

In the United States, modern regulations governing striker replacement began with the Supreme Court's 1938 decision in *NLRB v. Mackay Radio and Telegraph Co.*[54] In that ruling, the Court determined that struck employers were entitled to hire replacement workers to continue running their business. The language of the ruling created an equivalence between the right to strike enshrined in the Wagner Act on the one hand, and the employer's property rights on the other:

> Although Section 13 of the Act provides, "Nothing in this Act shall be construed so as to interfere with or impede or diminish in any way the right to strike," it does not follow that an employer, guilty of no act denounced by the statute, has lost the right to protect and continue his business by supplying places left vacant by strikers.

Under the guise of providing an evenhanded consideration of the rights of both parties, *Mackay Radio* fundamentally undermined the right to strike, by placing anyone who wished to exercise that right in the position of putting their economic livelihood at risk (Rogers 1990: 130–131).

---

[54] *NLRB v. Mackay Radio and Telegraph Co.*, 304 US 333 (1938).

In addition to its evenhanded consideration of employers' property rights, US law expanded the replacement workers' right to *refrain* from exercising their right to strike. Section 9 of the Taft-Hartley Act denied striking workers who had been permanently replaced the right to vote in representation elections in their workplace. This provided an incentive for strikebreakers to file for a decertification election, where they could eliminate the union and keep the jobs they had taken. The Landrum-Griffin Act restored strikers' right to vote, but only for twelve months from the beginning of the strike (McCammon 1990: 212–213).

The resulting policy regulating strikebreakers in the United States weakened workers' ability to exercise their right to strike, while strengthening employers' ability to withstand a strike and creating incentives for individual workers to engage in strikebreaking.

The regulations in Canada developed quite differently. There, some employers did hire replacement workers in the post-World War II decades, but rarely on a permanent basis. Strikers were generally rehired at the end of the strike. Where employers resisted, some provincial labor boards and courts acted to reinstate strikers. Other regulatory bodies came down on the side of employers' property rights. The status of replacement workers remained unclear in most jurisdictions until the 1970s (Logan 2002: 147–149).

Policies began to shift in favor of strikers in the 1970s. After initially favoring a *Mackay Radio*-style protection of employer rights in the 1970s, the Canadian Labour Relations Board moved in the 1980s and '90s toward a position that rejected the idea that employers had a unilateral right to replace striking workers. Meanwhile, most Canadian provinces enacted legislation prohibiting employers from permanently replacing strikers, and many provided at least limited reinstatement and voting rights to replaced workers. Most still allowed temporary strikebreakers, although Quebec's 1977 "anti-scab" law forbade all forms of replacement workers. British Columbia and Ontario followed Quebec's lead in 1993 (Logan 2002 :149–152).[55]

Overall, the US policy on strikebreakers offered a formally evenhanded consideration of the rights of strikers, employers, and replacement workers that substantively undermined the right to strike. Meanwhile, Canadian policy evolved over the course of the 1970s and '80s to restrict employers' ability to operate with strikebreakers, protect strikers' reinstatement rights, and shore up the right to strike.

---

[55] The Ontario law was repealed in 1995.

COMPARING STRIKE ACTIVITY IN THE UNITED STATES AND CANADA While US and Canadian policies surrounding strikes and replacement workers have diverged, particularly since the 1970s, what remains unclear is the extent to which these diverging policies had actual effects on strikes and unionization rates in both countries. How then has strike activity changed over time in the United States and Canada, and to what extent can we attribute these changes to the policy changes discussed above? Most importantly, can we detect a link between changes in strike activity and changes in union density?

Figures 2.15 and 2.16 compare strike activity in the United States and Canada along two different metrics: 1) the number of workers involved in strikes; and 2) the number of person-days idle due to strikes. Both

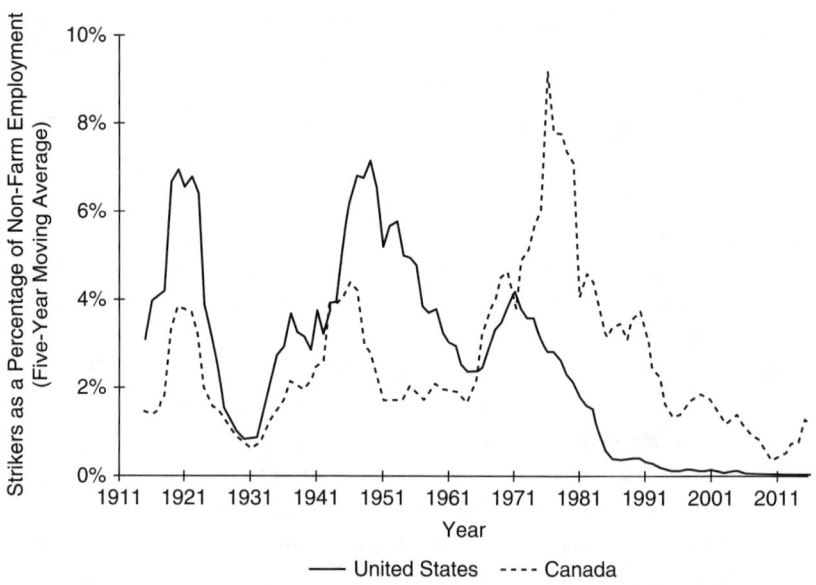

FIGURE 2.15 Strikers as a percentage of nonfarm employment in the United States and Canada, 1911–2016 (five-year moving average)
Sources, US: Historical Statistics of the US Millennial Edition, Table Ba4954-4964, Bureau of Labor Statistics, http://www.bls.gov/news.release/wkstp.to1.htm (1911–1981). Federal Mediation and Conciliation Service, https://www.fmcs.gov/resources/documents-and-data/ (1984–2014). Sources, Canada: Historical Statistics of Canada, Table E190-197 (1901–1975); Strategic Policy, Analysis, and Workplace Information Directorate, Labour Program, HRSDC (1976–2011), "Chronological Perspective on Work Stoppages," http://srv131.services.gc.ca/dimt-wid/pcat-cpws/recherche-search.aspx?lang=eng

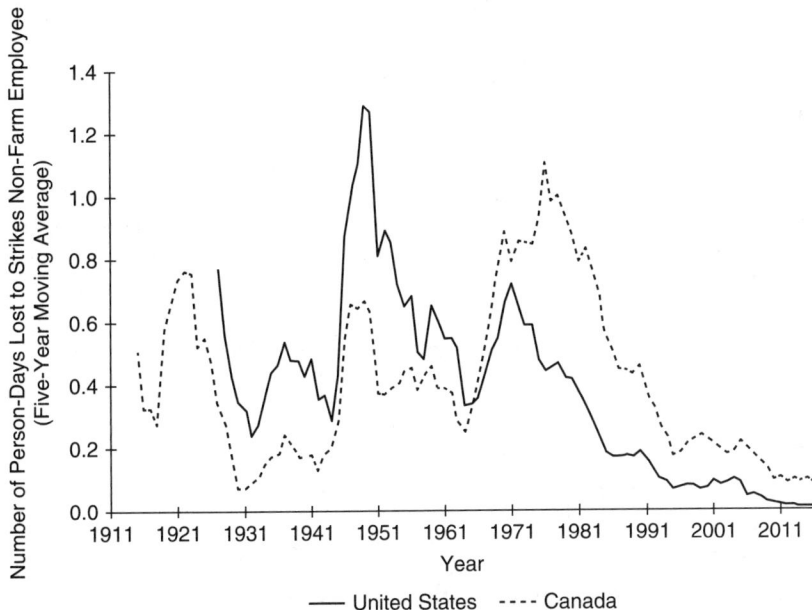

FIGURE 2.16 Number of person-days lost to strikes per nonfarm employee in the United States and Canada, 1911–2016 (five-year moving average)
Sources: Same as Figure 2.15

measures are expressed as a percentage of the nonagricultural workforce to improve comparability. The graphs display five-year moving averages to show the overall trend more clearly.[56]

What both figures show is that strike rates in both countries followed similar paths for most of the twentieth century, with the United States experiencing somewhat higher rates through the 1970s. Then, in the 1970s strike rates plummeted in the United States, while they exploded in Canada. That Canadian spurt proved to be short-lived though, and strike rates there too began to drop precipitously by the late 1970s and early 1980s. However, the 1970s surge placed Canadian strike rates firmly above those in the United States for the next forty years, reversing the prior trend.

The 1970s were an important turning point for strike frequency in both countries. Rates declined in both countries, but have remained consistently higher in Canada compared to the United States. How do we

[56] The underlying data for these charts are reported in Table A.5.

interpret this divergence, followed by decline in both countries? More importantly, how might this affect union density? As Robinson (1993: 40 n. 17) explains, the relationship between strikes and union power is complex:

> [T]he relationship between labour-movement power and strike levels is not linear. Rather, it is more like an inverted U-curve. When unions are few and fragmented – too weak to hold successful strikes – then strike levels are very low. Conversely, when unions are so powerful that strikes will cost employers much more than they can hope to gain, employers will bargain much more assiduously, and again strike levels will be very low (Hibbs 1987; Shalev 1980). So it is in the medium ranges of labour-movement power where strike levels tend to be higher. And within this medium range, greater union power will be associated with more strikes (Snyder 1977).

Interpreting strike data therefore requires a careful engagement with the historical and political specifics of the cases under examination. This is all the more important when trying to relate strike activity and measures of unions' organizational strength, such as union density. Since both strike activity and union density change over time, unions in a given country could be at different points along the inverted U-curve at a given historical moment, lending different interpretations to strike rates at that moment. Moreover, strike rates and union density are not simply a function of the relative power of labor and capital at a given point in time.

An additional factor is the role of the state. A more laissez-faire, less protective state labor regime would tend to tighten the relationship between strikes and union power, as unions and employers are left to battle each other in an economic test of strength. By contrast, a more interventionist, more protective state labor regime would tend to decouple the relationship between strikes and union power, as unions are able or required to use state-sanctioned nonstrike mechanisms to resolve disputes, while state policies limit unions' ability to strike, as well as employers' ability to break strikes.

This means that the relationship between strikes and union density is not simply a measure of economic or organizational power. It can also serve as an indicator of the *institutional strength and legitimacy* of the labor regime in question. A weaker labor regime will be characterized by a stronger relation between strike rates and union density, whereas a stronger labor regime will be characterized by a weaker relation between the two.

How does this relationship look in the United States and Canada? Figure 2.17 tracks the annual percentage-point difference between union density (the percentage of nonagricultural workers who were union

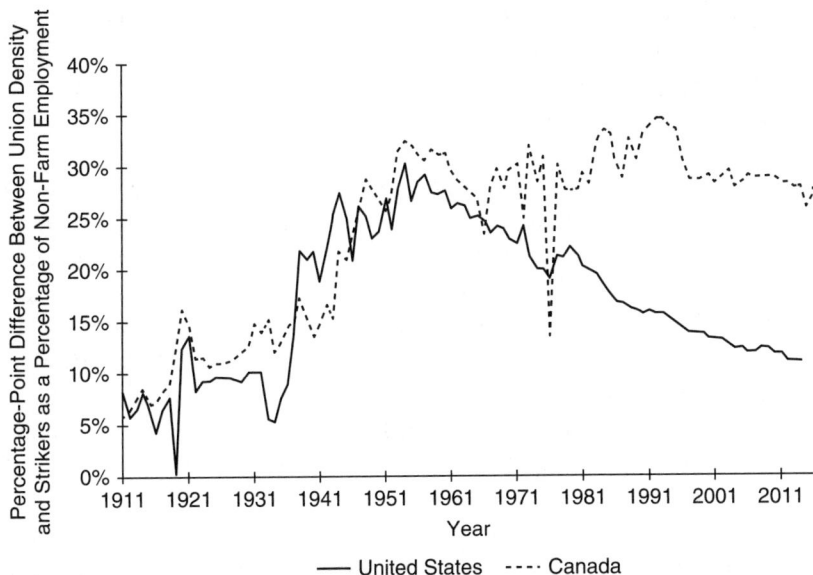

FIGURE 2.17 Percentage-point difference between union density and strikers as a percentage of nonfarm employment in the United States and Canada, 1911–2016
Source: For union density, Appendix A. For strike data, see Figure 2.15

members in a given year) and strike rates (the percentage of nonagricultural workers who were on strike that year). Mathematically, a rising trend line means that the relation between union density and strike rates is growing weaker, while a falling trend line means that the relation is strengthening. Substantively, a rising trend line suggests that unions' organizational strength is increasing, while their reliance on exerting economic power through strikes is diminishing. This is what we would expect to see with a more legitimate and institutionalized labor regime. A falling trend line suggests that unions' organizational strength is more dependent on exercising the strike weapon. This is what we would expect to see with a less legitimate, weakly institutionalized labor regime. It is important to emphasize that a falling trend line could result from a situation in which militant unions are adding members and striking a lot, or from a situation in which weak unions are losing members and not striking much.

As we would expect to see, the US line increased dramatically from the mid-1930s through the mid-1950s, as the Wagner Act regime took hold and allowed unions to consolidate membership gains without necessarily resorting to strikes. Strikes were still frequent in this time period, but membership grew much faster. In Canada, we see a similar dramatic increase, except that the spike only starts in the mid-1940s, when the Canadian labor regime gets established.

Starting in the mid-1950s, both lines remained high, but started to decline. The lines began to diverge in the mid-1960s, although it is important to note the periodic sharp downward spikes in Canada from the mid-1960s through the mid-1970s. This reflects the massive strike waves in Canada that were unmatched in the United States. After the mid-1970s, the trend diverged in both countries, with the line steadily declining in the United States, and rebounding to unprecedented high levels in Canada. This reflects the fact that strike rates plummeted in both countries, but without affecting Canadian union density nearly as much.

Given what we know about the timing and development of US and Canadian labor law, we can interpret this divergence in union density/strike rate differences as a divergence in labor regime strength and legitimacy. In the United States, an eroding labor regime eviscerated the strike weapon while giving employers a freer hand to attack unions, leading to union decline. In Canada, a stronger and more legitimate labor regime shored up Canadian union membership, even as labor militancy declined.

Based on the foregoing analysis, we can conclude that there is clear evidence showing that differences in labor law regimes have contributed to US and Canadian union density divergence. In terms of rules governing union certification, first contract negotiation, union security, and strike activity, the current Canadian labor regime provides relatively greater protections to workers and their unions than the US regime. At the same time, it places relatively stronger constraints on employers' ability to intervene in workers' efforts to exercise their collective bargaining rights. These differences have led to union density decline in the United States, and relative stability in Canada.

However, the analysis also shows that these labor regime differences have not always existed. Indeed, in several respects Canadian labor policy has historically been less favorable to unions than US policy. But whereas the US labor regime eroded over time, the Canadian labor regime strengthened. This change happened in the 1970s and '80s, with the advent of card-check certification and speedy certification election rules, first contract arbitration, mandatory agency shop laws, and anti-scab legislation. The labor regime divergence has led to a situation where US employers can – and do – essentially behave as if labor laws no longer exist. By contrast, Canadian employers, whatever their personal anti-union biases might be, must recognize that "here there are rules."

In terms of explaining union density divergence, the challenge then is not simply to note that labor regimes differ in the United States and Canada. Nor is it sufficient to note that employer hostility has increased in the United States, but not in Canada. Rather, what needs to be explained is *why* the US labor regime eroded so much more than in Canada? Labor regimes do not exist in isolation. Rather, they both affect and reflect societal pressures and power imbalances (Atleson 1994: 463). Thus, what really needs to be explained are the causes underlying shifts in those pressures and power imbalances. The central question then becomes much broader: why did working-class power erode less in Canada than in the United States?

Some have attempted to tackle this broader question regarding the overall context shaping labor relations in the United States and Canada. They have focused in large part on key differences in political institutions, national characters, and internal union cultures. Our next step is to evaluate these competing explanations of differences in US and Canadian working-class power.

3

Working-Class Power in the United States and Canada

The previous chapter showed that current differences in labor policies create a relatively more hospitable climate for unions in Canada compared to the United States. However, we also saw that these differences have not always existed and that the US labor regime eroded over time, while the Canadian regime strengthened. Explanations focusing on policy differences show that these differences have occurred, but they do not explain *why* they occurred.

This chapter evaluates explanations for why these differences in labor regimes have developed. They all focus on understanding the broader social and political forces that have enabled and constrained working-class power in both countries in different ways. They emphasize four key sets of differences: differences in political institutions, differences in national character, differences in internal union characteristics, and the different roles of racial divisions.

POLITICAL INSTITUTIONS

Explanations focusing on differences in political institutions emphasize how differences in all three branches of government eroded the US labor regime while maintaining or reinforcing the Canadian regime:

- In the legislative realm, they highlight the lack of a labor party in the United States, as compared to the role that Canada's labor party, first the Cooperative Commonwealth Federation (CCF) and later the New Democratic Party (NDP), has played in promoting more pro-labor policies and advancing working-class interests more generally.

- In the executive realm, they highlight how differences in the structure and administration of labor policy in both countries led to labor regime erosion in the United States and labor regime stability in Canada.
- In the judicial realm, they highlight how the tighter integration of the US labor adjudication system into the regular court system, particularly its greater exposure to judicial review, eroded US labor law over time. Meanwhile, the Canadian labor adjudication system's greater autonomy left it more insulated from the regular courts, allowing greater stability over time.

Party Differences

Parties, Institutional Arrangements, and Electoral Threats

Many explanations for why Canadian unions are relatively stronger than their US counterparts focus on the role of the CCF/NDP as a labor-based political party (Adams 1989; Bernard 1994; Bruce 1989; Chaison and Rose 1990; Maki 1982; Rose and Chaison 1996; Taras 1997). Although it has usually played the role of a third party, as opposed to governing, analysts contend the CCF/NDP has been able to pressure governing parties to take action, particularly in times of electoral insecurity for the governing party (Bruce 1989). Importantly, Bruce's study showed that the CCF/NDP was able to exert political influence for pro-labor reforms at a much lower electoral threshold than its most comparable US equivalent, non-Southern Democrats (1989: Tables 1 and 2).

Bruce attributes the CCF/NDP's ability to exert influence at lower electoral thresholds, as well as conservative forces' inability to roll back progressive labor legislation over time, to differences in how parties function in Canada's parliamentary system, as opposed to the presidential system in the United States (1989: 133–135). In a parliamentary system, because the governing party's ability to rule is contingent on retaining the confidence of the legislature, i.e. to not be outvoted on issues of major importance, party discipline is essential. Each individual Member of Parliament functions primarily as a party representative, and bloc voting is the norm. In such a system, the ruling party is extremely sensitive to shifts in the balance of power in the legislature, especially when they threaten its majority. Under such conditions, ruling parties can be pushed to adopt policies to which they had previously been opposed. Moreover, under conditions of strict party discipline, parties cannot merge without the minority partner sacrificing its autonomy. According to the argument, this has prevented the two usual major parties, the Liberals and Conservatives,[1] from allying against the minority CCF/NDP to roll back progressive labor legislation, while also preventing breakaway coalitions between one party and more conservative members of another party.[2]

Parties play a different role within the US presidential system. With the executive's and governing legislative party's power to rule not dependent on sustaining legislative majorities, party discipline is much less important (Patterson and Caldeira 1988). This creates more room for different, even opposing, regional and sectional interests to be represented within the same party. Rather than functioning primarily as representatives of their party, US legislators function more as individuals. In such a system, party affiliation matters, but it is counterbalanced by other pressures, namely those of reelection and constituency satisfaction (Mayhew 1974; Turner and Schneier 1970). Additionally, it allows individual legislators to function as "policy entrepreneurs" (Kingdon 1984; Walker 1974), denying party leaders the virtual monopoly over policy initiatives and agenda setting that exists in the Canadian majority-rule parliamentary system. It also creates numerous access points through which outside interest groups can seek to shape legislation.

The challenge with the presidential system is that each policy initiative requires its sponsors to cobble together a new coalition with enough votes to pass the desired legislation. The cobbling process often involves significant favor trading, logrolling, and revision/dilution of bill provisions in order for sponsors to secure enough votes for the bill to pass. This lack of coordination and party discipline creates large numbers of veto points for legislation (Moe and Caldwell 1994), making it far more difficult for the governing party, or any other group, to move their policy agenda through the legislature. It also makes changing existing policies via the legislative process more difficult.

Parties and the Organization of Interests
While parties exert influence through the institutional and electoral threat effects that Bruce describes, these are not the only ways they do so. Parties

---

[1] As will be explored in greater detail below, the Conservative Party appears under a variety of different and ever-changing names over the course of Canadian political history.
[2] Manitoba, Saskatchewan, and British Columbia have proven to be exceptions to this trend in party systems. In each case, a strong NDP has led to a de facto merger of the Liberals and Conservatives, with the Liberals largely disappearing in Manitoba, the Conservatives vanishing in British Columbia, and both forming a new party in Saskatchewan (Evans and Smith 2015).

also influence politics by forging coalitions, organizing interests, and shaping political agendas (De Leon et al. 2015, 2009; Gramsci 1978; Kingdon 1984). In the Canadian context, the NDP has served to put labor's concerns on the national agenda, and has provided a political vehicle for labor and progressive social movement organizations (Bernard 1994).

Granted, the labor-movement-party relationship is far from harmonious, and other scholars have been far more caustic than Bernard in their assessments of the NDP (Camfield 2011; Evans 2012; Panitch 1992; Savage 2010). Nevertheless, the problems that exist are slight when compared to those that scholars have identified as resulting from the lack of a labor party in the United States (Brenner 1985; Davis 1980a; Draper 1989; Lipsig-Mumme 1989; Milton 1982; Moody 1985, 1988; Piven and Cloward 1977; Salvatore 2012; Winders 2005).[3]

These analyses relating US labor's weakness to the lack of a labor party emphasize one of two factors. First, some argue that unions' political alliance with the Democratic Party channeled the disruptive power of class conflict into electoral activity, thus undermining the very source of labor's political power (Piven and Cloward 1977). Although these accounts do convincingly show that this kind of channeling occurred, such tensions between electoral and mobilizational strategies are a common feature of party–union relations in other countries, going back many years (Michels 1915; Przeworski 1985b, 1985a). They have certainly been present in Canada, where union leaders have at times subordinated and even undermined labor mobilization in favor of electoral mobilization on behalf of the NDP (Camfield 2011; Carroll and Ratner 1989; Evans 2012).

The second factor relates to the structure of political coalitions that have resulted from the labor–Democratic Party alliance. The central argument is that labor's abandonment of an independent labor party project in favor of an alliance with the Democrats undermined labor's political power by making it structurally dependent on hostile or unreliable coalition partners within the Democratic Party, particularly reactionary, racist Southern Democrats (Farhang and Katznelson 2005). This in turn hampered labor's ability to mobilize for a broader political program of

---

[3] This list of citations is far from comprehensive, and only includes works that specifically mention the link between the lack of a US labor party and labor union weakness. The literature addressing the broader question of why there is no labor party in the United States will be addressed in Chapter 4.

universal social benefits and protections that would benefit the working class as a whole. Instead, it turned inward, focusing on winning benefits for its own members, thus helping to create a privatized "shadow welfare state" that excluded nonunion members (Gottschalk 2000; McCarthy 2017). This undermined labor's ability to position itself as the defender of broad class interests and cut it off from broader social movements, leaving it vulnerable as a narrow special interest within the Democratic Party (Brenner 1985; Davis 1999; Moody 1988). Labor's position as a special interest not only undermined possibilities for broader social policy, but also left labor policy itself politically contentious, weakly institutionalized, and vulnerable to erosion over time (Draper 1989; Gross 1995; Winders 2005).[4]

While we will leave a fuller evaluation of the parties and political coalitions thesis for later, for now we can note that it holds promise and specify conditions it would have to meet to serve as an adequate explanation for diverging US–Canada union density. First, it must be able to explain the diverging policy trajectories in both countries, with the US labor regime eroding after its establishment with the Wagner Act in 1935 and the Canadian labor regimes stabilizing or strengthening after

---

[4] There are certainly those who defend the labor–Democratic Party alliance, viewing it as relatively analogous to labor–Social Democratic Party alliances in other countries (Dark 1999; Harrington 1972). For them, the alliance has remained a source of strength, even as labor has weakened. Their central evidence for their argument is labor's ever more central role in the Democrats' electoral mobilization strategy. It is certainly well documented that the union vote is an essential part of any Democratic electoral victory, as is the large amount of money that unions pour into Democratic Party coffers (Center for Responsive Politics, 2012; Erikson, Lancaster, and Romero 1989; Masters and Delaney 2005; Silver 2011). What is less clear is the extent to which labor's increasing electoral importance as a source of money and votes has translated into substantive influence on policy. On this account, labor's track record is one of consistent failure. To be sure, labor played a key role in the political coalitions that enacted the New Deal and Great Society programs that form the basis of the US welfare state as it exists today. It is also true that labor had to compromise with its coalition allies to get reform legislation passed, meaning that it had to settle for less than it would have liked. This is a normal part of politics. But two things stand out as less normal when comparing the US case to labor's role in enacting social welfare legislation in other countries. First, US labor had to compromise much more with factions within its own political coalition – particularly Southern Democrats. Second, labor got very little in return for its compromises. Labor consistently mobilized to elect political allies and get Democratic legislation passed, but their coalition partners did not return the favor by going to bat for labor's demands, particularly around labor law reform (Gross 1995; Heideman 2016; Lichtenstein 2010). Given that our primary interest in this book is to understand the factors contributing to labor's declining organizational power over time, the evidence in favor of the thesis that labor's alliance with the Democratic Party has mitigated what would otherwise be an even deeper decline is weak.

their establishment in the 1940s. Second, it must be able to explain the timing of union density divergence starting in the mid-1960s. Specifically, the explanation must account for why the presence of a party founded in the mid-1930s explains a divergence in union density that occurred thirty years later.

Altogether, differences in the configurations of political parties and institutions in both countries offer plausible explanations for union density divergence, although they require further investigation. The main shortcoming of such accounts is that they take current party systems for granted. It may be true that having versus not having a labor party matters for the shape of politics and policy in the two countries, but what is left unanswered in these accounts is *why* a labor party managed to take root in Canada, and not the United States?

Executive, Administrative, and Judicial Differences

In order to explain why the US labor regime eroded over time, while the Canadian one remained stable, some have pointed to differences in the very structures of those regimes and how they were built. Block's survey of labor regime variation in the United States and Canada identifies five specific areas of difference: "(1) the method of unfair labor [practice] case intake (the General Counsel); (2) the role of judicial review; (3) tripartism in the [labor] boards; (4) [policy] evolution by legislation; and (5) board involvement in resolving disputes during contract negotiations" (1993: 8).[5]

Case Intake. Block emphasizes the particular role played in the US case intake system by the NLRB General Counsel (NLRB-GC), a position established in 1947 with the passage of the Taft-Hartley Act. The NLRB-GC functions as does a federal prosecutor in the regular court system, bringing complaints of labor violations to the board. Appointed for a five-year term requiring Senate approval, the NLRB-GC is structurally independent of the NLRB. The position was established based on the idea of separating the prosecutorial and judicial functions of the NLRB, in keeping with US legal principles of due process.

---

[5] Many studies have examined various institutional aspects of the US and Canadian labor regimes. However, most focus on one specific institutional aspect, and few explore the comparative US–Canada framework. I use Block's survey here as a synthesis of this broader body of work. Unless otherwise noted, the description of institutional differences between US and Canadian labor regimes derives from Block.

While this reproduction of the regular courts' separation of functions in the name of due process may appear equitable, Block shows that the arrangement disproportionately favors employers when transposed into the realm of labor relations. The problem is that the vast majority of charges filed with the NLRB are filed against employers. As such, the NLRB-GC functions as the de facto representative for unions before the board. This creates a barrier to unions' ability to access the board to hear their grievances. It creates a two-step process: if a union believes that an employer has violated the law, it must first make a case to the NLRB-GC that a violation has occurred. The NLRB-GC then has the unappealable right to decide whether or not the case has merit. If the NLRB-GC decides that the case lacks merit, the case dies, and the union has no further recourse. If the NLRB-GC decides that the case has merit, the case proceeds, with the NLRB-GC prosecuting the case before the board. However, in doing so, the NLRB-GC removes control over the handling of the case from the union involved, as the case now becomes the responsibility of the NLRB-GC's office. The union's voice before the board is mediated through the NLRB-GC.

Employers do not have similar constraints. The basic assumption of the validity of employer property rights means that employers can continue engaging in activities they believe to be legal until a judgment is rendered. This means that the facts on the ground almost invariably remain in the employer's favor while the case is proceeding, aside from the rare case where the union can get an injunction to stop the employer's activity (Godard 2004: 24). Also, to the extent that employers represent themselves before the board, they do so directly, unmediated by a third party analogous to the NLRB-GC. They retain full control over their defense against the charges filed with the board.

The institutional arrangements are different in Canada. There is no analogue to the NLRB-GC, meaning that both unions and employers have direct, unmediated access to labor boards. This creates a more egalitarian system, where both sides can have their issues decided by the board in question. Comparing NLRB cases with cases in the federal jurisdiction, Ontario, and British Columbia at various points between 1975 and 1992, Block finds that 93.4 percent of US cases are closed before reaching the formal hearing stage, as opposed to between 59 percent and 81.2 percent for the Canadian jurisdictions (1993: Table 1). He interprets this difference to mean that unions have a relatively easier time getting their cases heard in Canada as compared to the United States. The combination of employers being able to continue the challenged status quo, and imbalances in the two parties' access to labor boards, creates conditions that tilt more in employers' favor over time.

Judicial Review. The two labor regimes also differ in their level of integration with the regular court system. In the United States, the supremacy of judicial review means that NLRB decisions are only enforceable by the courts, any NLRB decision is appealable to the courts, and courts will consider both procedural and substantive aspects of the case in weighing their decision. In Canada, the doctrine of parliamentary supremacy ensures that legislatively-mandated labor boards are granted much greater judicial deference and autonomy. Board decisions are appealable through the regular courts, but judicial review is limited to procedural questions in most cases. Canadian labor boards generally serve as the final and binding arbiter when it comes to regulation of the industrial relations system.

Broader US judicial review matters because, in considering substantive matters of labor cases, judges can adjudicate the issue based not only on questions of labor law, but also questions of property and contract law. Thus, collective labor rights are often overridden by the individual property rights of employers (Estlund 2007; Flynn 1995; Weiler 1984; Winter 1968). This in turn can erode union protections under labor law, and create advantages for employers.

Additionally, more expansive judicial review creates huge incentives for employers to appeal and delay as much as possible. If an employer receives an unfavorable ruling at the board level, they can continue to appeal the ruling in the regular court system, all the way to the US Supreme Court. Meanwhile, the employer's status quo remains in place, weakening workers' resolve to keep fighting. This in turn creates ever-greater opportunities for labor regime erosion over time, as employer appeals chip away at pro-union interpretations of the law. Such opportunities for appeal do not exist to the same degree in Canada. To the extent they do, more circumscribed concepts of judicial review mean that courts give greater deference to the collective rights enshrined in labor law, usually leaving it to parliaments to make substantive amendments. This limits opportunities for courts to prioritize employer property rights over workers' collective labor rights and reduces employers' incentive to drag out the appeal process.

Tripartism. US and Canadian labor regimes also differ in the structure and composition of their labor boards. In the United States, the NLRB is structured as a quasi-judicial body, with five members serving as neutral arbiters over the cases that come before them, along the lines of the Supreme Court. Board members are appointed to five-year terms, subject to Senate confirmation. While nominally neutral, the fact that members are political appointees remains very salient throughout their tenure. NLRB members are commonly known as "Democratic" or "Republican" appointees, and they cast their votes accordingly (Turner 2005). By contrast, labor boards in all eleven Canadian jurisdictions have a tripartite structure, meaning that they have equal numbers of representatives of workers and employers, with a "neutral" chair representing the state.[6]

The partisan structure of the US board means that board actions are politicized along partisan lines, while judicial review creates a body of precedent that constrains the board's scope of action, and weakens the durability of the board's own precedents. Conversely, the Canadian tripartite structure explicitly acknowledges the different and competing interests of labor and management, and creates an institutionalized forum within which those competing interests can be addressed. Additionally, having labor and management representatives on the boards ensures that both have a stake in the maintenance of the boards as institutions, and it limits employers' ability to question the legitimacy of the boards.

Policy Evolution by Legislation. All Canadian jurisdictions have amended their labor statutes numerous times in the decades since World War II, with an especially active period of reform in the 1970s and '80s that strengthened union protections. As discussed in the section on parties above, the parliamentary system of strict party discipline creates strong disincentives in Canada toward conservative political factions allying to defeat pro-labor initiatives, meaning that the general tendency is toward institutionalizing and strengthening existing labor law.

By contrast, the US presidentialist system of broad and unstable party coalitions creates major obstacles to legislative reform of labor law, and the lack of a labor party electoral threat diminishes any impetus for pro-labor policy reform. As a result, the letter of the law has only been changed a total of three times: first, the Wagner Act itself in 1935; second, the Taft-Hartley Act in 1947; and third, the Landrum-Griffin Act in 1959. Both legislative amendments of the Wagner Act eroded the Act, counter to what

---

[6] Links to each labor board, containing detailed information about board composition, can be found at http://pslrb-crtfp.gc.ca/labour_relations_board_e.asp (accessed July 26, 2017). While only six of ten provincial boards had adopted a tripartite structure at the time of Block's paper in 1993, all Canadian jurisdictions now have tripartite boards.

happened in Canada. Important labor law reform efforts failed despite strong support in 1977 and 2010. But the vast majority of labor policy change in the United States has not occurred in the legislative realm at all. Rather, it has occurred through legal interpretation, as the Wagner Act has been "judicially deradicalized" over time (Klare 1977).

Board Involvement. Canadian state agents intervene much more in the industrial relations system than their US counterparts. While this often takes the form of suppressing strikes through back-to-work legislation, it also manifests in stronger curbs on employer behavior. Mechanisms such as compulsory conciliation and first contract arbitration constrain employers' ability to resist unions' bona fide efforts to engage in collective bargaining. The lack of such compulsions in the United States gives employers a freer hand to fight unions.

Taken together, differences in administrative, executive, and judiciary institutions provide some convincing mechanisms to explain labor regime erosion in the United States and labor regime stability in Canada. However, as with differences in policies discussed above, many of these institutional differences have evolved over time and have led to different outcomes at different points in time.[7]

Additionally, as with labor law itself, institutional arrangements often reflect as much as shape existing social power dynamics. For example, it may be true that more expansive judicial review in the United States leads to greater consideration of employer property rights in labor law decisions than in Canada. But courts have privileged workers' union rights over employers' property rights at certain points, as in *Republic Aviation v. NLRB*,[8] decided in 1945, only to reassert employer property rights as in *Lechmere, Inc. v. NLRB*, decided in 1992.[9] What factors shaped these diametrically opposed judicial interpretations? Similarly, the case intake

---

[7] Block's analysis of cross-national institutional differences was essentially a snapshot of the institutional arrangements in both countries between the mid-1970s and the early 1990s, a period when labor regimes improved in Canada and eroded in the US. But as a thought experiment, consider how scholars of Canadian industrial relations might have used the same institutional differences to explain Canada's generally more restrictive labor regime in earlier periods.

[8] *Republic Aviation v. NLRB*, 324 US 793 (1945), which gave union organizers limited access to employer property.

[9] *Lechmere, Inc. v. NLRB*, 112 S. Ct. 841 (1992), which held that employers' right to exclude from their property trumped unions' right under Section 7 of the NLRA to engage in "concerted and protected" activity. Note that between *Republic Aviation* and *Lechmere*, there was a series of cases where justices debated the tradeoffs between employer property rights and unions' labor rights. A thorough discussion of this debate is beyond the scope of this work, but can be found in (Estlund 1993).

system, less interventional style, and partisan composition of the NLRB may be consequential, but those institutional characteristics were in place decades before union density began to decline. What changed about the environment in which these institutions were embedded to bring about union decline? In short, an adequate explanation of diverging labor regimes must integrate an analysis of institutional differences with an analysis of the political forces that shape those institutions.

NATIONAL CHARACTERISTICS

The national characteristics hypothesis attributes union density divergence between the United States and Canada to fundamental, long-standing differences in national values. According to this approach, Canada's more protective labor regime, as well as its stability over time, is a function of the country's more collectivist, Tory values and traditions, which trace back to its stronger historical ties to Britain. By contrast, the United States' weaker labor regime, as well as its erosion over time, is a function of the country's more individualist, laissez-faire values and traditions, which are less hospitable to the collective endeavors such as trade unions. This in turn traces back to the revolutionary tradition in the United States, which decisively broke from European feudal traditions and charted a different, "exceptional" path (Lipset 1989; Lipset and Meltz 2004).

A comprehensive analysis of the national characteristics hypothesis, tracing its origins back to the eighteenth century and beyond, is well beyond the scope of this work.[10] Instead, to evaluate the national characteristics hypothesis' capacity to explain divergent labor regimes, we can limit ourselves to two critical questions. First, to what extent do Canadians and Americans actually differ in their values when it comes to issues that might affect attitudes about unions and labor regimes? Second, if such differences exist, how might they contribute to the observed institutional divergences?

Do US and Canadian Values Actually Differ?

The first problem in assessing the extent to which the two countries actually differ in their values around collectivism and individualism is measuring those values. Most scholars tend to rely on survey data, which

---

[10] For a systematic and sympathetic critique, see Kaufman 2009.

is laden with problems of sampling methodology, question wording, coder reliability, and more. But in this case, because Lipset himself based much of his own argument about US–Canada differences on survey data, to the extent that survey data exists whose findings counter Lipset's, this would challenge the general validity of the national characteristics hypothesis.

The survey data presented is taken from the first five waves of the World Values Survey (WVS), which were administered between 1981 and 2009.[11] Results are pooled across all survey waves, as the same questions were not necessarily asked in each wave. This does not allow us to track changes in values over time. However, given that the surveys were all administered during a time period when cross-national union density divergence was already very evident, we would expect to see significant differences in values if value differences played a role in the divergence.

To get at cross-national values differences that would be salient to union and labor regime strength, I chose questions that highlight three sets of issues: 1) attitudes toward institutions, particularly unions, business, and government; 2) beliefs about individuals' control over their personal fates and the importance of individual freedom; and 3) attitudes about the proper role of government.

The results are reported in Figures 3.1, 3.2, and 3.3, with more detailed results provided in Appendix A. The WVS either asks respondents to rank on a scale of 1–10 how much they agree with a statement, or to place themselves on a scale of 1–10 between two opposing statements. So, for example, for the first question a respondent would rank on a scale of 1–10 the degree to which they agree with the statement "I have confidence in government." For the second question, a respondent would score a "1" for agreeing with the "low-score" statement that "success is more about luck and connections," and a "10" for agreeing with the "high-score" statement that "hard work brings success." Figure 3.1 charts the percentages of "high-score" respondents, meaning those who either agree most with a statement, or those who agree with the statement coded as scoring a "10" on a 1–10 scale. Figure 3.2 charts the percentages of "low-score" respondents, meaning those who agree least with a statement, or those who agree with the

---

[11] Specific years were as follows: Wave 1: Canada 1982, US 1981. Wave 2: Canada 1990, US 1990. Wave 3: Canada N/A, US 1995. Wave 4: Canada 2000, US 1999. Wave 5: Canada 2005, US 2006. There was a Wave 6 of the World Values Survey administered between 2010 and 2014, but Canada was not included in that wave. As such, I have decided to omit results from that wave.

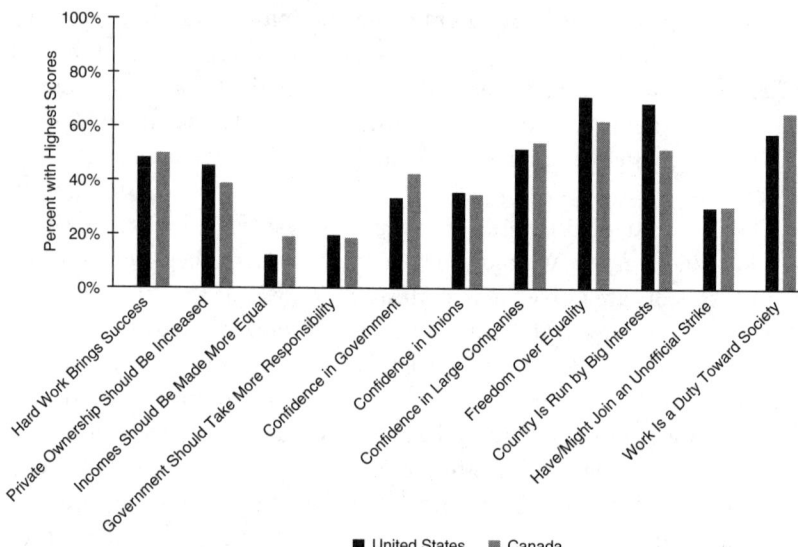

FIGURE 3.1 Pooled results of highest scores of selected measures from the World Values Survey for the United States and Canada
Source: World Values Survey, www.worldvaluessurvey.org/WVSContents.jsp

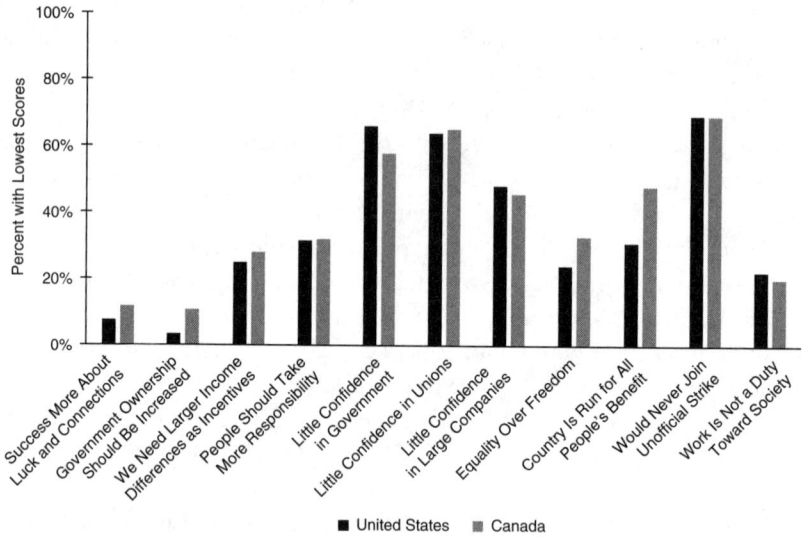

FIGURE 3.2 Pooled results of lowest scores of selected measures from the World Values Survey for the United States and Canada
Source: World Values Survey, www.worldvaluessurvey.org/WVSContents.jsp

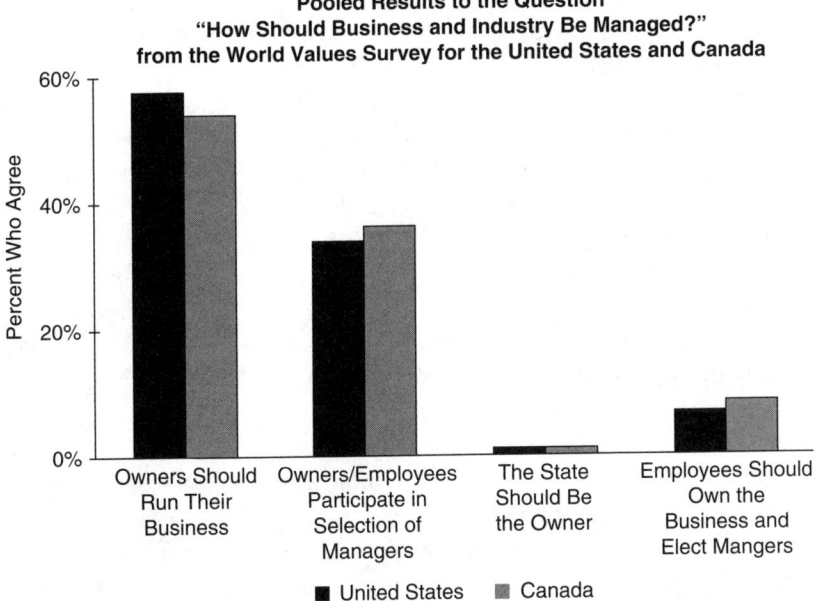

FIGURE 3.3 Pooled results to the question "How should business and industry be managed?" from the World Values Survey for the United States and Canada
Source: World Values Survey, http://www.worldvaluessurvey.org/WVSContents.jsp

statement coded as scoring a "1" on a 1–10 scale. Figure 3.3 reports responses to a single question with four possible answers.

Overall, US and Canadian respondents differ little in their reported attitudes. On five out of the eleven questions, the responses were virtually identical, and in most other cases, differences were slight. Taking the eleven "positive" and eleven "negative" responses together, in only four of the twenty-two cases does the size of the difference in responses exceed 30 percent.

Looking more closely at the results, we see that attitudes toward large companies and unions are roughly similar. Just over half express confidence in large companies, and approximately 35 percent express confidence in unions. More Canadians however express "a great deal" or "quite a lot" of confidence in government, 42.3 percent compared to 33.7 percent in the United States In both cases though, strong majorities express little confidence in government.

A large majority of both US and Canadian respondents valued freedom over equality, with 71.7 percent valuing freedom more in the United States, compared to 62.4 percent for Canada. People in both countries also believed that success could result from individual effort. Just shy of half of respondents in both countries agreed with the idea that "in the long run, hard work usually brings a better life." On the opposite end of this spectrum, just 11.8 percent of Canadians agreed more with the statement that "hard work doesn't generally bring success – it's more a matter of luck and connections," as compared with 7.5 percent of US respondents. Respondents in both countries believed that their work as individuals was important to society as a whole, with 57.8 percent of US respondents and 65.4 percent of Canadian respondents agreeing that "work is a duty towards society."

But while many believe that they can get ahead individually through hard work, they seem to doubt their ability to have a broader impact on society as a whole. Majorities in both countries agreed that their country is largely run by "big interests." The difference in magnitude between the two countries is quite striking here, with nearly 70 percent of Americans agreeing, compared with just over 50 percent of Canadians. This could be interpreted as evidence of the anti-authoritarian streak that is taken to be a central part of American cultural values, although it also seems at odds with their professed faith in democratic governance.

This raises the question as to what to do to rein in the "big interests," bringing us to questions dealing with the proper role of government. For both US and Canadian respondents, the proper role seems to be "limited." Large majorities in both countries express distrust in government. Most express more faith in the power of privately owned business, with 45.6 percent of Americans and 38.9 percent of Canadians agreeing that private ownership of business should be increased, as compared to 3.2 percent of Americans and 10.5 percent of Canadians who believe that government ownership should be increased. While the percentage of Canadians who believe in more government ownership is more than three times higher than the percentage of Americans, the overall percentages for both countries are very small, especially compared to those who believe in expanding private ownership of business. Moreover, when asked who should "take more responsibility" (for what exactly is not specified), people in both countries choose "people" over "the government" by substantial and virtually identical margins – 31.6 percent to 19.6 percent in the United States, and 32.2 percent to 18.5 percent in Canada. While the US response may be predictable, the virtually identical Canadian response is not what one would expect from a country that ostensibly is more eager to embrace more collectivist, statist policy approaches.

An initial look at the results about income inequality might suggest that Canadians are more willing to embrace government assistance, as 36 percent more Canadians than Americans believe that "incomes should be made more equal" (presumably through government intervention, although this is not specified). But for both countries, only a small minority of respondents express this belief, 19.1 percent in Canada and 12.2 percent in the United States. Moreover, the interpretation gets trickier when we consider the opposing statement in the question about income inequality. By a margin of 28 percent to 25.1 percent, more Canadians than Americans agree with the statement that "we need larger income differences as incentives."

If Canadians and Americans do not necessarily believe in government intervention to address inequality, a surprisingly large number in both countries seem open to quite radical versions of self-help. According to the survey, 30.8 percent of Canadians and 30.5 percent of Americans claim they either have joined or would join an *unofficial* strike, i.e. a wildcat strike, which by definition would be illegal according to most Canadian laws.[12]

Finally, an interesting finding reported in Figure 3.3 involves a question about how business and industry should be managed. The results support the idea that both Americans and Canadians strongly support private ownership and unfettered management control, with 53.9 percent of Canadians and 57.7 percent of Americans agreeing that "owners should run their business." However, a closer look shows that support for management prerogative is far from universal. Fully 44.9 percent of Canadians and 41 percent of Americans agreed that workers should exercise some form of control over management. More specifically, 36.5 percent of Canadians and 34 percent of Americans agreed that "owners and employees should participate in the selection of managers," whereas 8.4 percent of Canadians and 7 percent of Americans agreed that "employees should own the business and elect managers."

Taken together, these survey results show two countries whose values are much more similar than they are different. To the extent that US and

---

[12] Of those surveyed, 6.4 percent of Canadians and 4.2 percent of Americans claimed to have actually joined an unofficial strike. Given the tremendously low strike rates in both countries in the time period of this survey, these numbers seem suspiciously high. Even so, the fact that the numbers in both countries are very similar speaks against the idea that differences in values are driving labor relations trends in either country, and in favor of the idea that institutional structures are shaping outcomes, in spite of whatever underlying values and beliefs might exist.

Canadian responses do differ, it is not by much, and not necessarily in the ways that the national characteristics hypothesis would predict. Given the magnitude of difference in union density that was already evident by the earliest days of the World Values Survey in 1981, we would expect to see much wider differences in expressed values if they were in fact a critical force driving the US–Canada divergence.

It is important not to draw too many conclusions from the results of a single set of surveys. As Lipset himself has shown, it is also quite possible to draw different conclusions about US–Canada values differences based on other questions posed in other surveys. At most, the fact that WVS results find little evidence of cross-national difference raises some doubts as to the plausibility of the national characteristics hypothesis.

How Can Value Differences Explain Union Density Divergence?

Even if we were to grant that differences in national values do exist, we would still be faced with the important problem of explaining a variable with a constant: How can the same set of differing values produce similarity over one stretch of time, then difference? More specifically, if deep and abiding differences in US and Canadian national values were so important in shaping unions and labor regimes, why then did the divergence between the two only appear in the mid-1960s?

Certainly, the same factors can produce different outcomes at different points in time, as they interact with different historical contexts and political dynamics. In the case at hand, partisans of the national characteristics hypothesis account for this problem of divergence by conceptualizing the New Deal era from the 1930s to 1960s as the "exception to the exception," a period when, in response to deep crisis and economic threat, Americans briefly became more accepting of collectivist ideas and policies, including labor unions. As the New Deal era subsided, the explanation goes, traditional individualistic American values reasserted themselves, and support for unions fell.

To what extent does this "exception to the exception" thesis hold? If it were right, it would show three things. First, that prior to the New Deal era, Canadian unions were stronger than in the United States. Second, that during the New Deal era, there was a broad shift in values among all sectors of society that was more sympathetic toward unions. And third, that those values shifted back to traditional laissez-faire individualism as union density declined.

FIGURE 3.4 Union density, United States and Canada, 1911–1934
Source: See Appendix A

The Pre-New Deal Period, 1911–1934
Were Canadian unions stronger than their US counterparts prior to the New Deal? Figure 3.4 tracks union density in both countries between 1911 and 1934, the year before the passage of the Wagner Act. For the pre-Depression years, density in both countries was relatively similar, differing by little more than two or three percentage points in any given year.

In the early years of the Depression, there did seem to be a divergence. Canadian density rates rose from 13.1 percent in 1930 to 16.7 percent in 1933, while US density rates fell from 10.7 to 9.5 percent, leaving a gap of more than seven percentage points. However, upon closer inspection, this divergence in the early Depression years is more likely the artifact of relatively greater employment losses in Canada, i.e. shrinkage of the denominator, as opposed to any sort of surge in union membership. Figures 3.5 and 3.6 track year-to-year percentage changes in nonagricultural employment and union membership. They show that between 1930 and 1933, nonagricultural employment fell by 36.8 percent in Canada, compared to 16.2 percent in the United States. Union membership fell by a greater margin in the United States in that same period, 22.6 percent, as

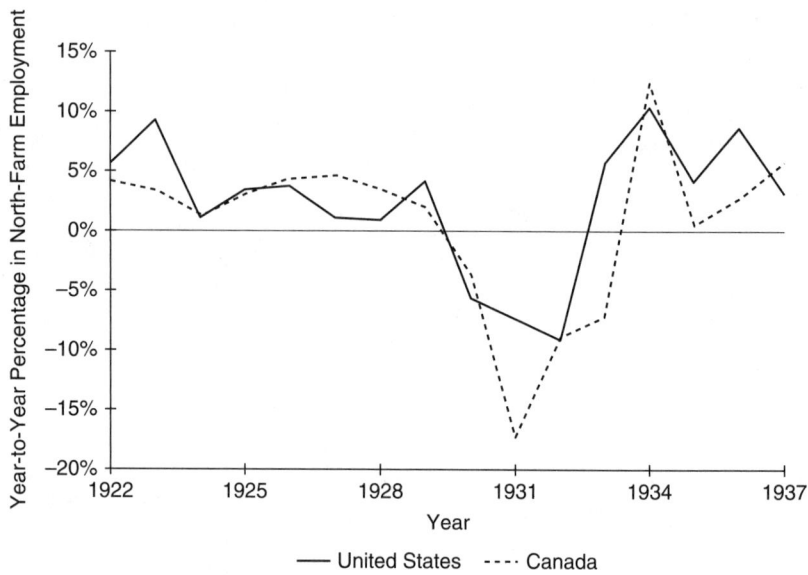

FIGURE 3.5 Year-to-year percentage change in nonfarm employment in the United States and Canada, 1922–1937
Source: See Appendix A

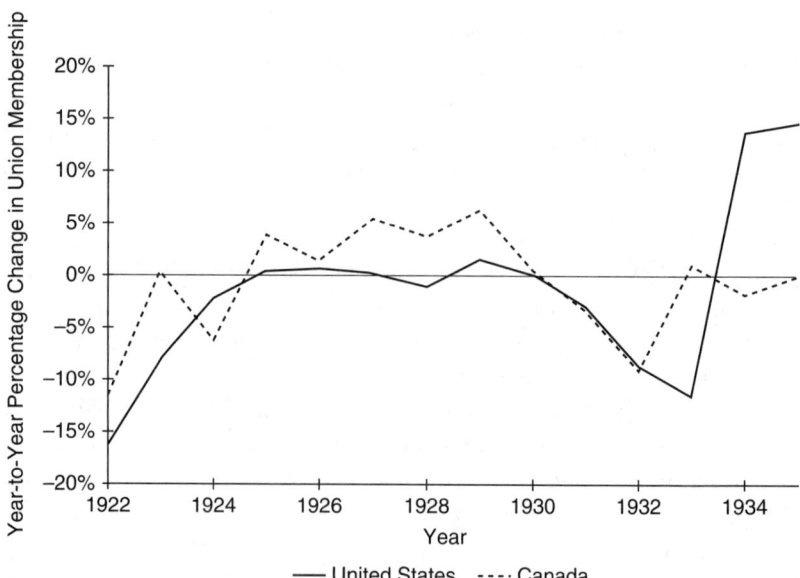

FIGURE 3.6 Year-to-year percentage change in union membership in the United States and Canada, 1922–1935
Source: See Appendix A

compared to 10.7 percent in Canada. However, the relatively larger magnitude of the drop in the Canadian denominator dwarfed the relatively smaller drop in the numerator, leading to a brief widening of the union density gap in the early Depression years.

In the decades prior to the passage of the Wagner Act then, it is difficult to make a convincing case that either US or Canadian unions displayed greater organizational strength. It may be true, as Lipset and others document, that there were differences in this period in terms of Canadian labor's greater tolerance of socialism, as well as the Canadian government's deeper involvement in labor relations (Horowitz 1968; Lipset and Meltz 2004). However, these differences were not enough to make a difference in union density. Instead, there was a period of relative cross-border similarity. Thus, the "exception to the exception" hypothesis comes up short in its first task, mis-specifying the initial conditions of union strength in both countries prior to the passage of the Wagner Act.

The New Deal Period: The Exception to the Exception?

The second test for the "exception to the exception" thesis involves its characterization of the New Deal period, which we can roughly characterize as the thirty years between the passage of the Wagner Act in 1935 and the beginning of US–Canada union density divergence in 1965. In this period, the argument goes, US unions were able to grow and remain strong because of a temporary shift in national values brought on by the trauma of the Great Depression. This led to a greater acceptance of collectivist ideas and policies, including support for labor unions. Meanwhile, in Canada, collectivist values and a more interventionist state already ensured protections for unions, providing them a favorable environment in which to grow.

To evaluate this characterization, we have little in the way of reliable data that surveys individuals' values over time and how those values shifted to favor individualism or collectivism. But our primary interest is not in individual attitudes, but rather in how the overall political and institutional environment shaped working-class organizational power. What we can use then, is evidence from key players in the development and maintenance of the US and Canadian labor regimes in this period. This would include government policymakers as well as representatives of unions and employers. We can examine to what extent these actors were operating in an environment governed by more collectivist or more individualist values.

THE UNITED STATES   For advocates of the national characteristics hypothesis, the more collectivist environment that prevailed in the New

Deal period is encapsulated in the idea of a postwar labor–management accord. According to this idea, unions and employers achieved a consensus in the postwar period. Employers agreed to recognize unions' right to exist, and to provide regular wage and benefit increases to union members, including decent pensions and health care coverage. In exchange, unions agreed to recognize management's "right to manage," and to limit overt displays of force, particularly strikes. Together, labor and management were to forge a mature relationship of mutual respect, based on their mutual interests in promoting economic prosperity (Bok and Dunlop 1970; Edwards and Podgursky 1986; Kerr 1960; Lester 1958). To the extent that the national characteristics hypothesis holds, we would expect to find evidence that such a labor–management accord existed and shaped actors' expectations and behaviors in this New Deal period.

It is clear that industrial relations scholars of the period took the existence of such an accord for granted, and that this belief shaped their expectations and behaviors. We can see an early articulation of this view in the work of Clinton Golden and Harold Ruttenberg, two staff members of the Congress of Industrial Organizations (CIO)'s Steel Workers Organizing Committee (SWOC).[13] Writing in the early years of World War II, just a few years after the passage of the Wagner Act and several years before the labor upheaval and backlash that would follow the end of the war, Golden and Ruttenberg laid out an optimistic vision for the future of labor–management relations in the United States:

We believe that American industry is on the threshold of a new era in human relations – the greatest period in union-management relations. The turmoil and strife of the last decade have merely reflected the transitional character of the relations between workers and management. Out of this transitional period is emerging a new capacity on the part of those in industry, regardless of their different positions, in point of view of responsibility and authority, to work together as a unit – literally with a singleness of purpose and of action for the attainment of a common objective (Golden and Ruttenberg 1942: xxi).

Embodying the vision they projected in their book, both Golden and Ruttenberg moved on from SWOC to play different roles as prominent

---

[13] The CIO was a labor federation founded in 1935 that split from the American Federation of Labor (AFL) over the question of organizing strategy. Although there were important exceptions, the AFL was generally committed to organizing skilled workers by craft or occupation, whereas the CIO proposed organizing workers by industry, regardless of their particular craft or skill level. The two merged in 1955 to form the American Federation of Labor-Congress of Industrial Organizations (AFL-CIO), which exists to this day (Galenson 1960; Zieger 1995).

figures in the postwar US industrial relations landscape. Golden first became a government labor advisor before assuming the executive directorship of the Harvard Trade Union Program, while Ruttenberg went on to a career in management with several different companies. Both continued to be strong advocates of labor–management cooperation and consensus building through the collective bargaining process.

By the late 1950s, it appeared that the world Clinton and Ruttenberg predicted had come to pass. Richard Lester opened his 1958 book, tellingly entitled *As Unions Mature*, with what seemed to be a self-evident assessment of the current state of affairs for unions:

Trade unionism in America has come of age. Some 18 million workers are enrolled in its ranks. The power and influence of unions penetrate not only the workplace but also the financial centers, the community chest, and even foreign aid. It may be idle to argue whether we have arrived at a "laboristic society" – the term Sumner Slichter applies to a community in which an employee viewpoint predominates. But, obviously, labor organization has become part of the dominant economic and cultural pattern of our day (Lester 1958: 3).

As a result of this process, Lester argued, labor management relations had begun to "settle down" and enter a new period of stability and maturity. For its part, he noted, "[e]mployer opposition to unions, especially in large firms and urban areas, seems to have been decreasing during the past two decades" (1958: 54). On the union side, as the environment for labor became more comfortable, they lost "some of the militancy and rambunctiousness that characterized them before World War II" (29). Overall, Lester observed that "life at both levels [legislative and socio-economic] seems more conductive to comity than enmity, to industrial peace than to union-management strife" (1958: 48–49).

It was when that seemingly stable climate began to change in the 1970s and '80s that industrial relations scholars began speaking explicitly of a "labor–management accord." They used this term retrospectively to refer to the postwar world that was disintegrating before their eyes. As Richard Edwards and Michael Podgursky described it,

The labor accord was an implicit, mostly unwritten *modus vivendi* between unions and large employers ... The accord constituted the "rules of the game" in industrial relations, and the contention, bargaining, and conflict that occurred between employers and workers were played out within these rules (1986: 19).

The problem was that "the accord's most important requirement was a certain degree of cooperation," but that cooperation was becoming harder to find. "Specifically," they argued, "management has shown an increasing willingness to abandon the accord; it has instituted a retreat from collective bargaining" (1958: 19). Similarly, Barry Bluestone and Bennett Harrison published a series of influential books where they spoke of a "Great U-Turn" in the 1970s and '80s, as management abandoned its previous cooperative stance (Bluestone and Harrison 1990).

This narrative of the establishment and dissolution of the labor–management accord between the New Deal and the 1970s quickly became the standard account of what had happened to US industrial relations among scholars and experts in the field. For them, it was clear that the three decades following World War II constituted an "exception to the exception" in that the dissolution of the accord seemed to be a reversion to the bare-knuckles system that predated the Wagner Act.

Along with industrial relations experts, many labor union leaders believed in the idea of a postwar labor–management accord. We already saw the optimistic predictions of SWOC staffers Golden and Ruttenberg regarding the future of postwar labor–management relations. With the end of the war, US labor leaders explicitly sought to establish the trade-off between labor's collective bargaining rights and management's control of the enterprise as the basis of a new postwar consensus. At a labor–management conference organized by the White House in November 1945, AFL President William Green laid out the terms of this agreement:

Labor's basic right to organize and bargain collectively and the full acceptance of that right by the employers stands side by side with the right of employers to manage their enterprise and direct its operation without interference. That right should be respected and wholeheartedly accepted by all labor. It is for us to provide means whereby this right can be clearly defined and accorded universal acceptance throughout industry (Green 1945).

Perhaps no other event symbolized the new era of the labor–management accord more that the "Treaty of Detroit," the name given to the 1950 contract agreement between the United Auto Workers (UAW) and General Motors. It was important firstly for *how* it was negotiated. In contrast to the protracted, public, and acrimonious negotiations that had marked previous auto agreements, as well as agreements in steel, mining, meatpacking, and elsewhere, the Treaty of Detroit was negotiated quickly and secretly among top-level union and company officials, in a businesslike fashion. Second, it was important for *what* was negotiated. For their part, autoworkers received unprecedented increases in their overall standard of living. The agreement guaranteed not only regular wage increases on top of an automatic cost-of-living adjustment, but also pension and health benefits. In exchange, GM got stability and control. Unlike previous contracts, the 1950 agreement lasted for an unprecedented five years. Additionally, the union gave GM complete control over management and production decisions.

The mainstream media viewed the agreement as a watershed, making analogies with Henry Ford's five-dollar-a-day wage and lauding it as "industrial statesmanship of a very high order." As sociologist Daniel Bell famously remarked in *Fortune*, "GM may have paid a billion for peace. But it got a bargain ... General Motors has regained control over one of the crucial management functions – long range scheduling of production, model changes, and tool and plant investment" (Bell 1950: 53). For his part, UAW President Walter Reuther hailed the agreement as "the most significant development in labor relations since the mass production industries were organized," seeing it as evidence of a "maturing relationship" between the union and the company (quoted in Lichtenstein 1995: 280).

Five years after the Treaty of Detroit, the US labor movement gave further evidence of its growing maturity by resolving the bitter internal struggle between the rival AFL and CIO labor federations. Out of this resolution emerged a combined organization, the American Federation of Labor-Congress of Industrial Organizations (AFL-CIO). The president of this new federation was former AFL chief George Meany, who rose through the ranks of the plumbers' union.

In a gesture that itself illustrated labor leaders' priorities in this new era of maturity and moderation, one of Meany's first acts as AFL-CIO president was to address the convention of the National Association of Manufacturers (NAM), one of the primary US employer associations. In his remarks, he made plain the extent to which he, and by extension the leadership of his newly merged federation, believed in the basic idea of the accord: free collective bargaining between unions and management, based on a mutual understanding of shared interests:

We have a tremendous vital interest in the maintenance of a free way of life and we feel the employer has the same interest ... We have this stake, and I am quite sure that management has the same stake in this system under which we live. We cannot maintain a free trade union under any other system, and we do contend that through the free trade union system that we have built up the standards of life of the American worker. We may take nothing away from management. We know that management ingenuity and resourcefulness have made their contribution, but we feel that we have made our contribution (Meany 1955: 3).

While there were more conservative, Meany-like and more progressive, Reuther-like visions of the accord, labor leaders generally acknowledged and acted as if a labor–management accord was in effect in the decades following World War II.[14]

That changed in the 1970s. As employer attacks increased, labor leaders could no longer dismiss them. The labor–management accord they thought they had was coming unraveled. Perhaps the best-known recognition of this new state of affairs is the 1978 letter that then-UAW President Douglas Fraser wrote to his fellow members of the Labor-Management Group, an independent government advisory board set up to discuss broad economic policies. In offering his resignation to the group, he expressed his sense of betrayal at the dismantling of the labor–management accord:

> I believe leaders of the business community, with few exceptions, have chosen to wage a one-sided class war today in this country – a war against working people, the unemployed, the poor, the minorities, the very young and the very old, and even many in the middle class of our society. The leaders of industry, commerce and finance in the United States have broken and discarded the fragile, unwritten compact previously existing during a past period of growth and progress (Fraser 1978).

As with the industrial relations scholars, the fact that labor leaders felt betrayed in the late 1970s suggests that they previously thought they had a deal.[15] Thus, it seems reasonable to suggest that, along with the experts, labor leaders too believed in the existence of the postwar accord.

---

[14] The extent to which the idea of the accord percolated to the rank and file is somewhat unclear. One imperfect metric is to look at strike rates, which can give some sense of how much workers were adapting to a new era of labor–management cooperation. At first glance, it seems that workers did in fact stop picketing as much and let contract negotiations happen at the bargaining table. The percentage of the nonagricultural workforce involved in strikes plummeted from a postwar high of nearly 10 percent in 1946 to a low of 1.5 percent by 1963. However, a closer look at the statistics shows that this is a somewhat selective reading of the numbers. The 1946 figure was especially high, and the 1963 figure was exceptionally low for that period. If we take a broader view, we see that until around 1956, strike rates in the "mature" postwar period stayed at or above levels seen during the "rambunctious" 1930s. They then declined through the late 1950s and early 1960s, but then promptly returned to 1930s levels or higher for much of the late 1960s and early 1970s. It was only in the mid- to late 1970s that US strike rates truly plummeted – well after any semblance of a " labor-management accord" had begun to unravel.

[15] Note that this sense of betrayal did not lead labor leaders to try a different strategy, perhaps one hearkening back to the mobilization and confrontation that characterized the labor movement of the 1930s. Rather, US union leaders "doubled down" on the idea of labor-management partnership. If employers no longer wanted it, labor leaders would do their best to woo them back. The result was a seemingly endless chain of concessions that have eroded pay, benefits, and working conditions for unionized workers, all in the name of labor–management "partnership" (Davis 1999; Moody 2007).

What then of government? For those in charge of administering labor–management policy at the time that Golden and Ruttenberg were articulating their vision for the future, they seemed to share that vision. However, they also seemed to realize that there would be a potential problem in realizing that vision: getting employers on board. A 1942 speech by National War Labor Board public member (and future Republican Senator) Wayne Morse to the American Bar Association embodies this attitude. Speaking before a group composed primarily of those who counseled management, he issued a call for a farsighted, consensual approach to labor relations:

The forward-looking employers of America today recognize that unions are here to stay. Instead of fighting them and trying to destroy them, they recognize that the struggle of the common man since feudal times to organize into collective bargaining groups for the purpose of improving his economic status, constitutes a social force or movement that cannot and should not be destroyed. The progressive employers of America recognize that organized labor is essential to our system of free enterprise ... Furthermore, progressive American employers know that the majority of American labor leaders and union members are basically conservative and can be counted upon to oppose any movement in the future which seeks to supplant our existing economic system (Morse 1942: 3).

By the end of the war, government leaders claimed to see evidence of a new era of labor–management partnership. In accepting Secretary of Labor Frances Perkins' resignation, President Truman complimented her on her service, noting that "the rights of labor as a partner in the system of private enterprise have been more firmly established than ever before. There has been created a cooperative relationship between industry and labor in the United States which has been largely instrumental in turning out the weapons of war" (Truman 1945).

Less than two decades later, the cooperative relationship seemed to be in good shape. In accepting a 1962 report from his President's Advisory Committee on Labor-Management Policy on the state of collective bargaining, President Kennedy noted approvingly,

The fact that public, labor, and management representatives are in unanimous agreement that collective bargaining is an essential element of economic democracy is a mark of our progress as a Nation when contrasted with the disagreements on this subject in the not too distant past. The fact that all agree on the necessity that collective bargaining be responsible and responsive to the public, or common, interest is a symbol of the maturity of the parties to the collective bargaining relationship (President's Advisory Committee on Labor-Management Policy 1962: inside cover).

By the late 1970s, government officials could not ignore the erosion of the stability they once knew. This was most apparent after the Carter administration's failure to enact its proposed 1977 labor law reform bill, which died in the Senate despite Democratic majorities in both houses (Cowie 2010). Reflecting on this setback, Labor Secretary Ray Marshall sensed that the battle over the bill amounted to an effort to turn back the clock on the postwar period. He accused the bill's opponents of refusing to discuss the substance of the bill, instead making it "a battleground to refight the union-recognition questions of the 1930s" (ABA Journal 1978: 1345). Expressing consternation at how completely the ostensible postwar consensus had vanished, he remarked that "this entire issue points out to us the need to give the American people a refresher course in the basic principles of industrial democracy and collective bargaining" (ABA Journal 1978: 1345).

Thus far, it seems that industrial relations experts, labor leaders, and government officials all held to the belief that an unspoken but very real labor–management accord existed for the roughly three decades between the end of World War II and the end of the 1970s. It also seems that, as the environment shifted in the 1970s, these groups all felt that employers were the ones who were changing. It was the employers who were backing away from collective bargaining, away from the unspoken deal between labor and management.

How then did employers see the postwar period? To what extent did they heed Morse's call to be forward-looking and admit, albeit temporarily, that "unions are here to stay"? More broadly, to what extent did employers in this period act as if there were a labor–management accord in effect?

This is the key question for evaluating the "exception to the exception" thesis for the US case. If employers acted as if a labor–management accord were in effect in the postwar period, then it would be plausible to claim that the accord was real. It would fit an account of the postwar period that characterized what happened as a broad across-the-board shift in values that temporarily mitigated classic American values of individualism and laissez-faire. However, if employers resisted that notion and only adapted to circumstances out of perceived necessity, then the claim of a legitimate postwar labor–management accord loses validity. An accord, after all, only exists if all parties acknowledge its existence.

It is difficult to gauge employer acceptance of unions and more collectivist social policy in the postwar period. The question has sparked a wide-ranging and lively debate ever since the 1970s, when increased employer aggression led many to suspect that the labor–management accord, to the extent it existed, was coming undone. Part of the problem is that employers did not, and do not, speak with one voice. Unlike other capitalist democracies, there was, and is, little peak-level employer organization. There were certainly organizations of employers, such as the National Association of Manufacturers (NAM) and the US Chamber of Commerce (USCC), but these were not always necessarily representative of employer views (Swenson 2004).[16]

As advocates for the existence of the postwar accord point out, there was a small but influential coterie of "corporate liberals" who played important roles in shaping postwar labor and social policy (Harris 1982; Hawley 1978; Mizruchi 2013). It could be that this stratum of corporate liberals provided the base for the employer end of the labor–management accord.

However, this would overlook the extent to which US employers consistently and systematically sought to undermine unions and labor policy in the postwar period. As it turns out, Morse's fear that not all employers would be so "forward-looking" was well founded. Although corporate liberals did exist, and some employers did resign themselves to the idea that "unions are here to stay," a significant stratum adamantly resisted any attempts to achieve consensus. This stratum may have represented a minority at first, but quickly gathered steam through the 1950s, and expanded dramatically beginning in the 1960s through the collective bargaining crisis of the 1970s.[17]

Initially NAM served as an organizational hub for employer intransigence. They had played a leading role in opposing the labor reforms of the 1930s, and while they lost that initial battle, they saw great opportunities in the postwar period not for labor–management cooperation, but for the reestablishment of business dominance. Mere days after the German surrender in May 1945, NAM began strategizing. A May 11 memo opened by saying that:

---

[16] This is not to imply that labor spoke with a single voice. To the contrary, there were plenty of inter- and intra-union disputes in this period, with Reuther and Meany often playing starring – and opposing – roles. However, on the question of the labor–management accord, there was general agreement among union leaders as to its existence and benefit, certainly more so than on management's side.

[17] In addition to the evidence cited below, broader accounts of postwar employer intransigence can be found in (Harris 1982; Nissen 1990; Phillips-Fein 2009).

Today industry has the greatest opportunity that it has had since 1932. It can:

- reverse the trend of the past twelve years
- regain economic leadership for private enterprise
- insure tremendous nation-wide demand for public policies that are good for business.

It can execute one of the biggest coups that industry possibly could undertake with an excellent chance of putting businessmen back in a position of leadership in the national economy – with the blessing of the White House (NAM NIIC 1945: 1).

Realizing that some employers may have grown accustomed to more cooperative or government-directed approaches since the arrival of the New Deal, the authors noted that such a campaign would require systematic organizing:

This calls for the biggest mobilization of free enterprise in the history of the country excluding, perhaps, the present war. Prior to 1933, it would have been the natural thing for business to assume such leadership. But now business must be "sold" on taking over a job that is rightfully its own (NAM NIIC 1945: 3).

Publicly, the climate in the immediate postwar period was such that even NAM representatives had to pay lip service to the value of collective bargaining. At a November 1945 meeting of the President's Labor-Management Advisory Committee, USCC head and noted corporate liberal Eric Johnston offered a full-throated endorsement of labor–management cooperation and free collective bargaining. Following Johnston, NAM President Ira Mosher also spoke of the value of collective bargaining, although he qualified his remarks by expressing "serious misgivings as to the manner in which it is being practiced" (Mosher 1945: 21).

More important than Mosher's characterization of collective bargaining was his characterization of the meeting itself. While other speakers spoke of it as a meeting of representatives from labor and management, facilitated by the state, Mosher disputed the representative structure of the group. Proposing instead that all delegates were there "as representative American citizens, called to this task by the first citizen of this land," he viewed the function of the group and its participants as "purely advisory – inspirational if you please" (Mosher 1945: 24).

Although this may at first appear to be merely a word preference, Mosher's proposed reframing had a much deeper symbolic significance in terms of characterizing labor–management relations. In redefining the group as an advisory committee of American citizens, as opposed to representatives of labor and management, Mosher was refusing to recognize labor leaders', and by extension labor unions', role as worker representatives. Implicit in this refusal was a rejection of the idea that unions had any business intervening in workplace decisions, or even that they had any legitimate purpose whatsoever.

This systematic attempt to undermine labor's representative claims became clearer and more widespread over time. NAM representatives would refuse to appear in public fora with union leaders, or if they did, they would do so only in an individual capacity, not as management representatives (National Association of Manufacturers 1953). When President Eisenhower convened his President's Labor-Management Public Advisory Committee in 1953, consisting of five members each from labor, management, and the "public" (meaning academics), the meeting ground to a halt almost immediately over the question of its representative function (Labor-Management Public Advisory Committee 1953). Whereas labor members such as Reuther, Meany, and Mine Workers President John L. Lewis argued that they were meeting in a representative capacity and should work together to come to mutual decisions about policy questions under consideration (9–11), employer representatives were united in their opposition to such an approach. After meeting over lunch, the employer representatives unanimously agreed that they would refuse to participate in any decision-making, and that "[m]embers came to the committee as individuals – each one to give his considered opinion" (15). Despite Secretary of Labor Martin P. Durkin's suggestion that he and the president "were ... desirous of having some opinion as a group" (15), management remained intransigent, and the meeting collapsed.

NAM's lack of representativeness in this immediate postwar period was partially due to legitimate differences of opinion among employers, but was also part of a deliberate strategy on the part of NAM to delegitimize labor. Employers could present themselves as owners of businesses as well as members of business associations, but union leaders only had a function in terms of their capacity as representatives of groups of workers (Offe and Wiesenthal 1980). By denying all participants' representative capacity, they were undermining labor's very base of existence.

Employer recalcitrance remained strong through the 1950s. Under the twin slogans of "free speech" and "right to work," employers successfully mobilized to enact right-to-work laws in six more states (for a total of eighteen), and obtained NLRB rulings allowing them greater latitude to intervene in union representation elections (Aaron 1962). In the aftermath of the McClellan Committee hearings to investigate organized crime influence in the union movement, employers successfully organized to place further restrictions on labor via the 1959 Landrum-Griffin Act. By this time the resistance had spread far beyond NAM. The Chamber of Commerce took a more hard-line turn after Johnston's departure. In the 1960s, new organizations such as the National Right-to-Work Committee also joined the fray. The management watchword in that decade was "concentration of union power." In the 1962 report of the President's Advisory Committee on Labor-Management Policy, several employer representatives – writing as individuals, of course – inserted addenda warning of the dangers arising from such concentration (President's Advisory Committee on Labor-Management Policy 1962).

By the late 1960s, employer resistance had reached the point where some mounted an all-out campaign to abolish the NLRB entirely. A Department of Labor report stated that "the new campaign is well-financed, closely coordinated, and aggressively enlisting private and public support" (US Department of Labor 1968: 1). It noted that "the prime mover of the campaign is certainly the US Chamber of Commerce, which has formed a closely woven, united front with the NAM and 35 national trade associations" (1). The strategy for the campaign, they reported, "is to create a groundswell of complaints about the NLRB and 'excessive' union power which, they hope, will create an atmosphere hospitable to far-reaching legislative changes"(1). That particular campaign was unsuccessful, but its very existence and scope speaks to an environment governed far less by an "unwritten *modus vivendi*" than by a deep and abiding animosity toward labor and any type of regulatory protections for labor – the kind of animosity that labor leaders and industrial relations experts would only recognize a decade later.

This is not to say that there were no accommodating employers in this period, or that unions were unable to establish stable collective bargaining relationships. What is at issue is whether it makes sense to characterize what happened in the postwar period as a broad shift in values that temporarily mitigated classic American values of individualism and laissez-faire, and led to greater acceptance of labor unions. The existing evidence does not fit a values-shift story for the postwar period. Almost immediately after the defeats of the 1930s, some employers regrouped and prepared to do battle once again in defense of their unfettered right to manage. These employers refused to recognize labor's legitimacy, let alone reach consensus with it. And it was this group of employers and their approach that gained in strength in the ensuing decades, achieving dominance by the late 1970s.

The persistence and growth of a group of recalcitrant employers is more consistent with a characterization of the postwar period as a cease-fire rather than a labor–management accord (Harris 1982; Nissen 1990). Management's values did not shift, although some took a progressive approach and embraced the new world of collective bargaining. Another group, concentrated around NAM, retained the recalcitrant approach, although they recognized in the early postwar period that the balance of forces was not in their favor. For the most part, employers pursued a realist strategy, where they engaged with collective bargaining, but sought as much as possible to turn the process to their advantage (Harris 1982: 131–135). This was particularly the case at the large industrial firms like GM. However, as soon as the balance of power was more in their favor, these firms shed their commitment to collective bargaining and adopted a more aggressive stance. And by the 1970s, employers were less constrained by what had become a weak and eroded labor regime.

In the US case then, the national characteristics hypothesis does not explain the postwar trajectory of labor relations as well as does a basic balance-of-power hypothesis. What remains to be explained are the dynamics underlying the shift in the balance of forces between labor and management in the postwar period.

CANADA According to the national characteristics hypothesis, Canada has more collectivist values, and those values are reflected in stronger unions and a more protective labor regime. In the postwar period, Canada fit this hypothesis well, with union density rising above 30 percent and staying above that threshold for the remainder of the period. It could be that collective values were undergirding that union density stability.

But there are two questions that the Canadian case raises for the national characteristics hypothesis. First, if Canada was in fact governed by more collectivist values and a greater propensity for state intervention, why then did Canadian workers have to fight for almost ten years longer than their US counterparts to win basic labor rights? Second, to what extent can we attribute postwar union density stability to collectivist Canadian values, as opposed to Canadian employers also pursuing a US-style realist strategy?

Looking first at the prewar period, although the modern Canadian labor regime was established nearly a decade after the US regime, proponents of the national characteristics hypothesis gloss over this decade-long time lag in their accounts. Most focus on the emergence of the CCF in the

1930s, then jump to the postwar period to discuss union growth (Lipset 1989: 166–170; Lipset and Meltz 2004: 39–44). There is little in these accounts about what *unions* were doing during the Great Depression and World War II. This is likely because the story of Canadian labor relations in this period does not fit well into the narrative of a "Tory-tinged" Canada, committed to more communitarian values.

While FDR's New Deal administration responded to the labor upsurge of the 1930s by creating legal mechanisms for union recognition and collective bargaining, the Canadian government responded with violence and repression. Conservative Prime Minister Richard B. Bennett accused union organizers of being Communist instigators, and vowed to crush them beneath the "iron heel of ruthlessness" (quoted in Jamieson 1968: 217). Under Bennett's watch, police arrested and deported organizers, ransacked union halls, and broke up union meetings (Imai 1981; Neatby 1972; Petryshyn 1982). Returning to the prime ministership in 1935, the Liberal William Lyon Mackenzie King approached "the labour problem" with a softer touch than Bennett, but adamantly refused to heed labor's calls for a Canadian Wagner Act (Fudge and Tucker 2001: 193; Thompson and Seager 1986).

Ironically, at least in light of the national characteristics hypothesis, King hesitated to implement comprehensive collective bargaining policies because of an ideological commitment to a value normally viewed as classically American: voluntarism (Fudge 1990). A classic corporate liberal himself, King had a long-standing interest in labor relations policy. He started his government career in 1900 as the editor of the *Labour Gazette*, the official journal of Canada's Department of Labour, and was quickly promoted to become Canada's first deputy minister of labour. He received a PhD in industrial relations from Harvard in 1909, and that same year, after winning a seat in Parliament in 1908, he was appointed Canada's first full-time minister of labour.

After losing his seat in 1911, he moved on in 1914 to serve as an industrial relations consultant for John D. Rockefeller. In that capacity, he helped Rockefeller craft a public relations response to the national outrage surrounding the Ludlow Massacre, in which at least thirteen people, including striking miners, women, and children, were either mowed down by machine guns or burnt alive. In keeping with his voluntarist ideas, King proposed a Joint Industrial Council (JIC), a forum in which workers and management could come together to discuss grievances. King's proposal subsequently became the template for the "American Plan," an open shop system of company unionism that spread throughout corporate America in the 1920s (Whitaker 1977b).

As Deputy Minister of Labour, King authored Canada's first effort at regulating labor–management relations, the Industrial Disputes Investigation Act (IDIA) of 1907. The IDIA sought to foster industrial harmony by providing a forum for negotiation and conciliation between labor and management. However, the structure of the law was entirely voluntary. There were no mechanisms compelling either side to negotiate or reach agreement. Although unions were very willing to negotiate, employers found little reason to aver themselves of the law, preferring instead their policy of hostility and intransigence toward labor (Fudge and Tucker 2001).

While the IDIA proved largely ineffectual in promoting collective bargaining, King took great pride in the law. He saw it as the embodiment of his philosophy of labor–management relations as articulated in his 1918 tome, *Industry and Humanity* (King 1918). As labor unrest heated up under his watch in the late 1930s, he expressed his sympathy for labor, telling himself that "to me it would be both an easy and an enjoyable battle to continue till the end of my life the fight for the rights of labour" (King 1937: 345). While he personally found employer and government repression of workers repugnant, he kept his faith in the ability of industrial voluntarism, as practiced through the IDIA, to create industrial peace.

With the advent of World War II, labor unrest continued to rise. In response, King's War Cabinet issued a set of voluntary collective bargaining guidelines, laid out in Order-In-Council PC 2685. But employers showed little interest in the guidelines, and unions complained loudly that the order was not working. In response, the cabinet issued a series of ever-harsher restrictions on workers' ability to strike. This only ramped up industrial conflict. Even so, the Canadian government refused to create any regulation that would compel employers to recognize and bargain with unions. Laying out the government rationale, Minister of Labour Norman McLarty explained that

> The Government has pursued this policy of non-compulsion during the war period and has tried to deal out even justice to both parties. It is felt that should employers be compelled to recognize and deal with trade unions that the question immediately arises as to whether employees should be forbidden to go on strike. If compulsion is adopted it must be applied to both parties and where rights are given responsibilities should definitely exist (McLarty 1941: 2).

Finally, in late 1943, as strike rates soared and the CCF began winning important electoral battles, King changed his mind. He realized that collective bargaining could only work if employers were compelled to recognize and bargain with unions. He announced plans for compulsory collective bargaining, and in February 1944, the Cabinet issued Order-In-Council PC 1003 (Camfield 2002; Fudge and Tucker 2001; McInnis 2002).

The history of Canadian unions and labor policy in the 1930s and early 1940s is a story that runs counter to what the national characteristics hypothesis would imply. Rather than being more accepting of collectivist labor rights, employers remained deeply attached to their individual rights of property and contract, and hostile to unions. Meanwhile, government actors committed to a voluntarist labor relations framework refused to compel union recognition or collective bargaining. Only under extreme political and economic duress did employers and government agents relent.

After World War II, Canadian employers continued with the baseline anti-union hostility they expressed before the war (Jamieson 1968; Pentland 1968).[18] Canadian employers looked south with interest when the Taft-Hartley Act was passed in 1947, and many pushed to get similar provisions enacted in Canada, particularly right-to-work language, prohibition of mandatory dues checkoff, and a ban on secondary picketing (Canadian Manufacturers' Association 1947a, 1947b). They were partially successful, keeping dues checkoff voluntary and imposing strike restrictions, but failed to get right-to-work language. The Canadian Manufacturers' Association (CMA) and other employer groups continued to push for a Canadian Taft-Hartley Act well into the 1950s, but were rebuffed (Anonymous 1948).

As the 1950s wore on, employer organizations lost steam, as they recognized that their battle for more restrictive labor laws was in vain. CMA's Ottawa representative, Willis George, articulated this sentiment in a 1954 report to headquarters regarding the latest round of legislative reforms. He noted that employers' near-universal adoption of the Rand

---

[18] As with the US case, we should be careful in ascribing too monolithic of a position to Canadian employers as a whole. However, in the course of my research I found that there was not as clear a delineation between corporate liberals and hard-liners in Canada as in the US. Rather, employer attitudes as a whole seemed to adhere to a deeply felt hostility to unions, albeit one that did not go as far as to deny their very right to exist, as we saw in the US case. Moreover, unlike in the US, where the NAM played a central role in sustaining and organizing the hardline pole of employer opinion, the CMA seems to have played a more moderating role, expressing sympathy with irate hardline employers, but not encouraging such attitudes. The CMA also seemed much more comfortable playing a representative role vis-à-vis unions and government than did the NAM.

Formula had rendered their organization's opposition to mandatory dues checkoff moot. Nonetheless, he continued,

> In spite of the present situation, I presume the CMA will oppose the Check-off being written into the legislation on the same grounds as we have made representations in the past, but we should not be realistic if we expected to be successful in our opposition, as the proposed amendment to the Act to include the Check-off has been yearly gaining more support and it is a foregone conclusion that the provision would carry if introduced in a Government bill (George 1954).

Employers also seemed to recognize unions' increased postwar clout. In response to an inquiry on the part of a concerned lumber executive as to "who or what is going to stop the [unions'] continued demands for higher wages and the check-off system?" (Campbell 1953), a CMA representative could only meekly reply that "[t]here was general agreement with your view, but it was recognized that it was a difficult matter on which to take action to put a stop to such demands on the part of unions" (Reburn 1953).

Although the main employer associations and large firms may have resigned themselves to having to deal with unions, this resignation was far from universal. As the Task Force on Labour Relations, headed by H.D. Woods, summed up in its report[19] on the "crisis of collective bargaining" in the late 1960s,

> On balance, we do not believe that most employers have a very positive orientation toward trade unions and collective bargaining. Although employers in general are prepared to accept the fact that these institutions are indispensable instruments in a modern industrial liberal democratic state, the majority would be more than pleased if they were to restrict their activities or confine them to enterprises other than their own (Canada Task Force on Labour Relations and Woods 1968: 91).

While the resignation of the Canadian employer associations stands in sharp contrast to the recalcitrance of the NAM and other US employer organizations, it should not be confused with a deeply held belief in the value of collectivist institutions. Rather, as in the United States, many Canadian employers pursued a realist strategy in the postwar period, whereby they accommodated unions and labor regulations only to the extent that it was required.

In the Canadian case then, the national characteristics hypothesis falls short as well. Canadian employers did not exhibit more collectivist

---

[19] We will return to the Woods Report in Chapter 6.

propensities, nor did state actors. Rather, both were constrained by a combination of political dynamics and institutional constraints. But what explains those shifting dynamics and constraints?

INTERNAL UNION CHARACTERISTICS

Explanations emphasizing the internal characteristics of the two national labor movements focus on the prevalence of a more progressive "social unionism" within the Canadian labor movement, as compared a more conservative "economistic unionism" in the United States. The most sophisticated articulation of this view is the work of Ian Robinson (1990, 1993). As he describes it, social unionism emphasizes a "moral economy" that "seeks to change the entire society and to advance the interests of many who are not union members," and articulates a "critique of the existing order ... that resonates with the values and experiences of most working people" (Robinson 1993: 21). By contrast, economistic unionism emphasizes selective incentives, meaning the individual benefits that can accrue to workers through union membership.

According to this approach, Canadian social unionism has better withstood employer and government attacks compared to US economistic unionism by changing the calculus of member involvement and action. As Robinson explains, "Economistic unionism is highly vulnerable to government and employer coercion because it is relatively easy for either of these actors to threaten penalties that more than outweigh the small economic benefits that the union can offer with its selective incentives" (1993: 22). Conversely, at an individual level, social unionism increases the benefits of union membership, making members and leaders more willing to resist government and employer coercion, and more willing to put greater effort into organizing the unorganized.

Why did social unionism prevail in Canada? Robinson traces it to differences in state responses to labor mobilization. In the United States, crucial labor reforms have generally been made "from above," with sympathetic politicians enacting legislation facilitating union organization. In Canada, crucial labor reforms have come "from below," as more hostile governments have been forced to grant labor rights under pressure from militant union mobilization. These different organizational contexts led to different organizational characters: whereas US unions became more dependent on finding sympathetic political allies with whom to strike bargains, Canadian unions learned the value of independent mobilization (Robinson 1993: 23–29). This pattern occurred at two critical moments in both movements' development: first at their institutionalization in the 1930s and '40s, and second at the time of public sector union expansion in the 1960s (Robinson 1993: 29–33).

For the first period of the 1930s and '40s, Robinson's key empirical evidence involves differences in the growth rates of competing union federations in both countries. In the United States, after the passage of the Wagner Act, the more economistic AFL outpaced the growth of the social unionist CIO. In Canada, labor's continued political exclusion gave the organizing advantage in this critical period to the social unionist Canadian Confederation of Labour (CCL) over the more economistic Trades and Labour Congress (TLC). While aggregate growth remained similar in both countries, this compositional difference – stronger economistic union growth in the United States, stronger social union growth in Canada – shaped the organizational character of the two labor movements differently, which in turn laid the groundwork for subsequent density divergence.

For the second period, he focuses on growth in public sector unionism, pointing out that in the United States, relatively weak public sector unions were granted basic union rights by sympathetic local, state, and federal governments, whereas in Canada, governments usually had to enact legislation to stem the tide of already-mobilized public sector workers. The resulting legislation differed quite sharply: in Canada, public sector workers won full collective bargaining rights, including the right to strike; in the United States, almost all legislation prohibited that right, and most put significant restrictions on the scope of collective bargaining rights. Additionally, public sector unionism's greater strength and influence in Canada in the 1960s accentuated the social unionist character of the labor movement as a whole compared to the United States, where public sector union influence was more muted (Robinson 1993: 33).

The internal union characteristics hypothesis has an advantage over the national characteristics hypothesis, in that it offers a historically contextualized explanation that can plausibly account both for initial union density growth and subsequent divergence. Rather than glossing over the events of the 1930s and '40s, it instead highlights them as a central part of the explanation. Its sophisticated analysis of the relationship between union mobilization and state response is also a strong point. Counter to popular current-day understandings of the Canadian state as generally more supportive of unions, a historical analysis shows not only that the Canadian state has often been more *hostile* to unions than the

US state, but suggests that it is precisely this state hostility that has strengthened the Canadian labor movement at key points in its development.

Where the internal union characteristics hypothesis falls short, however, is in its specification of the mechanisms driving movement divergence in both countries. The sharp distinctions that Robinson draws between the AFL/TLC and CIO/CCL, with the former representing economistic unionism and the latter representing social unionism, do not accurately capture the political dynamic of the period. In Robinson's account, it appears that the US CIO remained an advocate and practitioner of social unionism throughout its entire existence from the 1930s through the 1950s, and that it was simply eclipsed by the faster-growing AFL, which was a staunch defender of narrow business unionism.

This characterization has two problems. First, it overlooks the degree to which the transformation of the US labor movement in this period was in large part a consequence of a deradicalization *within* the CIO itself. As will be discussed in Chapter 4, it was the CIO unions that most aggressively pursued an alliance with the Democratic Party, in the process undermining efforts to sustain a social democratic party like the Canadian CCF. As will be discussed in Chapter 6, it was the CIO unions that most enthusiastically backed the no-strike pledge during World War II, which weakened labor's organizational power and created greater dependence on government favors (Kersten 2006; Lichtenstein 1982). And it was the CIO-affiliated UAW that agreed to the Treaty of Detroit. While industrial relations experts at the time saw it as a sign of growing union maturity, subsequent analysts saw that it signaled a decisive turn away from seeking broad-based gains for the working class as a whole in favor of particular benefits for union members (Davis 1980a; Lichtenstein 1989; Moody 1988). An adequate explanation of the organizational development of US unions must account for the decline of the "moral economy" of the CIO.

Second, it mischaracterizes the dynamics within the AFL at the time. While it is true that the AFL leadership tended toward a more conservative brand of unionism in general, the Great Depression had a radicalizing effect, even on it. In the early phases of labor's upsurge in 1933 and 1934, some within the AFL who soon bitterly resisted the CIO split saw great promise in what was happening. Take for example the normally stodgy AFL President William Green. As the AFL Executive Board met in 1933 to discuss its position on the National Industrial Recovery Act (NIRA), which would later form the basis of the Wagner Act, Green closed the meeting with his assessment of the AFL's central tasks:

Now is the time we ought to inaugurate a militant organizing campaign. This bill is the instrumentality through which we can tell workers what their rights are ... The workers must be organized to secure their rights and we, for our part, must carry the message to them ... The militant fighting spirit of the workers must be aroused. Even now men are beginning to strike. We can't stand still. We must go forward and we must become active immediately ... I am vitally impressed with the necessity of organization. We will center our attack on mass production industries with the means at hand. If the workers are not organized it won't be the fault of the American Federation of Labor (American Federation of Labor 1933: 16).

These hardly seem to be the words of a narrow, economistic unionist. Moreover, in terms of articulating a broader social vision, Green in speeches made around this time routinely called for increased aid to the unemployed, expanded public works programs, support for farmers, greater government support for housing, and more (Green 1934b). In making labor's case, Green was clear in saying that "I plead for workers, the poor and unprotected and for the protection and preservation of human rights" (Green 1934a: 6). Granted, this is far short of full-throated social unionism, but it suggests that Green did see room in the AFL for elements of a broader social unionist program.

Beyond Green, whose commitment to social unionism might have been shaky, there were more genuine social unionists within the ranks of the AFL leadership. David Dubinsky, whose International Ladies Garment Workers Union (ILGWU) pioneered industrial unionism and a broader vision for labor, supported the CIO, but never fully broke from the AFL (Parmet 2005). A. Philip Randolph and C.L. Dellums of the Brotherhood of Sleeping Car Porters (BSCP) led militant struggles for labor rights and racial justice on the railroads (Bates 2001). And at the local level, in cities like Minneapolis, Los Angeles, and San Francisco where the CIO had little reach, AFL-affiliated unions and central labor councils built community-based, working-class movements whose vision expanded beyond economism (Dobbs 1975; Faue 1991; Kazin 1986).

This changed in the latter part of the 1930s, as the AFL positioned itself as the more compliant, employer-friendly option to the CIO (M. Davis 1980a; Tomlins 1979). The change over the course of the 1930s shows a tactical malleability on the AFL's part, where it adapted to the legal-institutional environment into which it was incorporated. It suggests that the AFL's conservative tactics of the late 1930s were not an inherent part of its organizational characteristics. It was only once the Wagner Act machinery was firmly in place that the AFL could play its "sweetheart deal" game with employers fearful of being organized by the CIO. In a less institutionally stable environment, like the mid-1930s, the AFL leadership seemed capable of adopting a more social unionist outlook. It was the institutional context, as opposed to internal union characteristics, that was shaping union activity.

As for the Canadian case, the internal union characteristics hypothesis shares with many accounts of Canadian labor politics an account that takes the emergence of the CCF for granted, as well as its alliance with labor. But as will be discussed in Chapter 4, the emergence of the CCF as an established third party was far from a foregone conclusion in the 1930s. Also, the CCF's relationship with labor remained unsettled for most of the 1930s and '40s, and the alliance was fully consummated only in the late 1940s. An adequate explanation of the organizational development of Canadian unions must also explain the labor–CCF alliance.

Turning to the 1960s, Robinson's focus on differences in the growth of public sector unionism and the politicization of both labor movements is important, but again mischaracterizes the political and organizational dynamics at work. In Robinson's account, public sector unions are inherently political, as their members' livelihoods depend on political decisions. This, he argues, makes them more "more politicized than their private-sector counterparts in some respects, and their politics are more likely to favour state intervention for a variety of social and economic purposes" (Robinson 1993: 32).

But, as the US case shows, despite public sector unions' stronger structural ties to the political process compared to private-sector unions, there is nothing inherent about public sector unions that will make them mobilize politically for a broader class-wide agenda. Rather, mobilization strategies depend on a union's political orientation, which in turn depends on the political connections that a union makes. Unions that retain stronger connections to explicitly left-wing, class-based parties are more likely to articulate class-based political demands than those connected to non-class-based parties. Robinson recognizes this in emphasizing the importance of Canadian labor's link to the CCF/NDP, but the issue is broader than one party. In general, Canadian labor retained a stronger connection with the Left than did US labor, where that link was largely severed (Clawson 2003; Schenk and Bernard 1992). An adequate explanation of union density divergence must explain why that stronger link between labor and the Left persisted in Canada.

Overall, the internal union characteristics hypothesis goes a long way toward explaining US–Canada union density divergence. The key questions that remain unanswered are 1) why did the CCF get established in

Canada, and why did labor ally with it? And 2) why did the labor-Left alliance remain stronger in Canada than in the United States?

THE ROLE OF RACE

Finally, one crucial hypothesis we must consider is the role that race has played in shaping – and undermining – the US labor movement. The core of the argument is that white US workers' attachment to racial identities has often trumped their class identity, making class-based organizing especially difficult (Esch and Roediger 2009; Goldfield 1997; Griffith 1988; Hill 1996; Iton 2000; Roediger 1991).

At the outset, it is essential to emphasize that racism and exclusionary politics have marked both the US and Canadian labor movements (Creese 1988; Das Gupta 2007; Goldfield 1990; Goutor 2007; Hunt and Rayside 2000). Going back to the nineteenth century and continuing through much of the twentieth century, unions in both countries were enthusiastic backers of exclusionary policies toward certain immigrant groups, first those from Asian countries, and later those from Latin America. Native-born and indigenous workers of color fared no better, facing significant discrimination at the hand of unions. In both countries, the vanguard of racist exclusion was the craft-based unions in the AFL and TLC (Iton 2000; Palmer 1983). Similarly, employers in both countries have eagerly taken advantage of racial divisions to undermine worker solidarity and weaken union power (Goldfield 1993; Griffith 1988; Mathieu 2010).

Nonetheless, for those who have compared the two countries in depth, the consensus remains that racial divisions have had a more damaging effect on labor in the United States compared to Canada. At a basic level, until fairly recently fewer Canadians were people of color, creating fewer opportunities for racial divisions to undermine labor solidarity. In 1941, indigenous peoples made up 1.09 percent of the Canadian population, Asians 0.64 percent, and blacks 0.19 percent. Those percentages stayed relatively constant in the postwar decades, only increasing starting in the 1970s. By comparison, blacks made up 9.77 percent of the US population in 1940, with the "Other Races" category adding up to 0.45 percent. Those identified as "Hispanic," an ethnic identity comprised of people from all races, made up an additional 1.54 percent.[20] While the percentage of the US black population stayed relatively constant in the ensuing

---

[20] Since those of Hispanic ethnicity can be of any race, this percentage includes individuals already counted among the 10.22 percent of the population identified as nonwhite.

decades, the percentage of those classified as Asian and especially Hispanic expanded starting in the 1970s.[21]

Also, in Canada, indigenous peoples, the largest racialized minority group, were not fully proletarianized. While they did participate in the wage labor market, they blended paid work with independent production much more than other groups (Brownlie 2008; High 1996). As a result, the social cleavage between whites and indigenous peoples was less of a factor in the workplace and the labor market than in the United States, where workers of color comprised a larger part of the paid labor force.

But numbers only tell part of the story when it comes to race. Racial divisions and threats play powerful roles in the national imagination, even when the actual populations involved are small to nonexistent. We need only think most recently of President Trump's hyperbolic warnings about the threat of Mexican "illegals" streaming across the Southern border, or of Muslim "terrorists" bent on wreaking havoc inside the United States. Trump's rhetoric draws on long-standing fears of a racialized Other in the United States (Goldstein and Hall 2017; Omi and Winant 1986).

Compared with Canada, these racial divisions have played a more powerful role in the US national imagination. More specifically, race in the United States has been characterized by a sharp black–white dichotomy, fundamentally shaped by the legacy of chattel slavery and Jim Crow laws. This has "flattened" European ethnic divisions in the United States by subsuming them under a "white" racial identity to a greater extent than has happened in Canada, while accentuating the difference between the broad white identity and the other, black identity (Iton 2000; Kaufman 2009; Roediger 1991; Vickers and Isaac 2012).[22] As a result, class-wide efforts at cross-racial organizing in the United States have often foundered, weakening class-based organization as a whole.

Nonetheless, explanations focused on the role of racial divisions in weakening unions must be able to specify how, when, and under what conditions racial divisions undermined labor solidarity. Because as

---

[21] Canadian data: Statistics Canada, Table 075–0015 Historical statistics, origins of the population, every ten years. US data: Historical Statistics of the United States, Table Aa145–184. Population, by sex and race: 1790–1990 and Table Aa2189–2215. Hispanic population estimates, by sex, race, Hispanic origin, residence, nativity: 1850–1990.

[22] This is in no way meant to deny the existence of Latinx, Asian-American, or indigenous workers in the US, nor to minimize their valuable contributions to building workers' movements throughout US history. Rather, it is an analytical statement about the structure of racial divisions in the US The very fact that nonblack people of color must continuously struggle to get their historical contributions recognized speaks to the power of the black–white dichotomy in structuring US racial divisions.

checkered as labor's history has been in both countries when it comes to succumbing to racial divisions, some unions have managed to forge cross-racial class solidarity at certain times (Honey 2000; Zieger 2007). In the nineteenth century, the Knights of Labor organized across the color line (Gerteis 2007; Kealey and Palmer 1982). In the early twentieth century, the Industrial Workers of the World (IWW), One Big Union (OBU), and Workers' Unity League (WUL) made conscious efforts in both countries to organize workers of color, although those efforts were short-lived (Creese 1987; Foner 1970). Later on, many CIO unions, particularly those led by Communists, had greater success with interracial organizing (Brown and Brueggemann 1997; Goldfield 1993; Horowitz 1997; Stepan-Norris and Zeitlin 2003; Zeitlin and Weyher 2001). In the 1960s, the UAW played an important role in the fight for civil rights, as did public sector unions (Honey 2007; Isaac and Christiansen 2002; Jones 2013; McCartin 2006). Today, many unions in both the US and Canada are at the forefront of struggles for immigrant rights and racial justice (Hunt and Rayside 2007; Milkman 2006b; Voss and Bloemraad 2011). Without denying that each of these examples has important shortcomings, they still raise the question of why unions managed to unite workers across racial lines in some cases but not others?

Moreover, theories that highlight differences in the structure and intensity of racial divisions to explain the relative strength of US and Canadian unions confront the problem of explaining a variable with a constant: whatever cross-national differences exist, they did not have different effects on union density until the 1960s. Why didn't these differences matter as much prior to the 1960s?

To understand how, why, and when racial divisions mattered for explaining union density divergence, our analysis must focus on two key moments: 1) the moment of labor's institutionalization in the 1930s and '40s; and 2) the moment of density divergence in the 1960s. At both of these moments, we must look both at how race shaped the internal dynamics of labor unions, as well as the broader institutional environment, in order to see how it affected union density trajectories.

Looking first at internal union dynamics in the 1930s and '40s, the CIO made some strides in interracial organizing in basic industry, but results fell far short of the promise (Hill 1996). The critical moment was Operation Dixie, the CIO campaign to organize the South waged from 1946 to 1953 (Goldfield 1994; Griffith 1988; Honey 1992). The campaign required an interracial approach, and in some cases the CIO delivered. But its internal contradictions around questions of race proved to be its undoing. These contradictions were compounded by the fact that many of the CIO's best organizers and staunchest anti-racists were purged as part of postwar Red scares that dismantled the CIO's Communist-led unions (Stepan-Norris and Zeitlin 2003). Operation Dixie's failure in 1953 left an entire region of the country effectively de-unionized. And, as we saw in the section on sectoral shifts in employment, employers did increasingly relocate to these de-unionized areas over the course of the twentieth century. The defeat also coincided almost exactly with the beginning of the decline in US union density, and set the stage for the merger of the AFL and CIO. The merger in the United States – actually more of a reabsorption of the CIO into the AFL – effectively marked the end of the CIO's broader political program, and its retreat back into a more conservative business unionist model (Davis 1980a; Goldfield 1993).

As for the broader environment, race certainly played an important role in shaping key labor legislation in this period. The Wagner Act specifically excluded domestic and agricultural workers at the behest of white supremacist southern Democrats, who conditioned their support for Roosevelt's bill on that exclusion. At the time, both occupations were heavily composed of African Americans. Similarly, southern Democrats played a key role in overriding President Truman's veto of the Taft-Hartley Act, allowing it to become law. They were also major proponents of right-to-work laws, signaling to employers a more favorable, anti-union environment in those states. Operation Dixie tried to take on this racist Southern power structure, but ran into trouble due to the fact that the CIO's opponents in the South were also its ostensible New Deal coalition partners in Washington, DC, upon whose support they relied for key progressive legislation. The CIO's failure to organize the South left intact a system of white supremacy that constrained social reforms and anchored right wing politics for decades to come (Farhang and Katznelson 2005; Gall 1988; Katznelson 2013; Katznelson, Geiger, and Kryder 1993).

In the 1960s, the moment of divergence, US unions were challenged from within and without by the civil rights movement. Both old-line craft unions in the building trades as well as ostensibly more "modern" industrial unions issued from the former CIO were hit with discrimination lawsuits and forced to reform internal practices around hiring halls, seniority systems, membership criteria, and more (Frymer 2007; Hill 1996). Radical workers of color, often inspired by or directly involved with the Black Power movement, also organized insurgent reform movements within these unions (Brenner, Brenner, and Winslow 2010;

Georgakas and Surkin 1998). At the same time, the explosion of new unions in the public sector brought many more women and people of color into the labor movement, dramatically altering its complexion. These public sector unions also built alliances with the civil rights movement, most famously in Memphis, where sanitation workers striking in an effort to join the American Federation of State, County, and Municipal Employees (AFSCME) were joined by many civil rights leaders. Most notable among them was Dr. Martin Luther King Jr., who was assassinated in the course of supporting their struggle (Honey 2007; McCartin 2006).

Although these were positive changes for the US labor movement, they also exposed critical weaknesses. Within the labor movement itself, the public sector upsurge was significant, but not strong enough to reorient the movement's broader political orientation. The conservative, Cold Warrior business unionists around AFL-CIO President George Meany stayed in charge (Cowie 2010: 23–63).[23] Beyond labor, the civil rights movement and the employment discrimination legislation it fought for transformed union practices for the better. But the success and expansion of civil rights law, starting with the landmark *Brown v. Board of Education* decision in 1954, intensified the division between race and labor. Whereas earlier conceptions of civil rights law encompassed racial discrimination and labor rights, in the post-*Brown* era civil rights attorneys focused on dismantling Jim Crow racial segregation while ignoring workers' issues. This created two separate spheres of law – civil rights law and labor law – for remedying a set of problems that were intimately intertwined. While individual civil rights flourished starting in the 1960s, collective labor rights floundered. As a result, federal anti-discrimination legislation cleaned up labor unions and increased access for women and people of color within the labor movement at the precise moment that labor's power was collapsing (Frymer 2007; Goluboff 2007).

The importance of race in shaping union density trajectories in the United States becomes even more apparent when we incorporate the comparison with Canada. There, racial divisions certainly hobbled the movement's development at critical moments, but not to the same extent as in the United States. In the 1930s and '40s, without a Manichean black/white opposition, amplified and institutionalized by state power, Canadian workers and union organizers did not face the same kinds of

---

[23] For more on how the public sector union upsurge affected the US and Canadian labor movements, see Chapter 5.

barriers to multiracial organization that their US counterparts did, particularly in the South. And while Canadian workers did face hostile legislators, they were able to fight their anti-union political opponents head-on, unlike in the United States, where racist, anti-union southern Democrats were part of the same New Deal political coalition as labor.

In the 1960s, the public sector upsurge had a deeper and more transformative effect on the Canadian labor movement as a whole. Unlike in the United States, the new, militant public sector unions assumed a central leadership role in the Canadian Labour Congress (CLC) (Robinson 1993). In that capacity, they made anti-racism, feminism, and anti-discrimination policy a priority, both transforming the federation from within and mobilizing beyond the federation for broader social anti-discrimination policies. In so doing, they created a link between labor and civil rights law that was missing in the United States (Briskin 2008; Luxton 2001; Sangster 2010).

Clearly, differences in the organization of racial divisions do explain some of the US–Canada union density divergence. The key is understanding why and how they mattered at different points in time. For the period of the 1930s and '40s, US labor's ability to overcome racial divisions was hampered by its political alliance with racist southern Democrats, along with its purge of many of its best organizers and staunchest anti-racists as the result of Red scares. But why did US labor end up in the same political coalition with reactionary, anti-union, white supremacists? And why did the post–World War II Red scares have such a deep and lasting impact on US labor? As for the period of the 1960s, US labor's ability to overcome racial divisions was hampered by a divide between labor and the civil rights movement. Unlike in Canada, the social movements of the 1960s failed to permeate and transform the US labor movement to the same degree, largely keeping questions of racial justice off of the US labor leadership's agenda. But why did the civil rights movement, and the social movements of the 1960s more broadly, not have as transformative an effect on the US labor movement as they did on the Canadian labor movement? We will address these questions in Part II.

PART I

SUMMING UP

Existing explanations for why union density diverged in the United States and Canada after decades of similarity fall short. Looking first at structural explanations, common "service sector shift" arguments for union decline explain little, as employment in both countries has shifted toward the service sector, but without causing nearly as much union decline in Canada. Although the growth of public sector unionism in both countries did alter aggregate union growth trajectories, it did not conceal an underlying convergence in private sector density. Geographic shifts in employment, particularly manufacturing employment, affected US union density, but this raises the question as to why union density is so much more regionally clustered in the United States than in Canada.

Turning next to individual explanations, union density divergence is not the result of stronger anti-union sentiment in the United States. Polling data show relatively similar levels of public approval of unions over time in the United States and Canada, and there is a wide gap in both countries between individual preferences for union representation and actual levels of union representation. As for differences in employer opposition to unions, these are much more a function of the institutional environments in which employers operate than of actual differences in individual employer attitudes.

In terms of policy differences, macroeconomic policies such as monetary and trade policy had little effect on union density, but labor relations policy did. Canadian rules governing union certification, first contract negotiation, union security, and strike activity protect workers and their unions more than US rules, while putting more constraints on employers' ability to interfere with workers' efforts to exercise their collective bargaining rights. However, the rules in both countries have changed over time, with the US labor laws eroding and Canadian laws strengthening. The question then remains as to why the laws diverged?

Our analysis of the broader environment shaping working class power in both countries showed that differences in political institutions provide convincing mechanisms to explain density divergence. In particular, the presence of a labor party in Canada, and its absence in the United States, is critical. So too is the structure and administration of labor policy, particularly the relation between labor policy adjudication and the regular court system. But these institutions themselves have changed over time too, and that institutional change must be explained.

Differences in national characteristics, to the extent that they exist, do not explain union density divergence. Survey data for recent decades from the United States and Canada show similar beliefs about individualism, institutions, and the role of government, even as union density has diverged. Additionally, historical analysis based on the national characteristics hypothesis gets key questions wrong. Counter to the idea that the New Deal era constituted a temporary turn toward collectivist values, the "exception to the exception," the evidence shows that most US employers did not modify their values in a collectivist direction. Rather, they took a "realist" approach, accepting collective bargaining temporarily until the balance of power tipped back in their favor. Meanwhile, a militant segment of employers vociferously resisted unions throughout the entire period.

As for Canada, the national characteristics hypothesis does not explain the Canadian government's steadfast adherence to industrial voluntarism and its refusal to grant substantive labor rights in the 1930s and early '40s. Similarly, counter to what the national characteristics hypothesis would expect, Canadian employer behavior looked more like realist resignation to an unfavorable balance of power rather than an active embrace of more collectivist values.

The internal union characteristics hypothesis goes a long way toward explaining density divergence. Its accurate characterization of the relationship between state actors, labor militancy, and labor's organizational development is particularly helpful. Where it falls short is in its misspecification of the mechanisms driving labor movement divergence in both countries. Rather than simply being a story of the "economistic unionism" of the AFL besting the "social unionism" of the CIO in the United States, what needs to be explained is the deradicalization of the

CIO. And in Canada, the alliance between labor and the CCF, along with generally stronger ties between labor and the broader social movement left, must be explained, as they were not preordained.

Finally, differences in the structures of racial divisions played an important role in density divergence. The Manichean divide between black and white in the United States, reinforced by state power and the long-term effects of chattel slavery and Jim Crow, created greater internal and external obstacles for US unions. Meanwhile, the US civil rights movement did not transform the US labor movement as much as the social movements of the 1960s transformed Canadian labor. At the same time, the parallel success of US anti-discrimination law and erosion of labor law meant that unions became more racially integrated just as unions were declining. What remains to be explained is 1) why did US labor end up in the same political coalition with reactionary, anti-union, white supremacists? And 2) why did the civil rights movement, and the social movements of the 1960s more broadly, not have as transformative an effect on the US labor movement as they did on the Canadian labor movement?

From the foregoing analysis, we can distill three questions that are key to developing an adequate explanation of US-Canada union density divergence:

1) Why did Canadian labor forge a political alliance with the CCF at the same moment that US labor joined a political coalition that included reactionary, anti-union white supremacists?
2) Why did the social movements of the 1960s have a more transformative, reinvigorating effect on the Canadian labor movement than the US labor movement?
3) Why did the Canadian labor regime remain more stable over time, while the US labor regime eroded?

Answering the first two questions will take us beyond the world of unions and labor policy to explore the worlds of politics and social movements. However, once we have explored those other worlds, we will be better equipped to answer the last question, which will focus specifically on union density divergence.

In the process of answering these questions, we will develop what I have called the "political articulation" approach to explaining union density divergence in the United States and Canada. The next part of this book takes on that task.

PART II

POLITICAL ARTICULATION AND THE CLASS IDEA

This book's central argument is that understanding US-Canada union density divergence in the 1960s requires understanding the different processes of political articulation that occurred in the United States and Canada in the 1930s and '40s, as the working class was fully politically incorporated. I argue that these processes shaped relations between parties and classes differently, as well as relations between the broad political Left and the labor movement. They also affected the formation and development of different labor policy regimes and different labor movements in the United States and Canada. As a result, the class idea remained stronger in Canada, allowing Canadian labor to retain greater organizational stability than in the United States as the postwar ceasefire began to unravel in the 1970s. The result was union density divergence. In saying that the class idea remained stronger in Canada relative to the United States, I mean that social class remained a more salient and legitimate principle of political organization. Instances of class conflict were and are more likely to be expressed and recognized politically as such in Canada, rather than being filtered through another principle of political organization, such as partisan conflict, or blocked entirely from entering the political discussion, as happened in the United States.

This, I argue, was the result of two separate but related processes. On the union side, stronger links with the political Left and broader social movements encouraged Canadian labor to think of and articulate its demands more in class terms. On the government side, class representation was more built into Canadian political and policy institutions, enabling them to comprehend and process political questions in class terms. As class conflict flared in the late 1960s and early 1970s, it was both expressed as and understood as class conflict, leading to state responses aimed at shoring up labor policy. This reinforced labor's organizational capacity, as well as its institutional legitimacy. By contrast, in the United States, weakened links with the Left and broader social movements encouraged labor to think of and articulate its demands more in narrow "interest group" terms. And on the government side, class representation was eschewed in favor of either partisan representation or individual rights, making it difficult for state actors to understand political questions in class terms. As class conflict flared in the late '60s and early '70s, it was largely understood as a problem of individual worker alienation – a case of the "blue collar blues." Legislative efforts to address labor's faltering position failed, amidst perceptions that they were attempts to provide benefits for a Democratic Party "special interest."

In this second section, we will examine the complex back-and-forth between labor, capital, and the state that created such divergent political and institutional outcomes in the United States and Canada. The analysis will proceed in three steps, addressing each of the three central questions laid out at the end of Part I. First, in Chapter 4, we will look at how party–class relations diverged in both countries. The chapter explains why Canadian labor allied with a class-based political party, the CCF, at the very same moment that US labor abandoned efforts to establish a labor party, instead allying itself as a junior partner within the Democratic Party. Second, in Chapter 5, we will seek to understand why the social movements of the 1960s had a more transformative effect on unions in Canada than in the United States. To do so, we will examine how relations between labor and the Left diverged after World War II in both countries, and how that in turn shaped relations between labor and the New Left of the 1960s. Third, in Chapter 6, we will seek to understand why the US labor regime eroded while the Canadian labor regime remained more stable over time. To do so, we will examine conditions surrounding the formation of both regimes in the 1930s and '40s, how those regimes developed in the postwar period, and how they shaped the working-class upsurge and employer counteroffensive of the 1960s and '70s differently in both countries.

4

Party–Class Alliances in the United States and Canada, 1932–1948

One of the first things that any study comparing US and Canadian politics highlights is the difference in party systems: whereas the United States has a resolutely two-party system, Canada has a multiparty system. Importantly, Canada's multiparty system includes one, the New Democratic Party (NDP), which is a social democratic party with close ties to labor.

As we saw in Chapter 3, the presence of the CCF/NDP in Canada and the absence of a labor party in the United States had important consequences for how union power and labor policy developed in both countries over the course of the twentieth century. In Canada, the CCF/NDP created an electoral threat on the ruling parties' left flank, generating pressure for pro-labor reforms. It also provided an organizational vehicle for the class idea, keeping labor issues on the national agenda and legitimizing class-based demands. In the United States, the lack of a labor party meant that the Democrats faced no electoral pressure from their Left, while labor ended up as one interest group in a coalition that included anti-labor elements, particularly racist Southern Democrats. This makes the difference in party systems a key part of explaining US-Canada union density divergence.

The problem is that existing studies take this difference in party systems as given. They argue that US electoral institutions, individualist values, economic prosperity, and racial and ethnic divisions – or some combination thereof – ensured that a labor party would never take root there (Foner 1984; Laslett and Lipset 1974; Lipset and Marks 2000; Lowi 1984; Sombart 1976; Vössing 2012). To the extent a labor party had a chance, it was gone by the late nineteenth or early twentieth century (Archer 2007; Brody 1983). Meanwhile, Canada's parliamentary system, combined with its British, "Tory-touched" liberalism and a more racially and ethnically homogeneous working class, created more favorable terrain for labor parties, making the CCF's emergence appear natural, almost inevitable (Horowitz 1968; Lipset 1989). Indeed, historians have constructed a narrative where the emergence of the CCF in the 1930s becomes part of a long-standing Canadian tradition of independent class politics that is quite different from the tradition south of the border (McKay 2005; Palmer 1983; Penner 1977).

If long-standing differences in political cultures, electoral institutions, and intra-class divisions sufficiently explained cross-border differences in labor party support, we would expect to see consistently lower levels of support in the United States than in Canada. And yet, an analysis comparing existing US electoral data with newly-compiled Canadian data shows that this is not the case. Figure 4.1 tracks vote shares for independent left third parties (ILTPs) at the federal and state/provincial levels in the United States and Canada between 1867 and 2009.[1]

Instead of consistently different levels of ILTP support in both countries, we see divergence. From the late nineteenth century through World War I, ILTP support was *higher* in the United States than in Canada. From the end of World War I through the onset of the Great Depression, Canadian ILTP support pulled ahead of the United States, although Canadian support remained volatile and US support remained within past historical ranges.[2] Then, a decisive shift occurred in the 1930s: ILTP support collapsed in the United States, and took off in Canada.

---

[1] I define "independent left third party" (ILTP) as any party competing for electoral votes that was (1) organizationally unaligned with mainstream parties (Democrats and Republicans in the United States, Liberals and Conservatives in Canada); and (2) had a programmatic commitment to socialism or another left-wing ideology, or, for agrarian parties, emphasized collective, redistributive policies, as opposed to individualist policies of self-reliance. I use the broader term "ILTP" instead of "labor party" because of the long and fluid interrelationship in both countries between agrarian, labor, and socialist political organizing, making it difficult and analytically counterproductive to draw strong distinctions between them (Hild 2007; Kealey and Warrian 1976). A complete listing of Canadian ILTPs, as well as a discussion of the selection criteria used, can be found in Appendix A.

[2] While Figure 4.1 might suggest that ILTP support diverged after World War I, the postwar spike marked a period of volatility in the Canadian party system, rather than a lasting shift in ILTP support. The spike represents the meteoric rise of the Progressive Party at the federal level and the United Farmers movement at the provincial level. While these agrarian protest parties achieved impressive electoral gains initially, they proved fleeting (Heron 1998; Morton 1950). In no case were Progressive/United Farmer parties able to establish a lasting political presence, and none of these parties survived past 1935. It was only in the 1930s with the emergence of the CCF that ILTP support took hold in Canada.

These data challenge the idea that the success or failure of labor parties in either country was inevitable. Prior to the 1930s, the United States and Canada shared a track record of significant but failed attempts at establishing class-based political organization. The two countries then diverged in the ensuing years. By the end of World War II, Canadian labor had allied itself with the CCF, while US labor had decisively abandoned any labor party project and cast its lot with the Democratic Party. But in both cases, the formation of those different alliances was not a foregone conclusion.

Figuring out why ILTP support diverged in the United States and Canada in the 1930s therefore becomes an important first step in figuring out why union density diverged in the United States and Canada in the 1960s. Existing explanations for differing levels of ILTP support in the United States and Canada share what I call a *reflection model* of parties. They view party support as reflecting underlying factors, including differences in political cultures and ideologies, electoral institutions, and intra-class divisions. Without dismissing these differences, they cannot adequately explain the diverging ILTP support observed in Figure 4.1.[3]

The key to explaining US-Canada ILTP divergence involves focusing on the active role that parties play in shaping political cultures, conflicts, and class divisions – what I have referred to as an *articulation model* of parties. In this case, we must examine different ruling party responses to labor and agrarian protest sparked by the Great Depression, and the different processes of political articulation that resulted.

Parties ended up articulating new political coalitions in both countries, but with different results. In the United States, President Franklin D. Roosevelt and the Democrats adopted a *co-optive* response to farmer and labor insurgency. They used the Depression to broaden their coalition with appeals to the "forgotten man" and policy offerings that absorbed some working- and agrarian-class fractions. Simultaneously, New Deal labor and agricultural policies accentuated intra-class divisions and diverted energy from ILTP organizing. The result was ILTP collapse, with labor tying itself to a reactionary Southern agrarian bloc and incorporating itself as an interest group within the Democratic

---

[3] Also, it would be difficult to argue that either country had a deeper structural base for ILTP support. Levels of urban population, nonfarm employment, and union density all tracked each other closely in both countries leading up to the Great Depression. See Figures 2–4 in Eidlin 2016 and Figure 3.4 in this volume.

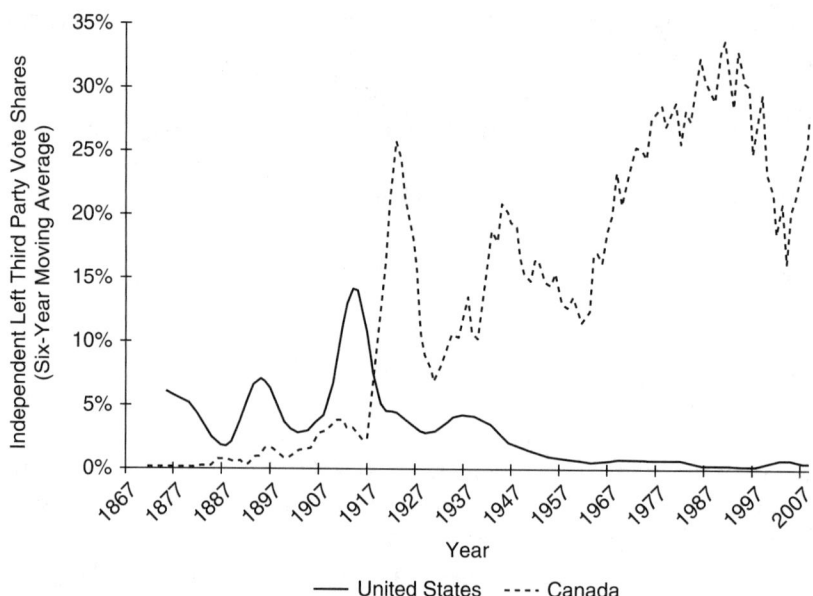

FIGURE 4.1 Independent left third party (ILTP) vote shares in the United States and Canada, 1867–2009 (six-year moving average)
Sources and list of included parties: See Appendix A.

Party. In Canada, the Liberal and Conservative parties shared a *coercive* response to the upsurge. Workers and small farmers were excluded, leaving room for the CCF to articulate an independent farmer–labor alliance. The result was ILTP takeoff, along with both groups' political incorporation as class representatives.

LIMITS OF EXISTING EXPLANATIONS

Existing explanations for differing levels of ILTP support in the United States and Canada fall short on three counts. First, many focus on long-standing cross-national differences in political cultures and electoral systems, which cannot by themselves explain ILTP divergence. Second, some rely on explanations that only hold in one country, not both, such as ruling parties' ability to absorb insurgent party challengers, or the role of critical elections in realigning political coalitions. Third, some overstate cross-national differences in levels of intra-class conflict that blocked independent working-class organization.

Difference, Not Divergence

Many explanations for why ILTPs took root in Canada but not the United States point to cross-national differences in political cultures and electoral systems. Cultural explanations contrast the individualist Lockean liberalism in the United States with Canada's more collectivist, "Tory-touched" liberalism, which was ostensibly more hospitable to socialist ideas (Horowitz 1968; Lipset 1989). As a result, Horowitz contends, "in the United States socialism was alien; in English Canada socialism was 'at home'" (1968: 58). Electoral systems explanations contend that the US presidentialist system was more hostile to multiple parties than was Canada's parliamentary system (Duverger 1954; Lijphart 1999; Lowi 1984), and the particularly open, ideologically flexible US two-party system allowed for "full inclusion" of labor, an option not available in Canada (Lipset and Marks 2000; Vössing 2012). These differences subsumed the political expression of class divisions within catch-all parties in the United States but not in Canada.

How might theories pointing to such long-standing differences explain the divergence in ILTP support reported in Figure 4.1? Defenders of the political cultures perspective might argue that Figure 4.1 masks a qualitative difference between US and Canadian socialist traditions. As Horowitz (1968: 24) summarizes, "In Canada, socialism is British, non-Marxist, and worldly; in the United States is it German, Marxist, and otherworldly." However, this fails to explain the timing of ILTP divergence. Did something change about the cultures of US and Canadian socialism in the mid-1930s? If so, what, and especially why?

Furthermore, emphasizing cross-border differences ignores the extent to which Canadian ILTPs often affiliated with US movements (Cook 1984; Glazer 1937; Kealey and Palmer 1982; Laycock 1990; McCormack 1977; Wiseman and Isitt 2013). Certainly, Canadian affiliates were independent from their US counterparts, but the fact that they were in the same organizations suggests cross-national differences were not as stark as cultural accounts would imply.

Similarly, although electoral system differences may have reinforced US-Canadian ILTP divergence after it got underway, they cannot explain the timing of divergence. Despite presidentialism and ruling parties' flexibility, US ILTPs enjoyed significantly more support prior to the mid-1930s than afterward. Likewise, despite parliamentarianism and more rigid parties, Canadian ILTPs took root only after the mid-1930s. Electoral system explanations also downplay US electoral structures, such as federalism, that might have provided more hospitable ground for ILTP development. The smaller scale of state-level government could have incubated nascent ILTPs by allowing them to build in areas where they enjoyed greater support. Federalism, for example, is often used to explain policy innovation in the United States (Ikenberry and Skocpol 1987) and the success of the CCF/NDP in Canada (Wiseman and Isitt 2007). All told, comparative arguments that rest on enduring national features cannot explain sudden changes in the direction or trajectories of individual cases.

Explaining One Case, Not Both

Other explanations for differences in US–Canadian ILTP support rely on factors that explain one case, not both. For example, some see the collapse of US ILTP support in the 1930s as part of a broader US tradition of ruling parties absorbing independent challengers. According to this argument, Roosevelt's New Deal coalition stole ILTPs' thunder by selectively adopting dissident movements' rhetoric and policies (Hartz 1955: 259–283; Lipset 1996: 86; Lipset and Marks 2000: 43–83). As for Canada, the argument goes, the Great Depression exacerbated existing inequalities within its more conservative, stratified class structure, which, combined with the rigidity of the Canadian party system, paved the way for the CCF (Lipset 1963).

Without denying the very real tradition of US ruling parties absorbing independent rivals, Figure 4.1 challenges such explanations. First, it shows that prior to the New Deal, ruling party absorption suppressed ILTP support only temporarily. Within a few years it would rebound. Why did the New Deal put an end to this pattern? Second, although the argument assumes that a similar thunder-stealing move was impossible for Canadian ruling parties, Canada's Liberal Party had a track record of absorbing Left challengers prior to the 1930s (Heron 1984, 1998; Morton 1950). Why did the Liberals fail to absorb the CCF?

One possibility is that the Left political climate was more threatening in the 1930s, making an absorption strategy riskier for the Liberals. However, the previous instance of absorption was in the aftermath of World War I, just a few years after the Russian Revolution sparked fears of communism around the world, two years after a general strike paralyzed the city of Winnipeg, and amid a major agrarian revolt (Heron 1998). Without diminishing the severity of the threat in the 1930s, absorption strategies were also risky after World War I. Additionally, the US ruling party faced a severe threat in the 1930s and *did* pursue an absorption strategy. Why did the Democrats, but not the Liberals, seek to absorb the Left challenge?

Party characteristics offer an explanation. Organizationally, the CCF did not suffer from the anti-partyism that undermined previous agrarian political efforts in Canada. Ideologically, its distinctive brand of socialism, mixing elements of British Fabianism, European socialism, social gospel, and agrarian radicalism, was coherent enough to pose a more primordial threat to the Liberals than past Left challenges. This predisposed them to try and defeat the CCF, not co-opt it. At the same time, CCF ideology was flexible enough to appeal to disparate groups. Ruling party hostility pushed these groups away, and CCF organization and ideology pulled them together (Horn 1980; McHenry 1950; Naylor 1993, 2016; Smith 1975: 231). For their part, the centrist Liberals saw better political opportunities to their right. As the ruling Conservatives collapsed in the mid-1930s, the Liberals positioned themselves not as a progressive alternative, but as the party of order against chaos (Whitaker 1977a). This left space for the CCF to build.

Another common explanation for US ILTP collapse focuses on the critical election of 1932 (Burnham 1970; Key 1955; Sundquist 1983). Proponents argue that this election realigned the party system to accommodate escalating social tensions, precluding the need for a new party. In this approach, critical elections reflect abrupt shifts in underlying social structures.

Critical elections certainly happen, and do reflect social and structural shifts, as the 1932 US election suggests. But the explanation does not work for Canada. There, although voters decisively repudiated governing parties in 1929 and 1935, neither election triggered party realignment. Instead, ruling party intransigence left room for the CCF to develop. Why did the tensions of the Great Depression trigger a critical realignment in the United States, but not in Canada?

Overstating Differences

Still other explanations for US-Canadian ILTP divergence overstate cross-border differences in intra-class conflict. Scholars of the United States contend that exceptional state and employer hostility toward labor, racial and ethnic divisions, and religious and socialist sectarianism blocked independent working-class organization (Archer 2007; Hattam 1993; Katznelson 1981; Voss 1993). By contrast, scholars of Canada argue that a more ethnically and religiously homogenous, less politically sectarian working class was better able to build ILTPs (Horowitz 1968).

Such divisions undoubtedly suppressed ILTP support in the United States, but Canadian workers were also divided along lines of craft, skill, religion, region, and ethnicity, and their organizations also experienced considerable internecine conflict (Heron 1996; Jamieson 1968; Kealey 1981; Palmer 1983). Additionally, characterizing the Canadian Left as predominantly British obscures its ethnic heterogeneity (Naylor 2006).[4] Without denying each country's distinctive character of intra-class divisions – particularly the different structure of racial divisions – these impeded ILTP development in both countries up until the 1930s. What changed in the 1930s to exacerbate divisions in the United States and mute them in Canada?

In summary, the central problem with reflection models is that they predict long-standing difference in ILTP support, but the evidence shows a pattern of divergence starting in the 1930s. Differences in US and Canadian cultures, ideologies, and institutions, while real, cannot explain this divergence. An adequate explanation starts from the idea that parties actively shape social cleavages and political coalitions: an articulation model of parties.

POLITICAL ARTICULATION AND ILTP DIVERGENCE

Given US political history, traditions, and institutions, the country was predisposed toward virtually nonexistent ILTP support. Similarly, Canada was predisposed toward stronger ILTP support. Prior to the 1930s, however, those differences were muted, with low but significant ILTP support in both countries. This changed in the 1930s: ILTPs collapsed in the United States and took off in Canada.

How does an articulation model explain this shift? Focusing on parties' central role in articulating political coalitions, it highlights how parties politically incorporated farmer and labor groups in both countries. As discussed in the introduction, "political incorporation" refers to the process whereby workers, farmers, and their organizations switched from being a problem for the state to police, to being a constituency for the state to address and administer (Collier and Collier 1991).[5]

In both countries, the political incorporation of workers' and farmers' groups occurred as a result of ruling party strategies to address labor and agrarian protest sparked by the Great Depression. Those parties had

---

[4] While the Canadian Left as a whole was quite heterogeneous, the CCF had a distinctly British influence. However, this British flavor actually impeded party growth among non-British immigrant workers, particularly in Quebec (Naylor 2006: 291).

[5] Incorporation differs from articulation in referring to the entry of new actors into the political arena, as opposed to the reconfiguration of existing actors. Incorporation can happen as part of an articulation process, as in this case.

managed such challenges in the past using a mix of repression and accommodation. As a result, up until that point both the United States and Canada had been exceptional among capitalist democracies as countries that had not politically incorporated their respective working and agrarian classes. All others had done so three or four decades prior (M. Davis 1980b; Laslett 1967; Penner 1977).

Farmer and labor groups were incorporated in both the United States and Canada over the course of the 1930s and 1940s, but in different ways: US farmer and labor groups were incorporated into the Democratic Party's New Deal coalition, whereas their Canadian counterparts forged an independent alliance within the CCF. The result in both cases was a farmer–labor coalition, but in the United States, the coalition undermined ILTP support, whereas in Canada it strengthened it.

Understanding why this happened requires examining parties' role in shaping political alliances. In the United States, Democrats adopted a *co-optive* response to farmer and labor protest, incorporating these constituencies into the New Deal coalition. In Canada, both mainstream parties adopted a *coercive* response, leaving these constituencies politically excluded and available for an independent left coalition. The parties' different approaches manifested in two ways:

1. *The structure of partisan conflict.* In the United States, FDR used the Great Depression to rearticulate the Democratic Party coalition, creating an opening to incorporate labor. In Canada, the Liberal and Conservative parties' responses to the crisis differed only in their degree of repressiveness toward farmer and labor groups. This foreclosed the possibility of incorporation.
2. *The political use of policy.* In the United States, New Deal labor and agricultural policy offered material benefits to some farmer and labor constituencies, while also undermining their independent political power by accentuating intra-class divisions. In Canada, the Liberal and Conservative parties' repression and neglect of farmer and labor constituencies left them excluded and available for an independent left coalition.

The Structure of Partisan Conflict

While the major social, economic, and political issue of the 1930s in both countries was the Great Depression, how the mainstream parties framed the Great Depression, and how they used it to mobilize voters, differed significantly. This shaped the structure of political coalitions and possibilities for ILTP organizing.

The United States

Roosevelt and the Democratic Party used the crisis of the Great Depression to mobilize working-class voters. Through invocations of the "forgotten man," FDR appealed to a working-class identity and positioned the Democratic Party as the "natural" home for such voters. In turn, workers identified the Democratic Party as their party, viewed Roosevelt as their "friend and protector," and voted accordingly. The result by 1940 was what author Samuel Lubell termed "a class-conscious vote for the first time in American history" (Lubell 1941: 9).

Lubell did not get it quite right. Figure 4.1 shows a long, if limited, tradition of class-conscious voting in the United States prior to the New Deal. The real change was the *form* that class-conscious voting took. Instead of being expressed through support for ILTPs, it was expressed via support for the Democratic Party. In identifying the Democratic Party as the appropriate vehicle for expressing workers' class interests, FDR's New Deal coalition eroded ILTP support in the United States.

The link between labor and the Democratic Party was not a foregone conclusion; rather, it was a political project whose outcome was anything but certain. In hindsight, to say that the Democratic Party used the Great Depression to mobilize working-class voters seems obvious. Similarly, FDR's New Deal is often seen as a necessary response to the Great Depression. What is forgotten is the degree to which these actions were contingent outcomes of political battles, and the degree to which historical alternatives were suppressed (Davis 1980b).

At the outset of the Great Depression, the Democratic Party was *not* the obvious home for working-class voters. Groups of workers were reliable sources of Democratic Party votes, but *not* as labor voters. Party allegiances were based on neighborhood, ethnic, or religious ties (Katznelson 1981; Shefter 1986). Union leaders, such as American Federation of Labor (AFL) head Samuel Gompers, often supported Democratic Party candidates, but this support was instrumental, based on a voluntarist philosophy of "reward your friends and punish your enemies" (Greene 1998: 274). It was not uncommon for union leaders to be lifelong Republicans, as was Mine Workers head and CIO founder John L. Lewis (Dubofsky and Van Tine 1977). Labor had not yet forged the alliance to the Democratic Party that was evident in the postwar years (Draper 1989; Greenstone 1969).

Additionally, working-class voters prior to the 1930s had a wider array of political choices. Granted, some were the orthodox Marxist groups that ostensibly made socialist politics "alien" in the United States, as Horowitz put it. At the same time, many were part of a home-grown "labor republican" tradition (Gerteis 2007; Gourevitch 2014; Montgomery 1980). Labor republicans drew on classic American themes of liberty and independence to argue that, even though workers had the formal trappings of freedom and equality, there was, as labor organizer George E. McNeill declared in 1877, "an inevitable and irresistible conflict between the wage-system of labor and the republican system of government" (quoted in Oestreicher 1988: 1259). They claimed that this conflict undermined workers' ability to exercise their rights as citizens in a democratic republic. Even though labor republicanism had waned by the turn of the century, its imprint remained in the distinctly US socialism of Eugene Debs (Salvatore 1982) and the farmer–labor parties of the early twentieth century (Brody 1983; Montgomery 1980; Oestreicher 1988).

ILTP organizing was in a lull in the early 1930s, but unrest was brewing. With unions in disarray and millions out of work, the field was open for more radical political elements, particularly the Communist Party, USA (CPUSA), to play a leading role in organizing working-class resistance to the crisis of the Great Depression (Cochran 1977). These efforts started among the unemployed, with CPUSA-led Unemployed Councils organizing mass marches, rallies, and eviction resistance actions across the country. Forging links with employed workers, they organized events like the Ford Hunger March in Dearborn, Michigan in 1932. There, unorganized autoworkers and the unemployed marched together and faced brutal repression at the hands of the police and Henry Ford's "Service Department" (Baskin 1972; Leab 1967). At the same time, textile strikes in North Carolina and coal strikes in Kentucky among others offered early signals of industrial unrest (Bubka 1970; Milton 1982: 27–29; Salmond 1995).

There were also stirrings among farmers. In the Midwest, a faction of the National Farmers Union (NFU) outraged at plunging commodity prices and rising farm foreclosures met in 1932 in Des Moines, Iowa, to found the Farmers' Holiday Association (FHA). The FHA ignited a series of militant farm strikes across the Midwest that summer which, although unsuccessful, nevertheless placed the farm crisis squarely on the public agenda (Shover 1965). In the South, the Alabama Sharecroppers' Union (ASU) began organizing in 1931, and in the West, ten major strikes involving agricultural workers were recorded between 1930 and 1932 (Gilbert and Howe 1991: 209–210).

The question was how this social unrest would find political expression. It was far from obvious that the Democratic Party would seek to mobilize these aggrieved constituencies.[6] Much of the party leadership was politically to the *right* of President Hoover. They attacked Hoover's handling of the Depression by accusing him not of inaction, but of wasteful deficit spending. Democratic National Committee chair John Raskob sought to downplay economic issues and focus on Prohibition. The party remained fractured along regional, religious, and urban/rural lines.

With Republican support crumbling amid the deepening economic crisis, Democrats knew the 1932 election was theirs to lose. But after decades of defeat, the question of how to forge a winning coalition remained. They had to unite urban progressives, Southern conservatives, and Western populists within the existing party, while also attracting new constituencies. Some in the party thought Roosevelt could do this.

In a May 19, 1932 memo outlining a speech he had written for Roosevelt, strategist Raymond Moley summarized his vision for the candidate's message. Stressing that "these are no ordinary times," he began by criticizing the Republican Party's handling of the Depression, charging that it had "neglected the 'Forgotten Man'" and that "[i]t is the party of reaction." He wrote that "the Democratic Party must present a clear alternative to the people of this country. It must be the party of liberal thought, planned action . . . ." Pointedly, he emphasized that "Democrats must not try to ape the fear stricken reaction of the Republicans," and warned that "[i]f the Democratic Party fails to offer a sound alternative of enlightened liberalism, the opposition may degenerate into wild and exotic radicalism" (Moley 1932).

Rhetorically, the speech built on a Moley-penned speech from April 7 in which Roosevelt first raised the idea of appealing to "the forgotten man at the bottom of the economic pyramid" (New York Times 1932b: 1). In terms of policy, it advocated a contradictory mix of centralized economic planning and budget cutting. The political goal was to attract independents and progressives from all parties, while remaining vague enough not to alienate conservative Democrats.

Roosevelt did alienate some conservative party leaders, including Raskob and 1928 presidential candidate Al Smith. They rejected what they saw as Roosevelt's class-laden rhetoric. Responding to Roosevelt's

---

[6] Accounts of the 1932 campaign taken from contemporaneous newspaper accounts and Cohen (2009); Craig (1992); Freidel (1990); Kennedy (1999); Leuchtenburg (1963); Moley (1932); Schlesinger (1957).

"forgotten man" speech, Smith declared, "I will take off my coat and fight to the end against any candidate who persists in any demagogic appeal to the masses of the working people of this country to destroy themselves by setting class against class and rich against poor" (New York Times 1932a: 6). Smith soon challenged Roosevelt for the presidential nomination. This made the Democrats' stance toward the Great Depression a key point of intra-party conflict, even as some Roosevelt supporters hoped his "forgotten man" appeals would be short-lived (Krock 1932).

Roosevelt withstood Smith's leadership challenge at a hard-fought convention, accepting the Democratic nomination with his promise of a "New Deal" for the US population. Building on Moley's strategy, Roosevelt blended social welfare liberalism with a conservative defense of states' rights and fiscal conservatism in the general election – including commitments to a 25 percent across-the-board cut in federal spending and a balanced budget. The contradictory mix confused Hoover, who accused FDR of being as changeable as "a chameleon on plaid" (quoted in Kennedy 1999: 102). However, Roosevelt's strategy worked, positioning the Democrats, according to a contemporary observer, as "the liberal party, the party which will restore the balance of power between the rich and the poor and bring prosperity to the 'forgotten man' as well as to the Wall Street banker" (Brown 1932: 197). This created an opening for Roosevelt to incorporate labor into the Democratic Party.

US labor was not yet incorporated by 1932, but the process was underway. Roosevelt's efforts to reconfigure the Democratic Party coalition created an opening for labor, but that move was not preordained. Rather, it was the outcome of factional challenges within the party that were amplified in the general election. Those challenges ensured Roosevelt's victory was perceived as a victory for the "forgotten man," creating the conditions to absorb labor into a broadened liberal Democratic Party coalition.

CANADA In Canada, neither the Liberal nor the Conservative Party used the Great Depression to mobilize new constituencies. Both excluded farmer and labor groups, leaving political space for the CCF to establish a new party around a socialist tradition that ran deep in Canada, but had not taken root organizationally.

Key to the CCF's success was its ability to articulate an independent farmer–labor alliance – even though that alliance had real limits (Naylor 2016). Prior to the CCF, worker and agrarian movements had foundered due to internal strife and political repression, or had been absorbed into mainstream parties. Distrust between and within farmer and labor groups had prevented an alliance of both forces (Anderson 1949; Brodie and Jenson 1988: 111–112; Eidlin 2015).

The economic and political situation for Canadian workers and farmers was bleak in the early 1930s (Horn 1984). With its National Policy predicated on tariff-protected industry in its central region and export of primary sector goods from its western and eastern peripheries, the Canadian economy was particularly vulnerable to fluctuations in international markets.[7] The collapse of world agricultural and manufacturing markets in the early 1930s sent the Canadian economy reeling. Regions dependent on export of primary staples had no markets in which to sell, which meant in turn that domestic, tariff-protected industry was deprived of its home market. Wheat prices, which accounted for nearly one-third of exports, fell by two-thirds between 1929 and 1932 (Leacy, Urquhart, and Buckley 1983: Series M228). Mean income for wheat-dependent Prairie farmers fell by an astonishing 94 percent between 1929 and 1934, and by 64 percent for farmers in other provinces. Wages in export industries fell by half, and even wages in domestic, tariff-protected industries fell by 37 percent (Lipset 1950: 123). Retail trade fell by a third between 1930 and 1933 across the country (Lipset 1950: 126).

Worker and farmer organizations were ill-equipped to address the crisis. Union membership stood at 13.1 percent of the nonagricultural workforce in 1930 and was fragmented among US-affiliated TLC unions, national unions affiliated with the All-Canadian Congress of Labour (ACCL), confessional Québécois unions affiliated with the Canadian Catholic Confederation of Labour (CTCC), the Communist-led Workers' Unity League (WUL), and numerous independent unions (Labour Canada 1980; Leacy et al. 1983: Series E175-177). Farmer organizations were internally divided on the question of political action (Anderson 1949; McMath 1995).

As for the government, neither major party grasped the depths of the crisis nor proposed policy solutions (Brodie and Jenson 1988: 148; Owram 1986: 161; Whitaker 1977a: 9–10). So deluded was Prime

---

[7] The National Policy was the Canadian government's economic development policy from Confederation through the early twentieth century. It sought to unite the northern colonies, create a domestic market, and facilitate development of a resource extractive, export-based economy. Its key features were railroad building, settlement incentives, and a tariff on imported manufactured goods (Brodie and Jenson 1988).

Minister William Lyon Mackenzie King that, even two months after being voted out of office due to the crisis, he could still write in his diary that "the country was happy and contented, [manufacturers] & labour alike but for the election propaganda" (King 1930: 237). Both Liberals and Conservatives remained ideologically opposed to government intervention in the economy (Brodie and Jenson 1988; Owram 1986; Whitaker 1977a).

Mackenzie King's Liberal government was replaced in 1930 by R.B. Bennett's Conservatives, but Bennett proved equally unable to address the crisis, doing little beyond increasing tariffs and proposing piecemeal and ineffectual proposals to shore up collapsing farm prices (Brodie and Jenson 1988: 162; Horn 1984: 7–9). Mainly he sought to scapegoat and target those who were organizing the poor and unemployed to demand relief. He revived Section 98 of the Criminal Code, which prohibited a broad array of "seditious" and "subversive" activities, and declared that such subversion was to be stamped out by "the iron heel of ruthlessness" (Jamieson 1968: 217). Under the Code's provisions, as mentioned in Chapter 3, prominent Communists were jailed and the party was banned, activists were deported, radical literature was censored, and meetings were routinely disrupted (Imai 1981; Petryshyn 1982; Roberts 1986). Bennett had groups of idled young male workers rounded up and shipped off to remote work camps. Under Communist/Workers' Unity League leadership, some of these unemployed workers organized the On to Ottawa Trek in 1935, which sought to journey by train from Vancouver in the west to the Canadian capital in search of economic relief. Their trek ended in Regina, Saskatchewan, where the Royal Canadian Mounted Police forcibly dispersed the riders under government orders (Hewitt 1995). Still, the Depression continued.

In a desperate attempt to stay in office, Bennett proposed an economic relief package in 1935 that he labeled a "New Deal." But it was too little, too late, and Mackenzie King's Liberals were returned to office later that year. Even then, as party supporter and McGill professor Brooke Claxton put it, the Liberals seemed "devoid of imagination, ideas, organizing ability and drive" (quoted in Owram 1986: 135). Neither party sought to invoke "forgotten man"-style class appeals, nor propose a new course for the country. Neither party reached out to farmer and labor groups; to the contrary, they tamped down protest even further. There was intellectual and political space for new ideas and new political formations to take hold (Brodie and Jenson 1988: 164; Brown 2007; Horn 1980: 11–13; Owram 1986: 161).

It was in this uncertain environment that the CCF took shape. The initial 1932 meeting in Calgary consisted of four groups: 1) agrarian populists from the United Farmers movements of Alberta, Manitoba, and Saskatchewan; 2) labor unions, represented by Aaron Mosher, head of the ACCL-affiliated Canadian Brotherhood of Railway Employees (CBRE); 3) representatives of local and provincial labor party organizations, along with a rump "Ginger Group" of Progressive and Independent Labour MPs; and 4) a group of Fabian academics from McGill and the University of Toronto, organized as the League for Social Reconstruction (LSR) (Lipset 1950: 114; McHenry 1950: 23–25). While each group had disparate interests and divergent analyses of the crisis and how to solve it, the specific conditions of the Great Depression, and the Canadian state's response to it, created the "common foe" (Penner 1977: 194) necessary to bring them together (Naylor 2016; Thompson and Seager 1986: 230–235).

FARMERS: THE NEED FOR A COALITION   Canadian farmers were no strangers to the politics of protest by the early 1930s. In successive waves dating back to Confederation, generations of farmers had organized to protect themselves from the vagaries of the market. In every instance though, farmer protest had ended in either dissolution or defeat.

The rise and fall of the Progressive Party in the early 1920s, although a failure, nevertheless marked a shift in Canadian farmer organizing. Taking advantage of the mainstream parties' disarray following World War I, it broke a layer of farmers away from the two-party system and left them open to other political alternatives (Archer 1990: 9–11; McMath 1995: 541). The experience of the Progressives showed that a solely farmer-based party could not succeed. What was needed was a reform coalition with urban workers. However, Canadian workers' organization remained in tatters following the violent state and employer counteroffensives of the post–World War I period, making such a coalition impossible in the early 1920s (Kealey 1992; Penner 1977: 174–175).

Farmer organizing continued throughout the 1920s, particularly through the formation of cooperative wheat pools in the Prairie Provinces. This process both revitalized and radicalized the farmers' movement in many areas. In Saskatchewan, the dynamic Farmers' Union merged with its more sedate rival, the Saskatchewan Grain Growers' Association (SGGA) to form the United Farmers of Canada (Saskatchewan Section), or UFC(SS) (Lipset 1950: 99–117; Solberg 1987: 198–202). Together with more moderate United Farmers organizations from Alberta, Manitoba, and Ontario, they would form the base of the agrarian constituency at the founding meeting of the CCF in Calgary.

The crisis of the Great Depression, and ruling parties' feeble response to it, led farmers to turn once again to search for political allies outside the major parties (F.W. Anderson 1949: 146–167). The agrarian groups remained acutely aware of the need for labor allies, but also of labor's weakened state. G.H. Williams, president of the UFC(SS), wrote to a colleague in 1930 that:

> In the political field the farmers have lacked the leadership to a very marked degree and there is no one who has appealed to the people's imagination as the leaders of the people's party in Canada ... Labor in Canada is very poorly organized ... Labor organizations in the industrial East ... is [sic] a local matter rather than a national one. *Were the workers really organized, I believe agriculture is sufficiently organized to carry her end of a political movement, but an agricultural group which ends at Winnipeg [i.e. does not include the industrial East] and has no means of communication with the industrial workers eastward is like an army with its left flank up in the air* ... The situation will not continue forever, and the time will come, having accomplished our economic development, we will carry them into the field of political legislation, but that time is not yet (Anderson 1949: 150, italics added).

One set of allies that was already available was the members of the Parliamentary Ginger Group, led by former Methodist minister J.S. Woodsworth. This group consisted of left-wing Progressive Party MPs who had refused to be absorbed into the Liberals, as well as a handful of Independent Labour MPs. These legislators in turn had connections with a loose network of provincially based labor parties, some of which had begun meeting starting in 1929 as the Western Conference of Labour Political Parties. In 1932, this group invited farmers' organizations to attend their meeting in Calgary, which is when the CCF was formed (Naylor 2016).

Another group in attendance at the Calgary meeting, the intellectuals of the League for Social Reconstruction (LSR), brought into the emerging coalition a new and critical element: a program and unifying vision for the party.

CCF "BRAINS TRUST": THE LEAGUE FOR SOCIAL RECONSTRUCTION
As the Great Depression challenged the legitimacy of capitalism as an economic system, and the mainstream social, political, and economic institutions proved unable to cope with the crisis, some middle-class intellectuals sought a new path forward. Small groups of academics at McGill University in Montreal and the University of Toronto, along

with other intellectuals and professionals, gathered beginning in 1930 to discuss proposals for change. In February 1932 the group drafted a manifesto and christened itself the League for Social Reconstruction (Horn 1980). The manifesto denounced capitalism as "unjust and inhuman, economically wasteful, and a standing threat to peace and democratic government." It called for the establishment of "a new social order which will substitute a planned and socialized economy for the existing chaotic individualism," that will end "the present glaring inequalities" and "eliminate the domination of one class by another" (Horn 1980: 28). The organization set up a branch structure, and members began to join from across the country, far afield from the main Toronto–Montreal axis.

Although initially constituted as a nonpartisan organization, LSR members observed the emergence of the CCF with great enthusiasm. Several members attended the 1932 Calgary meeting as observers, although they did not officially affiliate at the time. Soon there was discussion about affiliation though, and when Woodsworth approached LSR leaders Frank Underhill and Francis Scott about drafting the CCF's manifesto, they readily agreed. The product, unveiled and endorsed at the official founding convention of the CCF in Regina in 1933, became known as the Regina Manifesto. It echoed in many ways the same analysis and proposals contained in the LSR's manifesto. LSR members went on to amplify the themes of the Regina Manifesto in two subsequent books which proved quite influential: *Social Planning for Canada* (1935) and *Democracy Needs Socialism* (1938). LSR members like David Lewis also took on important leadership roles in the new party.

The intellectuals of the LSR provided ideological cohesion to the nascent CCF, and moved it into a position of moral and intellectual authority on the national political scene.[8] In contrast to the United States, where FDR's New Deal offered, if not a coherent program, at least "a feeling of high adventure, a sense of iconoclasm, genuine 'radicalism'" (Horowitz 1968: 32–33), the Canadian ruling parties offered little aside from unimaginative and timid conservatism. The LSR and CCF were able to fill the political and intellectual vacuum and became a pole of attraction. As the cadre of intellectuals who entered the

---

[8] As Naylor (2016) points out, their middle-class technocratic instincts also placed limits on the CCF's political vision, muting the labour socialist vision that animated many of its working-class founders.

Roosevelt administration were dubbed FDR's "Brain Trust," so too were the LSR-affiliated intellectuals of the CCF (Horn 1980: 46–47; Horowitz 1968: 33).

Unlike in the United States, neither Canadian mainstream party used the Great Depression to mobilize new constituencies. Demonized by the Conservatives and ignored by the Liberals, farmer and labor groups were pushed aside, leaving them available for an independent class-based political project.

The Political Use of Policy

In the United States and Canada, the structure of partisan conflict shaped possibilities for different political coalitions. But it was the political use of policy that cemented different outcomes. In the United States, New Deal labor and agricultural policy offered enough material benefits to secure Democratic Party loyalty among certain farmer and labor constituencies. Simultaneously, those policies undermined independent farmer and labor political organizing by exacerbating intra-class divisions. As a result, ILTP support collapsed. In Canada, the Liberal and Conservative parties' repression and neglect of farmer and labor constituencies left them excluded, pushing these groups toward the CCF. As a result, ILTP support increased.

The United States

In 1932, three years into the Great Depression, labor and agrarian unrest was simmering (Bernstein 1969; Gilbert and Howe 1991; Milton 1982; Shover 1965). For its part, US capital was in disarray, both conscious of the extent to which the economic order was in crisis, and unsure of how to restore it. Alexander Sachs, director of economic research for the Lehman Corporation, summed up the general feeling of capitalist malaise in a December 1932 letter to a cabinet member:

We are now faced in the United States ... with the question of the solvency not of any part but of our whole system ... The outstanding feature of this great depression is that the economic order developed since the Reformation and the Great Society developed since the Fall of the Roman Empire have come to be threatened, not by the destructive impact of external or natural forces, but by a spontaneous disintegration from within, because of an incipient failure of collective will and political wisdom, and because of lack of sound ideology on the part of the ruling classes and of the leaders. Now, the economic order in considerable areas in the United States and in the less developed countries is reverting to the feudalism and barter which ensued upon the breakup of the Roman Empire (quoted in Bernstein 1970: 14–15).

It was against this backdrop that Roosevelt took office in early 1933. Frustrated with both major parties' response to the crisis, farmer groups were turning to independent parties. They built on a tradition of agrarian political organizing (Brody 1983; Clemens 1997; Hicks 1933; Postel 2007; Sanders 1999), but they also had promising contemporary examples. In Minnesota, the Farmer–Labor Party regularly won state and federal office throughout the 1920s and claimed the governorship in 1931 (Gieske 1979; Haynes 1984; Valelly 1989). In North Dakota, although it had faded as a movement since its heyday in the 1910s and 1920s, the Nonpartisan League (NPL) remained enough of a force to get their candidate, William Langer, elected governor on the NPL ticket in 1932 (Huntington 1950; Lansing 2015; Morlan 1955). And while they were technically operating within the confines of the Republican Party, Wisconsin Governor Philip LaFollette and the agrarian progressives around him essentially functioned as a third party in state politics (Backstrom 1956; Miller 1982). Meanwhile, industrial workers remained politically up for grabs. There was little sign that either major party would address labor's grievances. Despite his "forgotten man" rhetoric, Roosevelt did not mention unions or collective bargaining rights during his 1932 campaign (Bernstein 1970).

FDR's initial policy solutions to the farm and industrial crises, the Agricultural Adjustment Act (AAA) and the National Industrial Recovery Act (NIRA), profoundly shaped agrarian and industrial class relations, along with ILTP organizing possibilities.

AGRICULTURE[9] The core of the AAA involved imposing production controls in exchange for farm subsidies, financed through a tax on agricultural processors. The goal was to increase farm prices. The focus on farm prices privileged agrarian elites, including large Midwestern corn farmers, Western growers, and Southern planters. Also, lack of federal state capacity meant that monitoring AAA compliance fell to county-level committees organized by the Agricultural Extension Service (AES) and the American Farm Bureau Federation (AFBF). These were dominated by larger, more prosperous farmers. Not only did this aggravate the elite bias in New Deal agricultural policy, but in building up the Farm Bureau, it consolidated a conservative agrarian bloc within the New Deal coalition.

---

[9] Discussion of New Deal agricultural policy draws on the following works: (Clemens 1997; Finegold and Skocpol 1995; Gilbert and Howe 1991; Hansen 1991; Hardin 1952; McConnell 1953; Saloutos 1969; 1974; Sheingate 2000; Young 1993).

At the same time, relief subsidies[10] and a farm foreclosure moratorium appeased family farmers. Reporting on an unsuccessful Farmers Holiday strike, an aide to Federal Emergency Relief Agency (FERA) head Harry Hopkins reported that "one thing that is contributing largely to its failure is the arrival of wheat allotment checks" (quoted in Lowitt and Beasley 1981: 97). Groups representing smaller "dirt farmers," such as the NFU, backed away from their past support for independent farmer–labor politics in favor of a moderate "agrarian liberalism" and integration into the New Deal coalition (Flamm 1994; McMath 1995: 531). By 1938, small farmer groups were wary of breaking from the Democrats. As a Wisconsin farmer leader who had previously backed independent politics editorialized, "I don't believe the rank and file of the farmers are going to give up what they have, no matter how little it is, unless they are cocksure of something better" (Hones 1938: 2).

Meanwhile, AAA policy left some agrarian groups completely excluded. Farm subsidies went only to landowners, leaving out tenant farmers, sharecroppers, and farmworkers. Given that Southern sharecroppers and tenant farmers, both black and white, were subject to Jim Crow–era voting restrictions, and Western farmworkers were often immigrant noncitizens, they were largely disenfranchised and could not serve as a viable base for a farmer–labor party.[11] Although groups like the Southern Tenant Farmers Union (STFU), the Cannery and Agricultural Workers Industrial Union (CAWIU), and the aforementioned Alabama Sharecroppers Union (ASU) led heroic struggles in this period, the combination of planter and grower violence and dynamics of Southern sharecropper dependency ensured their defeat (Alston and Ferrie 1993; Auerbach 1966; Grubbs 1971; Kelley 1990; Southworth 2002).

Overall, FDR's agricultural policies privileged agrarian elites, provided enough benefits to placate small farmers, and excluded tenant farmers, sharecroppers, and farmworkers. This undermined the agrarian constituency for ILTP organizing and encouraged absorption into the Democratic Party. At the same time, the AAA's consolidation of a conservative agrarian bloc within the New Deal coalition limited the reform possibilities of the farmer–labor alliance that did emerge in the United States.

---

[10] Subsidies were offered through the Federal Emergency Relief Agency (FERA), not the AAA.
[11] Nonetheless, Southworth (2002) shows that Southern tenant farmers and sharecroppers successfully organized to demand relief, and support for Socialist and Communist Party candidates was an important part of their protest.

INDUSTRY Section 7(a) of the National Industrial Recovery Act (NIRA), enacted in June 1933, asserted unions' right to organize and bargain collectively. Roosevelt resisted this provision but his advisors convinced him otherwise. Although Section 7(a) had no enforcement mechanism and employers vociferously opposed it, its symbolic value galvanized the labor movement (Bernstein 1970; Milton 1982). The number of strikes doubled between 1932 and 1933, from 852 to 1,672. Importantly, as workers sought to exercise their new rights under NIRA, union recognition replaced higher wages as the primary strike issue (Carter et al. 2006).

When NIRA was declared unconstitutional in 1935, Roosevelt's advisors pressed for a quick replacement policy. This was because, as one aide put it, "[c]ontinued confidence ... in the Administration's sureness of purpose, sense of direction and ability and willingness to act seems absolutely essential ... if the country is not to fall into political chaos between discordant groups of extremists" (Dickinson 1935: 5). The replacement policy was the National Labor Relations Act (NLRA), or Wagner Act, passed in July 1935. It resembled the NIRA but added enforcement mechanisms and banned company-dominated unions. Union membership exploded under the NLRA (see Figure 0.1).

The Wagner Act's perceived benefits drew labor toward Roosevelt. Simultaneously, business elites were abandoning him amid opposition to his proposed Second New Deal reforms. Deprived of business support, FDR reached out to labor for his 1936 reelection campaign (Bernstein 1970; Edelman 1961; Goldfield 1989a; Levine 1988; Milton 1982; Rubin, Griffin, and Wallace 1983). In April 1936, Clothing Workers President Sidney Hillman and CIO head John L. Lewis announced the formation of Labor's Non-Partisan League (LNPL). As Hillman explained to leaders of one of his union's largest locals,

> We hope that the [LNPL] will become a permanent institution. It will not practice non-partisan politics; it will be partisan, a labor program ... [I]n 1936, the League will work for the reelection of Roosevelt; after 1936 it will carry on with its own objectives. It is quite possible that even during 1936, Labor's Non-Partisan Political League while supporting Roosevelt will support candidates neither Democratic nor Republican, when it is possible to support a labor candidate (Hillman 1936a: 5–6).

Labor and the LNPL served as a key source of funds and votes for Roosevelt's landslide reelection. This strengthened labor's ties to the Democratic Party, while weakening its traditional voluntarist position (Bruner 1936; Derber and Young 1961; Greenstone 1969; Stark 1936;

Washington Post 1936). Key labor figures rose to prominence as Democratic Party advisors and officials. For example, Hillman served on the National Industrial Recovery Board, and Teamsters President Daniel J. Tobin was appointed chair of the Labor Division of the National Democratic Campaign Committee (Fraser 1991; New York Times 1936). Although some labor leaders continued to voice support for an independent party, the new era of government access dampened that support in practice. As Hillman (1936b: 1–8) explained to his union's executive board,

> The position of our organization is known: that we are for a labor party[12].... But in the last two years things have happened ... We have participated in making the labor policy of this administration ... We know that [NIRA] meant the revival of our organization ... We know that the defeat of the Roosevelt Administration means no labor legislation for decades to come ... The re-election of Roosevelt will not solve all our problems, but it will give us a breathing spell.

As with New Deal agricultural policy, FDR's industrial policy articulated labor constituencies to the Democratic Party coalition. At the same time, it exacerbated intra-class divisions that hampered class-based organization outside that coalition. Specifically, the NLRA crystallized differences between the AFL and CIO by pitting rival federations against each other over the Act's implementation and interpretation. This drew organizational energy away from ILTP organizing and sabotaged cross-union political collaboration, particularly at the local level. Paradoxically, these divisions solidified the labor–Democrat alliance at a moment when labor seemed poised to organize for independent class politics.

Frustrated with the disconnect between Democratic Party rhetoric defending labor rights and the reality of Democratic governors using state troops to break strikes, workers began organizing local labor parties across the country in the mid-1930s (Davin and Lynd 1979). At the same time, state-level ILTPs were gaining traction:

- In Minnesota, the Farmer – Labor Party expanded its influence, where by 1934 it held not only the governor's office, but both US senate seats and a majority of the Congressional delegation (Gieske 1979; Haynes 1984; Valelly 1989).
- In Wisconsin, the de facto party inside the Republican Party founded the Progressive Party in 1934. Inspired by the legacy of longtime

---

[12] Hillman's Amalgamated Clothing Workers of America (ACWA) was the primary backer of the New York-based American Labor Party (ALP).

senator and 1924 independent presidential candidate Robert M. LaFollette, Wisconsin Progressives took seven congressional seats in 1934. Additionally, LaFollette's son Philip was reelected governor on the Progressive Party ticket, and his brother, Robert Jr., was elected to the US Senate (Backstrom 1956; Miller 1982).

- In Washington and Oregon, Commonwealth Federations inspired by the CCF's example to their north captured their state Democratic Parties and proposed plans for independent political action (Acena 1975; Davis 1980a; Haynes 1986; Lovin 1975).
- In California, Upton Sinclair's EPIC (End Poverty in California) movement mobilized around a socialist program independent of the main political parties, with Sinclair winning 37 percent of the vote in the three-way 1934 California gubernatorial election (Mitchell 1992).

Aiming to create a national farmer–labor party movement, Wisconsin Progressive Congressman Thomas R. Amlie organized the Farmer–Labor Political Federation (FLPF) in 1933, then the American Commonwealth Federation (ACF) in 1935 (Lovin 1971, 1975; Rosenof 1974).

Workers backed FDR in 1936, but labor support for ILTPs grew as post-election frustration with Roosevelt set in. His cuts to public works spending and tax hikes prompted a "Roosevelt Recession" in 1937 that threw millions out of work. His overly even-handed response first to the Flint auto strikes of 1936 to 1937, then to the "Little Steel" strikes in May, 1937, prompted John L. Lewis to remark that "it ill behooves one who has supped at labor's table and who has been sheltered in labor's house to curse with equal fervor and fine impartiality both labor and its adversaries when they become locked in deadly embrace" (Lewis 1937: 6). Many also complained of Roosevelt's foot-dragging with key labor legislation in the new Congress (Bernstein 1970; Manly 1937; New York Times 1937). By that point Lewis was hinting strongly at forming an independent farmer–labor party, stating that "it becomes increasingly imperative that the farm population and millions of workers in industry must learn to combine their strength for the attainment of mutual and desirable objectives" (Lewis 1937: 6).

Amid growing dissatisfaction with Roosevelt, Wisconsin Governor Philip LaFollette announced his plan for a new group, the National Progressives of America (NPA) (LaFollette 1938). But this group went nowhere, folding after the 1938 elections. Most state-based ILTPs and

Amlie's organization also collapsed. Roosevelt ran with strong labor support in 1940, solidifying the labor–Democrat alliance over the course of his third term. By the 1948 election, the CIO was passing resolutions congratulating itself for rejecting "the attempts of the [Henry A.] Wallace third party adherents to divide our movement," confirming "the correctness of our decision to abstain from and discourage any move in the direction of a third party," (Congress of Industrial Organizations 1948: 11–13) and pledging its full support to President Truman (Gieske 1979; Lichtenstein 1982; Lovin 1971; McCoy 1957; Rosenof 1974; Valelly 1989).

To understand this ILTP collapse at a moment when support for independent political action was increasing, we must examine the NLRA's role in crystallizing and exacerbating intra-class divisions. Both labor federations benefited organizationally from the NLRA, growing tremendously in this period (Tomlins 1979). However, certain provisions, particularly those granting the National Labor Relations Board (NLRB) the power to determine appropriate bargaining units, created a focal point that amplified divisions between the AFL and CIO.[13] AFL leaders complained that the Act was biased in the CIO's favor, and vice versa. In their efforts to defeat the CIO at all costs, the AFL allied with employers and conservative farm interests to weaken key provisions of the NLRA and the proposed Fair Labor Standards Act (FLSA) (Davis 1980a; Herrick 1946; Milton 1982).

These inter-federation attacks spurred organizational growth but hampered political organizing. Rival federations had to defend their turf, distracting from efforts to channel workers' dismay with the Democrats into ILTP support. The internecine conflict paralyzed local labor councils, one of labor's main political vehicles. The AFL purged all CIO affiliates from the councils and withdrew support from CIO-sympathetic candidates. This defunded many local and state-level labor party movements. The combination of inter-organizational conflict and resource diversion undermined the base for ILTP support. The Democratic Party was now the only game in town, decisively suppressing ILTP organizing in the United States (Davis 1980a; Fraser 1989; Lovin 1971).

Canada
The Great Depression radicalized Canadian workers and farmers, sparking increased labor and agrarian militancy. But unlike in the United States, increased militancy did not win concessions from the

---

[13] Recall from Chapter 2 that a bargaining unit is a group of workers eligible to bargain collectively and be represented by the same union. AFL unions defined bargaining units by craft; the CIO defined them by industry.

state, nor did it lead ruling parties to propose labor or agrarian policy reforms (Fudge and Tucker 2001; MacDowell 1978). To the contrary, increased militancy provoked further state violence and harassment. Canadian ruling parties' repression and neglect of labor and agrarian constituencies foreclosed the possibility of absorbing them, and created an opening for the CCF to articulate an independent farmer–labor alliance.

POLICY OF REPRESSION AND NEGLECT   Unlike in the United States, Canadian ruling parties' response to the Great Depression excluded farmer and labor constituencies. For farmers, the National Policy continued to aggravate. Its protective tariffs and railroad subsidies benefited Eastern industrialists, bankers, and railroad magnates, while leaving farmers indebted and vulnerable to international price fluctuations. Prime Minister Bennett's policies of increased tariffs and meager farm subsidies closed off more markets to Canadian farmers but did little to bolster collapsed farm prices (Brodie and Jenson 1988; Horn 1984; Neatby 1972).

As for labor, Bennett and his provincial counterparts offered paltry unemployment relief along with an ample dose of state repression. Police and troops broke up strikes, and provincial and federal leaders jailed and deported union organizers and seized union property. King reversed some of Bennett's most egregious anti-labor policies upon returning to office in 1935, but he rebuffed calls for a Canadian Wagner Act. Provincial and federal governments enacted some labor regulations, but nothing approaching the NLRA (Abella 1973; Fudge and Tucker 2001; Petryshyn 1982; Whitaker 1986).

GREATER ORGANIZATIONAL UNITY   The Conservative and Liberal parties' policies not only excluded farmer and labor constituencies, but also unified them. Unlike in the United States, there were no policy reforms to divide agrarian and working-class fractions, creating an opening for the CCF.

By the mid-1930s, the CCF held promise as the organizational expression of a new politics in Canada based on a class alliance of labor and farmers. This was signaled by early electoral strength in British Columbia, where the party polled 31.5 percent of the vote in 1934, and in Saskatchewan, where the CCF was able to form the Official Opposition by 1938 (Lipset 1950: 146; Young 1976: 152).

However, serious problems remained. First, there was the issue of agrarian support. Although United Farmers groups from four provinces attended the 1932 Calgary meeting, three – those from Alberta, Manitoba, and Ontario – had all disaffiliated from the CCF by the end of the decade. They were uncomfortable with the overly socialist rhetoric of the Regina Manifesto, as well as the generally radical orientation of the group in practice. Only the Saskatchewan farmers remained (Naylor 2016).

Second, there was the problem of regionalism. Aside from a few LSR intellectuals in central Canada, the CCF was overwhelmingly Western in composition. It would be difficult to contend on the national political stage without spreading their organization eastward, particularly into Ontario. Additionally, the party's support for a strong federal government did not play well in Quebec, and their lack of outreach to the francophone population ensured that they would remain a marginal political presence in that province.[14] This would have serious consequences for the party's future development (Brodie and Jenson 1988: 170–172; Lewis 1943: 471–472; Naylor 2006, 2016; Penner 1977: 57–59).

Third, and perhaps most importantly, there was the problem of labor representation. Although the party conceived of itself as a farmer–labor alliance – its official name was Cooperative Commonwealth Federation (Farmer-Labour-Socialist) – in reality the "labour" component in the 1930s consisted almost exclusively of regional labor party organizations, not actual trade unions. In fact, organized labor as a whole kept an arms-length relationship with the CCF for the party's first decade (Abella 1973: 73–74; Logan 1948: 433). Most Canadian labor leaders stuck to the old voluntarist model (Fudge and Tucker 2001: 196; Logan 1948: 433). CBRE and ACCL head Aaron Mosher did attend the 1932 Calgary meeting and the 1933 Regina convention, but he did not formally affiliate either organization with the CCF (Barnes 1960: 254–256; McHenry 1950: 163–166). Given the federalized structure of the CCF, there actually was no formalized way for national-level organizations such as trade union federations to affiliate. The CCF did allow union locals to affiliate, but very few had done so by the end of the 1930s (Barnes 1960: 252–253; Palmer 1983: 215). The farmer–labor alliance within the CCF remained more rhetorical than real.

---

[14] This remained a problem until the "Orange Crush" federal election of 2011, where the NDP won fifty-nine of seventy-five seats in Quebec (Laycock and Erickson 2015).

The upsurge in class conflict in the mid-1930s galvanized Canadian labor. Inspired by the CIO upsurge in the United States, Canadian workers organized under the CIO banner, even though US CIO officials were largely unaware of Canadian efforts, let alone supporting them (Abella 1973: 4–5). Despite lacking any equivalent to the US Wagner Act, Canadian union membership spiked by 36 percent between 1935 and 1937 (see Figure 0.1).

Canadian labor's struggle against the state for recognition had a unifying effect. While many of their parent unions in the United States split into rival AFL and CIO federations that engaged in bitter internecine conflicts, Canadian unionists joined together to protest the lack of basic labor rights. The TLC only expelled its CIO unions in 1939, two years after the US split, and then only under direct pressure from the AFL. Importantly, the TLC did not purge local labor councils when it expelled its CIO affiliates, leaving local councils available to affiliate with the CCF (Forsey 1958: 82).[15] Also, unlike in the United States, Canadian CIO unions sought reunification with the TLC from the start. While the TLC rebuffed these overtures, the Canadian CIO did increase labor's organizational unity by merging with Mosher's ACCL to form the Canadian Congress of Labour (CCL) in 1940 (Abella 1973: 33–53; Galenson 1960: 49–72). The Canadian state's refusal to recognize labor rights did not dissolve inter-federation rivalries, but it did mute their political significance.

OPENING FOR CCF[16] While state intransigence to Canadian labor's demands fostered greater organizational unity, it also blocked the possibility of labor's co-optation into the ruling party coalition. It did so by pushing supporters of political voluntarism within labor toward official support for the CCF (Forsey 1958; Horowitz 1968: 166–185).

---

[15] Few local labor councils and local unions actually affiliated with the CCF (Forsey 1958). The important point is that the question of affiliation, as well as the councils' political activity, was less of a flashpoint of contention between the TLC and CCL than it was between the AFL and CIO, where conflict crippled the councils.

[16] This section focuses solely on the affiliation of the CCL with the CCF. The TLC maintained its nonpartisan position throughout this period, although its leaders were sympathetic toward the CCF. At the time of the TLC-CCL merger to form the Canadian Canadian Labour Congress (CLC) in 1956, the two federations compromised on the question of CCF affiliation, leaving the question to the discretion of each union and other subordinate bodies. However, with the transformation of the CCF into the NDP in 1961, the CLC officially affiliated itself with the new party (Forsey 1958; Horowitz 1968).

As the question of labor's role in politics became more urgent, some CCL officials like Mosher and Steel Workers Organizing Committee (SWOC) head Charles Millard advocated closer ties with the CCF. Others, like United Electrical Workers (UE) Canadian President C.S. Jackson, were more influenced by the politics of the Communist Party of Canada (CPC). Still others, most notably CCL Secretary-Treasurer Pat Conroy, continued to insist on labor's traditional nonpartisan role in politics. These three positions coexisted uneasily for several years, until the strains of class conflict and state repression during World War II brought them to a head (Abella 1973: 73–77; 139–140).

Unlike in the United States, where Roosevelt's wartime labor policy successfully absorbed the labor leadership and tightened the labor–Democratic Party alliance (Lichtenstein 1982), King's wartime labor policy further alienated Canadian labor. Recognizing the need to secure labor's cooperation to ramp up wartime production, King's war cabinet issued Order-in-Council PC 2685, stating that workers in war industries should have collective bargaining rights.[17] However, the order was merely advisory, provided no enforcement mechanism, and was universally ignored by employers. Additionally, as with the previous Great War, labor was systematically excluded from any wartime planning agencies, despite repeated entreaties to be included (Fudge and Tucker 2001: 229–230).

This exclusion politicized wartime class conflict. State repression of strikes exposed the gap between the promises of stated government policy and the reality of steadfast government intransigence. At their 1941 convention, as the AFL and CIO agreed to no-strike pledges for the duration of the war, the CCL chose a different path:

The [CCL] believes in the observance of contracts, and is therefore opposed to any strike where it is clearly and definitely established that such a strike is unjustified. The Congress desires to point out, however, that the refusal of employers to accept the Labour policy of the Government with regard to the right to bargain collectively often creates situations beyond the control of the Congress, but for which the Government has the remedy through the enforcement of its stated policy (Canadian Congress of Labour 1941: 23).

---

[17] Just prior to entering the war in September 1939, Mackenzie King invoked national emergency powers under the War Measures Act. This circumvented Parliament and concentrated power in the hands of the federal Cabinet. As such, all wartime legislation was created not by parliamentary procedure, but by cabinet edict (Fudge and Tucker 2001).

Escalating industrial conflict across Canada in 1942 and 1943 created many situations beyond the control of the CCL leadership. The number of strikes nearly doubled between 1941 and 1943 (Labour Canada 1977). King's response was a series of Orders-in-Council further restricting picketing and strikers' civil liberties (Camfield 2002; Fudge and Tucker 2001; Jamieson 1968; MacDowell 1978; McInnis 2002).

Spiraling class conflict led to a breakthrough in political support for the CCF in Ontario, where the Liberal Hepburn government was trying to smash the CCL. The harbinger of change was a February 1942 by-election in the deep Tory blue riding of York South, where CCF candidate Joseph W. Noseworthy defeated former Prime Minister and Conservative Party leader Arthur Meighen (Granatstein 1967). But the real CCF success in Ontario came in the provincial election of August 1943, when the party won thirty-four seats in Parliament, enough to form the Official Opposition (Caplan 1963: 102–104). Reflecting on the results, King wrote in his diary that

> The CCF have made a telling run in all industrial constituencies, particularly where there has been political unrest, making clear the combination of the industrial CIO with the political CCF ... The collapse of the Liberal Party in Ontario ... may be the beginning of the end of the power of the Liberal Party federally ... [Results may] show some members of the government the necessity of being less extreme in their attitude toward labour (King 1943a: 598).

Having branched out beyond their Western agrarian base and allied with the industrial working class in Ontario, the CCF no longer had "its left flank up in the air." It was now a much more serious electoral threat for the Liberals. Their success showed voluntarist labor leaders that a class-based political party could be viable.

Declaring that he was "sick and tired of going cap in hand to Mackenzie King to get Labour policies adopted," Conroy backed a resolution at the 1943 CCL convention recognizing the CCF as the "political arm of labour" (Canadian Congress of Labour 1943: 53–56). Conroy was a reluctant CCF supporter, and only came down decisively in favor of independent political organization at the 1946 convention, after a series of factional disputes with Communist Party supporters. The Liberals' intransigence toward labor and the CCF's demonstration of its electoral viability pushed Conroy and his voluntarist supporters toward CCF affiliation (Abella 1973: 73–80; Canadian Congress of Labour 1946: 79–81). The ruling parties' policies of repression and neglect prevented labor's absorption.

Instead, it allowed the CCF to articulate an independent farmer–labor alliance, paving the way for ILTP support to take root in Canada.

CONCLUSION

The first step in figuring out why union density diverged in the United States and Canada in the 1960s involves explaining one of the most consequential political differences between the two countries: the presence of a labor party in Canada, and its absence in the United States. Existing explanations for union density divergence show how this difference mattered, but take the difference itself for granted. That's because most theories of party systems in the United States and Canada view the difference as all but inevitable, due to long-standing differences in political cultures and electoral institutions.

But there was nothing inevitable about the failure or success of labor parties in the United States and Canada. Even if we grant cross-border differences in political cultures and electoral institutions, the data showed that ILTP support was similar in both countries prior to the 1930s. It was only in the 1930s that the two countries diverged, with ILTP support collapsing in the United States, and taking off in Canada. Existing explanations for differences in US-Canada ILTP support have difficulty accounting for this divergence.

To explain ILTP divergence in the United States and Canada, we must focus on the active role that parties play in shaping political cultures, conflicts, and class divisions – the process of political articulation. In the case at hand, the Great Depression sparked labor and agrarian militancy in both the United States and Canada. The upsurge reshaped politics, as farmers and labor forged political alliances in both countries. But those alliances affected ILTP support differently. In the United States, farmer and labor groups were absorbed into the Democratic Party's New Deal coalition, undermining ILTP support. In Canada, the Liberals' and Conservatives' failure to absorb those groups left space for the CCF (precursor to the NDP) to articulate an independent farmer–labor alliance, bolstering ILTP support.

In both countries, ruling party responses to the Great Depression played central roles in articulating these political coalitions. In the United States, FDR and the Democratic Party pursued a *co-optive* approach. They used class-inflected appeals and policy offerings to incorporate certain farmer and labor constituencies while marginalizing and dividing others. In Canada, the mainstream parties pursued a *coercive* approach. Neither used the Great Depression to mobilize new constituencies, and their policies of repression and neglect foreclosed the possibility of absorbing farmer and labor protest.

Labor's absorption into the Democratic Party in the United States and its alliance with the CCF in Canada also signaled a shift in the structure of political representation in both countries. In Canada, the CCF (later the NDP) created an institutionalized base for the articulation and defense of class-based political demands. Beyond creating a pro-labor political pressure point, it also embedded the class idea more deeply in unions' political and organizational practice. It enabled unions to think of themselves not simply as groups representing their specific membership, but more broadly as *class representatives*. In the United States, labor's absorption into the Democratic Party also absorbed labor into the world of interest group politics. The lack of class-based political representation undermined the class idea, preventing US labor from thinking of, let alone defending its interests in class terms. Instead, it began its postwar transformation into a *special interest,* whose organizational interests would remain institutionally tenuous and politically volatile.

While different processes of political articulation set the two movements on different paths in the 1930s and '40s, those paths had not yet diverged. The second step in explaining why union density diverged in the United States and Canada involves examining the different relationships between labor and the broader political Left that developed in both countries in the postwar decades. This allowed 1960s social movements to have a more transformative effect on Canadian labor than in the United States, which in turn left Canadian unions better prepared to counter the employer offensives of the 1960s and '70s.

5

Repression and Rebirth

Red Scares and Labor's Postwar Identity, 1946–1972

> Why should we worry about organizing groups of people who do not want to be organized? If they prefer to have others speak for them and make the decisions which affect their lives without effective participation on their part that is their right ... Frankly, I used to worry ... about the size of the membership. But ... I just stopped worrying about it, because to me it doesn't make any difference ... The organized fellow is the fellow that counts.
>
> George Meany, President, AFL-CIO (U.S. News and World Report 1972: 27–28)

> We can't leave things the way they are and just be content with talking about them. We must mobilize misery to combat misery, mobilize poverty to combat poverty, mobilize the indebted to combat indebtedness, mobilize the betrayed to end betrayal, mobilize the exploited to vanquish exploitation. And that starts with mobilizing ourselves.
>
> Marcel Pepin, President, CSN (1968: 116)[1]

It would be hard to find two labor leaders more different than George Meany and Marcel Pepin. The first, born in New York in 1894, was the son of a plumber. After learning his father's trade and obtaining his journeyman's certificate, he rose through the union leadership ranks to become AFL president by 1952. He negotiated the merger of the AFL and CIO in 1955, and remained the unified federation's president from its founding until weeks before his death in 1980 (Robinson 1981).

---

[1] Author's translation of: "Il ne faut pas laisser les choses comme elles sont et nous contenter d'en parler. Il faut mobiliser la misère pour combattre la misère, la pauvreté pour combattre la pauvreté, les endettés pour combattre l'endettement, les trahis pour éliminer la trahison, les exploités pour vaincre l'exploitation. Et il nous faut d'abord nous mobiliser nous-mêmes."

Meany embodied conservative US business unionism. With his trademark cigar and gruff manner, he relished his role as a power player in Washington. A staunch racist and anti-Communist, Meany had little time for left-wing social issues or social movements, although he maintained a strong interest in US foreign policy (Buhle 1999; Lewis 2013). He dismissed anti-Vietnam war union activists as "Communist dupes," and he sabotaged progressive Democrat George McGovern's 1972 presidential campaign, which he colorfully described as being overrun by "people who looked like Jacks, acted like Jills and had the odors of Johns" (quoted in Perlstein 2010: 695). He fought for the "organized fellow," but that fight did not extend very far. He once bragged to a group of employers that he had "never had anything to do with a picket line" (Meany 1955: 1).

Meanwhile, Meany's vision for labor remained squarely in the here and now, with no broader horizon. He opined that "the labor movement doesn't work with goals here and there … [I]t just goes forward and it looks for anything that it feels is possible and that the conditions call for" (quoted in *US News and World Report* 1972: 31).[2] He wholeheartedly embraced labor's position as a "special interest group," on a par with General Motors or any other group seeking to maximize its self-interest.

The second, born in Montreal in 1926, was also the son of a blue-collar worker. But where Meany left high school to learn his trade, Pepin continued his education, earning a master's degree in industrial relations from Laval University in 1949. He then went to work for what was at the time called the Confédération des travailleurs catholiques du Canada (CTCC, Canadian Catholic Confederation of Labour), organizing primarily textile and metal workers. In 1961, Pepin was elected general secretary of a de-confessionalized CTCC, now renamed the Confédération des syndicats nationaux (CSN, Confederation of National Trade Unions). He was elected CSN president in 1965, remaining in office until 1976. From 1973 to 1981, he was president of the World Confederation of Labour (WCL). Then, from 1980 until his retirement in 1990, he served as a professor of industrial relations at the University of Montreal (Grondin 2015; Rouillard 1981).

Pepin espoused a brand of militant unionism tied to a transformative socialist vision. He threw the CSN's support behind the social movements of the 1960s and '70s, opening what he called a "second front" for social

---

[2] To be fair, one thing that Meany felt was possible and that the conditions called for was national health insurance. But that speaks more to the scope of what was considered politically possible in the early 1970s than it does to labor's broader political vision.

justice outside the workplace. As part of this, the CSN fought for social housing, the unemployed, and women's rights. Inside the workplace, Pepin's CSN led an explosion of public sector organizing, culminating in the "Common Front" of 1972, a ten-day province-wide general strike involving three labor federations. Pepin not only mobilized hundreds of thousands of workers for that strike, but he continued leading it from jail after the provincial government locked up all three labor federation leaders. Unlike Meany, Pepin had plenty to do with picket lines, and he had a much broader vision for labor's role in society (Pepin 1968; Rouillard 1981). For Pepin, labor was a class representative.

It would be a mistake to read too much into this comparison of two individual labor leaders, as each represents an extreme case. There were more liberal and even radical labor leaders in the United States, and more conservative ones in Canada. Nevertheless, the comparison does tell us something about where things stood with the US and Canadian labor movements in the late 1960s and early 1970s, right at the moment of union density divergence. Meany sat atop a sclerotic AFL-CIO bureaucracy that was uninterested in organizing and actively hostile toward social movements of the period. Pepin led a dynamic labor upsurge that organized tens of thousands of new workers and was bolstered by organic links to social movements. The union density statistics may not have diverged much by this point, but the organizational cultures certainly had.

How did this happen? At first glance, the answer might seem obvious: the combination of McCarthyite Red Scares and the Cold War decimated and delegitimized the US Left,[3] leaving conservative anti-Communist crusaders like Meany in charge of the labor movement. In Canada, postwar Red scares did not have as much of an impact on labor or the Left, leaving more space for militant unionists like Pepin to develop.

This is true as far as it goes. Postwar Red scares and the Cold War did have a more devastating effect on labor and the Left in the United States than in Canada, and this did shape labor–Left relations differently in both countries. In terms of the effect of postwar Red scares, the US story is well known. Fear of alleged Communist "subversives" provided the justification for a widespread, state-sponsored attack on individual leftists and left organizations, including left-led labor unions. The attack dealt a crippling blow to class-based organization in the United States, eliminating or marginalizing a generation of left organizers, activists, and intellectuals,

---

[3] I use the term "the Left" as a catchall term to describe the universe of left-wing parties, organizations, and social movements in both countries.

and leaving a lasting mark on US political culture (Breitzer 2009; Cherny, Issel, and Taylor 2004; Schrecker 1998, 1999). What is less known is that in Canada, a similar fear of Communist subversion, driven by the discovery of actual Soviet spies in the Canadian government, also sparked a wave of political repression, which also included purges of left-led unions (Whitaker 1984; Whitaker and Marcuse 1994). However, by all accounts, these Red scares, while serious, did not approach the level of McCarthyism south of the border.[4]

As for how Red scares affected postwar labor–Left relations, there was a starker divide between the two in the United States compared to Canada. Some layers of the 1960s New Left and labor activists in both countries supported each other's struggles (Levy 1994; Palmer 2009), but the Canadian New Left retained more structural and generational ties to the class politics of the Old Left – often to the dismay of Canadian New Leftists (Gray 1965). As tensions flared between labor and the New Left in the United States over the Vietnam War, racism, and feminism, connections between segments of labor and the New Left in Canada grew stronger.[5] Newly radicalized national unions in both English Canada and Quebec declared their independence from US-based parent unions, linking up with nationalist, feminist, and other social justice movements. In English Canada, this coalition expressed itself politically as the Waffle, an explicitly socialist caucus within the labor-based New Democratic Party (NDP) that mounted a strong challenge for party leadership (Bullen 1983). In Quebec, it culminated in the 1972 Common Front, led by Pepin, among others. Although these movements subsided, they inflected Canadian left politics and social movement organizations with a stronger class character than existed south of the border. The class idea remained more prevalent in Canada (Finkel 1997).

The question we need to ask is why. Why did postwar Red scares have a more devastating effect in the United States, and why did they shape

---

[4] Following Ellen Schrecker (1998: x), I use the term "McCarthyism" broadly to encompass not only the specific acts of Senator Joseph McCarthy, but the entire "anti-Communist crusade ... that dominated American politics during the late 1940s and 1950s."

[5] Recent research shows that popular conceptions of a chasm separating labor and the anti-war New Left, best symbolized by the notorious "hardhat riots" in 1970, were overblown. There were in fact significant anti-war currents within the labor movement, and many workers disapproved of the pro-war "hardhat" demonstrations. Nonetheless, the riots did represent a strong pro-war current within US labor, certainly within influential layers of the union leadership. Unlike in Canada, these more conservative currents held broader sway over labor's political direction and over its relations with New Left organizations. For more on labor–New Left relations, see Levy (1994); Lewis (2013).

postwar labor–Left relations the way they did? Again, the answer might seem obvious. According to scholars of American political culture, McCarthyism tapped into a deep-seated conservative individualism, tied to a characteristically American suspicion of elites (Fried 1997; Schrecker 1998). This gave the Left at best a tenuous foothold in American political culture, temporarily bolstered by the crisis of the Great Depression and the New Deal (Lipset 1996). While McCarthyism's overzealous trampling of individual liberties may have been an overreach, its attack on the Left was a reassertion of classic American individualism over an inherently "foreign" collectivist ideology. Moreover, it fit into a broader history of Red scares and left repression going back well into the nineteenth century (Friedman 1991; Shefter 1986). As for Canada, it would make sense that postwar anti-Communist Red scares would not have as pervasive and destructive an impact on the political Left as in the United States, given its more collectivist political culture and greater amenability to socialist ideas. Socialism and the class idea were simply more "at home" in Canada.

Putting McCarthyism in historical perspective challenges this narrative. As we saw in Chapter 4, the Left had a similar organizational foothold in both countries prior to the 1930s, based in the unions and the broader working class. Labor and the Left faced similar levels of repression too. Governments and employers on both sides of the border frequently deployed military, police, and private mercenary forces to tamp down Left and labor militancy. Indeed, prior to World War II, both countries followed a similar pattern: explosions of labor and Left movements, followed by violent state and employer repression, followed by labor and Left rebirth.

That pattern was broken after World War II. While McCarthyism was in one sense just another chapter in the history of labor and Left repression, it marked a point of divergence for the United States and Canada. In the United States, McCarthyism differed from previous episodes of labor and Left repression in two critical respects. First, it severed the link between the labor and the Left. As a result, the New Left that emerged in the 1960s differed from previous Left movements in its lack of a strong base in the unions and the working class. Second, it severed the link across Left generations. Whereas previous Left movements drew inspiration, leadership, and personnel from past generations, much of the New Left defined itself in opposition to the class politics of the Old Left. In Canada, the postwar pattern was more similar to previous waves of Left repression and rebirth. Red scares hobbled the Left and weakened labor, but they did not sever the link between labor and the Left. As a result, the Canadian New Left retained closer ties to labor, lending Canadian labor a stronger social movement character.

What made McCarthyism such a turning point between the United States and Canada? It was a consequence of the different processes of political articulation that we examined in Chapter 4: labor's absorption into the Democratic Party coalition in the United States and its alliance with the Cooperative Commonwealth Federation (CCF) in Canada.

In the United States, labor's absorption into the New Deal coalition left the Communist Party, USA (CPUSA) as the closest approximation of a mass class-based political organization. However, its wartime "Popular Front" reorientation away from class politics and toward enthusiastic enforcement of the US government's wartime production policy, particularly the no-strike pledge, alienated the CPUSA from its working-class base. This left it isolated and vulnerable to attack in the postwar period. McCarthyism exacerbated this divide between the Left and the organized working class. It mobilized state power to dismantle left-led unions via the Taft-Hartley Act, Congressional investigations, and prosecution of suspected Communists. The *prior* collapse of independent class-based political organization described in Chapter 4, combined with the political use of policy, enabled McCarthyism to have the particularly devastating impact it did, driving a wedge between labor and the Left, and decimating a generation of Left leadership. The result was a labor movement purged of its best organizers, with conservative leaders like George Meany left in charge to manage its decline.

In Canada, the establishment of the CCF left *two* competing mass working-class parties, the CCF and the Communist Party of Canada (CPC). The anti-Communist CCF leadership offered itself to the governing Liberals as a "loyal Left," and the Liberals in turn delegated to them the task of policing the rest of the postwar Left. In this capacity, the CCF leadership attacked and purged Communist labor unions and political opponents with gusto. But recognizing that Cold War anti-Communist hysteria could easily be turned against them, the CCF leadership also took steps to ensure that it did not get out of hand. For their part, the Liberals sought to keep persecution of suspected Communists centralized under their control and avoid the kind of public spectacle they observed in the United States. Crucially, the Liberals resisted employer demands for a Canadian Taft-Hartley Act, which allowed Communist-led unions in Canada to persist organizationally even after they had been expelled from the major Canadian labor federations. Both the CCF and Liberal parties' interest in retaining political control mitigated the effects of the postwar Red scares in Canada. Crucially, the CCF's (later the NDP's) persistence as a class-based political organization maintained an infrastructural base for class politics through the difficult early years of the Cold War. It ensured that the link between labor and the Left, while strained, was not severed. As the New Left emerged in the early 1960s, it did so in connection with the NDP, although that connection was often tense. As the New Left developed and radicalized throughout the decade, the NDP provided an arena for political conflict to unfold and to connect different constituencies organizationally to labor. The result was a more class-inflected New Left and a labor movement more committed to mobilizing, with prominent leaders like Marcel Pepin.

WHAT MADE MCCARTHYISM DIFFERENT?

Echoing a commonly held view, Ellen Schrecker (1998: x) described McCarthyism as "the most widespread and longest lasting wave of political repression in American history." Even though its last vestiges petered out over six decades ago, the anti-Communist crusade of the late 1940s and 1950s left an indelible impression on American political culture.

Why did McCarthyism have this pervasive, lasting influence? The standard explanation is that it was yet another chapter in a history of hostility to Communism and class politics in the United States. As narratives of American exceptionalism are quick to point out, radical left politics have held at best a tenuous foothold in US political culture. Even at the height of the CPUSA's influence, party membership never exceeded much more than 100,000 nationwide. Given the long-standing US tradition of state repression of left-wing political movements following wars, it was likely that some sort of anti-Communist backlash would have developed after World War II. Adding to that tradition, the onset of the Cold War, which tied Communism to the new Soviet enemy, made such a backlash all the more inescapable (Preston 1994; Shefter 1986; Voss 1993).

But there was something different about McCarthyism. Compared to previous waves of left repression in the United States, McCarthyism stands out in three ways:

First, its lasting effect on US political culture. While other previous and subsequent waves of political repression put civil rights at risk, ruined lives and careers, and narrowed political debate, none other has approached McCarthyism's iconic space in the public lexicon (Caute 1979; Schrecker 1998).

Second, its effect on the relation between the Left and the working class. Prior to McCarthyism, left-wing political movements were grounded in either the agrarian or working classes (Dubofsky 1969; Shannon 1967). While systematic detailed membership data for left political organizations is difficult to obtain, data that do exist are illustrative. For example, a 1908 survey of the US Socialist Party's membership revealed that over 60 percent identified their occupation as either "craftsman" or "laborer," and an additional 17 percent identified themselves as farmers. Only 4.7 percent identified as "professionals" (Pischel 1909). Postwar left-wing movements lacked a strong working-class base. This led to leftist ideologies being identified largely with urban intellectual elites and *counterposed* to the working class, a fact deftly exploited by a nascent neoconservative movement in the latter part of the twentieth century (Perlstein 2010). At the same time, certain strata of postwar left intellectuals concluded that the working class, far from being the social base for left politics, was in fact a conservative constituency, salvageable only by an enlightened union leadership (Harrington 1972).

Third, the generational divide it created on the Left. Prior to McCarthyism, nascent left movements drew leadership and mentorship from generations of activists involved in past defeated movements. McCarthyism created a generational gap between the "Old Left" of the 1930s and '40s and the "New Left" of the 1960s and '70s.[6] As former

---

[6] Following John McMillian and Paul Buhle (2003: 5), I use a more focused definition of the New Left in this chapter as a "mostly white student movement that promoted participatory democracy, crusaded for civil rights and various types of university reforms, and protested against the Vietnam War." This is purely for analytical clarity, as the white student Left and the black-led civil rights movement were intertwined throughout the 1960s and '70s. A wide array of scholarship on the civil rights movement has shown that Black communities were better able than their white counterparts to preserve intergenerational continuities in the leadership of their movement. But even there, the character of the leadership shifted as a result of McCarthyism. Much of what is now known as the "early civil rights movement" of the 1930s and '40s was based in the Communist Party and several key CIO unions. However, the purges of Communist unions, the decimation of the Communist Party, and the failure of the CIO to organize the US South dissolved the nascent "urban/ labor/left/civil rights coalition" that was forming, and meant that the postwar civil rights movement was largely deprived of a working-class base. Instead, the organizational base of the movement was the black church, although certain individual labor and left leaders from the previous period certainly played central roles (Goldfield 1997; Isaac and Christiansen 2002; Korstad and Lichtenstein 1988).

Students for a Democratic Society (SDS) activist Michael Schwartz explained,

> When the white student movement started out in the early sixties, the Civil Rights movement inspired us, but we didn't have anyone to tell us how to organize or even whom to organize. The left was a barren wasteland; there was no "Old Left." The progressives from the 30s or 40s, if they were around, were invisible and inactive, probably terrified. McCarthyism had just wiped everything out. It really felt like we were starting from scratch (Schwartz 2011).

This is not to say that there was no generational continuity at all between the Old and New Lefts in the United States. To the contrary, as historians such as Maurice Isserman (1993) and Peter Levy (1994) have shown, some Old Leftists and labor leaders played important if underappreciated roles in the formation of the New Left. However, these accounts also illustrate two major differences between Old/New Left collaboration and previous cross-generational left collaborations. First, at the organizational level, activists in previous defeated movements joined the organizations of the nascent movements; old Knights of Labor (KOL) later showed up as Socialists and "Wobblies," as members of the Industrial Workers of the World (IWW) were called. They in turn later showed up in the CPUSA and CIO. By contrast, Old Leftists and New Leftists kept to their own distinct organizations. Second, at the political level, with a few exceptions, the Old Leftists that engaged with the New Left had largely abandoned independent class politics, either integrating with the Democrats or steering clear of party politics entirely.

How do we explain these distinguishing characteristics of McCarthyism? One plausible explanation would point to the particularities of the Cold War and the socioeconomic changes of the postwar world. According to such an account, the reality of the Soviet Union as a competing nuclear power gave the threat of Communist subversion more bite, while economic expansion, suburbanization, and the rise of "post-industrial society" reduced the political salience of class issues, thus allowing cultural and generational conflicts to come to the fore (Bell 1973; Dahrendorf 1959).

The Canadian comparison raises questions for such an account. Canada shared with the United States similar past cycles of left repression and rebirth. Likewise, its postwar government feared the threat of Soviet subversion. Furthermore, Canada experienced a similar postwar economic expansion, along with similar sociocultural shifts, as occurred south of the border. And yet, postwar Red scares did not have as pervasive

Similar Histories of Left Repression

We see similar trajectories in both countries in the pre-McCarthyism period. The birth pangs of North American industrial capitalism in the late nineteenth century gave rise to a variety of forms of agrarian and working-class protest on both sides of the border. Organizations like the Knights of Labor, Patrons of Industry, and others organized in both the political and economic realms, creating vibrant movements that challenged the dominant political forces of the day. While these movements heaved under the weight of a variety of internal contradictions, state and employer repression were key to their ultimate demise in both countries (Fine 1928; Fink 1983; Kealey and Palmer 1982; 1986; Palmer 1983; Voss 1993).

As working-class protest took on a more explicitly socialist cast in the late nineteenth and early twentieth century, so too did it attract more attention from state investigators. In both countries, immigration officials harassed and deported foreign-born radicals as "undesirables." In both countries, federal police forces monitored suspected "seditious" activity, including infiltrating radical organizations, opening personal mail, mounting prosecutions for criminal conspiracy, and more.[7] Government surveillance and repression intensified with the onset of World War I. The Canadian government even arrogated to itself extraordinary wartime powers of censorship, arrest, and detention, which it used on suspected socialists and radical labor organizers. The massive postwar strike wave of 1919 triggered a major backlash and Red scares in both countries that were exemplified by the execution of the Palmer Raids, the smashing of the Seattle General Strike in the United States, and the dismantling of the Winnipeg General Strike in Canada (Heron 1998; Kealey 1992; McCormack 1977; Penner 1977; Preston 1994).

Government repression of leftists and labor activists in both countries intensified once again during the Great Depression, as outlined in the previous chapter (Davin and Lynd 1979; Hewitt 1995; Petryshyn 1982; Roberts 1986; Zieger 1995). It continued with the onset of World War II, as the US government used the 1940 Smith Act to arrest and prosecute

---

[7] In the United States, this was the Federal Bureau of Investigation (FBI). In Canada, it was the Dominion Police and Royal Northwest Mounted Police (RNMP), later known as the Royal Canadian Mounted Police (RCMP).

What Made McCarthyism Different? 201

hundreds of Trotskyist and Communist leaders and activists (Haverty-Stacke 2016; Kohn 1994). In Canada, as had happened in World War I, the federal government claimed extraordinary authority under the War Measures Act, replacing rule by Parliament with rule by Privy Council decree. In 1940, the government declared the Communist Party illegal and interned suspected Communists (Whitaker 1986).

Similar Postwar Communist Threat

As in the United States, the Canadian government feared internal Communist subversion after World War II. Indeed, actual Soviet espionage was first uncovered in Canada. In September 1945, Soviet cipher clerk Igor Gouzenko defected, revealing that a network of Soviet spies had infiltrated several Canadian government agencies (Black and Rudner 2006). The Canadian government convened an official investigation under the auspices of the awkwardly-titled "Royal Commission to Investigate the Facts Relating to and the Circumstances Surrounding the Communication, by Public Officials and Other Persons in Positions of Trust of Secret and Confidential Information to Agents of a Foreign Power," commonly referred to as the Kellock-Taschereau Commission. The commission named at least twenty-two suspected Soviet spies, including thirteen civil servants. While only eleven of twenty trials ended in convictions, several on lesser charges, the proceedings brought the "Red Menace" to the fore politically. Among those convicted and jailed was Fred Rose, the only Communist member of Parliament (Whitaker and Marcuse 1994: 56–72).

As in the United States, the postwar Red scare led to political attacks and purges throughout Canadian society (Whitaker and Marcuse 1994: 161–243). Importantly for our purposes, this wave of attacks included a purge of Communist-dominated labor unions from the Canadian Congress of Labour (CCL) and the Trades and Labour Congress (TLC) that mirrored a US purge of Communist-dominated unions from the Congress of Industrial Organizations (CIO) (Abella 1973).

But despite similar histories of left repression, and similar postwar Communist threats, what is striking is the different effects that postwar Red scares had in both countries. Without diminishing the real impact that Red scares had on the lives of many Canadians, the levels of hysteria associated with McCarthyism simply did not reach the same level in Canada. As Reg Whitaker and Gary Marcuse, the preeminent scholars of the Cold War in Canada, wrote,

It is generally accepted that there was not a great deal of McCarthyism, as such, in Canada. There was no Senator McCarthy, no House Un-American Activities Committee. There were would-be McCarthys, but they misfired ... [T]here was a great deal of anti-Communism, but it was more likely to be *official* anti-Communism, sanctioned by the state and contained within the "legitimate" boundaries of state-sponsored activities (Whitaker and Marcuse 1994: 282).

Additionally, at a generational level the legacy of the Canadian Red scares was not as lasting. Culturally, McCarthyism has become an integral part of the US (and Canadian) political lexicon that remains salient to this day. By contrast, the postwar Red scares in Canada are largely of interest to historians of the period. Whereas the scholarship and popular writing devoted to the study of McCarthyism is vast, the historiography related to Canada's place in the Cold War is thin. Organizationally, the continued presence of the CCF created a generational link between the Old Left of the 1930s and the New Left that was to emerge in the 1960s (Isitt 2011; Wiseman and Isitt 2007).

Finally, and most importantly for our purposes, the Canadian Red scares did not erode the base for class politics. As shown in the previous chapter, electoral support for class-based political parties (primarily the CCF, and later the NDP) expanded in the postwar period. While the CCF experienced a period of decline in the 1950s, leading to its reconstitution as the NDP, it remained a legitimate and viable political party.

Relative both to previous waves of political repression in the United States, as well as to Cold War Red scares in neighboring Canada, McCarthyism stands out for its lasting generational and political effects. Why then was McCarthyism as pervasive and lasting as it was in the United States?

EXPLAINING DIVERGENT RED SCARE EFFECTS

To understand the lasting generational and political effects of McCarthyism, it is not enough simply to look at Cold War paranoia or deep-seated fears of ostensibly foreign socialist ideologies. Whatever real fears of socialism existed in the United States, they did not prevent the reemergence of class-based political organizing in the pre–World War II period as they did in the postwar period. And the Canadian example shows that it was possible to have Cold War anti-Communist witch hunts without the same pervasive and lasting effects that McCarthyism had on US political culture and organization.

What amplified the effect of McCarthyism compared to postwar Red scares in Canada was the way that parties and policies reconfigured the relationship between the Left and the working class differently in both countries. In terms of parties, the critical factor was the presence or absence of a non-Communist independent Left party. As for state policies, the key factor was the presence or absence of policy regulating Communist participation in labor unions.

The United States: Left Party Absence with Anti-Communist Policy

The Democrats' absorption of independent labor and agrarian parties in the 1930s left the CPUSA as the most prominent remaining left independent political organization. This absorption had two consequences. First, in the broader political culture, it linked the idea of independent left politics with CPUSA-style Communism. As Communism came to be identified as the mortal enemy, this further delegitimized independent left politics more generally. Second, within the CPUSA, the party's "Popular Front" strategy of the late 1930s and 1940s prioritized political unity with mainstream "bourgeois" parties to defeat fascism over independent class politics. Rhetorically, this led the CPUSA to deemphasize its own class politics in favor of a broad "progressive" coalition (Post 1996).[8] Organizationally, it led the CPUSA to lend enthusiastic support to governmental wartime production policy, including enforcing no-strike pledges in key industries and assembly line speedup. This alienated the CPUSA's working-class base. Although party membership expanded during the war, exceeding 100,000 members, the class composition of the party shifted as it tempered its class-based appeal (Glazer 1961: 114–116). Thus, the absorption of the non-Communist left and the politics of the Popular Front narrowed the political space for class politics, while also driving a wedge between the party and the organized working class (Glazer 1961; Lichtenstein 1982; Post 1996; Schrecker 1998; Starobin 1972).

---

[8] The CPUSA's Popular Front strategy was part of an international strategy developed and promulgated by the Soviet Comintern. Thus, Communist parties around the world adopted this same strategy, but not all suffered the same loss of legitimacy. Even in the case of countries like Canada where the CPUSA was delegitimized, it did not lead to the same loss of legitimacy for independent class politics more generally. The particularly devastating consequences of the CPUSA's Popular Front strategy in the US context resulted from the CPUSA being isolated as the sole representative of independent left politics. Without a non-Communist independent left, the postwar anti-Communist purges virtually eliminated independent left political organization in the United States as a whole.

Policy-wise, the passage of the anti-union Taft-Hartley Act in 1947 further deepened the split between labor and the Left. Its loyalty oath provision required all union officials to sign affidavits certifying that they were in no way affiliated with the Communist Party or any related organization. Those unions whose officials refused to sign such affidavits were denied legal recognition and the ability to claim protections under Section 9(h) of the now-revised National Labor Relations Act (NLRA). This created a mechanism not only to purge Communist-led unions from the main labor federations, but to deprive them of institutional resources and undermine their organizational legitimacy. Once the CIO expelled Communist unions from its ranks in 1949, it chartered new non-Communist unions to raid the membership of the expelled unions. Using Section 9(h), these non-Communist unions were able to petition for representation elections at firms represented by Communist-led unions where the incumbent union did not appear on the ballot. As a result, major Communist-led unions such as the United Electrical Workers Union (UE), the Farm Equipment Workers (FE), the United Mine, Mill, and Smelter Workers of America (UMMSWA), and the International Fur and Leather Workers Union (IFLWU) saw their memberships decimated. Most were forced to merge into larger, non-Communist unions, and those that did not were reduced to shells of their former selves. In either case, state policy enabled anti-Communists to forcibly remove left leadership from their positions of power within the organized working class.[9] This institutionalized split undermined the working-class base that had sustained past left-wing political movements, leaving what remained of the Left isolated and politically vulnerable. Also, in expelling Communists from the labor movement, US labor lost many of its best organizers and staunchest anti-racist fighters. This weakened labor's willingness and ability to organize across racial lines, further undermining unions' long-term strength (Stepan-Norris and Zeitlin 2003).

Canada: Left Party Presence without Anti-Communist Policy

In Canada, the ruling Liberals were firmly committed to combating the perceived Communist menace. At the same time, they looked south to the United States with alarm and consciously sought to avoid a descent into McCarthyite paranoia. In an effort to balance fighting Communism and the potential social destabilization of McCarthyism, the Liberals centralized

---

[9] The International Longshore and Warehouse Union (ILWU) was a notable exception to this trend (Kimeldorf 1988).

control over the management of Canadian Red scares. As one senior official put it, the goal was "to strike a happy medium between the dangers of unrestricted witch-hunting, on the one hand, and a too casual approach to the security problem on the other" (quoted in Whitaker and Marcuse 1994: 187). Unlike in the United States, no maverick political entrepreneurs were able to take up the anti-Communist crusade as their own. Those who tried, such as Opposition Conservative leader George Drew, found themselves marginalized and outmaneuvered by the Liberals on the anti-Communist issue.[10] Additionally, Canada's security service, the RCMP, remained under the supervision and control of the Privy Council[11] – unlike in the United States, where J. Edgar Hoover was able to achieve a degree of bureaucratic autonomy and use his investigatory powers to indulge his "Communists under every bed" fantasies (Schmidt 2000; Theoharis 2002).

For its part, the CCF leadership offered itself as a "loyal left" to the ruling Liberals, and it took on the role of policing the rest of the Left and the labor movement. This weakened those segments of the Left targeted by the Red scares, but also kept the scope of Red scares in check. The Liberals did not want to lose control over the process, and the CCF leadership knew that anti-Communist witch-hunts could be used against them if taken too far (Whitaker and Marcuse 1994: 269–272).

As for the Communist Party of Canada (CPC), it pursued a similar wartime Popular Front policy as in the United States – even though the federal government banned it in 1940. This included support for a no-strike pledge, production speedup, and ironically, the same Liberal King government that had banned them. These positions placed CPC policy to the right of the mainstream Canadian labor leadership, which refused to take a no-strike pledge for the war and threw its support behind the CCF in 1943.[12] As in the United States, the CPC's Popular Front policy undermined its ability to articulate class-based politics while also alienating its base in the

---

[10] While a deeper analysis is beyond the purview of this chapter, a central reason for Drew's inability to mobilize politically around the anti-Communist issue was the impossibility of a conservative anti-Communist coalition between Drew's Protestant, Anglo Conservatives and those of the Catholic, Francophone Union Nationale in Quebec. Here the two parties' commitments to old national cleavages proved too deep to overcome (Whitaker and Marcuse 1994).

[11] The Privy Council is the executive body made up of the prime minister and top-level cabinet ministers, assisted by its own staff of career civil servants.

[12] Neither Canadian labor federation, the Trades and Labour Congress of Canada (TLC) and the Canadian Congress of Labour (CCL), took a no-strike pledge during the war. However, as outlined in Chapter 4, only the CCL officially endorsed the CCF, although the party did enjoy support among certain layers of the TLC leadership.

working class. However, the presence of the CCF in Canada meant that the marginalization and missteps of the CPC did not fundamentally undermine the basis for class politics in Canada as they did in the United States, nor did they drive as much of a wedge between the political Left and the organized working class.

Crucially, the Liberals rebuffed employer entreaties to enact a Canadian version of the Taft-Hartley Act. King's successor as prime minister, Louis St. Laurent (also a Liberal), emphatically declared that "No one will ever convince me Canada needs a Taft-Hartley Act ... I believe the right to organize is a good thing, not only for labour but also for society" (quoted in Whitaker and Marcuse 1994: 195).

The lack of a Canadian equivalent to Taft-Hartley meant that the purge of Communist-led unions had a different effect than in the United States. There was a vicious and systematic purge of Communist-aligned unions and their leaders from the CCL, just like in the United States. The purged unions included many of those purged in the United States, including UE, FE, UMMSWA, and more. The key differences were that 1) those leading the purges were CCF partisans, as opposed to Democratic Party–aligned liberals; and 2) the lack of any equivalent to Taft-Hartley Section 9(h) allowed Communist-led unions to survive, albeit in weakened form, even after being purged from the major labor federations (Abella 1973).[13] Together with the survival of the CCF, this preserved a class-based left political infrastructure in Canada, helping to shelter a "militant minority" that sustained a link between the Left and the working class, and served as a generational bridge between the Old and New Lefts (Isitt 2011).

MCCARTHYISM AND THE NEW LEFT

How then did these different legacies of postwar Red scares influence the development of the New Left in both countries? The 1960s New Left looked very similar in the United States and Canada in many respects.

---

[13] It remains an abiding contradiction of both the CPUSA and CPC that, in spite of their Popular Front rhetoric and action in support of policies that undermined class politics, particularly during the war, Communist-led unions nonetheless remained some of the most militant working-class organizations in the postwar period. As Stepan-Norris and Zeitlin (2003) show for the US case, this contradiction was often the result of a disconnect between party officials rigidly enforcing the party line and CPUSA-influenced union leaders who remained committed to workplace militancy. This contradiction is important for understanding how the party's policies could serve to undermine the basis for class politics, while the destruction or survival of CPUSA-led unions remained a crucial factor for preserving an organizational infrastructure for class politics in the postwar period.

Both emerged out of youth discontent on college campuses, in reaction to the fears of nuclear holocaust, and out of a desire to break out of the stifling conformity that had characterized the postwar period. Both counterposed themselves to an "Old Left," by which they meant the class-based communist and socialist movements of the prewar period. As with previous left movements, there was also significant cross-border cross-pollination, with Canadian organizations drawing inspiration and organizational strength from their US counterparts (Kostash 1980; Levitt 1984; Milligan 2014; Palmer 2009).

But there was an important difference between the Canadian and US New Lefts: the Canadian New Left grew up in the face of an Old Left that was still very much an organizational presence. Although weakened by the effects of the Cold War, the CCF had managed to establish itself as a political presence, reconstituting itself as the New Democratic Party (NDP) in 1961.[14] Additionally, the less effective anti-Communist purges in Canadian unions left in place a "militant minority" of independent left-wing labor leadership. By contrast, the US New Left grew up against an Old Left that, by that time, was more of an idea than a reality. As Schwartz termed it in the quote above, the perception among US New Leftists was that "the Left was a barren wasteland." While subsequent historical research has challenged the extent of this barrenness, the perception among New Leftists at the time was real (Breines 1989; Jezer 1982).

The New Left and Electoral Politics

We can see this cross-border difference in the discussions within the New Left in both countries surrounding their relationships to the major parties. The US New Left was decidedly critical of the structure of the US party system. The 1962 Port Huron Statement of the Students for a Democratic Society (SDS), widely regarded as a seminal statement of the US New Left, proclaimed that

The American political system is not the democratic model of which its glorifiers speak. In actuality it frustrates democracy by confusing the individual citizen, paralyzing policy discussion, and consolidating the irresponsible power of military and business interests (SDS 2015: 246).

---

[14] A key part of the transformation from the CCF to the NDP involved strengthening the explicit relationship between the party and the Canadian Labour Congress (CLC), the labor federation that emerged out of the 1956 merger of the TLC and CCL.

The US New Left rejected the idea of the Democratic Party as a primary vehicle for social change. It sought to develop a new politics independent of the two-party system, based on a coalition of students, the urban poor, and African Americans (Gray 1965). But with the question of a labor party far removed from the US political landscape by this point, the most that SDS was able to propose in terms of concrete political options was the establishment of a genuine two-party system characterized by substantive political differences between the parties. The hope was for an ideological party realignment, with the conservative Southern Dixiecrats expelled from the Democratic Party, leaving the party as a true progressive coalition. However, SDS's experience working with the Mississippi Freedom Democratic Party and their failed attempt to be seated at the 1964 Democratic Convention disabused many New Leftists of the possibility of working within the Democratic Party (Gosse 2005; Heideman 2016).

The Canadian New Left also grappled with the question of how to relate to electoral politics, but their challenge was different from that of their US counterparts. The presence of the NDP fundamentally altered the terms of the discussion. Organizationally, the NDP provided an incubator for the development of the Canadian New Left. While hard numbers are difficult to find, both contemporary reports and more recent scholarship note that a large portion of the Canadian New Left emerged out of the NDP youth wing (Gonick 1965; Gray 1965; Palmer 2009). The relationship between Old and New Leftists within the NDP was contentious. Some Canadian New Leftists envied the political independence that the US New Left enjoyed, seemingly unencumbered by ties to stifling official party structures (Gray 1965). Nonetheless, the NDP created an organizational and generational link between the Old and New Lefts, and between the Left and the organized working class, that was largely absent in the United States. As the Canadian New Left sought to emulate its southern neighbors' efforts to reinvent social relations and develop a new politics in the 1960s, it did so while remaining tied to an organizational infrastructure based on class politics.

The "Turn to the Working Class"

The political and organizational consequences of this key US–Canada difference became apparent over the course of the 1960s, as the New Lefts in both countries radicalized.

In the United States, New Left activists grew increasingly frustrated with their inability to end the war in Vietnam, to address deep economic inequalities, to move beyond the formal racial equality of the Civil Rights Act, and more. As a result, elements within the New Left began to question their ability to effect meaningful social change as a largely student-based movement. For a tiny but memorable minority, the solution to students' relative lack of "social weight" involved rejecting US society and turning to individualized acts of violence, organized as Weatherman (Jacobs 1997). For many, the solution was a political rapprochement with the Democratic Party via the Robert Kennedy and Eugene McCarthy presidential campaigns, although the Chicago police riot at the 1968 Democratic Convention underscored the limits of such an approach (Breines 1989; Gitlin 1987; Katsiaficas 1999).

But for a small but significant segment of the US New Left, the solution was to return to the decidedly Old Left idea of the centrality of the working class as the key agent of social change, albeit updated for the world of the late 1960s. Inspired by the alliance of students and workers on display in France in May 1968, along with anti-colonial struggles in Asia, Africa, and Latin America, these radicalized, college-educated New Leftists advocated a "turn to the working class." Concretely speaking, this often meant pulling up roots, moving to industrial areas to take factory jobs, and becoming shop floor organizers, a process known as "colonization" (Elbaum 2002). The hope was to establish links with a newly restive industrial working class, which was beset with a wave of shop floor unruliness and outright rebellion (Brenner et al. 2010; Cowie 2010).

While colonization as a strategy had many shortcomings, chief among them was the yawning gap it exposed between labor and the New Left. Initially separated by the chasm of McCarthyism, the two had grown apart both organizationally and politically in the ensuing decades. The US New Left of the late 1960s embarked on its turn to the working class as outsiders. Their organizational vehicles consisted of tiny revolutionary grouplets, to which they largely unsuccessfully sought to recruit actual workers.[15] This model of organizing often served to reinforce the

---

[15] Some important exceptions that were more successful in bridging the worker–student divide were the union reform caucuses that developed in several key industrial unions in the 1970s, including the International Brotherhood of Teamsters (IBT), the United Auto Workers (UAW), the United Steel Workers of America (USWA), and the United Mine Workers of America (UMWA), among others. While these formations were often heavily influenced and staffed by college-educated New Leftists, they were not explicitly revolutionary or leftist organizations. Unlike many revolutionary groupings of the time, they

existing divide between the Left and the organized US working class, as well as the Old and New Lefts (Mauss 1971).[16]

In Canada, New Leftists also came to see the importance of allying with sectors of the working class (Milligan 2014). They too took inspiration from the worker–student alliance in France, as well as the anti-colonial struggles unfolding in the Third World. But unlike in the United States, the configuration of party systems and geopolitics in Canada ended up strengthening ties between labor and the Left.

Looking first at party systems, the continued presence of the CCF/NDP in Canada meant that the radicalization of the New Left over the course of the 1960s did not exacerbate the divide between labor and the Left to the same degree as in the United States. While the Canadian Left certainly had radical grouplets, as the United States did, the NDP provided an attractive institutional vehicle for leftists who wanted to orient toward the working class that was unavailable south of the border. In certain cases this took the form of so-called entryist groups, where left grouplets would operate within the NDP as an organized faction in an attempt to attract members to their own group (Isitt 2011; Webber 2009). More broadly though, New Left radicalization led to several efforts to articulate a more radical worker-student coalition within the NDP itself. In 1965, an organized Left Caucus challenged the leadership of the New Democratic Youth at its convention. According to a chronicler of the event,

> [The Left Caucus'] draft programme called for Canada's withdrawal from NATO, the immediate nationalization of basic and key sectors of the economy, ultimate workers' control of factories, student and faculty representation on all governing bodies of the universities, and the recognition of Quebec's right to self-determination (Gray 1965: 23).

The Left Caucus challenge itself came close, but proved unsuccessful. However, it was the prelude to a much more serious and sustained effort to redefine the politics of the NDP along more radical lines: the Movement for an Independent Socialist Canada, more commonly known as the Waffle.

---

sought to appeal to and organize workers around concrete shop-floor issues, as opposed to broad political positions. But even in these cases, few of the caucuses survived the 1970s, with the notable exception of Teamsters for a Democratic Union (TDU) (Brenner et al. 2010; Georgakas and Surkin 1998).

[16] Not all New Leftists who made the turn to the working class took rank and file jobs. Some sought to bridge the gap between labor and the New Left by taking staff jobs with labor unions. While this strategy ultimately proved more successful in terms of the career longevity of those who chose that path, it involved less of a labor-Left alliance and more of an absorption of individual New Leftists into the labor movement (Ganz et al. 2004).

From its formation in 1969 to its expulsion from the NDP in 1972, the Waffle pushed to make the NDP, in its own words, "a truly socialist party." It saw the core mission of the NDP to be "building of a mass base of socialists, in factories and offices, on farms and campuses" (NDP Waffle 1969: Point 2). In 1971, Waffle leader James Laxer came close to unseating longtime party stalwart David Lewis as NDP leader at the party's convention. Laxer took Lewis to a fourth ballot, capturing 37 percent of the delegate votes on that final ballot. This showed the Waffle to be far more than the fringe group that the NDP leadership had painted them to be (Bullen 1983; Morton 1986). By comparison, no left group in the United States had a similar degree of influence within a major party.

As for the effect of geopolitics, issues surrounding the Cold War, particularly US involvement in the war in Vietnam and other Third World decolonization struggles, focused greater attention on the United States' position as an imperial hegemon. In Canada, the reaction against this took the form of a new left nationalism, with Anglophone and Francophone variants.

In English Canada, the focus was on criticizing US control of the Canadian economy and the resulting threat to Canadian independence. Broad concern about US economic domination developed in Canada around the proceedings of the Task Force on Foreign Ownership and the Structure of Canadian Investment, created in 1967 by the Liberal government of Lester B. Pearson. The task force's report, commonly known as the Watkins Report (1968) after the task force's chair, University of Toronto economist Mel Watkins, attracted national attention. It explored in detail the degree to which foreign/US ownership was pervasive, including "external ownership of well over half of all manufacturing industries, and close to all assets in the high value manufacturing industries, plus over half of all mining assets" (Marchak 1985: 674). The Watkins Report was followed in 1970 with the publication of Kari Levitt's *Silent Surrender: The Multinational Corporation in Canada* (1970),[17] which inaugurated the intellectual tradition in Canada known as the "New Canadian Political Economy" (Clement 1996).

For Watkins personally, chairing the task force had a radicalizing effect. It drove him to play a leading role in the formation of the Waffle and the drafting of its manifesto, which declared that

American corporate capitalism is the dominant factor shaping Canadian society. In Canada, American economic control operates throughout the formidable

---

[17] Perhaps not coincidentally, Levitt is the daughter of Karl Polanyi.

medium of the multi-national corporation. The Canadian corporate elite has opted for a junior partnership with these American enterprises. Canada has been reduced to a resource base and consumer market within the American Empire (NDP Waffle 1969: Point 6).

Contemporary scholars have criticized this left nationalism for its blindness to Canada's own role in global imperialism (Gordon 2010; Kellogg 2015). But its focus on class exploitation and the economics of global capitalism created fertile ground for uniting segments of labor and the New Left. Organizationally, this was facilitated by the fact that the labor–Left alliance was happening within the NDP and newly radicalizing Canadian unions, particularly in the public sector, as discussed in detail below (Bullen 1983; Palmer 2009).

In Quebec, as in English Canada, growing nationalist consciousness and New Left radicalization strengthened the tie between the Left and the working class. But here the focus was more explicitly on Quebec's colonial status, and the national oppression of the Québécois at the hands of English Canadian capital. Drawing inspiration both from the Black Power movement in the United States, as well as anti-colonial liberation movements, the Québécois Left transformed itself over the course of the 1960s and '70s into the most militant, class-conscious, and broad-based Left movement in North America (Mills 2010). Central to this process was the transformation of Québécois labor unions – particularly the formerly Catholic CSN – and their close alliance with the political left. The CSN became one of the main driving forces behind the "Quiet Revolution," a process of social reform in Quebec that shook off the pervasive conservative influence of the Catholic Church and challenged Anglophone social and economic dominance (Confédération des syndicats nationaux and Centrale de l'enseignement du Québec 1987; Rouillard 1989; Thwaites 2007).

Across Canada, the combination of a Left that survived postwar Red scares with more organizational ties to the working class, and a New Left imbued with class-inflected nationalism, laid the foundation for closer ties between labor and the Left than existed south of the border.

THE NEW LEFT AND LABOR'S IDENTITY

Postwar relations between labor and the Left in both countries also reshaped labor's conception of itself. This in turn affected labor's mobilizing capacity.

In the United States, labor's abandonment of political independence in favor of an alliance with the Democratic Party, combined with the Cold War isolation from the Left and social movements, encouraged it to think of itself and act as an interest group. As such, it largely limited itself to making economic improvements at the bargaining table in the postwar decades, while looking for political reforms using inside influence and lobbying. As its influence within the Democratic Party weakened, labor was unprepared to return to a more mobilizational strategy. Its independent organizing capacity had been sapped by decades of behaving as a responsible interest group. The intensified employer and government attacks on labor beginning in the 1970s exposed labor's underlying organizational weakness, allowing employers to wage what UAW President Douglas Fraser (1978: 1) despairingly called a "one-sided class war."

In Canada, labor also sought to behave "responsibly," to achieve economic improvements at the bargaining table, and to lobby the legislature. But labor's greater political independence through its alliance with the NDP, combined with closer ties to broader left social movements, encouraged it to think of itself and act as more of a class representative. As a result, it retained a degree of independent organizational capacity that was lacking in the United States. Labor continued to fight more for broader social reforms, while also mobilizing political pressure outside the halls of Parliament. This greater organizational capacity in turn left Canadian labor better equipped to withstand the increased employer and government attacks on labor beginning in the 1970s.

Two factors in particular reinforced cross-border political differences in labor's internal characteristics: 1) differences in the role of public sector unionism; and 2) the differing effects of nationalism. While the rise of public sector unionism reinvigorated both labor movements at least temporarily, the effect was much more transformative in Canada than in the United States. As for nationalism, US labor's tight integration into the Cold War consensus alienated it from the social movements of the period, while Canadian labor's ties to a resurgent nationalism in English Canada and a national independence movement in Quebec reinforced labor's movement-oriented character.

Public Sector Unionism

Canada: Movement Revitalization

The new Canadian public sector unions transformed the character and complexion of the Canadian labor movement. Often formed out of bitter struggles and closely linked with new social movements, particularly feminism, they reinjected a dose of 1930s-style movement building and class consciousness into the Canadian labor movement as a whole. It was often through public sector unions that the linkages between labor and the New Left were formed (Luxton 2001; Sangster 2010; Warskett 1997).[18]

Public sector unions soon came to play an influential role in the CLC. Partially this was a result of their sheer numerical growth. But in their vocal push for a broader social agenda and closer political ties with the NDP, they alienated the most conservative elements within the Canadian labor movement, namely the twelve building trades unions. This group left the CLC in 1981, and nine of the twelve soon formed the rival, more conservative Canadian Federation of Labour (CFL).[19] The exodus of the conservative building trades further bolstered the power and influence of the public sector unions within the CLC, allowing them to steer the federation as a whole in a more progressive direction (Robinson 1993: 32).

Finally, as inherently national unions, as opposed to the US-headquartered "international" unions that previously dominated Canadian labor, the public sector unions tied into the growing trend toward greater national autonomy for Canadian unions in the 1960s and 1970s. As detailed below, the turn toward autonomy allowed Canadian labor to express a greater social movement character, unencumbered by the conservative policies of its southern counterpart.

The United States: Movement Dissipation

US public sector unions emerged out of the tumult of the 1960s, intimately tied to the civil rights movement, as most clearly illustrated by the 1968 Memphis sanitation strike (Honey 2007; McCartin 2006). As a result of the public sector upsurge, millions of women and African Americans joined the ranks of US labor, fundamentally transforming its complexion (Moody 1988: 82). For a time, it appeared possible that public sector unionism might also change the character of US labor. But by the mid-1970s, the movement energy from the public sector had largely dissipated.

---

[18] While Robinson argues that public sector unionism is inherently more politically progressive than private sector unionism, the example of public sector unionism in the United States belies his claim. Formerly militant activist public sector unions such as American Federation of State, County, and Municipal Employees (AFSCME) and 1199 have become among the most fervent supporters of labor's alliance with the Democratic Party at all costs, and they devote considerably more of their energy to electing Democratic politicians than supporting broader social movements or mobilizing for progressive policies. Far more important than the structural position of public sector unions is their political character, which is shaped both by the conditions surrounding union founding, and the political alliances those unions make.

[19] The CFL disbanded in 1997, with most of the affiliates rejoining the CLC.

Instead, most public sector unions followed their private sector counterparts in adopting an interest group orientation. Unlike other countries, including Canada, the growth of public sector unionism in the 1960s did not have a progressive "spillover" effect on the rest of the labor movement (Cowie 2010: 62).

Part of the explanation for the failure of public sector unionism to exert a more transformative influence on the US labor movement was external to labor. It had to do with the domestication and de-radicalization of the civil rights movement over the course of the 1970s (Marable 2007). To the extent that public sector unionism had a movement tinge, it was due to the influence of the Black freedom struggle. But as the civil rights movement became more bureaucratized and more incorporated into the Democratic Party, so too did the public sector unions (Davis 1986).

But there also was a component that was internal to the labor movement. That involved a factional struggle that unfolded within the AFL-CIO over the course of the 1960s. It pitted a conservative wing led by AFL-CIO President George Meany and his allies in the building trades unions against a liberal wing led by UAW President Walter Reuther. While Meany fully embraced the interest group/business unionist model, Reuther still held on to remnants of a social unionist vision. It was Reuther's UAW that made overtures to the social movements of the 1960s, paid for the placards for the 1963 March on Washington, provided a venue where Students for a Democratic Society could draft its Port Huron Statement, and attempted to position labor as a progressive counterweight within the Democratic Party. In the new public sector unions, Reuther saw a potential ally against the Meany faction. But Meany's skillful political maneuvering left Reuther isolated and outvoted, and in 1968 he pulled his UAW out of the AFL-CIO (Davis 1986; Lichtenstein 1995).

With Reuther gone, the public sector unions were isolated within the AFL-CIO. As *Time* magazine noted in reference to the influence of Jerry Wurf, firebrand President of the AFSCME, on the AFL-CIO's board, "the vote usually ranges from 25 to 1 to 34 to 1, depending on how many other union chiefs are present to vote down Jerry Wurf" (quoted in Cowie 2010: 62). Unlike in Canada, where the public sector unions were more uniformly movement-oriented and built up enough votes to influence the broader labor movement, the movement-oriented faction of public sector unionism in the United States remained small and marginalized. US labor remained committed to its role as a broker and interest group within the Democratic Party.

Diverging Nationalisms in the United States and Canada

The rise of public sector unionism in the United States and Canada pushed both labor movements in a more progressive, movement-oriented direction, although that movement dissipated in the United States. By contrast, nationalism in the 1960s and 70s pushed labor in the two countries in opposite directions. In Canada, economic nationalism in English Canada, along with sovereigntist nationalism in Quebec, had a radicalizing effect on labor, drawing it closer to the Left and social movements. In the United States, labor's firm embrace of Cold War nationalism, reinforced by its McCarthyite purge of its own left in the 1940s and '50s, entailed a full-throated defense of US intervention abroad, including the war in Vietnam. This alienated labor from the New Left and social movements. Moreover, in articulating a strident anti-Communism, labor's embrace of Cold War nationalism undermined its own moral and political legitimacy, as there was a fine line between making union demands and being accused of interfering with the "free market," the bedrock of what was then known as the "Free World."

Canada: Movement-Bolstering Nationalism

While Canadian workers had long been accustomed to being members of labor unions based in the United States, that practice came under scrutiny in the 1960s. Spearheaded by an upsurge in public sector unionization, Canadian workers began shedding their international union affiliations and joining new Canadian unions in greater numbers. Many of these national unions espoused more militant class politics, and fostered ties between the unions and New Left social movements, particularly the nascent feminist movement. Thus, the emergence of Canadian nationalism created conditions for a closer alliance between the New Left and segments of the organized working class (Luxton 2001; McInnis 2011; Palmer 1983; Sangster 2010; Warskett 1997).

Many Canadian officials of the major "international" labor unions (those headquartered in the United States) viewed this nationalist upsurge and the rise of the Waffle with alarm. They worried that the nationalist critique also posed the question of why Canadian workers should be subject to foreign rule. These leaders were also wary of angering their parent unions south of the border, which were often staunch supporters of US foreign policy (Robinson 1990: 286; Scott 1978).

Nonetheless, even those unions hostile to Canadian nationalism and the Waffle were sensitive to the critiques they raised. Starting in the early

1970s, the CLC adopted rules requiring greater Canadian autonomy over Canadian union affairs within international unions. This took the form of five "minimum Canadian standards," including among other things: provisions for election of Canadian union officers by Canadian union members, vesting responsibility for determining national policies with the Canadian leadership, and empowering Canadian officials to speak for Canadian union members. As part of asserting their political autonomy, Canadian unions also began raising critiques of US foreign policy (Robinson 1990: 282; Schenk and Bernard 1992: 45).

Meanwhile, as the Quebec nationalist movement radicalized over the course of the decade, the CSN served as a center linking together various social movements, particularly in major urban areas such as Montreal. Leaders like Marcel Pepin came to the fore, proposing a broader, more militant model of unionism, as embodied in his idea of the "Second Front" (Pepin 1968). Michel Chartrand, an open socialist and elected head of the powerful CSN Montreal Central Council in 1968, transformed that body into a hub of left social movement activity. It provided a home not only for those focused on labor issues but also for supporters of national liberation struggles in Angola, Mozambique, Palestine, and Vietnam, along with opponents of fascist regimes in Greece, Portugal, and Spain. So broad was the reach of the Central Council that historian Sean Mills notes that "the lines that separated labour and the left began to blur" (Mills 2010: 14). By 1972, the convergence of labor and the Left in Quebec culminated in the Common Front, an alliance of the three major Quebec labor federations[20] and community organizations that organized a ten-day province-wide general strike against the government (Confédération des syndicats nationaux and Centrale de l'enseignement du Québec 1987: 236–237).

Although not going as far as their Québécois brothers and sisters, more Canadian unions started declaring their independence from their US-based parent unions starting in the late 1960s. Between 1962 and 1982, membership in national unions more than tripled, from 503,229 to 1,625,949, while the percentage of all Canadian union members in

---

[20] There were (and remain) three major Quebec labor federations: the CSN; the Fédération des travailleurs et travailleuses du Québec (Quebec Federation of Labour, or FTQ), which primarily comprises international (US-based) unions; and the Centrale de l'enseignement du Québec (Congress of Quebec Teachers, or CEQ), primarily comprising teachers' unions. In 2000, the CEQ rechristened itself the Centrale des syndicats du Québec (Congress of Quebec Unions, or CSQ), in recognition of the fact that its membership had expanded beyond the teaching profession.

national unions surged from 33.2 percent of the total to 53.2 percent of the total (Canada Ministry of Supply and Services 1984: Table 1). That number has now risen to 69.7 percent (Employment and Social Development Canada 2016). A large part of this is the growth of public sector unions, but it is also a function of private sector workers forming national unions, such as the Canadian Auto Workers (CAW), which split off from the UAW in 1985 and is now known as Unifor.[21]

The growth of national unionism in English Canada and Quebec was tied to a growth in union militancy. In many cases, the CAW being the most dramatic, the break with the parent union was the result of a critique of the accommodationist, concessionary stance taken by the US parent union (Gindin 1995). Combined with the growth of movement-oriented public sector unionism, the move toward national unionism increased the organizational capacity of labor as a class representative.

United States: Movement-Blocking Nationalism

Whereas Canadian and Québécois nationalism strengthened their respective labor movements and reinforced their class identification, US nationalism weakened labor and reinforced its alliance with conservative forces within the Democratic Party. Central to this process was labor's postwar embrace of anti-Communism and US foreign policy.

As detailed above, McCarthyism and the Cold War drove a wedge between labor and the Left. This deprived labor of a broader social vision, while detaching the Left from its traditional working-class base. The AFL-CIO that emerged from the anti-Communist purges of the postwar period was a staunch ally not only of the Democratic Party, but of US foreign policy and the global fight against Communism. This had profound consequences for labor's organizational capacity. As a veteran organizer from the CIO's Operation Dixie reflected,

I think that by '48 – that was the [CIO] convention that finally told the story. You accept the Marshall Plan, you tie American labor to American foreign policy. Now it's a different thing when you strike. You're striking against your country. And now it's a different thing when you ask for wage increases (quoted in Griffith 1988: 158).

Put differently, labor's support for US foreign policy undermined its ability to articulate a broader social vision that could challenge the

---

[21] Unifor was the result of a 2013 merger of the Canadian Auto Workers (CAW) and the Communications, Energy, and Paperworkers (CEP) unions. Like the CAW, the CEP was the product of several unions that declared independence from their US-based parent unions (Keenan 2013).

ideological orthodoxy of the Cold War. Exercising basic labor rights could be construed as fundamentally unpatriotic, even treasonous.[22] Rather than reinforcing its organizational repertoire, US labor's political alliances limited that repertoire.

Additionally, labor's support for US foreign policy put it at odds with much of the New Left, which was leading the movement to end the war in Vietnam. This deprived it of potential allies and allied labor even more firmly with some of the most conservative, hawkish elements of the Democratic Party. To be sure, there were elements within US labor that were firmly against the Vietnam War, most notably Reuther, along with many of the public sector unions. They sought to retain labor's progressive social vision and saw labor's isolation from the movements of the 1960s as a problem. Nonetheless, they remained a minority within the AFL-CIO and were unable to shift federation policy (Lichtenstein 1995: 405–409; Robinson 1990: 286).

In sum, US nationalism tied labor to an ideology and set of policies that both undermined its organizational capacity and alienated it from potential allies. It narrowed labor's social vision, and reinforced its position as an interest group within the Democratic Party.

CONCLUSION

Not all US labor leaders were conservative, cigar-chomping power brokers like George Meany. Likewise, not all Canadian labor leaders were far-sighted militants like Marcel Pepin. But the fact that people like Meany and Pepin were able to rise to prominence as leaders in their respective labor movements speaks to the political and organizational shifts that were underway in the United States and Canada in the postwar decades. Meany embodied US labor's role as an interest group within the Democratic Party, while Pepin embodied Canadian labor's broader role as a class representative.

These shifts were a consequence of US labor's articulation to the Democratic Party's New Deal coalition in the 1930s. This weakened the link between the Left and the working class, a link that McCarthyism then severed. The absence of a class-based party and McCarthyism's severing of the link between labor and the Left accentuated the generational gap

---

[22] For many years, US labor's support for US foreign policy also involved undermining independent unions that the US government deemed too potentially hostile to US interests (Scipes 2010).

between the Old and New Lefts, and deprived the New Left of a class basis. As the New Left sought to re-forge a worker-student alliance in the late 1960s, Cold War politics and Democratic Party liberal hegemony served to deepen the divide between labor and the Left.

By contrast, in Canada, the continued presence of the CCF/NDP as a class-based political party retained a stronger link between the Left and the working class, mitigating the excesses of the postwar Red scare and retaining a class-based political infrastructure. While this did not ensure peaceful relations with the emerging New Left, it did ensure that the New Left would emerge in closer dialogue with the organized working class. As the Canadian New Left sought to reorient toward the working class, a resurgent Canadian left nationalism combined with the class-based political infrastructure of the NDP offered a framework for strengthening the link between the New Left and labor. The result was a Canadian labor movement better equipped than its US counterpart to mobilize against the employer offensive that got underway in the 1970s.

6

Class versus Special Interest

Labor Regimes and Density Divergence, 1911–2016

Comparing US and Canadian labor policy in the early 1960s, renowned McGill University industrial relations scholar H.D. "Buzz" Woods summarized the conventional wisdom of his time, noting that

> In general terms it can be said the Canadian policy is not as favorable to the promotion of collective bargaining relationships ... There has been a more positive attitude toward collective bargaining in the United States than in Canada (Woods 1962: 219).

By the 1990s, the conventional wisdom had shifted. In their comparison of US and Canadian labor policy, noted economists David Card and Richard Freeman observed that

> Despite [their] common heritage, Canadian laws have since become more favorable to unions while American laws have become less favorable. Under Canadian law it is easier to unionize ..., and management has less scope for expressing opposition to unionism. Firms cannot permanently replace strikers, and legislation in some provinces makes even temporary strike replacements illegal (Card and Freeman 1994:199).

This is the situation that VW workers in Chattanooga and Tim Hortons workers in Winnipeg faced (as discussed in the Introduction to this volume): a broken US labor policy that creates obstacles for workers who want to unionize, and a Canadian labor policy that, while far from perfect, still offers workers a modicum of protection. In Chapter 2, we examined in detail *how* labor policy has diverged in both countries. The question that remains is *why* the laws changed: Why did US labor laws erode, while Canadian laws improved?

Answering this question requires looking beyond the courts and legislatures that crafted and interpreted the laws. We must analyze the broader social and political context in which those laws were created and administered. David Kettler and his coauthors use the concept of "labor regime" to refer to this broader idea of laws embedded in sets of norms, principles, and sociopolitical relationships, which I will adopt (Kettler, Struthers, and Huxley 1990).[1] Understanding why the laws changed in both countries then becomes a question of explaining why the labor regimes diverged. Put differently, what changed about the norms, expectations, and political relationships surrounding labor law in Canada that better allowed unions to exert their organizational power than in the United States?

The divergence was a result of different processes of working-class political incorporation during the Great Depression and World War II: US labor was incorporated as an *interest group*, whereas Canadian labor was incorporated as a *class representative*. These different identities reflected different organizing logics that enabled or constrained labor's scope of action in each country. Canadian labor's role as a class representative fit into a *class idea* that broadened and legitimated its scope of action, while US labor's role as an interest group fit into a *pluralist idea* that narrowed and delegitimized its scope of action. Table 6.1 reproduces the table we saw in the Introduction, summarizing these different organizing logics.

The two organizing logics did not emerge fully formed, but rather developed over time. Their initial differences resulted from different ruling party responses to the working-class upsurge of the 1930s and '40s. As discussed in Chapter 4, US Democrats adopted a *co-optive* response to the upsurge, implementing reforms as a means of incorporating labor as an interest group within the New Deal coalition. Canadian ruling parties adopted a *coercive* response, reluctantly acceding to reforms under pressure nearly a decade later than their US counterparts. The resulting labor regimes, while formally similar, had different priorities: the US regime prioritized protecting workers' rights, while the Canadian regime prioritized enforcing industrial peace.

---

[1] Specifically, for Kettler et al., "labor regime" refers to "the institutionalized political organization of labour markets, comprising the patterned interactions among state (and possibly other legal administrative) agencies, employment-dependent labour, and employers" (1990: 169). It encompasses "not only the quasi-legalistic principles, norms, rules and decisionmakers around which the expectations of the relevant political actors converge in a given issue area over an identifiable period of time, but also ... the power constellations that condition the effectiveness of the institutionalized order in question" (167).

TABLE 6.1 *Differences in organizing logics*

Organizing Logic	Class Idea	Pluralist Idea
Group role – Labor	Class representative	Interest group
Group role – Capital	Class representative	Interest group/ individual employers
Group role – State	Mediator	Adjudicator
Rights	Collective	Individual
Bargaining	Group-based	Contract-based
Interests	Class/general	Special/particular
Institutionalization	High	Low
Politicization	Low	High

The US regime's rights focus created a sense that the state was protecting a particular group, leading to calls for "balancing" workers' collective bargaining rights against employer property and "free speech" rights. The rights framework also emphasized legal proceduralism, which concealed power imbalances inherent in the employment relationship beneath a formal legal equality. By contrast, the Canadian regime's focus on enforcing industrial peace encouraged more state intervention. This restricted labor's scope of action, but also insulated the regime from charges of pro-labor favoritism, and ensured greater employer compliance. Unlike the US labor regime, it emphasized conflict resolution over adherence to legal procedure, which entailed recognizing structural power imbalances between labor and management more explicitly.

At an organizational level, labor drew different lessons from these different processes of regime formation. US labor became more dependent on finding sympathetic political allies with whom to strike bargains, while Canadian labor learned the value of independent mobilization for class-wide demands.

As the labor regimes developed in the postwar decades, they mediated the relation between class conflict and politics differently. The class idea underpinning the Canadian regime provided a mechanism for translating class conflict into the political realm. Canadian state actors recognized worker unrest and protest as a *class* issue, and dealt with it as such. This led to a consistent pattern of worker protest being followed by government reform. In the United States, that process was blocked. Instead of being recognized as a class issue, worker unrest was misrecognized as the result of individual worker alienation, or the particular problems of a narrow Democratic Party "special interest." This left US labor policy less institutionalized and more subject to charges of partisan favoritism than in Canada.

The combination of a more protective labor regime and a labor movement more accustomed to winning gains through mass mobilization left Canadian labor better positioned to defend itself than its US counterpart when employers began a counter-offensive in the late 1960s. While US labor spiraled into decline, Canadian labor proved more resilient, leading to the divergence in union density rates.

LABOR REGIME FORMATION

The United States

Regime Formation Process: Granting Labor Rights

Although the Wagner Act was a response to an upsurge in working-class mobilization (Bernstein 1970: ch. 6; Goldfield 1989b), it was also part of a conscious reform project initiated from above by FDR's New Deal administration (Skocpol and Finegold 1990).[2] The initial basis for the Wagner Act, contained in Section 7 of the National Industrial Recovery Act (NIRA), was passed in 1933, soon after FDR's accession to office and before the tumult of 1934. While the NIRA had no enforcement mechanism, it nonetheless provided a symbolic endorsement of collective bargaining rights, which in turn led to an uptick in union organizing (Milton 1982). Once the NIRA was declared unconstitutional in 1935, the NLRA was immediately proposed as a replacement policy. It essentially reproduced Section 7 of the NIRA, but it added enforcement penalties and other mechanisms to compel employers to bargain with unions.

By that point, the labor unrest of the period was clearly on the minds of policymakers. However, just as important was the Administration's reputation. As a key advisor suggested to Labor Secretary Frances Perkins in discussing the need for legislation to replace the NIRA, "[t]he

---

[2] These two positions are usually counterposed to each other, often directly, as in the case of the competing articles by Goldfield and Skocpol & Finegold cited here. However, the very fact that there is a debate in the US case as to whether the NLRA was a response to labor insurgency or a top-down reform project speaks to the argument made here. Whereas it is at least possible to create plausible accounts of the formation of US labor policy that emphasize either working-class upsurge or autonomous state action, this is impossible for the Canadian case, as we will see in greater detail below.

maintenance of the prestige of the Administration is the one hope for the triumph of moderate and constructive policies, as against extremes of mob-policy on the one hand and reactionary policy on the other" (Dickinson 1935: 5). The NLRA was an effort to navigate between these two extremes.

Union density began to climb upon passage of the Wagner Act in 1935 but truly exploded after the Supreme Court declared it constitutional in 1937. The extent to which we can attribute this explosion in union density to the Act itself as opposed to unions' independent mobilization has been a matter of considerable scholarly debate (Barenberg 1993; Manza 2000; Piven and Cloward 1977; Rubin et al. 1983). Without adjudicating between these competing positions, the important point is that there was a broad sense among both labor and employer groups that the Wagner Act was something that the New Deal administration did *for* labor.

On the employer side, there was tremendous resistance to the Wagner Act, and it was only with the 1937 ruling declaring it constitutional that they gave it grudging acceptance. Even after outright repeal or overturning seemed to be off the table, employer groups continued with constant efforts to amend or undermine the law. Central to this strategy was an insistence that the NLRA was "biased" and "one-sided" in its structure and administration, lining government power up on the side of labor (Associated Press 1937; National Association of Manufacturers, 1938a). Invoking the danger of sagging business confidence in that period, two counsel for the National Association of Manufacturers wrote that "there will be little permanent improvement in business morale or confidence unless and until government again accepts the role of impartial umpire and proclaims to all groups alike that their efforts must be conducted within the bounds of law, reason, and fair play" (National Association of Manufacturers, 1938b: 7). Employer claims of "bias" and "one-sidedness" continued unabated through the 1930s and '40s, and played a key role in the move to create "balance" in labor policy with the Taft-Hartley Act in 1947.

On the union side, the presentation and passage first of Section 7 of NIRA, then the Wagner Act, created the impression that the administration was granting rights to labor. In discussing NIRA, AFL President William Green noted that "[w]hen the Congress of the United States carefully prepared and included Section 7A in the National Recovery Act, Labor believed that *it had been accorded* the legal and moral right to organize into unions of its own choice" (Green 1934b: 4, emphasis added).

More broadly, the pro-labor legislative proposals coming out of the Roosevelt administration almost immediately shifted many labor leaders' attention from mass mobilization in the workplace to lobbying in support of legislation. They believed that the legislative route held the greatest promise for ensuring labor's strength and long-term viability. One of the strongest advocates for such a legislative route was Clothing Workers President Sidney Hillman. In an April 1936 address to one of his union's key locals, he tackled the tension between mass mobilization and legislation head-on:

> Now you may come and ask me: why should we be concerned about the law? Why shouldn't we rely on our own power? ... I say to you that if labor is to make real progress, labor must have some legislative support. Of course, without it, we would continue to make some progress, just as we have in the past, but I mean <u>broad</u> progress ... If we are going to get ahead, we must have further legislation. We need more than legislation on the regulation of wages and hours. We need a legislative guarantee of the right to organize. We had 7a in the [NIRA] code, now we have the Wagner Act ... Labor must learn to use its economic and political power (Hillman 1936a: 1-4).

While many contemporary scholars have criticized US unions' narrow focus on labor law and insider politics, what is important to note here is that this focus emerged out of the very conditions of labor regime formation in the United States. The state's early and active involvement in responding to labor unrest with collective bargaining legislation created an impression that the laws themselves created greater union strength, as opposed to the laws being understood as the state's response to labor's show of force. This, combined with the New Deal administration's sustained courting of labor support, created incentives for seeking reforms through political allies as an interest group, as opposed to through independent mobilization as a class.

Regime Structure: Quasi-Judicial Nonpartisanship
While the conditions surrounding labor regime formation created certain impressions and expectations, the actual structures of the resulting regime also shaped its future development. Two key features were 1) its quasi-judicial structure, which emphasized legalistic procedure and integrated the regime more tightly into the regular court system; and 2) its "nonpartisan" structure, with NLRB members appointed by the president to serve as ostensibly impartial arbiters. The first element privileged legal acumen over conflict resolution, while also subjecting labor-related rulings to broader judicial review. The second element privileged partisan

representation (Democrats versus Republicans) over class representation (unions versus employers), leaving labor board decisions more vulnerable to charges of partisan bias. In each case, the result was a labor regime that deemphasized the specific power dynamics involved in class conflict, and instead substituted a formal equivalence between the parties involved.

While these elements of the US labor regime are taken for granted today, they were not inevitable. To the contrary, they represented a departure from initial labor regime structures. US labor boards initially combined case adjudication with labor-management conciliation services, which would have created an agency more generally concerned with expedient handling of labor-management relations as a whole. They also initially had a tripartite instead of a nonpartisan structure. Keeping those initial structures in place would have led to a much different labor regime – one much closer to that adopted in Canada.

QUASI-JUDICIAL STRUCTURE Initial attempts to establish an "industrial court" to adjudicate labor disputes emerged out of efforts to implement the 1933 NIRA. Section 7(a) of the NIRA was supposed to be self-policing, but the explosion of union organizing and strikes following its passage exposed the limits of self-policing (Morris 2005: 25). President Roosevelt established the National Labor Board (NLB) on August 5, 1933 to "consider, adjust, and settle differences and controversies" arising from labor strife (quoted in Morris 2005: 25). This broad and vague definition of the board's scope and function allowed for both adjudicative and conciliatory roles for the board.

As the board developed over the next two years, these dual roles remained part of the board's structure. Its primary focus was reaching agreement between the opposing parties. As an October 1934 NLRB[3] brief explained, "[p]rinciple ought not to be sacrificed to expediency, but on the other hand legalistic interpretations of 7(a) ought not to be insisted upon where genuinely harmonious relationships can best be brought about by agreement" (National Labor Relations Board 1934: 14).

Some within the Department of Labor (DOL) expressed concern about this hybrid structure. As one official argued, "the Board is supposed to exercise quasi-judicial authority or to act as an arbitrator, and should

---

[3] The NLRB itself predated the Wagner Act, established as it was by presidential order on June 29, 1934. The pre-NLRA NLRB was given the power "to make investigations, to hold labor elections, to hear cases of discharges of employees and to act as a voluntary arbitrator" (Roosevelt 1934).

refrain from weakening its own position by urging employers and employees to take steps which might bring about temporary peace but which are not based squarely on justice and legal rights" (US Department of Labor 1934b: 1). Some board members themselves also called for the separation of mediation and judicial functions, on the grounds that too deep involvement in specific cases could undermine the board's adjudicative authority (Associated Press 1934). Additionally, some DOL staff argued that the hybrid structure made it hard to divide up conciliation cases between the NLRB and the DOL, since it was often not apparent whether a case involved Section 7(a) issues until a hearing was held (US Department of Labor 1934b). But despite these concerns, what is important to note is that early iterations of US labor boards did adopt a hybrid adjudicative and conciliatory structure, and that there were advocates within the administrative branch for both hybrid and quasi-judicial structures.

By the time of the passage of the Wagner Act, the hybrid structure was gone, and the NLRB was a strictly quasi-judicial agency. In a memorandum prepared for President Roosevelt in advance of a meeting with new NLRB members, his aides outlined the NLRB's functions: "the work of the Board will be to decide specific cases and to refrain from research work ... In order to work harmoniously with agents in related fields, the Board should refrain from mediation or conciliation" (US Department of Labor 1935: 1).

According to the Wagner Act's primary author, this separation of adjudicative and conciliatory functions was largely "in the interest of clarity and simplification" (Casebeer 1987: 359). But there was also tension between those in the DOL who advocated a broader role for the board, including conciliation, and those on Senator Wagner's staff who saw the quasi-judicial nature of the board as a key source of its strength and independence. A key element of this quasi-judicial strength was the board's tight integration into the federal court system (Casebeer 1987: 345). The architects of the Act believed that quick access to the courts would facilitate enforcement, not hamper it.

However, it quickly became apparent to those charged with implementing the law, as well as those whom the law was designed to protect, that the NLRB's quasi-judicial structure came with significant costs. First, greater integration into the court system subjected labor board decisions to more extensive judicial review. This created a dynamic where judges would end up balancing workers' more novel collective rights established by the NLRA statute against more deeply entrenched individual rights of property and contract (Block 1993; Klare 1977). Second, it offered employers greater opportunities to focus on pursuing legal strategies to block unionization, as opposed to focusing on reaching settlements with unions. Sensing early on that this could be a problem, NLRB member Edwin Smith implored employers to let the administrative machinery work, arguing that

> [E]mployers will most satisfactorily further their relations with trade unions if they cease to think in terms of legal restraints which they may exercise against them. Successful dealing with trade unions depends on the growth of mutual confidence between the employer and his workers' representatives. Such confidence is never assisted by the fact that one party to negotiations sits with a lawyer at his elbow and his inward glance firmly directed at statutes and courts, seeking not for points of accommodation but for some means by which he can embarrass and frustrate the party of the second part (Smith 1937: 8–9).

Third, and most broadly, the quasi-judicial structure created a labor regime framework that privileged legal knowledge and expertise over knowledge of labor-management relations. This deemphasized the power imbalances inherent in the labor-management relationship by concealing them behind the formal equivalence of opposing parties under the law. NLRB member William Leiserson complained of this growing tendency as early as 1940:

> The problem is really more far-reaching than the NLRB itself. It threatens the whole idea of scientific investigation and administrative control ... As new administrative agencies have been created here, great numbers of lawyers have been recruited to man them [sic]. These have been trained in the new ideas about administrative law [emphasis in original] that are now current in the law schools. Their knowledge of labor relations ... is confined to decisions of courts on labor cases. They do not distinguish between the administrative procedures by which a Board carries on its own work and the decisions of the courts with respect to regulations that involve questions of due process of law. They therefore are concerned mainly with getting out rules of practice for the guidance of lawyers who have business before the Board, and they largely neglect the administrative regulations necessary for the intelligent handling of the cases and the personnel ...
> I have had occasion to say that it won't be long before we will have an association of practitioners before the Labor Board, to whose members both employers and unions will be forced to go to get the benefits of the Act because no layman could understand the legal practices and procedures. This is the trend here in Washington, and it threatens ... the whole idea of flexible and informed handling of modern economic problems by expert administrative agencies (Leiserson 1940: 2–3).

Smith's and Leiserson's concerns would prove prescient, as the NLRB evolved in an increasingly legalistic direction, tying up board proceedings in complex procedures and delays that ultimately favored employers (Block 1993).

REPRESENTATIONAL STRUCTURE   Between the passage of NIRA and the NLRA, FDR's administration vacillated between making labor boards tripartite, with representation from unions, employers, and "the public"; or nonpartisan, with representation by "neutral" experts.

The initial NLB was constructed as a tripartite panel, with three representatives each from labor and management, and Senator Wagner serving as the chair and representative of the state. Subsequent iterations of the national board, and many of the ad hoc regional and industry-specific boards that proliferated during the NIRA's short life, also employed a tripartite structure (Morris 2005; National Labor Relations Board 1934; US Department of Labor 1934a).

With the shift to the National Labor Relations Board, however, nonpartisanship replaced tripartism. Although Wagner's original bill for what would become the NLRA specified a tripartite board, that provision was gone by the time the bill passed in July 1935. The rationale was tied to the decision to separate out the board's conciliation and mediation work, and make it a purely quasi-judicial body (Gross 1981; National Labor Relations Board 1985). Those crafting the law ended up agreeing with a Chamber of Commerce representative, who argued that "because it is a judicial board, the NLRB should not be one in which 'some of the members directly represent one of the parties litigant and owe a duty to them ... It would be better to have the board constituted of members who owe a duty to no one, just like the Federal courts'" (quoted in Flynn:2000: 1383, n. 10). Echoing this sentiment, Labor Secretary Frances Perkins noted a few years later that

> it seems preferable to me to retain the present status of the Board as one completely representative of the public rather than to make it openly tripartite in character. The latter arrangement would inject partisanship into a situation in which it is extremely important to maintain as much impartiality as possible (Perkins 1939: 3).

The nonpartisan structure of the board created a situation where a great deal hinged on the individual actions of specific board members, and the degree to which they could maintain an aura of fairness and impartiality before the opposing parties. The ostensibly neutral status of each individual member left them open to charges of "imbalance" from opposing sides. Management embarked on a sustained campaign to discredit the board as "biased" and "one-sided." On labor's side, AFL unions charged that the board favored CIO unions, and CIO unions feared that the NLRB would fall too much under the sway of management influence (Booker and Coe 1986; Gellhorn and Linfield 1939). Noting what he considered a disturbing trend in 1939, CIO Secretary James B. Carey testified before the Senate that

> [A]t least a part of the personnel of the Board appears to have lost sight of the purpose of the Act and to have abandoned to a great degree the rigid and strict furtherance of those purposes, in order that they might indulge in playing politics – adjusting the principles of the law in an outrageous way to "pressure" and threats from the known and avowed enemies of the Act ... It is not beyond possibility that this kind of shabby manipulation of what is a good piece of legislation could very well turn the Act into a deterrent to industrial democracy (Carey 1939: F-2)

For his part, Roosevelt viewed such criticism from all sides as a sign that the board as a whole was fulfilling its duties in an impartial manner (Associated Press 1937). But what he overlooked was the degree to which such attacks signaled mistrust of the board on all sides.

The board's nonpartisan structure also ironically led to its partisan polarization. As political appointees with a vaguely defined mission to represent "the public," as opposed to the interests of labor or management, board members had an incentive to represent the interests of the administration that appointed them. This dynamic was initially less apparent, as Presidents Roosevelt and Truman hewed to the spirit of the NLRA by appointing neutral board members, usually career civil servants or academics. This changed under President Eisenhower, who appointed management-side labor attorneys to the board, and intensified under subsequent administrations (Flynn 2000).

Political appointment of NLRB members injected partisanship into the board's functioning. Members were not appointed as "labor" or "management" representatives, even though they often ended up being union-side or management-side labor lawyers. Rather, they were "Democratic" or "Republican" appointees. It was their *political* affiliation, not their class affiliation, that was most salient. This ensured that struggles over board nominations would remain politically contentious, as opposed to institutionalized within the routine administration of the US labor regime.

The New Deal administration's quick enactment of labor reforms reinforced the idea that the government was granting rights to labor. Meanwhile, the labor regime's quasi-judicial, nonpartisan structure set in place dynamics that would ensure the US labor regime's long-term politicization and delegitimization. It created a US labor regime governed by a *pluralist idea*, with labor functioning as a formally equivalent *interest group* within that regime. There was little recognition within that formally equivalent framework of the power imbalances inherent in the labor–capital relationship, let alone that labor might function as a class representative. At the same time, labor regime legalism created incentives to focus on parsing issues of law, while labor's focus on seeking influence as an interest group narrowed its scope of vision.

Canada

The conditions surrounding labor regime formation were quite different in Canada, as was the labor regime that emerged out of this early period. Whereas US labor dealt with a relatively sympathetic government that responded to the labor upsurge of the 1930s with reforms, Canadian labor faced a hostile state that responded with increased repression. It was only under the combined pressure of a massive wartime strike wave and an electoral threat from the ruling party's left flank that it acquiesced to labor reforms. Unlike in the United States, there could be no debate about whether labor reform came "from above" or "from below": labor rights were forcibly extracted from a hostile government via labor's independent economic and political mobilization (MacDowell 1978). Accordingly, Canadian labor drew different lessons from its struggle for industrial legality, learning the value of winning gains through mass mobilization. Meanwhile, the resulting labor regime focused on maintaining industrial peace rather than adjudicating legal rights (Fudge 1990; Robinson 1990, 1993).

Regime Formation Process: The Effects of Exclusion
Canadian labor remained politically excluded for nearly a decade longer than in the United States. As outlined in Chapter 4, the Canadian government responded to the crisis of the Great Depression and resulting working-class unrest with a policy of repression and neglect. There was little in the way of relief or public works programs to mitigate the economic impact of the Depression, but ample violence against those who protested their impoverished condition (Horn 1984; Manley 1998; Neatby 1972; Petryshyn 1982; Roberts 1986; Thompson and Seager 1986).

When William Lyon Mackenzie King retook the Prime Minister's office in 1935, he toned down the level of state repression but refused labor's demands for a Canadian Wagner Act. In keeping with his views on labor–management relations, and his steadfast belief in the continued validity of the 1907 Industrial Disputes Investigation Act (IDIA), which he drafted, King clung to the notion that union recognition and contract negotiation should be voluntary. He could not abide the idea of injecting government compulsion into labor–management relations (Fudge and Tucker 2001; MacDowell 1978; Wells 1995a).

It took World War II to disabuse King of his voluntarist notions. In order to assure guaranteed wartime production, King's war cabinet issued Order-in-Council 2685, which laid out a framework for establishing collective bargaining and union representation in war industries, but with no enforcement mechanisms. While King and his government were reticent to compel collective bargaining, they showed no such reticence when it came to imposing mandatory wartime wage controls. Employers flagrantly disregarded the collective bargaining recommendations, while labor continued to strike both for recognition and to protest wage controls. The government responded with increasingly stringent wartime restrictions on striking, but to no avail. Strikes continued to escalate (Camfield 2002; Fudge and Glasbeek 1995; Fudge and Tucker 2001; McInnis 2002).

The final straw occurred when the wartime class conflict on the shop floor spilled over into the political realm, as described in Chapter 4. Reflecting on a series of defeats at the hand of the Cooperative Commonwealth Federation (CCF) in 1943, King wrote that "it may well be that losses to the CCF and Labour[4] ... will cause some of our people to realize that labour has to be dealt with in a considerate way" (King 1943b: 623). By mid-September, King had convinced his cabinet of the need for compulsory collective bargaining policy, and in February 1944, almost 10 years after passage of the Wagner Act, the cabinet enacted PC 1003, which created a Wagner Act-style mechanism for certifying union representation and enforcing collective bargaining rights (Fudge and Glasbeek 1995; Fudge and Tucker 2001).

Ten additional years of political exclusion and delay created a Canadian labor regime that differed in important ways from its US counterpart. Whereas the US labor regime sought primarily to adhere to legal procedure and promote statutory rights, the Canadian regime was primarily concerned with enforcing industrial peace. There was little talk of defending workers' rights; labor legislation was a means of controlling workplace militancy. In exchange for recognizing unions and facilitating collective bargaining, the Canadian labor regime imposed strict restrictions on strikes and union certification. Employer attempts to complain of

---

[4] King is referring to the Labour Progressive Party, as the Communist Party of Canada was known at the time.

US-style labor regime "imbalance" largely fell on deaf ears, and legal proceduralism was limited (Anonymous 1948; Logan 2002; McInnis 2002: 28–42).

Political exclusion also reshaped Canadian labor. Not only did it leave space for labor to ally with the CCF, as we saw in Chapter 4, but it reduced opportunities for labor to achieve gains through influencing sympathetic political leaders. Whereas US labor leaders were faced with the tantalizing prospect of being granted a seat at the table, nothing of the sort was on offer for Canadian labor leaders. By necessity, labor had to remain focused on building its organizing and mobilizing capacity (Robinson:1990: 222–229).

This difference became apparent during World War II. By that point, US labor was already incorporated as a loyal junior partner within the ruling New Deal coalition. One of President Roosevelt's first acts after the bombing of Pearl Harbor was to call a meeting of labor and management representatives to ensure continuous wartime production. At that meeting, both AFL and CIO representatives agreed to a no-strike pledge for the duration of the war (Taft 1959: 219–221). However, wartime speedup and wage controls virtually guaranteed an increase in strike activity, regardless of any pledge. Sure enough, strike rates spiked in 1942 and 1943. In their roles as partners in the war coalition, FDR's administration called on US labor leaders to enforce the no-strike pledge. They responded by launching campaigns to squelch the strike wave and reimpose industrial peace. This drove a wedge between the leadership and the rank and file, undermining labor's mobilizing capacity and reinforcing its reliance on government action to achieve gains (Kersten 2006; Lichtenstein 1982).

In Canada, Prime Minister Mackenzie King sought to emulate Roosevelt in extracting a no-strike pledge from labor to ensure wartime production. Union leaders demanded Wagner Act-style collective bargaining laws in exchange. King only offered the voluntary provisions of PC 2685, so labor leaders rebuffed his no-strike pledge (Abella 1973). As in the United States, the combination of wartime production speedup, wage controls, and state-imposed strike restrictions provoked an eruption of strikes across Canada. But without any duty to the government to police their ranks, Canadian labor leaders used the wartime strike wave to pressure the government to accede to their demands for labor legislation. Rather than driving a wedge between the leadership and the membership, as in the United States, Canada's wartime strike wave had a galvanizing effect, unifying rival factions, officials, and members in a common goal of achieving industrial legality (Robinson 1990: 243–252).

The postwar strike wave that shook both countries amplified these cross-border differences. US union leaders used the postwar strike wave as a "safety valve" to vent rank and file discontent while demonstrating to government officials their ability to serve as "responsible" bureaucrats (Davis 1980a: 66–68; Zieger 1995: 212–227). By contrast, in Canada the postwar strike wave served to keep the membership mobilized and to pressure the government for permanent labor rights. Since PC 1003 was an emergency edict issued under the Canadian Privy Council's wartime powers, it was by definition temporary and set to expire with the end of the war. Canadian workers' postwar mobilization ensured that the gains won under PC 1003 would be institutionalized in more permanent legislation. The result was the 1948 Industrial Relations and Disputes Investigation Act (IRDIA), which formed the basis of the postwar labor retime and became the template for analogous provincial legislation (MacDowell 1978: 194–195; Robinson 1990: 254–255).

This galvanizing effect of Canadian labor's political exclusion had little to do with any inherently more social unionist vision on the part of Canadian union leaders. To the contrary, Canadian union leaders were every bit as eager as their US counterparts to portray themselves as "responsible," to police their membership, to get a seat at the table of government decision-making, and more. There simply was no opportunity to do so. In an ironic twist, Canadian union leaders wanting to become responsible and compliant could only get the government to listen by engaging in disruptive, confrontational tactics.

We can get a flavor for this problem from correspondence between CCL Secretary-Treasurer Pat Conroy and an official in the powerful Department of Munitions and Supply (DMS), regarding a 1944 situation at Anaconda Brass in Toronto, where workers were consistently rejecting company efforts to extend the work day. Expressing dismay at the constant flow of new workers that were outvoting the (presumably more "responsible") "usual steady union group," Conroy explained his predicament:

The main point is that if the Union is to do a good job, it needs a wider coverage so that the workers may be held responsible to the Union. Through this our Union might do a better job of convincing the workers of the need for a longer work day. If they had union shop or recognition on a scale that would enable them to control the employees in the sense of doing a better job, they would be glad to cooperate (Conroy 1944: 1).

Conroy clearly wanted to establish the kind of routine, well-established collective bargaining relationships that characterized many industrial plants in the postwar decades. But without proper legal mechanisms in place for controlling labor, Conroy could only get the government's ear to propose such ideas when the workers he represented engaged in "irresponsible" disruptive activity.

Adding to this basic irony, Canadian union leaders striving for "responsibility" could only make a credible case to government officials as to their ability to control their members by retaining the support and loyalty of the membership – which meant more mobilizing and confrontational rhetoric. Unlike in the United States, where absorption into the New Deal coalition gave labor leaders an alternate base of legitimacy, Canadian labor leaders' legitimacy remained based largely upon membership support (Camfield 2002: 162; Robinson 1990: 246–255; Yates 1993: 58–64).

Overall, the conditions surrounding labor regime formation in Canada led to a labor regime that was primarily focused on enforcing industrial peace, as opposed to defending labor rights as in the United States. For labor, these conditions accentuated an organizational focus on building class independence and militancy, as opposed to influence-seeking within the ruling party. Political exclusion left space for an alliance with an independent, class-based political party, while galvanizing labor mobilization around demands for labor rights. This ensured that the wartime strike wave in Canada bolstered union power, instead of undermining it as in the United States. The result was a Canadian labor movement more imbued with the class idea.

Regime Structure: Conciliation and Tripartism

Two key differences with the US regime stand out which enabled the Canadian regime to retain greater stability over time: 1) unlike the US NLRB, Canadian labor boards retained both adjudicatory and conciliatory functions; and 2) unlike the NLRB's "nonpartisan" structure, most Canadian labor boards were established as tripartite representative bodies.

ADJUDICATION AND CONCILIATION   In the United States, once policymakers decided that the NLRB would serve as a quasi-judicial body, the chief concern was to make that body resemble an actual court as much as possible. To do that, legislators separated the NLRB's adjudicatory and conciliatory functions, housing the conciliatory functions initially in the

United States Conciliation Service (USCS), a unit within the Department of Labor.[5] Mimicking the courts' administrative structure constricted the board's action within a narrow legalistic framework, and undermined labor's ability to defend its interests by concealing the power imbalances inherent in the employment relationship behind formal legal equality.

In Canada, policymakers' central focus in crafting the Canadian labor regime was imposing industrial peace (Fudge and Tucker 2001: 261). The Canadian government only turned to establishing compulsory union recognition and collective bargaining as a last resort, after their initial strategy of placing ever-stricter limits on workers' ability to strike had failed. For them, maintaining judicial impartiality was less important than controlling labor militancy and preventing strikes. The resulting policies granted labor recognition and collective bargaining rights, but at the cost of severe limits on labor's scope of action. Strikes would only be allowed after a period of compulsory government conciliation, as well as a "cooling off" period, and union leaders were required to take measures to quell unlawful worker protest (Wells 1995a). Given the way that union recognition and strike suppression were intimately intertwined in the creation of the Canadian labor regime, it made sense to establish a more fluid relationship between adjudicatory and conciliatory functions at both the federal and provincial levels.[6]

But just as in the United States, the labor regime's structure was not inevitable. Canadian policymakers settled on keeping adjudication and conciliation more intertwined only after experimenting with a strictly judicial labor board. One of the first attempts at establishing a labor board in Canada was the Ontario Labour Court, created in 1943, prior to the proclamation of PC 1003. Going beyond the quasi-judicial

---

[5] The Taft-Hartley Act removed the USCS from the DOL, establishing it as its own independent agency, the Federal Mediation and Conciliation Service (FMCS). This further entrenched the strict separation between labor adjudication and conciliation in the United States.

[6] To be clear, adjudicatory and conciliatory functions remain organizationally distinct in Canada, as in the United States. At the federal level, for example, there is a Canada Industrial Relations Board (CIRB) and a Federal Mediation and Conciliation Service (FMCS). The difference has to do with the relation between the two agencies, and the degree to which mediation and conciliation is built into the union recognition process supervised by the labor board. In Canada, the existence of first contract arbitration provisions automatically inserts the conciliation service into the recognition process in a way that is unheard of in the United States. Efforts at reforming US labor law, such as the failed Employee Free Choice Act (EFCA) of 2007–2010, would have actually created a more Canadian-style relationship between the adjudicative and conciliatory branches of the US labor regime, as it contained provisions for first contract arbitration.

structure of the NLRB, it was established as an actual branch of the High Court of Ontario, staffed by High Court judges, who rotated in and out for two-week periods. The system was designed to ensure strict impartiality and clearly defined legal authority. However, it quickly ran into difficulties. Strict legal interpretations and rules of evidence did not always fit union certification cases. Specific expertise in labor relations was important for settling contentious labor–management conflicts. Judges lacked this expertise, and with two-week stints serving on the Labour Court, could not develop expertise on the job. Federal policymakers drew on the Ontario experience as they crafted the policy that would serve as the postwar template for the federal and provincial labor regimes. They explicitly rejected the Labour Court model in favor of a quasi-judicial administrative structure. But unlike the US quasi-judicial structure, it incorporated conciliatory functions (MacDowell 1978).

As in the United States, the Canadian labor regime's quasi-judicial structure channeled shop floor conflict into the narrow confines of legal interpretations (Camfield 2002; Fudge and Glasbeek 1995; McInnis 2002; Wells 1995b). However, the closer link between adjudication and conciliation led to important differences. It reduced the regime's focus on maintaining judicial impartiality, which laid the groundwork for greater state intervention in labor disputes. This constrained labor's ability to exercise its economic power (Panitch and Swartz 1984, 2003). At the same time, it had three more salutary effects. First, it constrained employers' ability to disregard the law, as the state took a more active role in maintaining the integrity of the collective bargaining process in the name of industrial peace (Block 1993: 26–27; Logan 2002: 145–149). Second, the threat of state intervention prevented labor leaders from developing the idea that the state served to protect labor rights. Third, more direct state intervention by definition brought class conflict more explicitly into the political realm. In politicizing class conflict, state intervention created a broader, more unified target for labor's ire, one that larger groups of workers could see might directly affect them. This in turn fostered a relatively more independent, oppositional class consciousness in Canada, as would become apparent in the upsurge of the 1960s and '70s.

TRIPARTISM Canadian policymakers opted for a tripartite representational structure for most of their labor boards. Unlike the US "nonpartisan" structure, which politicized labor board decisions along party lines, the tripartite structure reinforced the Canadian labor regime's legitimacy and stability over time. Having labor and management representatives on the boards ensured that both parties felt that their views were fairly represented, and that both had a stake in the maintenance of the boards as institutions (Block 1993; Kumar 1993). This was particularly important for limiting management's ability to question the very legitimacy of the boards, as happened in the United States. The tripartite structure also explicitly recognized and institutionalized the distinct class interests of labor and capital. This made it harder for employers' individual property and contract rights to trump workers collective labor rights. It also mitigated, but did not eliminate, the tendency toward narrow legalism more prevalent in the nonpartisan, quasi-judicial NLRB (MacDowell 1978: 195). At a more symbolic level, the tripartite structure also promoted labor's identification as a class representative, while undermining employers' ability to portray business interests as the general or "public" interest.

As with the decision to combine adjudicative and conciliatory functions, policymakers' decision to opt for a tripartite structure was closely related to their goal of imposing industrial peace. Although class representatives would not be legal experts, policymakers believed that their greater familiarity with the dynamics of industrial relations would facilitate reaching agreements, avoiding strikes, and ensuring greater compliance with board decisions.

While Canadian employers bitterly resented the government's imposition of compulsory collective bargaining, by the end of the 1940s they were generally resigned to its inevitability. Instead of full-fledged resistance to the new labor regime as a whole, management pursued a strategy of seeking policy amendments that would work in its favor. None of the reforms were aimed at changing the tripartite structure of the boards. In stark contrast to US employers, who challenged the very notion that employers could serve in a representative capacity on government advisory boards, Canadian employers by the end of the 1940s had largely accepted this idea (Fudge and Tucker 2001; McInnis 2002).

Canadian ruling parties' intransigence delayed labor regime formation by nearly a decade compared to the US. Labor rights had to be forcibly extracted from a hostile state as a result of escalating labor militancy. This reinforced for labor the value of independent organization and militancy to influence state policy from without. Meanwhile, the labor regime's blending of adjudication and conciliation, along with its largely tripartite structure, set in place dynamics that would ensure the Canadian labor regime's long-term stability and legitimacy. It created a labor regime governed by a *class idea* in which labor functioned as a *class representative*. The regime explicitly recognized class divisions and class interests, as well as the structural power imbalance inherent in the labor–capital relationship. While the regime's formal structures encouraged a degree of bureaucratic legalism, its more interventionist form politicized class conflict, encouraging a broader political vision for labor.

LABOR REGIME DEVELOPMENT: EROSION VERSUS STABILITY

Given the different conditions surrounding labor regime formation in the United States and Canada, the political alliances for labor that resulted, and the different labor regime structures that emerged out of that process, what were the consequences for labor regime development and union strength?

Here we must focus on how both countries' labor regimes shaped the way that class conflict translated into the political realm. In Canada, the labor regime's conciliation-focused, tripartite structure meant that class issues were recognized as such. Worker protest translated into political pressure for reform, leading to periodic policy adjustments to contain class conflict within institutional channels, regardless of the political party in power. At the same time, the labor regime's focus on enforcing industrial peace recognized class power imbalances and restricted employers' ability to manipulate the collective bargaining process. As a result, postwar class conflict strengthened the Canadian labor regime's stability and legitimacy.

In the United States, the process of translating class conflict into politics was blocked. The quasi-judicial, nonpartisan structure of the US labor regime meant that class issues were translated as questions of legal rights, partisan interests of a Democratic Party constituency, or as individual problems unrelated to politics. This impeded legislative efforts at labor policy reform by making them appear to advance "special interests," or by dissipating the political effect of worker protest.

With legislative reform blocked, the formal US labor regime structure remained frozen. However, the regime continued to erode through judicial and administrative interpretations of the law. Those shifted toward balancing employers' "right to manage" and "free speech" rights against workers' collective bargaining rights, while emphasizing legal proceduralism. The rights-based regime favored employers by concealing class power imbalances and not restraining employers' ability to manipulate the collective bargaining process. As a result, postwar class conflict weakened the US labor regime, leaving it less institutionalized and more politically contentious.

1940s and 1950s: Policy Development and Interpretation

United States: "Balancing" Management and Worker Rights

The US labor regime continued to develop based on trends that emerged in the 1930s. The focus on mimicking the forms of legal procedure and due process transferred a template based on individual rights into an area of law fundamentally based on collective rights. This submerged the power imbalances inherent in the employment relationship, creating a formal equivalency between labor and capital as interest groups.

The first major postwar indicator of this trend was the Taft-Hartley Act. Coming after employer setbacks in the 1930s and early '40s, it was part of a concerted effort by management to reassert its "right to manage" as a counterbalance to labor's right to collective bargaining (Harris 1982; NAM NIIC 1945). A central part of employers' strategy in pushing the bill was their focus on correcting the perceived "imbalance" of the Wagner Act's promotion of collective bargaining rights, and the "irresponsibility" of labor's postwar strike wave.

The language of "balance" and "due process" permeated the law. Section 14(b) "balanced" the right to join a union with the right to *refrain* from joining a union, paving the way for right-to-work laws and undermining union security. The separation of prosecutorial and adjudicative functions of the NLRB with the creation of the Office of the General Counsel was done in the name of establishing "due process." But this primarily served to limit labor's direct access to the board by mediating its access through the General Counsel (Block 1993). And, while not directly related to formal legal equivalence, the anti-Communist affidavit included in Section 9(h) implicitly undermined the legitimacy of working-class-based demands, tying them to a treasonous Communist ideology.

Key to employers' efforts to reimpose balance was the establishment of a new legal doctrine known as "employer free speech." Creating an analogy to political campaign speech, employer free speech rights balanced unions' right to make their case to workers against management's right to make their case against them. Implicit was the idea that unionization is not an independent decision for workers to make among themselves, but rather a campaign where workers choose between two opposing and external forces: the union and the company. In the interest of ensuring that workers hear both sides of the unionization argument, employer free speech in practice legalized a variety of employer intimidation tactics that have since become standard fare in the union avoidance playbook (Bronfenbrenner 2009; Secunda 2012).

The doctrine originated in Section 8(c) of the Taft-Hartley Act, but its application remained contentious for several years. The NLRB initially sought to strike a balance between ensuring access to "both sides" of the unionization argument and protecting workers from intimidation with its *Bonwit Teller* decision.[7] It created a labor relations version of the federal "equal time" provision for parties and candidates in elections. The courts looked dimly upon that decision, although they did not go so far as to overturn it. However, that did happen in 1953 after a change in NLRB personnel. Ruling in its *Livingston Shirt*,[8] *Peerless Plywood*,[9] and *Chicopee Manufacturing Co.*[10] decisions, the new NLRB rejected the logic of *Bonwit Teller*, affirming instead a broad employer right to free expression over the course of union election campaigns. In creating an analogy with political free speech rights and formal equality under the law, the new NLRB overlooked noted jurist Learned Hand's earlier observation that "[w]hat to an outsider will be no more than the vigorous presentation of a conviction, to an employee may be the manifestation of a determination which it is not safe to thwart"[11] (Aaron 1962; Adell 1965).

The new NLRB's rulings also signaled a shift in the functioning of the board more generally. Eisenhower broke with the nonpartisan tradition established by Roosevelt and Truman, instead appointing experienced management-side labor attorneys. Board appointees no longer represented a disinterested idea of "the public," but rather the political agenda of the president who appointed them. As the *National Association of Manufacturers' Law Digest* noted, "They [the NLRB] seem to have proceeded on the assumption that since they were appointed by a new Administration they had a license to overhaul any or all of the Board's policies" (quoted in Draper 1989: 34). While the Kennedy board overturned several of the Eisenhower board's most pro-management rulings, the federal courts intervened to reassert employer free speech rights (Adell 1965). Thus, while board partisanship made rulings more politically contentious and vulnerable to being overturned by subsequent boards, court oversight gave an advantage to more conservative, legalistic, and above all individualist interpretations of the statute. This dynamic intensified as the partisan divide sharpened under President Reagan, and NLRB

---

[7] *Bonwit Teller, Inc.*, 96 N.L.R.B. 608 (1951).
[8] *Livingston Shirt Corp.*, 107 N.L.R.B. 400 (1953).
[9] *Peerless Plywood Co.*, 107 N.L.R.B. 427 (1953).
[10] *Chicopee Manufacturing Co.*, 107 N.L.R.B. 106 (1953).
[11] Quoted in *Federbush Co.*, 121 F.2d 954, 957 (1941).

appointments are now regularly a flashpoint of partisan conflict between Democrats and Republicans (Draper 1989; Flynn 2000; Turner 2005).

This new, more politicized board structure was qualitatively different from the tripartite boards of the wartime and pre-Wagner period. First, the salient divide on the new board was party identification, not class; rather than being management and union representatives, board members were primarily Republican or Democratic appointees.[12] Instead of recognizing distinct class interests, this partisan structure reduced class interests to partisan special interests. Second, board appointees were almost invariably attorneys, not actual union or management representatives. As such, their appointment virtually guaranteed an intensification of adherence to formal legalism on the board, as opposed to the more flexible reconciliation of opposing interests that is supposed to occur on a tripartite board.

Canada: Recognizing and Regulating Class Conflict

The Canadian labor regime's emphasis on enforcing industrial peace seriously restricted labor's scope of action, erecting stiff barriers for union certification and striking, and demanding "responsibility" from union leaders to prevent labor unrest. But the regime's focus on industrial peace also reinforced recognition of class divisions through its tripartite structures, while restricting employer behavior as well. Additionally, greater state intervention increased government sensitivity to class conflict. The result was a labor regime that encouraged labor mobilization, resulting in a dynamic of class conflict leading to legislative responses aimed at routing conflict back into institutional channels.

After PC 1003's proclamation in 1944, the next major step in the development of the Canadian labor regime was the establishment of union security provisions. This mirrored cross-border differences in the initial establishment of collective bargaining rights. In the United States, the Roosevelt administration offered "maintenance of membership" clauses[13] at the outset of World War II in exchange for adherence to a no-strike pledge and enforcement of production quotas (Lichtenstein 1982:

---

[12] Certainly, Democratic appointees have tended to represent labor's interests, and Republican appointees have tended to represent management's interests. But this is not their *primary* identification. Within this board structure, class ends up getting refracted through party identification.

[13] As mentioned in Chapter 2, note 30, maintenance of membership clauses do not require union membership as a condition of employment, but do require that those workers who join the union retain their membership for the duration of the collective bargaining agreement currently in effect.

78–81). In Canada, the Rand Formula provisions were extracted from the state as part of the settlement of a bitter 99-day strike in 1945 by UAW members at the Ford plant in Windsor, Ontario (Fudge and Tucker 2001: 283–287; Yates 1993: 51–54). The conditions under which union security was won affected both regimes' long-term stability. In the United States, union security provisions were caught up in the anti-labor backlash following the war, as the Taft-Hartley Act outlawed the closed shop and allowed right-to-work laws, that is, the open shop. In Canada, the Rand Formula diffused across the country and became institutionalized (Fudge and Tucker 2001: 293).

Aware that PC 1003 was due to expire soon after the war, Canadian workers kept pressure on the government to craft a more permanent postwar labor regime (Robinson 1990: 254–255). That came in 1948 with the passage of the federal IRDIA, accompanied by similar legislation in each of the 10 provinces. Compared with Taft-Hartley, passed one year before, the IRDIA was more restrictive in terms of union certification and limits on striking. However, it lacked the hallmarks of the Taft-Hartley legislation: right-to-work provisions, the anti-Communist affidavit, and employer free-speech protections.

This was not for lack of trying on the part of Canadian employers. To the contrary, they aggressively sought to incorporate Taft-Hartley-style provisions into the Canadian legislation, both at the federal and provincial levels. Quebec employers actually succeeded in including an anti-Communist provision in that province's legislation, and BC employers managed to win provisions for criminally prosecuting strikers (Canadian Manufacturers' Association 1947a; 1947b; Fudge and Tucker 2001: 295–297; McInnis 2002: 161–169; Stewart and Dalton 1948).

But Canadian policymakers rebuffed such employer proposals. They thought that the IRDIA was not as "unbalanced" as the Wagner Act, and therefore did not require a Taft-Hartley-style correction. As Deputy Minister of Labour W. Elliott Wilson noted, "Canada has been fortunate in that it has not gone to extremes. The pendulum has not swung too far in either direction" (Anonymous 1948). They also did not feel that specific anti-Communist legislation was necessary because, as discussed in Chapter 5, they were confident that the CCF could do a good job of policing and containing the Communist left on its own (Fudge and Tucker 2001: 298). Eight out of 11 Canadian jurisdictions did eventually adopt some form of employer free speech protection, but these protections have remained much more narrowly circumscribed than in the United States, and are counterbalanced by extensive employer interference prohibitions (Adell 1965; Doorey 2007; McPhillips 1982).

As the Canadian postwar settlement solidified, a tug-of-war developed between labor and capital, mediated through state legislation. Labor unrest led to state intervention, which would then culminate in legislative amendment of labor laws. For example, even though employers in Quebec and British Columbia were able to win more draconian restrictions on labor than other provinces in the late 1940s, militant strikes subsequently succeeded in repealing many of those restrictions (Isitt 2011; Rouillard 2004).

1960s: Extending Collective Bargaining to the Public Sector

The differences between the formation and development of private sector labor regimes in the United States and Canada in the 1930s and '40s repeated themselves when public sector labor regimes took shape in the 1960s. As before, US public sector workers were granted various forms of union rights relatively early by sympathetic politicians. Meanwhile, Canadian public sector workers had to fight for longer, and extracted their collective bargaining rights from a reluctant, often hostile state. The result was a more domesticated labor movement in the United States, and a more mobilized movement in Canada.

United States: Granting Public Sector Labor Rights

The large-scale extension of collective bargaining rights to US public sector workers began in a few states such as California, Massachusetts, and Wisconsin in the late 1950s.[14] The most significant early breakthrough was President Kennedy's Executive Order 10988, issued in 1962, which extended limited collective bargaining rights to federal government workers. However, public sector unionism did not begin to grow significantly until the late 1960s (Freeman 1986; Lewin and Goldenberg 1980; McCartin 2006; Miller and Canak 1988; Najita and Stern 2001).

In all these cases, public sector collective bargaining rights were largely granted by sympathetic Democratic Party politicians. The new laws varied significantly in their scope, ranging from rights to "meet and confer" with

---

[14] Municipal workers in certain large cities had started unionizing earlier, as had teachers and health care workers, many of whom are in the public sector. Nonetheless, public sector organizing on any significant scale only began in the 1960s.

management all the way to binding arbitration. Generally, the laws governing public sector unionization tended to be weak, and none granted the right to strike (Freeman 1986: 46–47; Robinson 1993: 29–30).

The fact that it was sympathetic politicians granting public sector collective bargaining rights often gave the impression that they were offering payback to loyal constituencies. This was literally true in some cases, as with Kennedy's proclamation of EO 10988, which was understood as a reward in exchange for union support in the 1960 election, particularly in the hotly contested state of Illinois, which Kennedy barely won (Miller and Canak 1988). The conditions surrounding the establishment of public sector collective bargaining rights reinforced the political perception of labor as a narrow special interest.

Canada: Extracting Public Sector Labor Rights

The Canadian government only began extending collective bargaining rights to public sector workers in the mid-1960s, starting with postal workers. As with private sector workers in the 1930s and '40s, Canadian public sector workers had begun organizing as far back as 1889, but had faced opposition and intransigence from government officials. Quebec Premier Jean Lesage summarized the government's imperious attitude when he declared in 1962 that "the Queen does not negotiate with her subjects" (quoted in Boivin 1972: 705). Instead, the federal Civil Service Commission unilaterally determined wages and working conditions in the public sector. While the federal government did begin consulting its workers via advisory groups in the 1940s, and permitted dues checkoff for employee associations as of 1953, full-fledged collective bargaining in the public sector remained far off.

The turning point was in 1963, when the Conservative government of John Diefenbaker rejected the Civil Service Commission's wage proposals, triggering a rebellion among federal workers. Coincidentally, the government also lost the confidence of Parliament that year, leading to elections where the Conservatives were replaced by the Liberals, now led by Lester B. Pearson. Upon taking office, Pearson appointed a Preparatory Committee on Collective Bargaining in the Public Service to design a new public sector collective bargaining policy. The question now was no longer if, but how to implement collective bargaining in the public sector.

The Preparatory Committee's proposals included full collective bargaining rights with recourse to binding arbitration and no right to strike.

However, events soon overtook the Committee, as postal workers staged a massive, popularly supported walkout in 1965. This showed the government that strike restrictions may be ineffective, while also increasing demand for the right to strike among other groups of public sector workers. As a result, the Preparatory Committee modified its proposals, adding a mechanism to allow public workers the right to strike (Arthurs 1968; Lewin and Goldenberg 1980).

The revised proposals provoked a backlash among employers and their political representatives. They were appalled at the idea of allowing government workers to go on strike, and warned of the dire consequences that it would entail. But by this point, Pearson understood the need to grant full collective bargaining rights to public sector workers, including the right to strike. As he explained to a Member of Parliament who wrote to complain about the proposed legislation,

> After very careful consideration, my colleagues and I concluded that in the existing climate of public opinion in this country, and especially in the Province of Quebec, to introduce legislation which failed to provide civil servants with bargaining rights comparable, in the philosophical sense, to those available to other employees in the private sector, would court not only extreme opposition from the ranks of organized labour, but far more dangerous, a wave of serious unrest in the Public Service.
>
> Nobody wants chaos and disorder in the ranks of the civil service. My colleagues and I have concluded that the threat of such disorder is not academic, and that it is a good deal less likely to occur in a realistic bargaining relationship rooted in law than it would be if we attempted to make work stoppage illegal in all circumstances. My own feeling is that if public servants are to be told that under law they can never strike, one may be precipitating the very thing one is trying to prevent (Pearson 1966: 1–2).

Pearson's logic was fully in keeping with the central tenets of the Canadian labor regime as it was established in the 1940s: above all, avoid disorder and ensure industrial peace. It also captures the dynamic of labor protest followed by legislative reform that characterized the postwar development of the Canadian labor regime in general.

The resulting federal legislation, the Public Service Staff Relations Act (PSSRA), was enacted in 1967. Its basic outlines bore a strong resemblance to the private sector IRDIA: full collective bargaining rights, including the right to strike for most public sector workers, together with strict limits on strike authorization and a strong burden of "responsibility" on union leaders for controlling shop floor militancy. Like the IRDIA, the PSSRA was to be administered by a tripartite board, known as the Public Service Staff Relations Board (PSSRB).

Once the PSSRA was in place, unionization of the public sector exploded, reaching close to 80 percent of public workers by the 1980s. Similar laws were also enacted in the provinces, allowing provincial and municipal workers to join the burgeoning Canadian public sector labor movement.

1960s–1970s: State Responses to Working-Class Upsurge

The late 1960s marked a decisive shift in the character of class conflict in both countries. Strike rates began to spike in the mid-1960s after declining fairly consistently in the years following World War II.[15] This signaled a new wave of working-class unrest, a fraying of whatever truce or understanding existed in the postwar decades.

Even though the upsurge of class conflict may have looked similar in both countries, it was interpreted in very different ways, with different consequences for each labor regime. In Canada, it was seen as a "crisis of collective bargaining," a crisis in class relations that required a state policy intervention. The result was a new series of policy reforms that strengthened the Canadian labor regime. In the United States, worker unrest was understood primarily as a crisis of the individual worker, related to workers' increasing sense of alienation in an increasingly "postindustrial" society (Bell 1973). While state actors did weigh policy options, they were all related to alleviating workers' problems *as individuals*. There was no sense of workers' problems being a class issue, tied to a broader set of social relations and power dynamics. As such, worker unrest did not translate into pressure to address what was by then a severely weakened labor regime. Instead, US labor was left in the 1970s trying to persuade increasingly unreliable allies in the Democratic Party to pass a new round of reform legislation, again making labor appear as a special interest lobbying for legislative favors.

Canada: Class Issues as Class Issues

Faced with growing working-class unrest, including crippling strikes at key employers such as the postal service and the railroads, the Canadian government was concerned about the danger of chaos and disorder. State actors understood the unrest as symptomatic of a crisis of institutions, the institutions that were essential for reproducing and maintaining social order.[16]

---

[15] See Figures 2.15 and 2.16.
[16] For more detailed accounts of the labor unrest of the 1960s in Canada, see (McInnis 2011).

The state's response was to convene a special Task Force on Labour Relations in 1966. It would analyze the causes underlying the wave of working-class unrest, and propose policy changes. The task force was chaired by H.D. "Buzz" Woods, the McGill industrial relations professor introduced earlier. Over the next two years, Woods coordinated a massive, multipronged, comparative and historical analysis of all aspects of the Canadian industrial relations system and its role in Canadian society as a whole. Tapping the expertise of dozens of leading scholars, the task force commissioned no fewer than 73 ancillary reports, while committee members traveled abroad to examine industrial relations systems in the United States and several European countries (McInnis 2011: 276).

The final report, issued in December 1968, confirmed government fears: wide-scale worker unrest was symptomatic of "a crisis of confidence in the present industrial relations system" (Canada Task Force on Labour Relations and Woods 1968: 3). The system was straining under the weight of employers whose stated support for collective bargaining was belied by their recalcitrance on the shop floor, a new generation of workers challenging the authority of their elected union leaders, and a government that increasingly resorted to coercive labor injunctions to impose its will. The task force saw in the unrest "a sense of frustration that the social, economic and political institutions of society are not pressing effectively for the removal of the disparities [in availability of human rights]" (Canada Task Force on Labour Relations and Woods 1968: 39).

While sympathetic to workers' plight, the committee nonetheless viewed increasing worker protest with alarm. Of particular concern to them was their observation that "worker dissatisfaction sometimes runs as deeply against the union and collective bargaining as against management" (Canada Task Force on Labour Relations and Woods 1968: 98), undermining union leaders' ability serve as "responsible" representatives. Indeed, the committee noted with dismay that "militant behaviour has paid off frequently in recent years, even where union membership militancy has taken illegal forms," and that "once having tasted the fruits of their militancy, union members may find it irresistible to display that militancy again" (103).

Despite these challenges to its authority, the task force came down firmly in favor of shoring up collective bargaining as an institution, "not only because of its virtues ... but also because we see no alternative that is compatible with the heritage of Western values and institutions" (Canada Task Force on Labour Relations and Woods 1968: 137). They lauded the role that collective bargaining had played in extending democracy to the industrial sphere, reducing "the disparity between the rights of the individual as a worker and his rights as a citizen." Going further, they noted that "the curbing or elimination of arbitrary authority in the hands of management has been one of the greatest contributions of unions and collective bargaining." (97).

The challenge for the task force was to shore up the legitimacy of the industrial relations system by maintaining "a minimal degree of consensus with respect both to the fundamental tenets of the industrial relations system, and to its current operational framework of rules and regulations, without which it cannot hope to endure" (93).

To that end, the committee proposed a lengthy series of reforms to the structure and functioning of Canadian collective bargaining. These proposals, while not all adopted, set a new pattern for the Canadian labor regime. This was symbolized most clearly by its recommendation to add a preamble to the Canada Labour Code positively affirming the state's commitment to collective bargaining as an institution (Canada Task Force on Labour Relations and Woods 1968: 138). In addition to shaping the subsequent development of federal labor law, the Woods Report served as a template for many of the province-level labor reforms that occurred over the course of the 1970s – the reforms that scholars now identify as contributing to US-Canada union density divergence (Weiler 1980).

While the substance of these labor law reforms was certainly important in and of itself, what is of particular interest for our purposes is how the Woods Task Force reinforced the previously established pattern of labor regime development in Canada. Convened in response to mass worker unrest, out of a concern for maintaining industrial peace and social order, the task force recognized the worker unrest as a class issue, related to structural power imbalances in society. In response, it proposed a series of policy reforms aimed at addressing those structural power imbalances, albeit in a way that constrained both labor and management's scope of action. The result was a labor regime that strengthened over the course of the 1970s and '80s.

US: Class Issues as Individual Alienation

As worker unrest spread in the United States in the late 1960s and early 1970s, it attracted increasing attention from both the state and the media.[17] But whereas the unrest was interpreted as a class issue in

---

[17] For detailed accounts of the labor militancy of this period, see (Brenner et al. 2010; Cowie 2010).

Canada, it was largely interpreted as a problem of individual alienation in the United States. Rather than seeking to examine the possible structural causes behind the rash of wildcat strikes, policy advisors and reporters alike chose to plumb the depths of workers' psychology to understand the problem.

The favored term was the "blue-collar blues," a blanket label applied to everything from frustrated life expectations, to depression caused by the mind-numbing organization of work, to the perceived loss of power and status of blue-collar work (Goodling 1970; New York Times 1970). The turn to psychology was necessary because the very idea that it could be a problem related to class was excluded a priori. As Nicholas von Hoffman explained,

> As a class, these people have no solidarity, no awareness of themselves as a group apart as a group with a special destiny. Because they're not a class in anything like the Marxist use of that term, they're highly unpredictable people. It's impossible to assume that they will act in certain ways according to their perceived class Interest (Hoffman 1971: B1).

The Nixon administration took notice of the emerging problem. In a 1970 memorandum prepared for Secretary of Labor George Schultz entitled "The Problem of the Blue-Collar Worker," Assistant Secretary for Policy, Evaluation, and Research Jerome M. Rosow outlined a diagnosis of the problem and a possible course of treatment. Echoing the popular media of the time, Rosow emphasized twin threats: the "economic squeeze" and the "social squeeze." The economic squeeze centered around workers' eroding purchasing power as a result of increasing family obligations and inflation, combined with limited possibilities for upward job mobility. The social squeeze focused on how blue-collar workers now felt like low-status "forgotten people ... unsure about their place in the 'mainstream' of American society" (Rosow 1970: 8).[18]

Importantly, Rosow asserted that "people in the blue-collar class are less mobile, less organized, and *less capable of using legitimate means to either protect the status quo or secure changes in their favor*" (1970: 7, emphasis added). As he excluded *a priori* the idea that the problem was class-related, so too did he exclude the idea that workers have any independent means at their disposal to better their situation. This is not likely the result of an anti-union animus on Rosow's part, as he proposed plenty of policies in the memo that would undoubtedly be branded as "socialist"

---

[18] Notice the echoes of Roosevelt's "Forgotten Man" speech.

were they to be proposed today. These included family subsidies for child care and ensuring the right to higher education for children of blue-collar workers. Rather, it is more indicative of the erasure of the class idea in the United States by this time. The idea that unions could play a role in shaping broad social issues was virtually unthinkable. Instead, both economic and social problems were framed at the level of the individual.

The erasure of the class idea was equally on display in the Nixon administration's next attempt at addressing the "blue-collar blues," a 262-page report issued in 1972 entitled *Work in America* (HEW Task Force 1972). Written by a special task force convened by the Secretary of Health, Education, and Welfare (HEW), the report explored in depth the broad role of work in society, workers' collective psychology, the effects of work on personal health, and more. Its detailed policy proposals outlined plans for the redesign of work to make it less alienating, along with full employment and job retraining policies. What was missing from *Work in America* was unions. The section called "The Role of Trade Unions," the only section that discussed unions, was all of two pages long, and focused mostly on how unions had also contributed to the problem of worker alienation, and now found themselves to be targets of workers' ire, along with management (HEW Task Force 1972: 112–114).

The contrast with the Woods Report is striking. Whereas the entire crisis in Canada was conceived of as a crisis of the industrial relations system,[19] a system in which unions were an essential constitutive part, the crisis in the United States was conceived as a problem of individuals in their relation to society as a whole. There was no acknowledgment in this conceptual model of groups, let alone classes, or power dynamics between groups. As such, it is understandable that unions barely merited any mention in the discussion.

Since the worker upsurge of the 1960s was interpreted not as a class issue, but as a problem of individuals, the policy solutions did not address

---

[19] This is not to say that alienation was not an issue in Canada. To the contrary, the Woods Report devoted several pages to a discussion of the alienation of modern work life. The key difference is that they viewed this alienation also as a product of the broader crisis of confidence in the industrial relations system. Implicit in its analysis was the idea that unions could and should have a role to play in addressing worker alienation: "Unions, like management, have failed in this new and more challenging area, although they have responded comparatively well to worker concerns about their terms and conditions of employment and their subordinate status in relation to their employers. To some extent this failure is due to the fact that unions and collective bargaining were not designed to handle problems growing out of the nature of work itself" (Canada Task Force on Labour Relations and Woods 1968: 97–98).

labor policy or labor–management power dynamics. Workplace protest in the United States did not translate into policy reform, as it did in Canada.

This is not to say that there was no need for labor policy reform. To the contrary, labor regime erosion and union decline was painfully evident by the 1970s. But with the labor regime incapable of translating worker pressure into policy reform, labor had to continue its inside game of seeking influence as an interest group within the Democratic Party. The problem was that the Democratic Party was distancing itself from labor by the 1970s, becoming less and less reliable as an ally even as labor's dependence on the party was increasing (Brenner 1985; Davis 1986). As such, despite having a Democratic president and Democratic control of both houses of Congress, the 1977 Labor Law Reform Bill died when it failed to withstand a Senate filibuster in 1978 (Cowie 2010: 296–298).

The failure of the Labor Law Reform bill starkly exposed labor's limited power within the Democratic Party coalition, while also illustrating how the political system viewed labor. In what is now a well-worn tactic, those opposed to the law attacked it as a favor for a narrow special interest, namely unions. Typical of this approach was a letter from a Wyoming employer to President Carter, who wrote,

> It has always been my understanding that the President of the United States was elected to serve the total population, and not just one special segment. On this issue, 75 percent of the nation's employees, whom you are also supposed to represent, are not unionized by choice. And yet, you exercise the power and influence of your office in support of the union position in this matter. It is obvious that the financial support of the labor organizations is buying your support and influence (Zook 1978: 1).

While employers would be expected to attack legislation designed to facilitate unionization, what is significant is the degree to which this identity of labor as a special interest was pervasive not only among employers, but among labor's ostensible allies in government. Administration support for the bill came more from a desire to placate a key constituency as opposed to a belief in the need to shore up collective bargaining rights. As such, when other political priorities came up, they took precedence over labor's interests, and the Administration did not do all in its power to overcome Senate resistance to the bill (Cowie 2010: 292–295).

After the 1978 labor law failure came events more commonly identified with US union decline: deregulation, the Reagan revolution, and the PATCO strike. But these landmark events only exposed the weakness of a labor regime that had been eroding for decades.

The differing responses to the working-class upsurge of the late 1960s and early 1970s in the United States and Canada illustrate how much labor regimes had already diverged in both countries by that point. Whereas the Canadian labor regime allowed for an effective translation of class mobilization into the political realm, leading to regular policy reforms, the US labor regime consistently mistranslated class mobilization into the political realm, diffusing labor's independent political pressure. While Canadian labor gained benefits from increased mobilization, US labor continued its turn inward, relying ever more on retaining its flagging influence within the Democratic Party.

CONCLUSION

Much research has shown how current differences in labor law make it harder to unionize in the United States than in Canada. What has remained unexplained is why, despite starting from similar frameworks, US labor law weakened over time, while Canadian labor law strengthened. Explaining why the laws diverged is essential to explain why union density diverged in the United States and Canada.

Labor law divergence resulted from differences in the character and timing of ruling party responses to working-class upsurge during the Great Depression and World War II. In the United States, Roosevelt enacted reforms early as a means of quelling unrest and absorbing labor into the New Deal coalition. In Canada, Liberal and Conservative governments alike resisted reforms, responding to labor unrest with increased coercion. Mackenzie King's Liberals only enacted reforms under duress nearly a decade later than in the United States, in the face of a crippling wartime strike wave and a growing electoral threat from the CCF.

The resulting labor regimes, while formally similar, were governed by different logics. The US regime was governed by a *pluralist idea* focused on promoting workers' collective rights. The Canadian regime was governed by a *class idea* focused on containing class conflict. Within those regimes, US labor was treated as an *interest group*, while Canadian labor was treated as a *class representative*.

Labor regime differences led to differences in how those labor regimes perceived and processed working-class issues. In Canada, working-class issues were understood as such. Worker unrest translated into policy reforms, which strengthened the Canadian labor regime over time. In the United States, that translation process was blocked. Working-class issues were mistranslated as either questions of legal rights to be balanced against competing employer property and free-speech rights, the narrow special interests of a key Democratic Party constituency, or personal problems unrelated to politics. In each case, this mistranslation diffused the political effect of worker unrest, and weakened the US labor regime.

The differences in political incorporation and regime development led to a Canadian labor regime that legitimized class issues and facilitated addressing them, and a US labor regime that delegitimized class issues and prevented addressing them. As employer aggression flared in both countries in the 1970s, the Canadian regime held employers in check and better protected workers' collective bargaining rights. Meanwhile, the US labor regime proved incapable of reining in employers and protecting workers' rights. As a result, union density stabilized in Canada in the ensuing decades, while collapsing in the United States.

Conclusion

In an era of widening inequality, labor unions remain one of the few tools available to right the scales for those falling behind. But unions today are less able to do their job, beset by decades of weakness and organizational decline. Nowhere has this been more apparent than in the United States, where union density has sunk back to levels not seen since the early days of the Great Depression.

For its part, Canada has not been immune from global political and economic trends. Yet unions are currently much stronger there than in the United States, despite the two countries' many socioeconomic similarities. This was not always the case. For much of the twentieth century, unions in both countries followed similar tracks, diverging only in the 1960s. Understanding why Canadian unions have held their own can help explain why US unions declined, and can suggest strategies for reversing the trend.

Many of the standard explanations for US-Canada union density divergence fall short. It was not the result of differences in fundamental cultural values, nor of structural economic differences, nor of differences in individual preferences regarding unions and collective organization. Nor was it simply a function of differences in labor laws and policies. Rather, union density diverged as a result of differences in how the working class was politically incorporated in the United States and Canada during the Great Depression and World War II.

The social and political struggles of the 1930s and '40s forged two labor movements and two labor regimes that, although bearing a surface resemblance, were organized along different logics. In Canada, the working class was incorporated as a class representative. In the United States, it was incorporated as an interest group. This happened through what I have termed different processes of *political articulation*, the active work of parties in organizing political conflict and coalitions. Differences in how labor was political incorporated enabled or constrained labor's legitimacy and organizational capacity in different ways in both countries. Canadian labor's role as a class representative legitimized it and expanded its organizational capacity in the postwar decades, leading to union stability. Meanwhile, US labor's role as an interest group delegitimized it and undermined its organizational capacity, leading to union decline. Put differently, the class idea was more firmly embedded in politics, policies, and organizational practices in Canada relative to the United States.

But despite their differences, the fates of the US and Canadian labor movements remain closely intertwined. In these final sections, we will examine what has happened to both movements in recent decades, and close with some conjectures about what these developments hold for the future of the working class in the United States and Canada.

THE CLASS IDEA UNDER ATTACK

The period since the mid-1970s, often referred to as the "neoliberal" era, has been difficult for the working class and working-class movements around the globe. It has been a period of increasing state austerity, employer aggressiveness, job loss and employment instability, and income inequality, all in the name of increased economic "dynamism," "competitiveness," and free market orthodoxy (Albo 2009). For unions specifically, it has been a period of near-universal decline, as union density rates have dropped across virtually all industrialized countries (OECD 2017; Vachon, Wallace, and Hyde 2016).

However, there has been a good deal of cross-national variation in how neoliberal policies have affected working-class organization (Western 1995). In the case at hand, the effects have been much deeper and widespread in the United States compared to Canada. That is because the class idea, the degree to which class has served as a salient and legitimate principle of political organization, has been more deeply embedded in politics, policies, and practices in Canada relative to the United States. Nonetheless, attacks on unions and broader working-class movements have taken a toll in both countries.

US: Concessions, Partnership, and the Fleeting Search for Revival

The fate of the US labor movement since the mid-late 1970s has been well documented (Clawson and Clawson 1999; Davis 1999; Fantasia and Voss

2004; Moody 1988). It is the narrative underlying much of the existing industrial relations scholarship on union decline. Employer hostility, deregulation, Reagan and PATCO, plant closings, NLRB gridlock, and continued erosion of unions and collective bargaining have by now become standard elements of a story that speaks of the "disappearance" of the US working class (Cowie 2010). In the current environment it is virtually impossible even for analysts sympathetic to labor to speak of its current plight without at least implicitly calling into question its very viability (Dixon and Fiorito 2009; Moyers 2012).

Since Douglas Fraser somewhat belatedly recognized that labor was on the receiving end of a "one-sided class war" in 1979, the movement has struggled to figure out a response to the management onslaught. The initial response was one of retreat, starting with the contract that Fraser himself negotiated between the UAW and a nearly bankrupt Chrysler Corporation in 1979. For the first time in UAW history, Fraser agreed to contract concessions in the hope that they would save the financially troubled firm. The trend took off in earnest in the early 1980s, as company after company lined up to demand givebacks from their unions. Pattern agreements in steel, mining, meatpacking, auto, and other basic industries were dismantled, leaving the labor movement in disarray (Moody 1988; Slaughter 1983).

Over the course of the 1980s and into the 1990s, the new pattern of concession bargaining became institutionalized within a new regime of labor–management partnership. The centerpiece of this new regime was its focus on "employee participation" programs which, under the guise of improving the quality of work life, instead introduced a new form of workplace control known as "management by stress" (Arnold 1999; Fantasia, Clawson, and Graham 1988; Parker and Slaughter 1994). The emphasis on partnership, especially in a situation where management was clearly only interested in a partner it could control, undermined labor's ability to articulate and defend workers' interests by increasing its dependence on management beneficence and decreasing its class identity.

By the mid-1990s, the sense of organizational crisis within the US labor movement had reached a point where, for the first time in the history of the AFL-CIO, there was a contested election for the leadership. The challenger "New Voice" slate led by Service Employees International Union (SEIU) President John Sweeney defeated the incumbents, who represented the business union tradition passed down from George Meany. This led to new hopes for labor's organizational renewal, as scholars and progressives hailed Sweeney's call for a renewed focus on organizing (Clawson and Clawson 1999; Milkman 1998). New studies showed the benefits that innovative tactics and resource mobilization had on reversing union decline, and there was serious talk of possibilities for union renewal (Clawson 2003; Lopez 2004; Voss and Sherman 2000). Nonetheless, organizing remained exceedingly difficult and attacks on unions continued, as perhaps illustrated most devastatingly by the five-year Detroit Newspaper strike and lockout (Rhomberg 2012). Labor continued its downward spiral.

Talk of union renewal largely subsided by the mid-2000s as the AFL-CIO was wracked by internecine conflict that led to seven affiliates leaving to form the Change to Win Federation (CtW) in 2005. The CtW unions included three of the country's largest: SEIU, the International Brotherhood of Teamsters (IBT), and the United Food and Commercial Workers (UFCW). Although much of the press coverage focused on the personality conflicts behind the dispute, CtW advocates charged that the antiquated structure of the AFL-CIO left it ill-equipped to organize workers on a scale large enough to reverse labor's decline. While some analysts held out hope that the split might galvanize new organizing as unions competed for new members, union density continued its downward trajectory. Within a few years, several of the CtW affiliates reaffiliated with the AFL-CIO, and CtW had rebranded itself as less of a competing labor federation, and more of a "strategic organizing center" (Eidelson 2017a).[1]

Union political action in 2008 played a key role in getting Barack Obama elected as president. In exchange, labor hoped for passage of the Employee Free Choice Act (EFCA), the first effort at comprehensive labor law reform since the failed effort of 1977–1978. And yet, in a replay of the previous attempts, EFCA failed in Congress, despite a large majority in the House and a (just barely) filibuster-proof majority in the Senate. Labor's allies in the Democratic Party once again proved unreliable (Lichtenstein 2010; Lofaso 2011).

The 2010 midterm elections signaled a right-wing resurgence, as Republicans regained control of the federal House of Representatives, along with 25 state legislatures and 29 state governorships (National Conference of State Legislatures 2011). Unlike Democrats, who dithered on labor law reform, newly emboldened Republicans wasted no time in attacking unions. Wisconsin governor Scott Walker led the way with his

---

[1] For a more comprehensive analysis of the factors behind the split, see Chaison (2007); Estreicher (2006); Masters, Gibney, and Zagenczyk (2006); Milkman (2006a).

Act 10. Not only did it abolish "fair share" fees in the public sector, but it stripped public sector unions of the ability to negotiate about anything other than wage increases, limited pay raises to no more than the rate of inflation, and required annual union recertification votes.

The legislation sparked weeks of massive protests, including an occupation of the state capitol in Madison. Ultimately the legislation passed, as some protest leaders advocated channeling the protest energy into a campaign to recall Walker. In keeping with labor's weakened political standing, once the recall election campaign succeeded, the Democrats nominated as their standard-bearer Milwaukee mayor Tom Barrett. Not only was he the same candidate that Walker had just defeated in the 2010 election, but he refused to make labor rights a key recall campaign issue or even to commit to repeal Act 10 if elected. Barrett and his strategists did not want to be seen as in thrall to the labor "special interests," although they still expected labor's backing. Unsurprisingly, Barrett lost (Stein and Marley 2013; Yates 2012). Walker followed up his victories on Act 10 and the 2012 recall election with a right-to-work law for private sector workers in 2015 (Stein and Kissinger 2015).

President Obama won reelection in 2012, but labor's decline continued during his second term. Not only did union density continue to erode, but political attacks escalated at the state level. Indiana Governor Mitch Daniels passed a right-to-work law in 2012, after eliminating collective bargaining rights for public sector workers immediately upon taking office in 2005 (Davey 2012; Foley 2012). In Michigan, Governor Rick Snyder signed a right-to-work law in late 2012, which the state supreme court extended to public sector workers in 2015 (Egan 2015). Meanwhile, Snyder-appointed "emergency managers" took control of city governments across the state, tearing up city worker union contracts in the process (Blitchok 2012; MacGillis 2016). Ohio governor John Kasich tried to emulate Wisconsin's Act 10 with his own Senate Bill 5, although that law was overturned by popular referendum in November 2011 (McNay 2013). In Illinois, governor and former hedge fund manager Bruce Rauner has made attacking unions a centerpiece of his administration's efforts to create what he has called a more "business-friendly" climate in the state. He has sought to implement local "right-to-work zones" and eliminate "fair share" fees for state workers by executive order, although he has been blocked by a hostile legislature (Confessore 2015). West Virginia eliminated its law mandating that workers be paid a set "prevailing wage" on new construction projects, and passed a right-to-work law in February 2016, although the law remains blocked by court order (Associated Press 2016; MetroNews Staff 2017; Zuckerman 2017).

Still, there were some bright spots for workers' rights. At the Department of Labor, Wage and Hour Division head David Weil led a campaign to ratchet up enforcement and expand protections against wage theft, unpredictable scheduling, workers getting misclassified as independent contractors, and more (Penn 2016). The Obama NLRB issued rulings to hold franchisors more responsible for the labor practices of their franchisees, expedite certification elections, and recognize private university student workers' collective bargaining rights (Scheiber 2017). Meanwhile, "alt-labor" groups like the Restaurant Opportunities Center (ROC), National Domestic Workers Alliance (NDWA), OUR Walmart, the New York Taxi Workers Alliance (NYTWA), and the Coalition of Immokalee Workers (CIW) organized to win significant protections for groups of marginalized workers outside of traditional collective bargaining models (Eidelson 2013). Perhaps most impressive was the work of Fight for $15, which within a few years transformed the idea of a $15 minimum wage from a pipe dream into a reasonable target, and even a policy in some cities (Hannah 2016; Luce 2015).

Labor unions had a hand in all of these reforms, whether through financial backing, organizational support, member mobilization, or policy advocacy. Yet none of them were seen as labor victories, and none did much to reverse unions' own fortunes.[2] Nowhere has this been more apparent than with the Fight for $15. While the campaign has been remarkably successful in raising the minimum wage, the second part of its slogan – Fight for $15 *and a union* – has fallen by the wayside. Not only has the campaign not sparked union growth, but the unions that were instrumental in building the campaign have downplayed their role. Again, this is out of fear that linking the minimum wage fight to labor unions will undermine its legitimacy. As a result, few workers who have benefited from higher wages are aware of labor's role in securing those wage hikes. Similarly, Obama administration labor reforms appeared as enlightened policy decisions (or special interest favors, depending on one's perspective), not the product of labor mobilization. The result is what some have called "laborism without labor," wherein worker protection via government regulation expands as protection via worker organizing shrinks (Rosenfeld 2016a; Yeselson 2016).

This arrangement appears to suit segments of the Democratic Party elite, who are far more intrigued by the intricacies of policy design than the

---

[2] For examples of how media outlets have downplayed labor's role in the Fight for $15, see Harrell (2016); Pethokoukis (2016); Wallace-Wells (2016).

challenges of building worker power. Even as they continue to rely on unions as a critical source of funds and votes, their support for labor remains shallow and instrumental. This was driven home during the 2016 presidential campaign, when emails from Democratic nominee Hillary Clinton's campaign leaked. In one exchange, the candidate was asked to take a public stand against right-to-work laws. In response, her political director Amanda Renteria demurred, saying, "I like staying more at platitudes about what unions have done for workers." Campaign speechwriter Dan Schwerin replied with a helpful solution: "would a Tweet not do the trick here?" (Renteria and Schwerin 2015).

The contrast between the Clinton campaign's platitudes about labor issues and the candidate's concrete support for pro-business free trade policies and coziness with financial elites contributed to a Clinton "enthusiasm gap" among union voters, of which 43 percent voted for Trump. The gap was particularly pronounced in the critical counties in Michigan, Pennsylvania, and Wisconsin that put Donald Trump over the top in the Electoral College. This includes not only the much-discussed white segments of the working class who took a chance on Trump's faux populism, but also the tens of thousands of workers of color in cities like Detroit and Milwaukee who refused to fulfill their demographic destiny as taken-for-granted members of Clinton's base, and didn't vote at all (Ben-Shahar 2016; McQuarrie 2017; Rosenfeld 2016b; Tavernise 2016).

Upon taking office in January 2017, President Trump quickly ran into difficulty implementing much of his controversial agenda, thanks to a more unified Democratic opposition, skeptical courts, and an internally fractured Republican caucus. However, he and his Republican congressional counterparts had much less difficulty rolling back a slew of worker protections proposed or enacted under the Obama administration. These included an effort to raise the threshold above which salaried workers cannot receive overtime pay, regulations requiring federal contractors to disclose pay equity and workplace safety violations, rules on mine safety and exposure to beryllium, and mandates for private sector employers to collect and keep accurate data on workplace injuries and illnesses.[3]

This federal anti-worker offensive was mirrored at the state level, where newly installed Republican legislative majorities took aim at labor unions by passing right-to-work legislation in Missouri and

---

[3] For an overview of Trump administration policy changes related to worker rights and wages, see the Economic Policy Institute's Perkins Project on Worker Rights and Wages Policy Watch, at www.epi.org/policywatch/.

Kentucky, possibly making them the twenty-seventh and twenty-eighth right-to-work states (National Right to Work Committee 2017).[4] And in Iowa, lawmakers passed House File 291, which emulated Wisconsin's Act 10 in restricting public sector unions' ability to bargain over anything but wages, eliminating workers' ability to have their union dues deducted automatically from their paychecks, and requiring regular union recertification votes (Murphy 2017). Meanwhile, the AFL-CIO and large unions like SEIU have responded to the attacks with announcements of staff and budget cuts (Eidelson 2016; 2017b).

US labor's tactics and messaging may have changed over the past few decades, but the overall ideological framework has not. Labor remains stuck within its role as an interest group, reliant on influencing sympathetic politicians and negotiating ever-less-favorable terms with emboldened, aggressive employers. To the extent that labor has pursued more mobilizational strategies, debate about them has been at the level of technique and execution: how much to spend on organizing, how many organizers to hire, what tactics to use for greatest impact. With some exceptions, there has been little effort to develop a broader working-class identity. To the extent that labor leaders have dared talk about class, it has been in the context of "defending the middle class" or "working families," murky terms that both obscure the power relations underlying class differences between workers and employers in the workplace, and exclude marginalized segments of the working class like the poor and unemployed. The class idea remains elusive in the United States.

Canada: The Crisis of Class Organization

While many US labor scholars and union leaders look north to Canada as a model to which they aspire, there are growing signs that Canadian labor is in crisis as well (Camfield 2011; Jackson 2006). Although union density remains much higher than in the United States, there is increasing concern that Canadian labor's organizational power is eroding. Many unions, particularly in the private sector, are accepting concessionary agreements similar to those for which they criticized their US counterparts two decades ago. They have also backed away from the more militant rhetoric and

---

[4] This depends on what happens with West Virginia's 2016 right-to-work law, which is currently under appeal, as well as Missouri's law, which is blocked pending the result of a voter referendum scheduled for the November 2018 midterm elections. Additionally, a proposed right-to work law was defeated in the New Hampshire House of Representatives in February 2017 (Ancel 2017; Hicks 2017; Morris 2017).

action of the recent past, embracing instead the discourse of labor–management partnership (Rosenfeld 2009). And even in the public sector, some striking unions have failed to connect their struggles to the broader community or their own members, leaving them vulnerable to charges from anti-union public officials that they are merely "greedy special interests" (Camfield 2011; Ross and Savage 2013).

In the political realm, despite the NDP's historic positive role in articulating and defending labor's interests, it has faltered in recent years, and its relationship with labor has frayed. As with social democratic parties globally, the NDP has not been immune from the rightward tilt toward "Third Way" politics. NDP-led governments in Ontario, Manitoba, Saskatchewan, and British Columbia have proven all too willing to attack unions, particularly in the public sector, in the name of fiscal discipline (Bernard 1994; Camfield 2011; Pilon, Ross, and Savage 2011; Savage 2010). This has provoked rebukes and accusations of betrayal from labor leaders, and some prominent unions such as Unifor have gone so far as to sever their historic alliance with the NDP in favor of a more "strategic" approach to politics (Savage 2012).

More broadly, elements within the NDP have questioned the party's formal ties to labor, although delegates still voted to retain those ties at its 2011 party convention (Canadian Press 2011). So diluted has the class character of the NDP become that some analysts charge that "It is now virtually impossible to discern what sets an NDP government apart from those led by traditional parties of business" (Evans 2012). While the new NDP government in British Columbia gave some on the Left reason for hope, recent moves such as the government's approval of the environmentally sensitive Site C hydroelectric dam project have raised doubts (Ejeckam 2017; Kurjata 2017; Meissner 2017). At the federal level, Jagmeet Singh's victory in the 2017 NDP leadership race marked an important milestone, making him the first person of color to lead a major Canadian party. He brings a more youthful, vibrant image to the party, while the leadership contest he won signaled a leftward shift after previous leader Tom Mulcair's efforts to move the party further to the right. However, it remains unclear what Singh's message of "love and courage" will mean in terms of concrete policies or political direction (Austen 2017; Bruemmer 2017; Wherry 2017). Meanwhile, organizers behind the Leap Manifesto are evoking memories of the Waffle with their programmatic intervention to pull the NDP left on social, economic, and ecological issues (Canadian Press 2017a).

For its part, the Canadian state has become much more hostile toward labor. In the past, state intervention in labor disputes strengthened the

Canadian labor regime by reining in employer aggression and reinforcing the legitimacy of the overall collective bargaining framework. But in recent years, state action has eroded the Canadian labor regime. In their efforts to impose industrial peace, state actors have shifted from trying to "balance" union and employer interests to eliminating strikes at all cost. What Panitch and Swartz (2003) termed "permanent exceptionalism" has become more prevalent, as federal and provincial governments increasingly turn to "exceptional" forms of intervention, particularly back-to-work legislation, as a means of imposing order. This intervention has curtailed labor rights and undermined the Canadian labor regime's stated "rules of the game," as it makes clear that the state will discard those rules when they hinder its goals.

In sum, the class idea is under attack in Canada, just as it has been in the United States for decades. Significant elements within Canadian labor are moving away from their traditional role as class representatives fighting for broad social issues in favor of defensive battles to protect their narrow self-interest. Large segments of Canada's class-based political party have moved away from class politics and are becoming ever more indistinguishable from the mainstream ruling parties. And the Canadian state has felt less obligated to protect labor rights as a means of ensuring industrial peace, preferring instead a more explicitly coercive approach.

But despite these very real setbacks, the class idea remains more embedded in politics, policies, and practices in Canada compared to the United States. The institutional legacy of the political struggles of the 1930s and '40s, as well as the 1960s and '70s, still shapes the political terrain differently in both countries. Having said that, the problem of renewing class politics remains an open and hotly debated question in both countries, especially with the renewed focus on class and inequality in the years following the 2008 economic crisis.

What then is the future of class politics in North America? Is the class idea still relevant in the twenty-first century? If so, what must be done to revive it?

THE ROAD AHEAD

If we as a society care about the dangers of increasing economic inequality, job insecurity, and the erosion of democracy, then we must be concerned with rebuilding working-class power. A central part of this task must be rebuilding the very idea of the working class. Attacks on the working class over the past four decades have undermined that idea, not only in the United States and Canada, but across most capitalist democracies.

Rebuilding the class idea is not simply a matter of finding the right "messaging," or "framing" labor's issues in just the right way. It involves creating new, durable collective identities for labor, ones that recognize and encompass the working class as it exists today. While today's workers and unions can look to the past for promising examples, this must necessarily be a new endeavor.

The main lesson we can draw from the past is that such transformative collective identities are created, maintained, and reshaped through sustained collective action. These identities have taken many forms through the years: the labor republicanism of the Knights of Labor; the "One Big Union" of the Industrial Workers of the World; the industrial unionism of the early CIO; the slogan "I Am A Man," adopted by striking Memphis sanitation workers in 1968 as they fused labor and civil rights struggles; and CSN leader Marcel Pepin's vision of "the second front," to name a few. These ideas sparked mass mobilization, which in turn injected the ideas with greater potency.

More than anything, it is this combination of galvanizing ideas tied to durable, deep organization that is missing from today's labor movement, on both sides of the border. We can certainly find elements of each. Despite decades of decline, unions still have plenty of organizational infrastructure at their disposal, which must not be discounted (Ginsburg 2017). But this is not tied to compelling ideas or collective identities. Leaving aside forgettable efforts at doing so like AFL-CIO's "Union Yes!" and "Voice@Work" campaigns, even more sophisticated campaigns like SEIU's Justice for Janitors have not aimed to create a sense of collective identity among its members. Rather, they have aimed to create "public dramas" using scripted confrontations to shame corporate targets into making deals with union leaders (Chun 2009). Workers in such a model function not as a collective force driving the campaign, but as "authentic messengers" dispatched by union leadership to influence media coverage and public opinion (McAlevey 2016).

We have also seen galvanizing ideas take hold in recent years. These include the aforementioned Fight for $15, the powerful counterposition of "the 99 percent" versus "the one percent" that animated the Occupy movement, and Bernie Sanders' message of working-class justice and solidarity that fueled his improbable run for the Democratic Party's presidential nomination (Gould-Wartofsky 2015; Milkman, Luce, and Lewis 2013; Rosenblum 2017; Sanders 2016).[5] These, however, have lacked

---

[5] These movements have also taken hold in Canada to some extent. The Fight for $15 has been the most successful, pressuring the governments of Alberta and Ontario to enact

firm organizational links. In the case of Fight for $15, the organizational tie to unions was obscured. Occupy, for all its accomplishments in "changing the subject" and forcing economic inequality back onto the political agenda, foundered on its inability to build lasting organization. As for Sanders, he managed to emerge from his failed presidential bid as the most popular politician in the United States (Harvard-Harris Poll 2017). His organization, Our Revolution, currently claims over 400 local groups across the United States and several other countries, which are mobilizing around an array of progressive political issues (Our Revolution 2017). Initial results have been promising, but it is too early to assess the longer-term organizational effects of the Sanders campaign.

Historically, unions have used two methods to link ideas and organization: strikes and shop floor organization.[6] The first has gotten plenty of attention, grabbing headlines and filling the pages of labor history books. The second, while often overlooked, has been equally important, a necessary building block for the first. Even in cases where strikes seem spontaneous, cursory research will uncover the organizing work that preceded it. But beyond strike preparation, shop floor organization has been what gives substance to labor's well-worn slogan, "we are the union." It has created the setting for the everyday interactions that build trust, solidarity, leadership, and the confidence that members can act collectively. It was an essential part of union building efforts from the nineteenth century to the CIO, and lives on in certain pockets of today's labor movement (Ahlquist and Levi 2013; Briskin 2008; Camfield 2007; Montgomery 1979; Stepan-Norris and Zeitlin 2003; Uetricht 2014).

For the most part though, strikes and shop floor organization are things of the past. Even where strikes do happen, evidence suggests that they are no longer as effective as they used to be (Rosenfeld 2006).[7] Meanwhile, corporate consolidation, financialization, and restructuring means that

---

$15 per hour minimum wage policies (Kuitenbrouwer 2017). The difference, as Evans (2017) points out, is that minimum wage hikes in Canada have happened more in the context of policy advocacy, as opposed to movement building. Occupy encampments did sprout up across Canada (Rebick 2012). However, the NDP has not yet seen the emergence of an equivalent to Sanders, Britain's Jeremy Corbyn, or France's Jean-Luc Mélenchon.

[6] To these we could add a third, union culture. This is the practice of unions creating a social and cultural life for their members outside the workplace, whether it be through housing communities, sports leagues, hunting clubs, summer camps, radio shows, newspapers, medical clinics, and more. For some examples of union culture at work, see (Foner and North 2002; Fones-Wolf 2006; Katz 2011).

[7] For a counter to this argument, see Burns 2011.

power and authority have not just moved further up the organizational chart, but have disappeared into a hazy thicket of investment funds, shell companies, and merged mega-corporations. In this new environment, many argue that workplace organizing can only have limited effects. Unions' leverage must be exerted elsewhere, either in politics or capital markets (Voss 2015; Voss and Gaston 2016). Almost by definition, this analysis suggests that unions' primary activities must happen at the staff level, in the strategic research and legislative action departments – not in the workplace. Unsurprisingly, unions that subscribe to this analysis, most notably SEIU, have transformed themselves in ways that make their workplace presence even more remote (Eaton et al. 2011).

These changes in global capitalism are real. Any viable strategy for labor renewal must include global strategies that reach beyond the workplace to confront globalized capital. But there is also evidence that these economic changes are creating new forms of leverage for labor. The large manufacturing plants of the postwar period may be gone, but they have been replaced by huge concentrations of logistics workers employed in strategically located transportation hubs. Waves of corporate consolidation are bringing workers together on a larger scale,[8] while methods of "lean production" and increased reliance on fragile global supply chains are creating new opportunities for organizing. Meanwhile, unions retain strong concentrations of members in key cities, which have taken over factories' roles as sites of production and profit – as well as protest. Unions

---

[8] While these groups of workers may be brought together in the same workplaces, the new reality of today's "fissured workplaces," as David Weil (2014) calls them, means that their formal employment contracts are often divided among different layers of subcontractors and labor brokers. This poses an additional challenge to organizers, albeit one that unions have faced before. Historically, in industries like trucking, longshore, garment, film, and the building trades, which are characterized by large groups of small employers and/or layers of subcontractors, unions have forced employers to create employers' associations with which to bargain master agreements, or have negotiated "jobbers' agreements" which covered all subcontractors working for a target company (Appelbaum and Lichtenstein 2014; Dobbs 1973; Garnel 1972; Kazin 1988; Kimeldorf 1988; Segrave 2009). More recently, unions like SEIU and UNITE HERE have used strategic research and corporate campaigns to target the parent companies employing subcontractors in building services and hospitality, while smaller unions like the Farm Labor Organizing Committee (FLOC) and Coalition of Immokalee Workers (CIW) have pressured larger corporate entities to take responsibility for their subcontractors' wages and working conditions, and workers' centers have waged campaigns to organize fragmented groups of workers, including taxi drivers, domestic workers, street vendors, and more (Asbed and Sellers 2013; Barger and Reza 1994; Erickson et al. 2002; Milkman and Ott 2014; Zuberi 2007). Such efforts could be modified and expanded to confront other forms of fissured workplaces.

can position themselves in those areas as leaders of broad urban progressive coalitions that can address a wide array of working class needs – not just better wages and working conditions, but affordable housing and health care, decent schools, and more. Some already are (Greenberg and Lewis 2017; Moody 2017).

For the moment, these potential points of workplace leverage remain just that – potential. Turning that potential into actual worker power is far from given, and will require patient, dedicated organizing. The point is that workplace organizing is not only possible, but essential. And giving up on the possibility of workplace organizing is not only strategically short-sighted, but has troubling implications for labor, politics, and democracy more broadly.

If labor has no way of tying global leverage strategies to workplace organizing, then it is unclear how whatever agreements are worked out between corporations, governments, and unions can actually make daily life on the job better for workers. Agreements mean little without enforcement. At a basic level, workplace organization is necessary not only to make sure that corporations abide by their agreements, but to provide a check on management's unbridled authority. Janice Fine's work on the coproduction of enforcement[9] offers some clues as to how this might happen, but labor needs to prioritize workplace organization for these ideas to reach the necessary scale (Fine 2017).

More broadly though, if labor abandons the workplace, it implies that workers have no hope of shaping their own destiny, that they remain at the mercy of forces beyond their control, and that they must rely on others to do battle on their behalf. If this is the model of organization and social change that labor has to offer workers today, then the future is indeed dire. If unions are no longer capable of organizing workers on a mass scale to make their voices heard collectively, then that leaves workers vulnerable to demagogues like Donald Trump who proclaim that "I am your voice" (POLITICO 2016).

There are signs of other options. In the United States, there is the model proposed by the Chicago Teachers Union, which led a successful strike against Mayor Rahm Emanuel in 2012, and then used that power again in 2016 to get the mayor to back down without a strike (Ashby and Bruno

---

[9] Fine defines the coproduction of enforcement as a system wherein "government partners with organizations that have industry expertise and relationships with vulnerable workers," such as unions and workers centers, to monitor and enforce state labor regulations (Fine 2017: 359).

2016; Cherone 2016; Uetricht 2014). Another would be that of the Communications Workers of America (CWA) members who took on Verizon in a 45-day strike in the spring of 2016. Not only did they defeat the company's concessionary demands, but they managed to increase pension contributions and outsourcing protections, create new union jobs, and establish a foothold for the union in Verizon's wireless business (DiMaggio 2016).

In Canada, the Quebec Common Front of public sector unions continues to mobilize, more than four decades after its landmark 1972 general strike. In the fall of 2015, 420,000 workers (out of provincial population of 8.2 million) engaged in a series of rotating strikes against government austerity proposals. After months of mobilization and negotiation, they fended off the government's most damaging proposals. Although critics charged that the agreement fell short on several counts, the unions inflicted enough damage that Premier Philippe Couillard had to reassign the minister in charge of labor negotiations to a different portfolio in the aftermath (Lévesque 2016; Smith 2016).[10] For their part, 200,000 Ontario teachers engaged in a months-long "work to rule" campaign as part of their battle with Premier Kathleen Wynne in 2015. That, combined with a threat of rotating strikes, led to union victories on class size and professional development, along with pay raises. Two years later, their mobilizing capacity prompted the Wynne government to agree to a two-year contract extension to avoid the prospect of labor strife in the run-up to an anticipated 2018 election (Canadian Press 2017b; Morrow 2015; Singh 2015).

Admittedly, these are isolated examples, and do not yet approach the scale needed to respond to the challenges that labor faces in the coming years. But they show that it is still possible to organize, it is still possible to strike, and it is still possible to win. In each case, building a union culture and organization in the workplace was key. Broadening this kind of organizing model outwards could provide ways of reversing labor's fortunes.

Labor has a tough road ahead in both the United States and Canada. But despite the real challenges that exist, there are small openings for

---

[10] Some unions in the Common Front, or aligned with it, expressed their disapproval by holding out for better deals, and many on the Left criticized the Common Front leadership's reticence to escalate the mobilization and settle for a stalemate (for a sample, see *Nouveaux cahiers du socialisme* No. 16, "Bilan de luttes," pp. 190–221). But the very fact of such criticism and a willingness to hold out for more speaks to the greater level of labor movement confidence and strength that persists in Quebec.

rebuilding working-class power in both countries. The outcome remains uncertain, and there is good reason to be pessimistic about the future of the working class, both as an idea and as a reality. To the extent that there is hope, it lies in labor's ability to bring workers together and change their assessment both of what is possible, and what they are capable of – as a class.

APPENDIX A

Data

STATISTICAL SOURCES AND SELECTION

This book relies on a wide variety of statistical data sources that span over a century and come from two different countries. To the extent possible, I have sought to use data that is as reliable and as comparable as possible. In order to do so, I have had to make a variety of choices about which sources to use, how to compensate for missing data, and how to ensure data comparability. This appendix outlines how I selected and compiled the various data sources presented in this book. It also reports the full data tables upon which the charts in this book are based.

In some cases, I simply use complete data series compiled by governmental or other reputed statistical agency. For those cases, the full citation is provided with the relevant chart. However, in many cases, compiling a complete time series required combining and/or interpolating data from several different sources. This was particularly the case for data series on union density, vote shares, and goods versus service sector employment.

UNION DENSITY

Figure 0.1 tracks union density rates in the United States and Canada between 1911 and 2016. This required compiling time series data both for union membership and nonagricultural employment. I chose to use union membership as opposed to collective bargaining coverage as the numerator, so as to make the data as comparable as possible across time. Given that collective bargaining contract terms are determined at the firm level in both countries, and do not extend to entire sectors, the difference between membership and collective bargaining coverage numbers is quite small, usually between 1 and 2 percentage points, and does not substantively change the overall trajectory for union density in either country.

For both the United States and Canada, this involved combining data from a variety of sources. Additionally, there were specific issues involved in disaggregating union density by goods versus service sector employment, and by public versus private sector employment. I discussed some of those considerations in the text itself, but provide additional detail here.

United States

Union Membership. Data for union membership come from three sources:

1) For aggregate union membership from 1911 to 1972: The Bureau of Labor Statistics' series reporting "Union Membership, 1880–1999," which can be found in Table Ba4783-4791 of Susan B. Carter et al. 2006. *Historical Statistics of the United States Millennial Edition Online.* New York: Cambridge University Press, available online at http://hsus.cambridge.org/HSUSWeb/toc/tableToc.do?id=Ba4783-4791.

2) For aggregate union membership from 1973 to 2016, as well as public versus private sector union membership from 1973 to 2016 and state-by-state union density from 1964 to 2016: Estimates from the Census Bureau's Current Population Survey (CPS), as compiled by Barry T. Hirsch and David A. McPherson and reported at www.unionstats.com. For the years 1973–1981, data come from the May Current Population (CPS). For the years 1983–2011, data come from the CPS Outgoing Rotation Group (ORG) Earnings Files. There were no union questions in the 1982 CPS, so membership data for that year are interpolated by averaging membership figures for 1981 and 1983.

   State-by-state union density statistics for the years 1964 through 1972 are taken from Barry T. Hirsch, David A. Macpherson, and Wayne G. Vroman, "Estimates of Union Density by State," *Monthly Labor Review,* 124(7), July 2001: 51–55, and the remaining years from 1973 to 2011 are from the CPS. Note that the 1964–1972 estimates are direct estimates of union density. Underlying disaggregated data on union membership are unavailable from Hirsch et al. (personal communication with Hirsch, April 27, 2012). To create state-by-state membership estimates, I used employment figures from the Bureau of Labor Statistics' Current Employment Statistics as the denominator, and then multiplied reported employment by the density percentage figure that Hirsch et al. reported in their *Monthly Labor Review* article. Hirsch indicated that this would result in reasonable estimates for state-by-state union membership for these years (personal communication with Hirsch, April 30, 2012).

3) For public versus private sector union membership from 1960 to 1973 and state-by-state union membership from 1939 to 1963: Leo Troy and Neil Sheflin. 1985. *US Union Sourcebook: Membership, Finances, Structure, Directory*. West Orange, NJ: Industrial Relations Data and Information Services, Table 7.2, p. 7–4 (state-by-state) and Appendix A, pp. A-1-A-2 (public versus private)

Nonagricultural Employment. Data for US nonagricultural employment come from two sources:

1) For aggregate nonagricultural employment from 1911 to 1972, goods versus service sector employment, and public versus private sector employment from 1960 to 1972: Susan B. Carter et al. 2006. *Historical Statistics of the United States Millennial Edition Online*. New York: Cambridge University Press, Table Ba470-477, available online at http://hsus.cambridge.org/HSUSWeb/toc/tableToc.do?id=Ba470-477.

2) For aggregate nonagricultural employment, goods versus service sector employment, and public versus private sector employment from 1973 to 2016: Estimates from the Census Bureau's Current Population Survey (CPS), as compiled by Barry T. Hirsch and David A. McPherson and reported at www.unionstats.com.

3) For state-by-state employment from 1939 to 2016: Estimates from the Bureau of Labor Statistics' Current Employment Statistics (CES). Time series for certain states begin later than 1939, which required combining and interpolating CES data with other data sources:

   a. CES data for Illinois begin in 1947. To estimate data between 1939 and 1946, employment data from the 1940 Census, published in the 1944 Statistical Abstract of the United States were used for the 1939 data, and data for 1943 came from the 1950 Statistical Abstract. Intervening years were interpolated.

   b. CES data for Michigan begin in 1956. Employment data from the 1940 Census, published in the 1944 Statistical Abstract of the United States, were used for the 1939 data point. Data for 1949–1952 were taken from the 1953 Statistical Abstract of the United States. Remaining dates are interpolated.

   c. CES data for Minnesota begin in 1947. Employment data from the 1940 Census, published in the 1944 Statistical Abstract of the United States, were used for the 1939 data point. Data for 1943 are from the 1950 Statistical Abstract of the United States. Intervening dates are interpolated.

d. CES data for Alaska begin in 1960, and for Hawaii in 1958. Given their small size, I omit these two states from years prior to their appearance in the CES data.

Canada

Union Membership. Data for union membership come from the following sources:

1) For aggregate union membership from 1911 to 1975: *Directory of Labor Organizations in Canada*, as reported in F.H. Leacy, M.C. Urquhart, and K.A.H. Buckley. 1983. *Historical statistics of Canada*. Ottawa: Statistics Canada, available at http://www5.statcan.gc.ca/access_acces/archive.action?l=eng&loc=E175_177-eng.csv.

2) For aggregate and province-by-province union membership from 1976 to 1995: *Corporations and Labour Unions Reporting Act, Part 2*, (CALURA) as reported in Statistics Canada, Table 279-0026 – Number of unionized workers, employees and union density, by sex and industry based on the Standard Industrial Classification, 1980 (SIC), annual, available online at http://www5.statcan.gc.ca/cansim/a34?lang=eng&id=2790026&searchTypeByValue=1&mode=tableSummary&p2=35.

3) For aggregate union membership, goods versus service sector membership, and province-by-province membership from 1997 to 2016: *Labour Force Survey*, available online at http://www5.statcan.gc.ca/cansim/a34?lang=eng&id=2820078&searchTypeByValue=1&mode=tableSummary&p2=35.

4) For province-by-province union membership from 1941 to 1967: J.K. Eaton and Kebebew Ashagrie. 1970. Union growth in Canada, 1921–1967. Ottawa: Information Canada, p. 80.

5) For Canada public versus private sector membership from 1961 to 1989: Jean-Guy Bergeron. 1993. "Unionization in the Private Service Sector." PhD Dissertation, Centre for Industrial Relations. Toronto: University of Toronto, Table 2.1, p. 12. Membership data from 1990 to 1996 are interpolated.

Appendix A

Nonagricultural Employment. Data for nonagricultural employment come from the following sources:

1) Employment data for 1921 to 1967: J.K. Eaton and Kebebew Ashagrie. 1970. Union growth in Canada, 1921–1967. Ottawa: Information Canada, Table VI-A, p. 78.
2) Employment data for 1968 to 1976: George Sayers Bain, 1978. "Union Growth and Public Policy in Canada." Employment Relations Branch, Canada Department of Labour 1–50, Table 1, p. 3.
3) Employment data for 1976–1995: CALURA, Table 279–0026: Number of unionized workers, employees and union density, by sex and industry based on the Standard Industrial Classification, 1980 (SIC), available online at: http://www5.statcan.gc.ca/cansim/pick-choisir?lang=eng&p2=33&id=2790026.
4) Employment data for 1997–2016: Labour Force Survey, Table 282–0078: Employees by union coverage, North American Industry Classification System (NAICS), sex and age group, annual, available online at: http://www5.statcan.gc.ca/cansim/a34?lang=eng&id=2820078&searchTypeByValue=1&mode=tableSummary&p2=35.
5) For measurements of Canadian Transportation, Communications, and Utilities (TCU) sector measurements from 1961 to 1967: J.K. Eaton and Kebebew Ashagrie. 1970. Union growth in Canada, 1921–1967. Ottawa: Information Canada, Table IV, p. 74. TCU sector employment measurements, 1968–1975: Labour Gazette. For TCU sector employment measurements, 1976–1995: CALURA. TCU employment excludes "public utilities" subcategory in 1948 SIC, and "Utilities" subcategory in 1960 SIC. The size of the sector drops in 1976 due to a reclassification in the shift from the SIC to the NAICS system. For TCU sector union membership between 1980 and 1989, the data are not disaggregated by subsector as it is for previous years. In each previous year, membership in the "Public Utilities" and "Gas, Water, and Power Utilities" subcategories remains relatively constant around 50,000 members. Thus, to allow for rough comparability, I have subtracted 50,000 from the sector totals for 1980, 1984, 1986, and 1989.
6) Special Note on employment from 1911 to 1920. Labour Canada did not start collecting data on nonagricultural employment until 1921. Thus, there is a 10-year period from 1911 to 1920 where there are annual data on union membership, but not

nonagricultural employment. To create union density statistics for this period, I used 1911 census data on "gainfully employed" persons (subtracting agricultural employment) to create a union density data point for 1911. I then generated estimates for the years between 1911 and 1921 by linearly interpolating between the 1911 data point and the first Labour Canada estimate of the paid non-agricultural workforce in 1921. The 1911 census data were obtained from *Historical Statistics of Canada*, Series D8-85: Work force, by industrial category and sex, census years, 1911 to 1971.

TABLE A.1 *Union density, United States and Canada, aggregate and public vs. private, 1911–2016*

Year	United States			Canada		
	Aggregate	Public**	Private	Aggregate	Public	Private
1911	9.8	3.9	10.3	7.4		
1912	9.8	3.9	10.6	†		
1913	10.4	4.9	10.9			
1914	10.5	5.1	10.8			
1915	10.2	4.8	10.8			
1916	10.2	4.9	10.8			
1917	11.0	5.0	11.9			
1918	12.1	4.6	13.6			
1919	14.3	5.7	16.0			
1920	17.5	6.7	17.7			
1921	17.6	6.9	17.3	16.0		
1922	14.0	6.4	13.9	13.6		
1923	11.7	6.9	11.6	13.2		
1924	11.3	6.9	11.3	12.2		
1925	11.0	6.9	11.8	12.3		
1926	10.7	6.8	11.5	12.0		
1927	10.6	6.8	11.7	12.1		
1928	10.4	7.1	11.4	12.1		
1929	10.1	7.7	10.7	12.6		
1930	10.7	8.5	11.3	13.1		
1931	11.2	8.0	11.8	15.3		
1932	11.3	7.8	12.6	15.3		
1933	9.5	5.5	12.9	16.7		
1934	9.8	4.8	13.7	14.6		
1935	10.8	4.8	11.9	14.5		
1936	11.1	4.5	12.6	16.2		
1937	18.6	5.8	16.5	18.2		
1938	23.9	5.5	18.3	18.4		

(*continued*)

TABLE A.1 (continued)

Year	United States			Canada		
	Aggregate	Public**	Private	Aggregate	Public	Private
1939	24.8	6.0	18.9	17.3		
1940	23.5	6.4	20.3	16.3		
1941	25.4	6.7	22.6	18.0		
1942	24.2	7.4	24.9	20.6		
1943	30.1	8.0	28.4	22.7		
1944	32.5	8.8	29.8	24.3		
1945	33.4	9.8	30.5	24.2		
1946	31.9	11.3	29.8	27.9		
1947	31.1	12.0	30.7	29.1		
1948	29.6	12.1	30.1	30.3		
1949	30.0	12.1	29.9	29.5		
1950	29.0	12.3	29.6	29.0		
1951	31.5	12.0	30.7	28.4		
1952	31.2	12.0	31.5	30.2		
1953	32.5	11.6	32.2	33.0		
1954	33.3	11.4	31.9	33.8		
1955	31.9	11.4	31.5	33.7		
1956	32.1	11.1	31.1	33.3		
1957	31.7	10.6	31.1	32.4		
1958	31.5	10.6	29.7	34.2		
1959	30.8	9.4	28.6	33.3		
1960	30.0	10.8	31.9	32.3		
1961	28.6	10.6	31.9	31.6	16.4	33.8
1962	28.5	24.3	31.6	30.2		
1963	27.9	25.1	31.2	29.8		
1964	27.7	26	31	29.4		
1965	27.8	26.1	30.8	29.7		
1966	27.8	26.1	30.3	30.7	20.8	31.7
1967	27.9	27	30.5	32.3		
1968	28.1	27.3	29.9	33.1		
1969	27.4	26.9	29	32.5		
1970	27.6	32	29.1	33.6	32.4	32.2
1971	27.1	33	28.2	33.6		
1972	26.6	35.4	27.3	34.4		
1973	24.0	37.0	24.2	36.3		
1974	23.6	38.0	23.4	35.7	26.8	27.5
1975	22.2	39.6	21.5	36.8		
1976	22.1	40.2	21.3	32		
1977	23.8	38.1	21.7	33.3		
1978	23.0	36.7	20.7	32		
1979	24.1	37.0	21.2	32.1		
1980	23.0	35.9	20.1	32	55.0	29.3

(continued)

TABLE A.1 (continued)

Year	United States			Canada		
	Aggregate	Public**	Private	Aggregate	Public	Private
1981	21.4	34.3	18.7	32.4		
1982	*	*	*	32.9		
1983	20.1	36.7	16.5	35.2		
1984	18.8	35.7	15.3	34.9		
1985	18.0	35.7	14.3	34.3		
1986	17.5	35.9	13.8	34.5	57.0	24.2
1987	17.0	35.9	13.2	33.8		
1988	16.8	36.6	12.7	34		
1989	16.4	36.7	12.3	34.4	58.0	24.7
1990	16.1	36.5	11.9	35.1		
1991	16.1	36.9	11.7	35.5		
1992	15.8	36.6	11.4	35.5		
1993	15.8	37.7	11.1	34.9		
1994	15.5	38.7	10.8	34.2		
1995	14.9	37.7	10.3	34.6		
1996	14.5	37.6	10			
1997	14.1	37.2	9.7	30.9	69.8	19.0
1998	13.9	37.5	9.5	30.5	70.1	18.8
1999	13.9	37.3	9.4	29.9	70.4	18.1
2000	13.5	37.5	9	30.1	70.0	18.4
2001	13.5	37.4	9	30.2	71.4	18.2
2002	13.3	37.8	8.6	30.1	72.3	17.9
2003	12.9	37.2	8.2	30.1	72.0	18.1
2004	12.5	36.4	7.9	29.8	71.9	17.5
2005	12.5	36.5	7.8	29.8	71.0	17.5
2006	12.0	36.2	7.4	29.4	71.0	17.1
2007	12.1	35.9	7.5	29.3	71.0	16.8
2008	12.4	36.8	7.6	29.1	71.1	16.2
2009	12.3	37.4	7.2	29.4	71.2	16.2
2010	11.9	36.2	6.9	29.3	71.9	15.9
2011	11.8	37	6.9	29.0	71.0	15.8
2012	11.2	35.9	6.7	29.3	71.5	16.1
2013	11.2	35.3	6.7	29.2	72.0	15.9
2014	11.1	35.7	6.6	28.4	71.3	15.2
2015	11.1	35.2	6.7	28.6	72.4	15.0
2016	10.7	34.4	6.4	28.4	73.0	14.6

Thick line indicates break in series.
* There were no union-related questions on the US CPS survey administered in 1982
** For public sector union density between 1973 and 1978, there is a large discrepancy between the Troy-Sheflin series and the CPS series, which does not exist for the private sector. I chose to report figures from the Troy-Sheflin data until 1979 to create a smoother time trend.
† See note 6 under Union Density>Canada>Nonagricultural Employment in Appendix for explanation of union density from 1911 to 1920.

TABLE A.2 US union density organized by state (including right-to-work status), 1939–2016 (%, ordered by 2016 rank)

2016 Rank	State	RTW?	RTW Year	1939	1953	1960	1966	1971	1981	1991	2001	2011	2016	1939 Rank	Rank Change 1939–2016	Density Change 1939–2016	Rank by Density Growth/Loss
1	NEW YORK			24.7	35.6	31.9	34.5	33.1	29.4	29.4	26.9	24.1	23.7	12	+11	−1.0	10
2	HAWAII			2	14	20.8	24.6	29.7	35.4	29.1	23.2	21.6	19.7	51	+49	+17.7	1
3	ALASKA			15.4	52.7	46.8	37.3	33.5	33.7	21.6	22.1	22.2	18.5	27	+24	+3.1	6
4	WASHINGTON			43.2	54.2	45.6	40.8	39.7	31.5	23.2	18.8	19.3	17.8	2	−2	−25.4	49
5	CONNECTICUT			12	27.2	23.7	27.8	26.9	24.1	19.1	15.1	16.8	17.6	34	+29	+5.6	2
6	NEW JERSEY			17.1	35.9	27.9	37.8	35.6	25.0	24.4	19.6	16.2	16.1	23	+16	−1.0	11
7	CALIFORNIA			24.8	37	37.3	31.5	29.5	22.8	18.7	16.8	17.4	16.1	11	+5	−8.7	31
8	RHODE ISLAND			10.7	28	21.8	24.5	24.4	24.7	20.8	17.0	17.4	15.5	41	+33	+4.8	3
10	MICHIGAN	Y	2012	21.2	44.6	49.1	41.7	40.4	32.8	24.9	22.1	17.6	14.6	17	+7	−6.6	25
9	ILLINOIS			27.3	40.7	43.2	33.3	33.0	25.6	21.1	18.4	16.3	14.6	8	−1	−12.7	39
11	MINNESOTA			26.1	38.6	32.8	35.4	31.0	20.2	21.9	18.0	15.3	14.4	9	−2	−11.7	36
12	OREGON			31.8	44.3	41.8	36.8	33.3	18.3	19.5	15.8	17.5	13.7	4	−8	−18.1	46
13	OHIO			25.5	38	34.1	36.1	36.4	28.5	20.8	17.9	13.5	12.5	10	−3	−13.0	41
14	MASSACHUSETTS			16.2	30.4	21.6	25.8	25.2	26.6	17.6	14.9	12.5	12.1	25	+11	−4.1	17
15	NEVADA	Y	1951	19.3	31.2	37.4	30.0	33.4	28.5	18.4	16.9	14.7	12.1	19	+4	−7.2	27
16	PENNSYLVANIA			29	40.6	26.1	36.5	36.7	33.3	20.3	17.2	14.7	12.1	6	−10	−16.9	45
17	MONTANA			38.7	47.7	34.7	35.8	31.6	26.1	17.8	13.5	13.2	12	3	−14	−26.7	50
18	WEST VIRGINIA			43.6	45	28.5	35.7	34.2	38.3	19.5	14.7	13.9	11.9	1	−17	−31.7	51
19	DELAWARE			8.2	19.1	18.2	26.5	26.1	26.7	16.8	12.5	10.5	11.6	43	+24	+3.4	5
20	VERMONT			12	19.5	18.1	16.6	16.7	21.7	11.9	10.9	12.2	11.6	35	+15	−0.4	9
21	MAINE			7.6	22	15.2	22.6	21.2	20.1	18.5	13.0	11.4	11.5	45	+24	+3.9	4
22	KENTUCKY	Y	2017	23.5	25.3	25	25.0	24.2	21.5	13.5	11.5	9.0	11.2	13	−9	−12.3	37
23	MARYLAND			12.6	25.8	20.1	24.6	24.2	26.1	14.3	13.8	12.5	11	33	+10	−1.6	13

(continued)

24	INDIANA	Y	2012	23	41.3	33.1	40.7	38.8	27.8	19.5	14.7	11.3	10.5	14	-10	-12.5	38
25	COLORADO			18.5	28.2	23.6	21.1	18.4	14.4	9.9	9.2	8.2	9.9	20	-5	-8.6	30
26	MISSOURI			22.9	40.2	42.5	25.3	24.4	20.5	14.3	13.6	10.9	9.7	15	-11	-13.2	43
28	NEW HAMPSHIRE			7.7	25.2	18.4	23.0	20.7	19.4	11.7	9.7	11.2	9.5	44	+16	+1.8	7
27	DISTRICT OF COLUMBIA			22.6	21.5	18.7	18.3	18.0	19.4	15.0	16.8	8.4	9.5	16	-11	-13.1	42
29	IOWA	Y	1947	18.2	26	25.6	26.4	25.2	29.1	14.0	13.6	11.4	9.2	21	-8	-9.0	32
30	KANSAS	Y	1958	14.1	24.8	23.2	20.0	18.2	12.7	12.2	9.3	7.7	8.6	29	-1	-5.5	19
31	ALABAMA	Y	1953	16.7	25	17.3	21.5	22.1	18.4	13.5	10.0	10.0	8.2	24	-7	-8.5	29
32	WISCONSIN	Y	2015	30.9	29.3	35.3	32.7	31.1	24.5	21.1	16.6	13.5	8.2	5	-27	-22.7	48
33	NEBRASKA	Y	1946	13	20.3	22.1	22.5	20.8	21.0	11.0	8.1	8.1	7.5	32	-1	-5.5	20
34	MISSISSIPPI	Y	1954	6.8	15	11.9	14.0	14.6	11.2	8.3	5.5	5.0	6.7	48	+14	-0.1	8
35	NEW MEXICO			11.7	14.4	17.1	15.3	19.5	19.0	9.0	8.1	6.8	6.4	37	+2	-5.3	18
36	WYOMING	Y	1963	28.2	28.4	22.3	22.1	22.8	19.6	12.7	9.3	7.3	6.4	7	-29	-21.8	47
37	IDAHO	Y	1986	14.5	22.1	24.5	24.0	23.1	9.3	7.8	5.3	6.3	28	-9	-8.2	28
38	TENNESSEE	Y	1947	15.9	22.6	18.8	21.8	22.5	17.6	11.1	7.9	4.6	5.8	26	-12	-10.1	35
39	FLORIDA	Y	1944	11.9	16.5	13.1	13.5	14.1	11.7	8.9	6.7	6.4	5.7	36	-3	-6.2	24
40	NORTH DAKOTA	Y	1947	11.7	15.5	12.7	16.6	19.6	14.7	9.8	7.4	6.4	5.6	38	-2	-6.1	23
41	OKLAHOMA	Y	2001	11	16.7	13.6	15.6	16.7	11.4	10.4	8.5	6.5	5.4	39	-2	-5.6	21
42	SOUTH DAKOTA	Y	1946	7.6	14.4	8.7	14.1	16.5	16.8	9.2	6.0	5.2	5.3	46	+4	-2.3	14
43	UTAH	Y	1955	20.5	26.8	16.4	22.0	26.5	20.8	9.6	7.0	5.8	4.6	18	-25	-15.9	44
44	ARIZONA	Y	1947	17.4	27.7	27.2	16.9	16.2	10.8	7.8	6.1	6.0	4.5	22	-22	-12.9	40
45	VIRGINIA	Y	1947	13.4	17.8	11.5	15.5	15.8	13.2	8.8	5.4	4.6	4.3	30	-15	-9.1	33
46	LOUISIANA	Y	1976	9.8	19.7	18.4	17.6	17.0	14.1	8.0	7.9	4.5	4.2	42	-4	-5.6	22
48	TEXAS	Y	1947	10.9	17.4	15.1	12.9	13.3	8.6	6.6	5.8	5.3	4	40	-8	-6.9	26
47	ARKANSAS	Y	1947	13.4	21.9	14.3	15.3	15.1	8.0	10.4	6.4	4.3	4	31	-16	-9.4	34

(continued)

TABLE A.2 (continued)

2016 Rank	State	RTW?	RTW Year	1939	1953	1960	1966	1971	1981	1991	2001	2011	2016	1939 Rank	Rank Change 1939–2016	Density Change 1939–2016	Rank by Density Growth/Loss
49	GEORGIA	Y	1947	7.2	15.1	11.8	12.0	12.6	8.7	6.9	7.3	4.0	3.9	47	−2	−3.3	16
50	NORTH CAROLINA	Y	1947	4.4	8.4	5.3	7.7	8.5	8.0	5.3	3.7	2.9	3.1	49	−1	−1.3	12
51	SOUTH CAROLINA	Y	1954	4.2	9.4	5.8	6.4	8.8	8.1	5.3	4.9	3.4	1.6	50	−1	−2.6	15
	All STATES			21.2	32.5	28.6	28.4	27.2	21.7	16.3	13.7	11.9	10.8				
	Density Range			41.6	45.8	43.8	35.3	31.9	30.3	24.1	23.2	21.2	22.1				

Sources: 1939–1963: Leo Troy and Neil Sheflin. 1985. US Union Sourcebook: Membership, Finances, Structure, Directory. West Orange, NJ: Industrial Relations Data and Information Services, Table 7.2, p. 7–4. 1964–2016: Barry T. Hirsch, David A. Macpherson, and Wayne G. Vroman, "Estimates of Union Density by State," Monthly Labor Review, 124(7), July 2001: 51–55 (up-to-date data available at www.unionstats.com).

Information on right-to-work status taken from W. Robert Reed,. 2003. "How Right-to-Work Laws Affect Wages." *Journal of Labor Research* 24(4): 713–730, p.728, n. 7, and National Right-to-Work Committee, "State Right-to-Work Timeline," https://nrtwc.org/facts-issues/state-right-to-work-timeline-2016/. Note that Missouri and West Virginia are not included, as their right-to-work laws were still pending as this book went to press.

Note: South Dakota (1946), Nebraska (1946), and Florida (1944) all had constitutional amendments prohibiting union shops prior to the passage of the Taft-Hartley Act in 1947.

TABLE A.3 *Canadian union density by region, selected years, 1941–2016 (%)*

Year	1941	1951	1961	1967	1976	1981	1991	2001	2011	2016
Atlantic Provinces	19.2	24.7	26.9	25.7	32.3	36.3	39.3	32.2	33.9	30.1
Quebec	16.0	22.8	27.5	33.0	34.9	37.6	42.6	40.6	39.6	35.5
Ontario	13.0	23.7	29.5	31.0	30.2	29.8	32.5	27.9	28.2	25.2
Prairie Provinces	14.5	25.5	23.9	21.8	28.2	28.8	33.4	32.8	32.1	26.2
British Columbia	22.2	37.7	45.2	40.6	41.2	40.1	39.9	35.1	31.9	27.4
Total	18.0	27.5	31.1	31.9	32.4	32.8	36.1	32.3	31.7	28.4
Range	9.2	14.9	21.3	18.8	13.0	11.3	10.1	12.7	11.4	10.3

Atlantic Provinces: Newfoundland and Labrador, Prince Edward Island, Nova Scotia, New Brunswick
Prairie Provinces: Manitoba, Saskatchewan, Alberta
Sources: 1941–1967: J.K. Eaton and Kebebew Ashagrie. 1970. Union Growth in Canada, 1921–1967. Ottawa: Information Canada, p. 80. 1976–1995: CALURA (Statistics Canada. Table 279-0025 – Number of unionized workers, employees and union density, by sex and province, annual). 1997–2016: LFS (Statistics Canada. Table 282-0220 – Labour Force Survey estimates (LFS), employees by union status, sex and age group, Canada and provinces, annual)

GOODS VERSUS SERVICE SECTOR EMPLOYMENT

Table A.4 reports the data used in Figure 1.1, which tracks employment in the service sector in the United States and Canada between 1931 and 2016.

TABLE A.4 *Service sector employment as share of nonfarm employment, United States and Canada, 1931–2016*

Year	US	Canada
1931		58.74
1932		
1933		
1934		
1935		
1936		
1937		
1938		
1939	62.44	
1940	61.80	
1941	59.18	55.18
1942	57.04	
1943	55.99	
1944	57.20	
1945	59.75	
1946	61.39	
1947	60.60	
1948	60.90	
1949	62.45	
1950	61.71	
1951	60.98	55.63
1952	61.30	
1953	60.78	
1954	62.29	
1955	62.10	
1956	62.27	
1957	62.86	
1958	64.38	
1959	64.10	
1960	64.67	
1961	65.54	62.55
1962	65.50	62.74

(continued)

TABLE A.4 (*continued*)

Year	US	Canada
1963	65.85	62.71
1964	66.21	62.28
1965	66.17	62.77
1966	66.04	62.69
1967	66.81	64.09
1968	67.23	65.03
1969	67.53	65.24
1970	68.76	66.36
1971	69.72	66.79
1972	69.78	67.18
1973	69.51	66.90
1974	70.19	67.05
1975	72.34	68.48
1976	72.30	69.87
1977	72.19	70.43
1978	72.18	70.61
1979	72.20	70.42
1980	73.20	70.75
1981	73.58	71.14
1982	74.86	73.21
1983	75.51	73.86
1984	75.21	73.84
1985	75.82	73.98
1986	76.56	74.08
1987	77.02	74.26
1988	77.31	74.12
1989	77.75	74.16
1990	78.34	74.94
1991	79.17	76.41
1992	79.69	77.16
1993	79.97	77.79
1994	80.09	77.55
1995	80.28	77.28
1996	80.47	77.47
1997	80.57	77.10
1998	80.70	77.01
1999	81.07	77.03
2000	81.33	76.91
2001	81.93	77.27
2002	82.73	77.14
2003	83.26	77.39
2004	83.40	77.32

(*continued*)

TABLE A.4 (*continued*)

Year	US	Canada
2005	83.45	77.60
2006	83.49	78.17
2007	83.89	78.73
2008	84.45	78.99
2009	85.87	80.19
2010	86.38	80.33
2011	86.32	80.15
2012	86.27	79.95
2013	86.26	80.08
2014	86.16	80.25
2015	86.17	80.52
2016	86.32	80.85

Canadian data:
1931–1951: Historical Statistics of Canada, Series D8-85. Work force, by industrial category, census years, 1911 to 1971 (gainfully occupied 1911 to 1941, labour force 1951 to 1971), www.statcan.gc.ca/access_acces/archive.action?l=eng&loc=D8_85-eng.csv
1961–1975: Series D290-317. Civilian employment, by industry (1960 S.I.C.), both sexes and males, annual averages, 1961 to 1975, www.statcan.gc.ca/access_acces/archive.action?l=eng&loc=D290_317-eng.csv
1976–2016: Statistics Canada CANSIM, Table 282–0008 Labour force survey estimates (LFS), by North American Industry Classification System (NAICS), sex and age group, annual, http://www5.statcan.gc.ca/cansim/a26?lang=eng&retrLang=eng&id=2820008&&pattern=&stByVal=1&p1=1&p2=35&tabMode=dataTable&csid=;
US data: Bureau of Labor Statistics, Current Employment Survey, www.bls.gov/ces/

The US data are taken from the Bureau of Labor Statistics' Current Employment Statistics dataset, which is continuous from 1939 to the present.

The Canadian data are compiled from three different sources. Data for 1931, 1941, and 1951 are taken from Canadian census data, as reported in (Worton 1969: Table 1). To ensure comparability with the US BLS data, I have omitted data on agricultural employment, and reclassified utility workers as part of the service sector. I interpolated data between these data points from 1931 through 1960. From 1961 to the present, I use employment data from Statistics Canada's Labor Force Survey (LFS), which is a household survey. However, the LFS changed significantly in 1976, meaning that I combined two separate data series, one from 1961 to 1975, published in *Historical Statistics of Canada, Section D: The Labour Force* (Leacy et al. 1983), and another from 1976 to the present, available from Statistics Canada (Table 282–0008, http://estat.statcan.gc.ca).

PUBLIC VERSUS PRIVATE SECTOR EMPLOYMENT

The main definitional problem with public sector employment is that official employment statistics until relatively recently have focused on distinguishing between different types of jobs, rather than on determining whether those jobs were performed in the public or private sector. For the United States, the Bureau of Labor Statistics' (BLS) Current Population Survey (CPS), a household survey, began including questions intended to determine whether respondents were employed in the public or private sector in 1973. For Canada, Statistics Canada's Labor Force Survey (LFS), a similar household survey, only began including such questions in 1997. Prior to this, efforts at disaggregating public and private sector employment involved developing estimates based on certain sets of assumptions.

For the United States, the most extensive series of such estimates is that compiled by Troy and Sheflin (1985). Their series includes disaggregated estimates of public and private sector union density from 1929 to 1983, with a break in the series in 1962. For Canada, there are only periodic estimates of public sector unionism prior to 1997. Rose (1984) compiled disaggregated membership estimates going back to 1911, but did not calculate disaggregated union density statistics based on these numbers. Lipset and Meltz (2004) reported density statistics going back to 1960. Bergeron (1993) calculated disaggregated density statistics for select years between 1961 and 1989.

For both countries, the estimates involved calculations and assumptions based on union jurisdictions, i.e. the types of workers represented by a given union. This involves examining membership data as reported by individual unions. So for example, the membership of the Canadian Union of Public Employees (CUPE) or the American Federation of Government Employees (AFGE) would be classified as public sector union membership. The problem is that many unions represent members in both the public and private sectors. Thus, calculating public sector membership requires developing assumptions about the percentage of a given union's membership that is employed in the public sector. For the United States, Troy and Sheflin developed a percentage estimate of public sector membership for each individual union based on calculations from an unpublished 1978 BLS survey. They then applied this percentage to each union's membership, as reported in federally mandated forms, for the period from 1962 to 1982 (Troy and Sheflin 1985:3-2-3-3). For Canada, Rose sent out surveys to private sector unions to develop estimates of their public sector membership, which he then used to disaggregate the Canadian statistics (Rose 1984:88–89). Lipset and Meltz do not specify their methodology. Freeman et al. (1988) discuss the mechanics, as well as the advantages and drawbacks of different methods of calculating public sector union membership in detail.

A second problem with disaggregating public sector unionization involves defining what constitutes union representation. Collective bargaining in the public sector takes a wide variety of shapes, and has changed significantly over time. Initially, many public sector unions began as employee associations, and only later began engaging in more traditional union activities such as collective bargaining. A classic example of this is the National Education Association (NEA), which was founded in 1857 as a professional association, but only began engaging in collective bargaining in the 1960s (Troy and Sheflin 1985 3-3). There is also a wider variety of collective bargaining relationships in the public sector than in the private sector. In particular, there are more workers in so-called "agency shops" where membership is not required to be covered by the terms of a collective bargaining agreement. Reflecting this diversity of forms of unionization, the BLS's CPS survey began asking respondents whether they were members of "a union or an employee association similar to a union" beginning in 1977. By contrast, the Canadian LFS survey only asks respondents if they are union members. The US CPS also reports data on union membership and collective bargaining coverage, in order to account for workers in agency shops who are covered by the terms of a collective bargaining agreement, but are not members.

To create roughly comparable data series, I join the Troy and Sheflin and CPS data for the United States, and the Lipset and Meltz and LFS data for Canada. Due to limitations in the Canadian data, I begin the data series in 1961, the first year with data reported for both countries. While a more comprehensive data series would be preferable, beginning the series in 1961 is sufficient for two reasons. First, we know from Troy and Sheflin's and Rose's membership numbers that public sector unionism in both countries was not a significant portion of overall union membership prior to the early 1960s. In neither country did it surpass 13 percent of total union membership until the early 1960s, and for the majority of that period public sector membership was firmly in the single digits. As such, public sector union membership did little to drive overall union density statistics until the 1960s. Second, as we know from the aggregate union density data, the divergence between US and Canadian union density only began in 1964. Thus, beginning the series in 1961 does capture the complete period of density divergence, as well as the period immediately preceding it.

STRIKES

Table A.5 reports the data used in Figures 2.15 and 2.16.

TABLE A.5 *Number of workers involved in strikes, United States and Canada, total, as percentage of nonagricultural workforce, and person-days idle due to strikes, 1911–2016 (selected years)*

Year	# of Strikers		Strikers as % of Nonfarm Employment		Person-Days Idle Due to Strikes	
	US	Canada	US	Canada	US	Canada
1911	373,000	29,285	1.57	1.63	–	1,821,084
1916	1,600,000	26,538	6.00	1.42	–	236,814
1919	4,160,000	148,915	14.71	7.74	–	3,400,942
1921	1,099,000	28,257	4.10	1.44	–	1,048,914
1926	330,000	23,834	0.98	1.04	–	266,601
1931	342,000	10,738	1.09	0.53	6,890,000	204,238
1934	1,470,000	45,800	4.42	2.37	19,600,000	574,519
1936	789,000	34,812	2.10	1.75	13,900,000	276,997
1941	2,360,000	87,091	6.45	3.39	23,000,000	433,914
1943	1,980,000	218,404	4.65	7.44	13,500,000	1,041,198
1946	4,600,000	139,474	11.02	4.65	116,000,000	4,515,230
1951	2,220,000	102,870	4.63	2.79	22,900,000	901,911
1956	1,900,000	88,680	3.62	2.19	33,100,000	1,246,130
1961	1,450,000	97,959	2.68	2.15	16,300,000	1,336,080
1966	1,960,000	411,459	3.06	7.29	25,400,000	5,180,030
1971	3,280,000	239,631	4.60	3.31	47,589,000	2,854,480
1976	2,420,000	1,584,793	3.04	18.80	37,859,000	11,544,170
1981	1,081,000	341,612	1.18	3.59	24,730,000	8,850,040
1986	635,823	486,456	0.64	4.79	20,452,685	7,151,470
1991	196,138	253,581	0.18	2.38	9,694,068	2,516,090
1996	196,487	275,805	0.16	2.48	15,471,178	3,269,060
2001	282,896	221,203	0.21	1.76	32,209,021	2,202,740

(*continued*)

TABLE A.5 *(continued)*

Year	# of Strikers		Strikers as % of Nonfarm Employment		Person-Days Idle Due to Strikes	
	US	Canada	US	Canada	US	Canada
2006	69,662	42,314	0.05	0.31	4,120,282	792,923
2011	69,267	91,147	0.05	0.63	1,525,928	1,350,556
2016*	30,429	49,168	0.02	0.54	852,994	499,870

* *US data for 2016 is from 2014.*
Sources, strikes (US): 1911–1981: Historical Statistics of the US Millennial Edition, Table Ba4954-4964: http://hsus.cambridge.org/HSUSWeb/toc/tableToc.do?id=Ba4954-4964; 1984–2014: Federal Mediation and Conciliation Service, "Work Stoppages Ended 1984–2004" and "Work Stoppages Ended 2005–2014," available at www.fmcs.gov/resources/documents-and-data/

Sources, strikes (Canada): 1911–1945: Statistics Canada: Historical Statistics of Canada, Table E190-197; 1946–2016: Table 278–0015 Work stoppages in Canada, by jurisdiction and industry based on the North American Industry Classification System (NAICS), Employment and Social Development Canada – Labour Program.

Sources, employment (US): 1911–1937: Historical Statistics of the United States, Table Ba470-477. Labor force, employment, and unemployment: 1890–1990 [Weir]; 1938: Historical Statistics of the United States, Table Ba478-486. Labor force, employment, and unemployment: 1938–2000; 1939–2016: US Bureau of Labor Statistics Current Employment Survey.

Sources, employment (Canada): 1921–1945: Series D124-133. Labour force and main components, noninstitutional population and armed forces, 14 years of age and over, 1 June of each year, 1921 to 1960; 1946–1975: Series D146-159. Civilian labour force and main components, civilian noninstitutional population, 14 years of age and over, by sex, annual averages, 1946 to 1975; 1976–1995: CALURA Table 279–0026 Number of unionized workers, employees and union density, by sex and industry based on the Standard Industrial Classification, 1980 (SIC), annual; 1997–2016: Table 282–0223 Labour Force Survey estimates (LFS), employees by union status, North American Industry Classification System (NAICS) and sex, Canada, annual.

NATIONAL CHARACTERISTICS

Table A.6 reports the values used in Figures 3.1, 3.2, and 3.3.

TABLE A.6 *Comparison of US and Canadian values*

Question	US		Canada	
Hard work brings success[1]	Hard work brings success 48.5%	More about luck and connections 7.5%	Hard work brings success 49.9%	More about luck and connections 11.8%
Private versus state ownership of business[2]	Private ownership increased 45.6%	Gov't ownership increased 3.2%	Private ownership increased 38.9%	Gov't ownership increased 10.5%
Fix income inequality[3]	Incomes should be made more equal 12.2%	We need larger income differences as incentives 25.1%	Incomes should be made more equal 19.1%	We need larger income differences as incentives 28.0%
Government versus personal responsibility[4]	More gov't 19.6%	More personal 31.6%	More gov't 18.5%	More personal 32.2%
Confidence in government	Great deal/ quite a lot 33.7%	Not much/ none 66.2%	Great deal/ quite a lot 42.3%	Not much/ none 57.8%
Confidence in unions	Great deal/ quite a lot 35.9%	Not much/ none 64.1%	Great deal/ quite a lot 34.9%	Not much/ none 65.2%

(*continued*)

[1] Answer reports those scoring between a 1 and 3 and 8 and 10 on the question, where 1 signifies closest agreement with the statement "In the long run, hard work usually brings a better life," and 10 signifies closest agreement with the statement "Hard work doesn't generally bring success – it's more a matter of luck and connections."

[2] Answer reports those scoring between a 1 and 3 and 8 and 10 on the question, where 1 signifies closest agreement with the statement "Private ownership of business should be increased," and 10 signifies closest agreement with the statement "Government ownership of business should be increased."

[3] Answer reports those scoring between a 1 and 3 and 8 and 10 on the question, where 1 signifies closest agreement with the statement "Incomes should be made more equal," and 10 signifies closest agreement with the statement "We need larger income differences as incentives."

[4] Answer reports those scoring between a 1 and 3 and 8 and 10 on the question, where 1 signifies closest agreement with the statement "The government should take more responsibility," and 10 signifies closest agreement with the statement "People should take more responsibility."

TABLE A.6 (*continued*)

Question	US		Canada	
Confidence in large companies	Great deal/ quite a lot 51.7%	Not much/ none 48.3%	Great deal/ quite a lot 54.4%	Not much/ none 45.6%
Freedom or equality	Freedom 71.7%	Equality 24.1%	Freedom 62.4%	Equality 32.9%
Country is run by big interests versus for all people's benefit	Big interests 69.1%	All the people 30.9%	Big interests 52.0%	All the people 48.0%
Joining unofficial strikes	Have done/ might do 30.5%	Would never do 69.4%	Have done/ might do 30.8%	Would never do 69.1%
Work is a duty toward society	Strongly agree/ agree 57.8%	Strongly Disagree/ disagree 22.4%	Strongly agree/ agree 65.4%	Strongly disagree/ disagree 20.2%

Source: World Values Survey, www.wvsevsdb.com/wvs/WVSAnalizeStudy.jsp

VOTE SHARES

Figure 4.1 uses data from two separate sources. The first dataset comprises data on all votes cast for US House, Senate, and all statewide offices between 1876 and 2004. It was compiled by Stephen Ansolabehere, Shigeo Hirano, and James M. Snyder Jr., and forms the basis of Hirano and Snyder's paper analyzing the decline of third-party voting in the United States (Hirano and Snyder 2007). The data presented in Figure 4.1 comprise only vote shares for third parties that the authors identified as left-wing parties. According to the authors, "based on the historical literature and sources such as the *Biographical Dictionary of the American Left*, we classified each party as Left or Other (non-Left)" (2007: 2). The data exclude presidential votes to better focus on third party movements as opposed to individual candidates (2, fn. 6).

The second dataset comprises data on all votes cast in Canadian federal and provincial parliamentary elections between 1867 and 2009. I compiled this dataset from the sources listed in Table A.7:

TABLE A.7 *List of sources for votes cast in Canadian federal and provincial elections, 1867–2009*

Jurisdiction	Source
Federal	*History of Federal Ridings Since 1867*, www.parl.gc.ca/About/Parliament/FederalRidingsHistory/HFER.asp
Alberta	*A Century of Democracy: Elections of the Legislative Assembly of Alberta, 1905–2005* (Legislative Assembly of Alberta, 2006), and Elections Alberta, www.elections.ab.ca/Public%20Website/730.htm
British Columbia	*An Electoral History of British Columbia, 1871–1986* (Elections British Columbia, 1988), *Electoral History of British Columbia Supplement, 1987–2001* (Legislative Library of British Columbia, 2002), and Elections British Columbia, www.elections.bc.ca/index.php/resource-centre/reports/
Manitoba	*Historical Summaries, 1870 to 2006* (Elections Manitoba 2007), and Elections Manitoba, www.elections.mb.ca/en/Results/index.html
Nova Scotia	*Nova Scotia Provincial Elections 1867–2010* (Elections Nova Scotia 2011, http://electionsnovascotia.ns.ca/electionsstatistics.asp)
Ontario	*Electoral History of Ontario, Candidates and Results, with Statistics from the Records, 1867–1982* (Office of the Chief Election Officer, Province of Ontario, 1984), and Elections Ontario, www.elections.on.ca/en-CA/Tools/PastResults.htm
Prince Edward Island	Historical data obtained directly from Chief Election Officer Lowell Croken (e-mail dated September 8, 2010), and Elections PEI, www.electionspei.ca/provincial/historical/results/main.php
Quebec	Drouilly, Pierre, *Statistiques Électorales du Québec, 1867–1989* (Québec: Bibliothèque de l'Assemblée Nationale, 1990), and Élections Québec, http://www2.electionsquebec.qc.ca/corpo/francais/elections-generales-provincial.asp
Saskatchewan	*Provincial Elections in Saskatchewan, 1905–1986* (Chief Electoral Office, Province of Saskatchewan, 1987), *Report of the Twenty-Second General Election, October 21, 1991*, *Report of the Twenty-Third General Election, June 21, 1995*, and Elections Saskatchewan, www.elections.sk.ca/publications.php

Data for Newfoundland are excluded, as it did not join Confederation until 1949. Data for New Brunswick are also excluded because candidates in that province did not have party affiliations until 1935, and thus could not demonstrate any shift before and after the formation of the CCF. Similarly, the Yukon and Northwest Territories are excluded because candidates only began having party affiliations in the 1970s. Nunavut is excluded because it only became a territory in 1999.

Figure 4.1 reports vote shares using a six-year moving average. This smooths out data from off-year elections while preserving overall trends.

Figure 4.1 reports only vote shares for left-wing third parties. As with Hirano and Snyder, I used historical sources to distinguish left parties from other third parties. Table A.8 provides a complete list of included parties.

TABLE A.8 *List of Canadian left-wing third parties*

	Full Name
CLAB	Canadian Labour
CCF	Co-operative Commonwealth Federation
CPC	Communist Party of Canada
FARM	Farmer
FL	Farmer Labour
FUL	Farmer-United Labour
CCFIND	Independent Co-operative Commonwealth Federation
LABIND	Independent Labor
PROGIND	Independent Progressive
LAB	Labour
LF	Labour Farmer
LPP	Labour Progressive Party
MLP	Marxist-Leninist Party
NATLAB	National Labour
NDP	New Democratic Party
NPL	Non-Partisan League
OUVIND	Ouvrier indépendent
PDE	Parti de la démocratisation économique
POC	Parti ouvrier canadien
PATRON	Patrons of Industry
PROG	Progressive
PWM	Progressive Workers Movement
SOC	Socialist
SOCLAB	Socialist Labour
UF	United Farmers
UFA	United Farmers of Alberta
UFO	United Farmers of Ontario
UFOL	United Farmers of Ontario-Labour
UFL	United Farmers-Labour
UNPROG	United Progressive
UNREF	United Reform
UNREFM	United Reform Movement
UNITY	Unity

APPENDIX B

Archival Sources

- Confédération des syndicats nationaux (CSN) (Confederation of National Trade Unions (CNTU)) Library, Montreal, Québec
- George Meany Memorial Archives, Silver Spring, Maryland
- Hagley Library, Wilmington, Delaware
- Kheel Archives, Catherwood Library, Cornell University, Ithaca, New York
- Library and Archives Canada, Ottawa, Ontario
- National Archives, College Park, Maryland
- Robert F. Wagner Papers, Special Collections, Georgetown University, Washington, DC
- Walter Reuther Library, Wayne State University, Detroit, Michigan

APPENDIX C

Permissions

Sections of Chapters 1, 2, 3, and 6 adapted from Barry Eidlin. "Class vs. Special Interest Labor, Power, and Politics in the United States and Canada in the Twentieth Century." *Politics and Society* 43(2): 181–211. Copyright © 2015 by SAGE Publications. Reprinted by permission of SAGE Publications, Inc.

Sections of Chapter 4 adapted from Barry Eidlin. "Why Is There No Labor Party in the United States? Political Articulation and the Canadian Comparison, 1932 to 1948." *American Sociological Review* 81(3): 488–516. Copyright © 2016 by American Sociological Association. Reprinted by permission of SAGE Publications, Inc.

Sections of Chapter 4 adapted from Barry Eidlin. "Continuity or Change? Rethinking Left Party Formation in Canada," Chapter 2 in *Building Blocs: How Parties Organize Society*, edited by Cedric de Leon, Manali Desai, and Cihan Tuğal. Copyright © 2015 by the Board of Trustees of the Leland Stanford Jr. University. All rights reserved. Used by permission of the publisher, Stanford University Press, sup.org.

Sections of the Conclusion adapted from Barry Eidlin. "Labor's Legitimacy Crisis Under Trump." *Jacobin*, July 5, www.jacobinmag.com/2017/07/labor-movement-unions-trump-strikes-working-class-identity.

Bibliography

Aaron, Benjamin. 1962. "Employer Free Speech: The Search for a Policy," pp. 28–59 in *Public Policy and Collective Bargaining*, edited by J. Shister, B. Aaron, and C. Summers. New York: Harper & Row.

ABA Journal. 1978. "'Dangerous' Lobbies Sank Reform: Labor Secretary." *American Bar Association Journal* 64(9):1345.

Abella, Irving M. 1973. *Nationalism, Communism and Canadian Labour: The CIO, the Communist Party and the Canadian Congress of Labour, 1935–1956.* Toronto: University of Toronto Press.

Acena, Albert A. 1975. "The Washington Commonwealth Federation: Reform Politics and the Popular Front." PhD Dissertation, History, University of Washington.

Adams, Roy J. 1989. "North American Industrial Relations: Divergent Trends in Canada and the United States." *International Labour Review* 128(1):47–64.

Adams, Roy J. 1995. "A Pernicious Euphoria: 50 Years of Wagnerism in Canada." *Canadian Labour and Employment Law Journal* 3:321–355.

Adams, Roy J. 2008. "From Statutory Right to Human Right: The Evolution and Current Status of Collective Bargaining." *Just Labour: A Canadian Journal of Work and Society* 12(Spring):48–67.

Adell, Bernard. 1965. "Employer Free Speech in the United States and Canada." *Alberta Law Review* 4:11–35.

Adell, Bernard. 2003. "Secondary Picketing after Pepsi-Cola: What's Clear and What Isn't?" *Canadian Labour and Employment Law Journal* 10:135–159.

Ahlquist, John S., and Margaret Levi. 2013. *In the Interest of Others: Organizations and Social Activism.* Princeton: Princeton University Press.

Ahmed, Amel. 2013. *Democracy and the Politics of Electoral System Choice: Engineering Electoral Dominance.* Cambridge: Cambridge University Press.

Albo, Greg. 2009. "The Crisis of Neoliberalism and the Impasse of the Union Movement." *Development Dialogue* 51(January):119–132.

Alderson, Arthur S., and François Nielsen. 2002. "Globalization and the Great U-Turn: Income Inequality Trends in 16 OECD Countries." *American Journal of Sociology* 107(5):1244–1299.

Alderson, Arthur S., Jason Beckfield, and François Nielsen. 2005. "Exactly How Has Income Inequality Changed? Patterns of Distributional Change in Core Societies." *International Journal of Comparative Sociology* 46(5–6):405–423.

Alston, Lee J., and Joseph P. Ferrie. 1993. "Paternalism in Agricultural Labor Contracts in the US South: Implications for the Growth of the Welfare State." *The American Economic Review* 83(4):852–876.

American Federation of Labor. 1933. "Conference Held in Executive Council Chamber, A. F. of L. Bldg., Tuesday, June 6, 1933." *George Meany Memorial Archives* RG1-015 Office of the President, William Green Papers, 1888, 1909–1952, Series 1 Conferences, 1925–1944, Box-Folder 2–3 Industrial Recovery Bill 1933–06–06.

Anastakis, Dimitry. 2004. "Between Nationalism and Continentalism: State Auto Industry Policy and the Canadian UAW, 1960–1970." *Labour/Le Travail* 53 (Spring):89–126.

Anastakis, Dimitry. 2005. *Auto Pact: Creating a Borderless North American Auto Industry, 1960–1971*. Toronto: University of Toronto Press.

Ancel, Judy. 2017. "310,567 Signatures Block 'Right to Work' in Missouri." *Labor Notes*. September 18, www.labornotes.org/2017/09/310567-signatures-block-right-work-missouri.

Anderson, Elizabeth. 2017. *Private Government: How Employers Rule Our Lives (and Why We Don't Talk About It)*. Princeton: Princeton University Press.

Anderson, Frederick W. 1949. "Some Political Aspects of the Grain Growers' Movement, 1915–1935, with Particular Reference to Saskatchewan." MA Thesis, Department of Economics, University of Saskatchewan.

Anonymous. 1948. "No Canada Taft-Hartley Likely; Management Must Lead, Says Wilson." *Library and Archives Canada* CMA papers, MG28 I230, Vol. 118, Folder IRDIA (#8) Also BC AB NZ Ind Arb Act 1951–1953 #1.

Appelbaum, Rich and Nelson Lichtenstein. 2014. "An Accident in History." *New Labor Forum* 23(3):58–65.

Archer, Keith. 1990. *Political Choices and Electoral Consequences: A Study of Organized Labour and the New Democratic Party*. Montreal: McGill-Queen's University Press.

Archer, Robin. 2007. *Why Is There No Labor Party in the United States?* Princeton: Princeton University Press.

Arnold, Patricia J. 1999. "From the Union Hall: A Labor Critique of the New Manufacturing and Accounting Regimes." *Critical Perspectives on Accounting* 10(4):399–423.

Arthurs, Harry W. 1968. "Collective Bargaining in the Public Service of Canada: Bold Experiment or Act of Folly." *Michigan Law Review* 67:971–1000.

Asbed, Greg and Sean Sellers. 2013. "The Fair Food Program: Comprehensive, Verifiable and Sustainable Change for Farmworkers." *University of Pennsylvania Journal of Law and Social Change* 16(1):39–48.

Ashby, Steven K., and Robert Bruno. 2016. *A Fight for the Soul of Public Education: The Story of the Chicago Teachers Strike*. Ithaca: Cornell ILR Press.

Associated Press. 1934. "Text of Appeal to President – National Labor Board Chairman Says Unit Should Not Be Placed in Position of Mediator in Suggesting Intervention." *National Archives* RG174 General Records of the Department of Labor Secretary Frances Perkins, Box 86 Office of the Secretary Secy Frances Perkins, General Subject File 1933–1941 National Labor Relations Board to National Recovery Admin, Folder National Labor Relations Board September 1934.

Associated Press. 1937. "Roosevelt Denies 'Bias' in Labor Board; Doesn't Consider Wagner Act One-Sided." *New York Times*, July 28, 1.

Associated Press. 2016. "West Virginia Repeal of State Prevailing Wage Takes Effect." *West Virginia Public Broadcasting*, May 5, www.wvpublic.org/post/west-virginia-repeal-state-prevailing-wage-takes-effect.

Atkinson, A.B. 2003. "Income Inequality in OECD Countries: Data and Explanations." *CESifo Economic Studies* 49(4):479–513.

Atleson, James B. 1994. "Law and Union Power: Thoughts on the United States and Canada." *Buffalo Law Review* 42:463–500.

Auerbach, Jerold S. 1966. "Southern Tenant Farmers: Socialist Critics of the New Deal." *Labor History* 7(1):3–18.

Austen, Ian. 2017. "Jagmeet Singh, Canada's Newest Political Star, Lifts His Party's Hopes." *New York Times*, October 4, A, A7, nyti.ms/2yHWxvO.

Autor, David H., and David Dorn. 2013. "The Growth of Low Skill Service Jobs and the Polarization of the US Labor Market." *American Economic Review* 103(5):1553–1597.

Backhouse, Constance. 1980. "The Fleck Strike: A Case Study in the Need for First Contract Arbitration (1980)." *Osgoode Hall Law Journal* 18(4):495–553.

Backstrom, Charles H. 1956. "The Progressive Party of Wisconsin, 1934–1946." PhD dissertation, Department of Political Science, University of Wisconsin–Madison.

Bain, George S. 1981. *Certifications, First Agreements, and Decertifications: An Analytical Framework*. Ottawa: Labour Canada.

Barenberg, Mark. 1993. "The Political Economy of the Wagner Act: Power, Symbol, and Workplace Cooperation." *Harvard Law Review* 106(7):1379–1496.

Barger, W.K. and E.M. Reza. 1994. *The Farm Labor Movement in the Midwest: Social Change and Adaptation Among Migrant Farmworkers*. Austin: University of Texas Press.

Barnes, Samuel H. 1960. "Canadian Trade Unions and the Cooperative Commonwealth Federation." *Papers of the Michigan Academy of Science, Arts, and Letters* XLV(1959 meeting):251–264.

Baskin, Alex. 1972. "The Ford Hunger March – 1932." *Labor History* 13(3):331–360.

Bates, Beth T. 2001. *Pullman Porters and the Rise of Protest Politics in Black America, 1925–1945*. Chapel Hill: University of North Carolina Press.

Becker, Amanda and Bernie Woodall. 2014. "UPDATE 4-UAW Suddenly Retreats From Fight at Tennessee VW Plant." *Reuters*, April 21, www.reuters.com/article/vw-uaw-tennessee-idUSL2N0ND0B020140421.

Bell, Daniel. 1950. "The Treaty of Detroit." *Fortune* 42(1):53–55.

Bell, Daniel. 1960. *The End of Ideology: On the Exhaustion of Political Ideas in the Fifties.* Glencoe: Free Press.
Bell, Daniel. 1973. *The Coming of Post-Industrial Society: A Venture in Social Forecasting.* New York: Basic Books.
Beller, Emily, and Michael Hout. 2006. "Intergenerational Social Mobility: the United States in Comparative Perspective." *The Future of Children* 16(2):19–36.
Ben-Shahar, Omri. 2016. "The Non-Voters Who Decided the Election: Trump Won Because of Lower Democratic Turnout." *Forbes,* November 17, www.forbes.com/sites/omribenshahar/2016/11/17/the-non-voters-who-decided-the-election-trump-won-because-of-lower-democratic-turnout/.
Bentham, Karen J. 1999. "The Determinants and Impacts of Employer Resistance to Union Certification in Canada." PhD dissertation, Centre for Industrial Relations, University of Toronto.
Bentham, Karen J. 2002. "Employer Resistance to Union Certification: A Study of Eight Canadian Jurisdictions." *Industrial Relations* 57(1):159–187.
Bergeron, Jean-Guy. 1993. "Unionization in the Private Service Sector." PhD dissertation, Centre for Industrial Relations, University of Toronto.
Bernard, Elaine. 1994. "The New Democratic Party and Labor Political Action in Canada." *Labor Research Review* 1(22):98–109.
Bernstein, Irving. 1969. *Lean Years: A History of the American Worker, 1920–1933.* Boston: Houghton Mifflin.
Bernstein, Irving. 1970. *Turbulent Years: A History of the American Worker, 1933–1941.* Boston: Houghton Mifflin.
Black, J.L., and Martin Rudner. 2006. *The Gouzenko Affair: Canada and the Beginnings of Cold War Counter-Espionage.* Newcastle: Penumbra Press.
Blanchflower, David G., and Richard B. Freeman. 1992. "Unionism in the United States and Other Advanced OECD Countries." *Industrial Relations* 31(1):56–79.
Blitchok, Dustin. 2012. "Gov. Rick Snyder Has Signed New Emergency Manager Bill Into Law." Oakland Press, December 27, www.theoaklandpress.com/article/OP/20121227/NEWS/312279950.
Block, Richard N. 1993. "Unionization, Collective Bargaining, and Legal Institutions in the United States and Canada." *Queen's Papers in Industrial Relations* QPIR 1993–1994.
Bluestone, Barry, and Bennett Harrison. 1982. *The Deindustrialization of America: Plant Closings, Community Abandonment, and the Dismantling of Basic Industry.* New York: Basic Books.
Bluestone, Barry, and Bennett Harrison. 1990. *The Great U-Turn: Corporate Restructuring and the Polarizing of America.* New York: Basic Books.
Boivin, Jean. 1972. "La négociation collective dans le secteur public québécois: une évaluation des trois premières rondes (1964–1972)." *Relations Industrielles/Industrial Relations* 27(4):679–717.
Bok, Derek C., and John T. Dunlop. 1970. *Labor and the American Community.* New York: Simon and Schuster.

Booker, Gene S., and Alan C. Coe. 1986. "An Analysis of the Objectivity of the Criticisms of the National Labor Relations Board." *American Business Law Journal* 6(2):535–557.
Breines, Wini. 1989. *Community and Organization in the New Left, 1962–1968: The Great Refusal.* New Brunswick: Rutgers University Press.
Breitzer, Susan R. 2009. "Loved Labor's Losses: The Congress of Industrial Organizations and the Effects of McCarthyism." *History Compass* 7(5):1400–1415.
Brenner, Aaron, Robert Brenner, and Cal Winslow, eds. 2010. *Rebel Rank and File: Labor Militancy and Revolt From Below During the Long 1970s.* New York and London: Verso.
Brenner, Robert. 1985. "The Paradox of Social Democracy: The American Case." *The Year Left: An American Socialist Yearbook* 1:32–87.
Briskin, Linda. 2008. "Cross-Constituency Organizing in Canadian Unions." *British Journal of Industrial Relations* 46(2):221–247.
Brodie, M. Janine, and Jane Jenson. 1988. *Crisis, Challenge and Change: Party and Class in Canada Revisited.* Ottawa: Carleton University Press.
Brody, David. 1983. "On the Failure of US Radical Politics: A Farmer-Labor Analysis." *Industrial Relations: A Journal of Economy and Society* 22(2):141–163.
Bronfenbrenner, Kate. 1994. "Employer Behavior in Certification Elections and First-Contract Campaigns: Implications for Labor Law Reform," pp. 75–89 in *Restoring the Promise of American Labor Law*, edited by S. Friedman, R.W. Hurd, R.A. Oswald, and R.L. Seeber. Ithaca: Cornell ILR Press.
Bronfenbrenner, Kate, Sheldon Friedman, Richard W. Hurd, Rudolph A. Oswald, and Ronald L. Seeber, eds. 1998. *Organizing to Win: New Research on Union Strategies.* Ithaca: Cornell ILR Press.
Bronfenbrenner, Kate. 2009. "No Holds Barred: The Intensification of Employer Opposition to Organizing." Washington, DC: Economic Policy Institute Briefing Paper #235.
Bronfenbrenner, Kate, and Robert Hickey. 2004. "Changing to Organize: A National Assessment of Union Organizing Strategies," pp. 17–60 in *Rebuilding Labor: Organizing and Organizers in the New Union Movement*, edited by R. Milkman and K. Voss. Ithaca: Cornell University Press.
Bronfenbrenner, Kate and Tom Juravich. 1995. "The Impact of Employer Opposition on Union Certification Win Rates: A Private/Public Sector Comparison." Washington, DC: Economic Policy Institute Working Paper 113.
Brooks, Chris. 2016. "Organizing Volkswagen: A Critical Assessment." *WorkingUSA* 19(3):395–417.
Brown, Cliff and John Brueggemann. 1997. "Mobilizing Interracial Solidarity: A Comparison of the 1919 and 1937 Steel Industry Labor Organizing Drives." *Mobilization: An International Quarterly* 2(1):47–70.
Brown, E. Francis. 1932. "The Presidential Campaign." *Current History* 37(2):197–205.
Brown, Lorne A. 2007. "The Early CCF in Saskatchewan as the Political Vehicle of Left Agrarian Populism," pp. 169–200 in *The Prairie Agrarian Movement*

Revisited, edited by K.M. Knuttila and R.M. Stirling. Regina: University of Regina Press.

Brownlie, Robin J. 2008. "'Living the Same as the White People': Mohawk and Anishinabe Women's Labour in Southern Ontario, 1920–1940." *Labour/Le Travail* 61(Spring):41–68.

Bruce, Peter G. 1989. "Political Parties and Labor Legislation in Canada and the US." *Industrial Relations: A Journal of Economy and Society* 28(2):115–41.

Bruemmer, René. 2017. "NDP Leadership Candidates Call for a Return to Party's Roots." Montreal Gazette, March 26, www.montrealgazette.com/news/local -news/ndp-leadership-candidates-call-for-a-return-to-partys-roots

Bruner, Felix. 1936. "Labor's Napoleon: John L. Lewis, Once Conservative Labor Leader, Now Embarked on Venture Which May Lead to High Places – or Ruin." *Washington Post*, October 10, X9.

Bubka, Tony. 1970. "The Harlan County Coal Strike of 1931." *Labor History* 11 (1):41–57.

Buchmueller, Thomas C., John DiNardo, and Robert G. Valletta. 2002. "Union Effects on Health Insurance Provision and Coverage in the United States." *Industrial and Labor Relations Review* 55(4):610–627.

Budd, John W., and In-Gang Na. 2000. "The Union Membership Wage Premium for Employees Covered by Collective Bargaining Agreements." *Journal of Labor Economics* 18(4):783–807.

Buhle, Paul. 1999. *Taking Care of Business: Samuel Gompers, George Meany, Lane Kirkland, and the Tragedy of American Labor*. New York: Monthly Review Press.

Bullen, John. 1983. "The Ontario Waffle and the Struggle for an Independent Socialist Canada: Conflict within the NDP." *Canadian Historical Review* 64 (2):188–215.

Bump, Philip. 2017. "The Importance of a Cultural Blue-Collar Identity in Support for Donald Trump." *Washington Post*, June 5, www.washington post.com/news/politics/wp/2017/06/05/the-importance-of-a-cultural-blue-col lar-identity-in-support-for-donald-trump/.

Burnham, Walter D. 1970. *Critical Elections and the Mainsprings of American Politics*. New York: Norton.

Burns, Joe. 2011. *Reviving the Strike: How Working People Can Regain Power and Transform America*. Brooklyn: Ig Publishing.

California Teachers Association. 2014. "Not if, but When: Living in a World Without Fair Share." PowerPoint presentation, July, www.eiaonline.com/Fair Share.pdf.

Camfield, David. 2002. "Class, Politics, and Social Change: The Remaking of the Working Class in 1940s Canada." PhD dissertation, Social and Political Thought, York University.

Camfield, David. 2007. "Renewal in Canadian Public Sector Unions: Neoliberalism and Union Praxis." *Relations Industrielles* 62(2):282–304.

Camfield, David. 2011. *Canadian Labour in Crisis: Reinventing the Workers' Movement*. Winnipeg: Fernwood.

Campbell, Arthur H. 1953. "Campbell to Ferguson, October 2, 1953." Library and Archives Canada CMA papers, MG28 I230, Vol. 116, Folder Industrial Relations Labour Union Demands 1953.

Campolieti, Michelle, Chris Riddell, and Sara Slinn. 2007a. "Labor Law Reform and the Role of Delay in Union Organizing: Empirical Evidence From Canada." *Industrial and Labor Relations Review* 61(1):32–58.

Campolieti, Michelle, Rafael Gomez, and Morley Gunderson. 2007b. "Say What? Employee Voice in Canada," pp. 49–71 in *What Workers Say: Employee Voice in the Anglo-American Workplace*, edited by R.B. Freeman, P. Boxall, and P. Haynes. Ithaca: Cornell ILR Press.

Canada Ministry of Supply and Services. 1984. *1982 Annual Report, Corporations and Labour Unions Returns Act (Part II. Labour Unions)*. Ottawa: Canada Ministry of Supply and Services.

Canada Task Force on Labour Relations and H D. Woods. 1968. *Canadian Industrial Relations: The Report of the Task Force on Labour Relations*. Ottawa: Queen's Printer.

Canadian Congress of Labour. 1941. *Proceedings of the Second Annual Convention, September 8–12*. Hamilton, Ontario.

Canadian Congress of Labour. 1943. *Proceedings of the Fourth Annual Convention, September 13–19*. Montreal, Quebec.

Canadian Congress of Labour. 1946. *Proceedings of the Sixth Annual Convention, September 23–29*. Toronto, Ontario.

Canadian Foundation for Labour Rights. 2016. *Restrictive Labour Laws Directory*. Ottawa, Ontario, https://labourrights.ca/restrictive-labour-laws.

Canadian Manufacturers' Association. 1947a. "Freedom of Association Under the United States Labor Management Relations Act, 1947 (Taft-Hartley Act)." Library and Archives Canada CMA papers, MG28 I230, Vol. 121, Folder Labour Relations 1944–51.

Canadian Manufacturers' Association. 1947b. "Submission of the Canadian Manufacturers' Association to the Standing Committee on Industrial Relations of the House of Commons, with Respect to Bill 338." Library and Archives Canada CMA papers, MG 28 I 230, Vol. 117, Folder IRDIA 1947–48.

Canadian Press. 2011. "Layton Nixes Cutting NDP Ties to Labour Unions." *CTV.ca*, June 6, www.ctvnews.ca/layton-nixes-cutting-ndp-ties-to-labour-unions-1.659123#.

Canadian Press. 2017a. "Leap Manifesto: What Is It, and What Could It Mean for the NDP's Future?" *The Globe and Mail*, January 5, www.theglobeandmail.com/news/politics/leap-manifesto-what-is-it-and-what-could-it-mean-for-the-ndpsfuture/article29583796/.

Canadian Press. 2017b. "Ontario Elementary Teachers Ratify Two-Year Contract Extension." *The Globe and Mail*, March 4, www.theglobeandmail.com/news/national/ontario-elementary-teachers-ratify-two-year-contract-extension/article34207926/.

Caplan, Gerald L. 1963. "The Failure of Canadian Socialism: The Ontario Experience, 1932–1945." *Canadian Historical Review* 44(2):93–121.

Card, David, and Richard B. Freeman. 1994. "Small Differences That Matter: Canada vs. the United States," pp. 189–222 in *Working Under Different Rules*, edited by R.B. Freeman. New York: Russell Sage Foundation.

Card, David, Thomas Lemieux, and W. Craig Riddell. 2004. "Unions and Wage Inequality." *Journal of Labor Research* 25(4):519–559.

Carey, James B. 1939. "Statement by James B. Carey to the Senate Education and Labor Committee, November 2, 1939." *National Archives* RG174 General Records of the Department of Labor Secretary Frances Perkins, Box 135 Office of the Secretary Secy Frances Perkins, Conferences to Congress of Industrial Organizations, Folder Congress of Industrial Organizations.

Carnes, Nicholas. 2013. *White-Collar Government: The Hidden Role of Class in Economic Policy Making*. Chicago: University of Chicago Press.

Carnes, Nicholas. 2015. "Why Are There So Few Working-Class People in Political Office? Evidence From State Legislatures." *Politics, Groups, and Identities* 4(1):84–109.

Carroll, William K., and R.S. Ratner. 1989. "Social Democracy, Neo-Conservatism and Hegemonic Crisis in British Columbia." *Critical Sociology* 16(1):29–53.

Carter, Susan B., Scott Sigmund Gartner, Michael R. Haines, Douglas A. Irwin, Alan L. Olmstead, Richard Sutch, and Gavin Wright. 2006. *Historical Statistics of the United States Millennial Edition Online*. New York: Cambridge University Press.

Case, Anne, and Angus Deaton. 2017. "Mortality and Morbidity in the 21st Century." Washington, DC: Brookings Panel on Economic Activity, May 1.

Casebeer, Kenneth M. 1987. "Holder of the Pen: An Interview with Leon Keyserling on Drafting the Wagner Act." *University of Miami Law Review* 42:285–364.

Caute, David. 1979. *The Great Fear: The Anti-Communist Purge Under Truman and Eisenhower*. New York: Simon and Schuster.

Ceaser, James W. 2012. "The Origins and Character of American Exceptionalism." *American Political Thought* 1(Spring):3–28.

Center for Individual Rights. 2016. "Supreme Court Denies Friedrichs Petition for Rehearing." *Center for Individual Rights*, www.cir-usa.org/cases/friedrichs-v-california-teachers-association-et-al/.

Center for Responsive Politics. 2012. "Top Overall Donors | OpenSecrets." *opensecrets.org*, www.opensecrets.org/overview/topcontribs.php.

Chaison, Gary N. and Joseph B. Rose. 1990. "New Directions and Divergent Paths: The North American Labor Movements in Troubled Times." *Labor Law Journal* 41(8):591–596.

Chaison, Gary N. 2007. "The AFL-CIO Split: Does It Really Matter?" *Journal of Labor Research* 28(2):301–311.

Chen, Victor Tan. 2015. *Cut Loose: Jobless and Hopeless in an Unfair Economy*. Berkeley: University of California Press.

Cherny, Robert W., William Issel, and Kieran W. Taylor, eds. 2004. *American Labor and the Cold War: Grassroots Politics and Postwar Political Culture*. New Brunswick: Rutgers University Press.

Cherone, Heather. 2016. "Here's What Chicago Teachers Won & Lost in Contract Deal." *dnainfo.com*, www.dnainfo.com/chicago/20161014/gladstone-park/cps-chicago-public-schools-teachers-union-strike.

Chibber, Vivek. 2017. "Rescuing Class from the Cultural Turn." *Catalyst* 1(1):26–55.

Chun, Jennifer J. 2009. *Organizing at the Margins: The Symbolic Politics of Labor in South Korea and the United States*. Ithaca: Cornell ILR Press.

Clawson, Dan. 2003. *The Next Upsurge: Labor and the New Social Movements*. Ithaca: Cornell ILR Press.

Clawson, Dan, and Mary Ann Clawson. 1999. "What Has Happened to the U.S. Labor Movement? Union Decline and Renewal." *Annual Review of Sociology* 25(1):95–119.

Clemens, Elisabeth S. 1997. *The People's Lobby: Organizational Innovation and the Rise of Interest Group Politics in the United States, 1890–1925*. Chicago: University of Chicago Press.

Clement, Wallace, ed. 1996. *Understanding Canada: Building on the New Canadian Political Economy*. Montreal: McGill Queens University Press.

Cochran, Bert. 1977. *Labor and Communism: The Conflict That Shaped American Unions*. Princeton: Princeton University Press.

Cohen, Adam S. 2009. *Nothing to Fear: FDR's Inner Circle and the Hundred Days That Created Modern America*. New York: Penguin.

Collier, Ruth B., and David Collier. 1991. *Shaping the Political Arena: Critical Junctures, the Labor Movement, and Regime Dynamics in Latin America*. Princeton: Princeton University Press.

Confessore, Nicholas. 2015. "A Wealthy Governor and His Friends Are Remaking Illinois." *New York Times*, November 29, www.nytimes.com/2015/11/30/us/politics/illinois-campaign-money-bruce-rauner.html.

Confédération des syndicats nationaux (CSN) and Centrale de l'enseignement du Québec (CEQ). 1987. *The History of the Labour Movement in Québec*. Montréal: Black Rose Books.

Congress of Industrial Organizations. 1948. "Report of the Resolutions Committee." Proceedings of the Tenth Constitutional Convention, November 22–26, Portland, Ore.

Conroy, Pat. 1944. "Letter From Conroy to Carmichael (DMS Official), June 1, 1944." Library and Archives Canada CLC papers MG28 I103, Vol. 193, Folder 193-10 Federal Government Munitions and Supply Department of Part 1 1940–1944.

Cook, Ramsay. 1984. "Tillers and Toilers: The Rise and Fall of Populism in Canada in the 1890s." *Historical Papers/Communications historiques* 19 (1):1–20.

Cowie, Jefferson R. 2010. *Stayin' Alive: The 1970s and the Last Days of the Working Class*. New York: New Press.

Craig, Douglas B. 1992. *After Wilson: The Struggle for the Democratic Party, 1920–1934*. Chapel Hill: University of North Carolina Press.

Craver, Charles B. 2005. "The Labor Movement Needs a Twenty-First Century Committee for Industrial Organization." *Hofstra Labor and Employment Law Journal* 23:69–100.

Creese, Gillian. 1987. "Organizing Against Racism in the Workplace: Chinese Workers in Vancouver Before World War II." *Canadian Ethnic Studies-Etudes Ethniques au Canada* 19(3):35–46.

Creese, Gillian. 1988. "Exclusion or Solidarity? Vancouver Workers Confront the 'Oriental Problem'." *BC Studies: The British Columbian Quarterly* 80 (Winter):24–51.

Cullen, Jim. 2003. *The American Dream: A Short History of an Idea That Shaped a Nation*. New York: Oxford University Press.

Dahrendorf, Ralf. 1959. *Class and Class Conflict in Industrial Society*. Stanford: Stanford University Press.

Dark, Taylor E. 1999. *The Unions and the Democrats: An Enduring Alliance*. Ithaca: Cornell ILR Press.

Das Gupta, Tania. 2007. "Racism and the Labour Movement," pp. 181–207 in *Equity, Diversity, and Canadian Labour*, edited by G. Hunt and D.M. Rayside. Toronto: University of Toronto Press.

Davey, Monica. 2012. "Indiana Governor Signs a Law Creating a 'Right to Work' State." *New York Times*, February 2, A12.

Davin, Eric L. and Staughton Lynd. 1979. "Picket Line and Ballot Box: The Forgotten Legacy of the Local Labor Party Movement, 1932–1936." *Radical History Review* 1979–80(22):43–63.

Davis, Joe C. and John H. Huston. 1995. "Right-to-Work Laws and Union Density: New Evidence From Micro Data." *Journal of Labor Research* 16 (2):223–29.

Davis, Mike. 1980a. "Why the US Working Class Is Different." *New Left Review* I/123(September-October 1980):3–44.

Davis, Mike. 1980b. "The Barren Marriage of American Labour and the Democratic Party." *New Left Review* I/124(November-December 1980):43–84.

Davis, Mike. 1986. "The Lesser Evil? the Left and the Democratic Party." *New Left Review* I/155(January-February):5–36.

Davis, Mike. 1999. *Prisoners of the American Dream: Politics and Economy in the History of the US Working Class*. New York and London: Verso Books.

de Leon, Cedric, Manali Desai, and Cihan Tuğal. 2009. "Political Articulation: Parties and the Constitution of Cleavages in the United States, India, and Turkey." *Sociological Theory* 27(3):193–219.

De Leon, Cedric, Manali Desai, and Cihan Tuğal, eds. 2015. *Building Blocs: How Parties Organize Society*. Stanford: Stanford University Press.

DePillis, Lydia. 2014. "Auto Union Loses Historic Election at Volkswagen Plant in Tennessee." *Washington Post*, February 14, www.washingtonpost.com/news/wonk/wp/2014/02/14/united-auto-workers-lose-historic-election-at-chattanooga-volkswagen-plant/?utm_term=.4a2edce92362.

Derber, Milton, and Edwin Young. 1961. *Labor and the New Deal*. Madison: University of Wisconsin Press.

Devereux, Michael B. 2009. "Much Appreciated? The Rise of the Canadian Dollar, 2002–2008." *Review of Economic Analysis* 1(1):1–33.

Devinatz, Victor G. 2011. "The Continuing Controversy over Right-to-Work Laws in the Early Twenty-First Century." *Employee Responsibilities and Rights Journal* 23(4):287–293.

Dickens, William T., and Jonathan S. Leonard. 1985. "Accounting for the Decline in Union Membership, 1950–1980." *Industrial and Labor Relations Review* 38(3):323–334.

Dickinson, John. 1935. "Memo From Dickinson to Perkins: Course to Be Followed by Administration as a Result of Supreme Court Holding That National Industrial Recovery Act Is in Large Part Unconstitutional." National Archives RG174 General Records of the Department of Labor Secretary Frances Perkins, Box 86 Office of the Secretary Secy Frances Perkins, General Subject File 1933–1941 National Labor Relations Board to National Recovery Admin, Folder National Labor Relations Board December 1934.

DiMaggio, Dan. 2016. "Verizon Strike Shows Corporate Giants Can Be Beat." *Labor Notes*, www.labornotes.org/2016/06/verizon-strikers-show-corporate-giants-can-be-beat.

Dinsdale, Henry, and Dan Awrey. 2003. "Secondary Picketing in Canada: Thoughts for the Pepsi Generaion." *Queen's Law Journal* 29:789–808.

Dixon, Marc. 2008. "Movements, Countermovements and Policy Adoption: The Case of Right-to-Work Activism." *Social Forces* 87(1):473–500.

Dixon, Marc. 2009. "Limiting Labor: Business Political Mobilization and Union Setback in the States." *Journal of Policy History* 19(03):313–344.

Dixon, Marc. 2010. "Union Threat, Countermovement Organization, and Labor Policy in the States, 1944–1960." *Social Problems* 57(2):157–174.

Dixon, Marc, and Jack Fiorito. 2009. "Can Unions Rebound? Decline and Renewal in the US Labour Movement," pp. 154–174 in *Union Revitalisation in Advanced Economies*, edited by G. Gall. Basingstoke: Palgrave Macmillan.

Dobbs, Farrell. 1973. *Teamster Power*. New York: Pathfinder Press.

Dobbs, Farrell. 1975. *Teamster Politics*. New York: Pathfinder Press.

Doorey, David. 2013. "Why Unions Can't Organize Retail Workers." *Dooreys Law of Work Blog*, http://lawofwork.ca/?p=7061.

Doorey, David J. 2007. "The Medium and the Anti-Union Message: Forced Listening and Captive Audience Meetings." *Comparative Labor Law & Policy Journal* 29(2):79–118.

Draper, Alan. 1989. *A Rope of Sand: The AFL-CIO Committee on Political Education, 1955–1967*. New York: Praeger.

Dubofsky, Melvyn. 1969. *We Shall Be All: A History of the Industrial Workers of the World*. Chicago: Quadrangle Books.

Dubofsky, Melvyn, and Warren R. Van Tine. 1977. *John L. Lewis: A Biography*. New York: Quadrangle/New York Times Book Co.

Dunlop, John T. 1994. "Fact Finding Report: Commission on the Future of Worker-Management Relations." *Federal Publications*, http://digitalcommons.ilr.cornell.edu/key_workplace/276.

Duverger, Maurice. 1954. *Political Parties, Their Organization and Activity in the Modern State*. London and New York: Methuen and Wiley.

Eaton, Adrienne E., Janice Fine, Alison Porter, and Saul Rubinstein. 2011. *Organizational Change at SEIU, 1996–2009*. Washington, DC: Alvarez Porter Group.

Edelman, Adam. 2016. "Billioniare Donald Trump: I Am a Blue Collar Worker." *New York Daily News*, October 10, www.nydailynews.com/news/politics/billioniare-donald-trump-blue-collar-worker-article-1.2825716.

Edelman, Lauren B. 1990. "Legal Environments and Organizational Governance: The Expansion of Due Process in the American Workplace." *American Journal of Sociology* 95(6):1401–1440.

Edelman, Murray. 1961. "New Deal Sensitivity to Labor Interests," pp. 157–192 in *Labor and the New Deal*, edited by M. Derber and E. Young. Madison: University of Wisconsin Press.

Edsall, Thomas B. 2012. "White Working Chaos." *NY Times Campaign Stops: Strong Opinions on the 2012 Election* 1–7, http://campaignstops.blogs.nytimes.com/2012/06/25/white-working-chaos/.

Edwards, Richard. 1979. *Contested Terrain: The Transformation of the Workplace in the Twentieth Century*. New York: Basic Books.

Edwards, Richard and Michael Podgursky. 1986. "The Unraveling Accord: American Unions in Crisis," pp. 15–60 in *Unions in Crisis and Beyond: Perspectives from Six Countries*, edited by R. Edwards, P. Garonna, and F. Tödtling. Dover and London: Auburn House.

Egan, Paul. 2015. "Supreme Court Upholds Right-to-Work for State Workers." *Detroit Free Press*, July 29, www.freep.com/story/news/politics/2015/07/29/supreme-court-ruling-right-work-law-state-employees/30839363/.

Eidelson, Josh. 2013. "Alt-Labor." *The American Prospect*, January 29, www.prospect.org/article/alt-labor.

Eidelson, Josh. 2016. "Trump Triggers $100 Million Budget Cut by Nation's Second Largest Union." *Bloomberg Businessweek*, www.bloomberg.com/news/articles/2016-12-27/fear-of-trump-triggers-deep-spending-cuts-by-nation-s-second-largest-union.

Eidelson, Josh. 2017a. "@Eidlin Here's What Mary Kay Henry Told Me in 2013 on the Day It Was Announced UFCW Was Returning to AFL-CIO: https://t.co/spsisappgz." *Twitter*, July 20.

Eidelson, Josh. 2017b. "AFL-CIO Dismissing Staff Amid Declines in U.S. Union Membership." *Bloomberg Businessweek*, www.bloomberg.com/news/articles/2017-02-23/afl-cio-dismissing-staff-amid-declines-in-u-s-union-membership.

Eidelson, Josh. 2017c. "Unions Are Losing Their Decades-Long 'Right-to-Work' Fight." *Bloomberg Businessweek*, www.bloomberg.com/news/articles/2017-02-16/unions-are-losing-their-decades-long-right-to-work-fight.

Eidlin, Barry. 2014. "Class Formation and Class Identity: Birth, Death, and Possibilities for Renewal." *Sociology Compass* 8(8):1045–1062.

Eidlin, Barry. 2015. "Continuity or Change? Rethinking Left Party Formation in Canada," pp. 61–86 in *Building Blocs: How Parties Organize Society*, edited by C. de Leon, M. Desai, and C. Tuğal. Stanford: Stanford University Press.

Eidlin, Barry. 2016. "Why Is There No Labor Party in the United States? Political Articulation and the Canadian Comparison, 1932 to 1948." *American Sociological Review* 81(3):488–516.

Ejeckam, Chuka. 2017. "Seven Progressive Changes Coming to BC." *The Broadbent Blog*, www.broadbentinstitute.ca/seven_progressive_changes_coming_to_bc.

Elbaum, Max. 2002. *Revolution in the Air: Sixties Radicals Turn to Lenin, Mao and Che*. New York and London: Verso.

Elk, Mike. 2014. "After Historic UAW Defeat at Tennessee Volkswagen Plant, Theories Abound." *In These Times*, http://inthesetimes.com/working/entry/16300/after_uaw_defeat_at_volkswagen_in_tennessee_theories_abound.

Ellwood, David T. and Glenn Fine. 1987. "The Impact of Right-to-Work Laws on Union Organizing." *Journal of Political Economy* 95(2):250–273.

Employment and Social Development Canada. 2016. *Labour Organizations in Canada 2015*. Ottawa, www.canada.ca/en/employment-social-development/services/collective-bargaining-data/reports/union-coverage.html.

Epps, Garrett. 2016. "Will the U.S. Supreme Court Gut Public-Employee Unions?" *The Atlantic*, www.theatlantic.com/politics/archive/2016/01/will-the-supreme-court-gut-public-employee-unions/423666/.

Erickson, Christopher L., Catherine L. Fisk, Ruth Milkman, Daniel J.B. Mitchell, and Kent Wong. 2002. "Justice for Janitors in Los Angeles: Lessons from Three Rounds of Negotiations." *British Journal of Industrial Relations* 40(3):543–567.

Erikson, Robert S., Thomas D. Lancaster, and David W. Romero. 1989. "Group Components of the Presidential Vote, 1952–1984." *Journal of Politics* 51(2):337–346.

Esch, Elizabeth, and David Roediger. 2009. "One Symptom of Originality: Race and the Management of Labour in the History of the United States." *Historical Materialism* 17(4):3–43.

Esping-Andersen, Gøsta. 1990. *The Three Worlds of Welfare Capitalism*. Princeton: Princeton University Press.

Estlund, Cynthia. 2007. "The Ossification of American Labor Law and the Decline of Self-Governance in the Workplace." *Journal of Labor Research* 28(4):591–608.

Estlund, Cynthia L. 1993. "Labor, Property, and Sovereignty after Lechmere." *Stanford Law Review* 46:305–360.

Estreicher, Samuel. 2006. "Disunity Within the House of Labor: Change to Win or to Stay the Course?" *Journal of Labor Research* 27(4):505–511.

Evans, Bryan. 2012. "The New Democratic Party in the Era of Neoliberalism," pp. 48–61 in *Rethinking the Politics of Labour in Canada*, edited by S. Ross and L. Savage. Winnipeg: Fernwood Publishing.

Evans, Bryan. 2017. "Alternatives to the Low Waged Economy: Living Wage Movements in Canada and the United States." *Alternate Routes: A Journal of Critical Social Research* 28:80–113.

Evans, Bryan M., and Charles W. Smith, eds. 2015. *Transforming Provincial Politics: The Political Economy of Canada's Provinces and Territories in the Neoliberal Era*. Toronto: University of Toronto Press.

Fang, Tony, and Anil Verma. 2002. "Union Wage Premium." *Perspectives on Labour and Income* 3(9):13–19.

Fantasia, Rick, Dan Clawson, and Gregory Graham. 1988. "A Critical View of Worker Participation in American Industry." *Work and Occupations* 15(4):468–488.

Fantasia, Rick, and Kim Voss. 2004. *Hard Work: Remaking the American Labor Movement*. Berkeley: University of California Press.

Farber, Henry S. 1984. "Right-to-Work Laws and the Extent of Unionization." *Journal of Labor Economics* 2(3):319–352.

Farber, Henry S. 1985. "The Extent of Unionization in the United States," pp. 15–43 in *Challenges and Choices Facing American Labor*, edited by T.A. Kochan. Cambridge: MIT Press.

Farber, Henry S. 1990. "The Decline of Unionization in the United States: What Can Be Learned From Recent Experience?" *Journal of Labor Economics* 8(1):75–105.

Farber, Henry S. and Bruce Western. 2002. "Ronald Reagan and the Politics of Declining Union Organization." *British Journal of Industrial Relations* 40(3):385–401.

Farhang, Sean and Ira Katznelson. 2005. "The Southern Imposition: Congress and Labor in the New Deal and Fair Deal." *Studies in American Political Development* 19(Spring):1–30.

Faue, Elizabeth. 1991. *Community of Suffering and Struggle: Women, Men, and the Labor Movement in Minneapolis, 1915–1945*. Chapel Hill: University of North Carolina Press.

Ferguson, John-Paul. 2008. "The Eyes of the Needles: A Sequential Model of Union Organizing Drives, 1999–2004." *Industrial and Labor Relations Review* 62(1):3–21.

Fine, Janice. 2017. "Enforcing Labor Standards in Partnership with Civil Society: Can Co-Enforcement Succeed Where the State Alone Has Failed?" *Politics and Society* 45(3):359–388.

Fine, Nathan. 1928. *Labor and Farmer Parties in the United States, 1828–1928*. New York: Rand School of Social Science.

Finegold, Kenneth, and Theda Skocpol. 1995. *State and Party in America's New Deal*. Madison: University of Wisconsin Press.

Fink, Leon. 1983. *Workingmen's Democracy: The Knights of Labor and American Politics*. Urbana: University of Illinois Press.

Finkel, Alvin. 1997. *Our Lives: Canada after 1945*. Toronto: James Lorimer & Company.

Flamm, Michael W. 1994. "The National Farmers Union and the Evolution of Agrarian Liberalism, 1937–1946." *Agricultural History* 68(3):54–80.

Flora, Peter, and Arnold J. Heidenheimer. 1981. *The Development of Welfare States in Europe and America*. New Brunswick: Transaction Books.

Flynn, Joan. 1995. "The Costs and Benefits of Hiding the Ball: NLRB Policymaking and the Failure of Judicial Review." *Boston University Law Review* 75:387–446.

Flynn, Joan. 2000. "A Quiet Revolution at the Labor Board: The Transformation of the NLRB, 1935–2000." *Ohio State Law Journal* 61:1361–1793.

Foley, Elise. 2012. "Mitch Daniels: Public-Sector Unions Shouldn't Exist." *The Huffington Post*, www.huffingtonpost.com/2012/06/10/mitch-daniels-unions-public-sector-unions_n_1584396.html.

Foner, Eric. 1984. "Why Is There No Socialism in the United States?" *History Workshop Journal* 17(Spring):57–80.

Foner, Moe, and Dan North. 2002. *Not for Bread Alone*. Ithaca: Cornell University Press.

Foner, Philip S. 1970. "The IWW and the Black Worker." *The Journal of Negro History* 55(1):45–64.
Fones-Wolf, Elizabeth. 2006. *Waves of Opposition: Labor and the Struggle for Democratic Radio*. Urbana: University of Illinois Press.
Forrest, Anne. 2000. "What Do Women Want From Union Representation?" *Hecate* 26(2):47–61.
Forsey, Eugene. 1958. "The Movement Towards Labour Unity in Canada: History and Implications." *The Canadian Journal of Economics and Political Science / Revue canadienne d'économique et de science politique* 24(1):70–83.
Foster, James E., and Michael C. Wolfson. 2009. "Polarization and the Decline of the Middle Class: Canada and the U.S." *The Journal of Economic Inequality* 8(2):247–273.
Fowlie, Barry. 2017. Author's Phone Conversation with Barry Fowlie, Director, Workers United Canada Council, July 26, 2017.
Fraser, Douglas. 1978. "Douglas Fraser's Resignation Letter From the Labor-Management Group." 1–4, www.historyisaweapon.com/defcon1/fraserresign.html.
Fraser, Steve. 1989. "The 'Labor Question'," pp. 53–84 in *The Rise and Fall of the New Deal Order, 1930–1980*, edited by S. Fraser and G. Gerstle. Princeton: Princeton University Press.
Fraser, Steve. 1991. *Labor Will Rule: Sidney Hillman and the Rise of American Labor*. New York: Free Press.
Freeman, Richard B. 1986. "Unionism Comes to the Public Sector." *Journal of Economic Literature* 24(1):41–86.
Freeman, Richard B. 1988. "Contraction and Expansion: The Divergence of Private Sector and Public Sector Unionism in the United States." *The Journal of Economic Perspectives* 2(2):63–88.
Freeman, Richard B. 2004. "The Road to Union Renaissance in the United States," pp. 3–21 in *The Changing Role of Unions: New Forms of Representation*, edited by P.V. Wunnava. Armonk, NY: M. E. Sharpe.
Freeman, Richard B., and James L. Medoff. 1984. *What Do Unions Do?* New York: Basic Books.
Freeman, Richard B., and Joel Rogers. 1998. "*Worker Representation and Participation Survey (WRPS).*" Cambridge: National Bureau of Economic Research
Freeman, Richard B., and Morris Kleiner. 1990. "Employer Behavior in the Face of Union Organizing Drives." *Industrial and Labor Relations Review* 43(4):351–365.
Freeman, Richard B., Casey Ichniowski, and Jeffrey Zax. 1988. "Appendix A: Collective Organization of Labor in the Public Sector," pp. 365–398 in *When Public Sector Workers Unionize*, edited by R.B. Freeman and C. Ichniowski. Chicago: University Of Chicago Press.
Freidel, Frank B. 1990. *Franklin D. Roosevelt: A Rendezvous with Destiny*. Boston: Back Bay Books.
Fried, Albert. 1997. *McCarthyism: The Great American Red Scare: A Documentary History*. Oxford and New York: Oxford University Press.

Friedman, Gerald. 1991. "Worker Militancy and Its Consequences: Political Responses to Labor Unrest in the United States, 1877–1914." *International Labor and Working-Class History* 40(1):5–17.

Friedman, Gerald. 2015. "American Labor and American Law: Exceptionalism and Its Politics in the Decline of the American Labor Movement." *Law, Culture and the Humanities* 11(1):30–43.

Frymer, Paul. 2007. *Black and Blue: African Americans, the Labor Movement, and the Decline of the Democratic Party*. Princeton: Princeton University Press.

Fudge, Judy. 1990. "Voluntarism, Compulsion and the 'Transformation' of Canadian Labour Law During World War II," pp. 81–100 in *Canadian and Australian Labour History: Towards a Comparative Perspective*, edited by G.S. Kealey and G. Patmore. Sydney: Australian Society for the Study of Labour History.

Fudge, Judy. 2010. "Labour, Courts, and the Cunning of History." *Just Labour: A Canadian Journal of Work and Society* 16(Spring):1–8.

Fudge, Judy, and Eric Tucker. 2001. *Labour Before the Law: The Regulation of Workers' Collective Action in Canada, 1900–1948*. Don Mills: Oxford University Press.

Fudge, Judy, and Harry Glasbeek. 1995. "The Legacy of PC 1003." *Canadian Labour and Employment Law Journal* 3(4):357–399.

Galenson, Walter. 1960. *The CIO Challenge to the AFL*. Cambridge: Harvard University Press.

Gall, Gilbert J. 1988. *The Politics of Right to Work: The Labor Federations as Special Interests, 1943–1979*. New York: Greenwood Press.

Gamoran, Adam. 2001. "American Schooling and Educational Inequality: A Forecast for the 21st Century." *Sociology of Education* 74(Extra Issue: Current of Thought: Sociology of Education at the Dawn of the 21st Century):135–153.

Ganz, Marshall, Kim Voss, Teresa Sharpe, Carl Somers, and George Strauss. 2004. "Against the Tide: Projects and Pathways of the New Generation of Union Leaders, 1984–2001," pp. 150–194 in *Rebuilding Labor: Organizing and Organizers in the New Union Movement*. Ithaca: Cornell University Press.

Garden, Charlotte. 2016. "What Will Become of Public-Sector Unions Now?" *The Atlantic*, www.theatlantic.com/business/archive/2016/02/scalia-friedrichs/462936/.

Garnel, Donald. 1972. *The Rise of Teamster Power in the West*. Berkeley: University of California Press.

Gellhorn, Walter, and Seymour L. Linfield. 1939. "Politics and Labor Relations: An Appraisal of Criticisms of NLRB Procedure." *Columbia Law Review* 39(3):339–395.

Georgakas, Dan, and Marvin Surkin. 1998. *Detroit, I Do Mind Dying: A Study in Urban Revolution*. 2nd ed. Boston: South End Press.

George, Willis. 1954. "CMA Memo: George to Whitelaw Re: Federal Labor Legislation, January 13, 1954." Library and Archives Canada CMA papers, MG28 I230, Vol. 116, Folder Industrial Relations Disputes Investigation Act 1954.

Gerteis, Joseph. 2007. *Class and the Color Line: Interracial Class Coalition in the Knights of Labor and the Populist Movement.* Durham: Duke University Press.

Getman, Julius G., and F. Ray Marshall. 2000. "The Continuing Assault on the Right to Strike." *Texas Law Review* 79: 703–736.

Getman, Julius G. 2016. *The Supreme Court on Unions.* Ithaca: Cornell University Press.

Gieske, Millard L. 1979. *Minnesota Farmer-Laborism: The Third-Party Alternative.* Minneapolis: University of Minnesota Press.

Gilbert, Jess, and Carolyn Howe. 1991. "Beyond 'State vs. Society': Theories of the State and New Deal Agricultural Policies." *American Sociological Review* 56(2):204–220.

Gindin, Sam. 1995. *The Canadian Auto Workers: The Birth and Transformation of a Union.* Toronto: Lorimer.

Ginsburg, Matthew. 2017. "Nothing New Under the Sun: The New Labor Law Must Still Grapple With the Traditional Challenges of Firm-Based Organizing and Building Self-Sustainable Worker Organizations." *Yale Law Journal Forum* 126:488–502.

Gitlin, Todd. 1987. *The Sixties: Years of Hope, Days of Rage.* New York: Bantam.

Glazer, Nathan. 1961. *The Social Basis of American Communism.* New York: Harcourt, Brace & World.

Glazer, Sidney. 1937. "Patrons of Industry in Michigan." *The Mississippi Valley Historical Review* 24(2):185–194.

Godard, John. 2003. "Do Labor Laws Matter? The Density Decline and Convergence Thesis Revisited." *Industrial Relations* 42(3):458–492.

Godard, John. 2004. *Trade Union Recognition: Statutory Unfair Labour Practice Regimes in the USA and Canada.* London: UK Department of Trade and Industry.

Golden, Clinton S., and Harold J. Ruttenberg. 1942. *The Dynamics of Industrial Democracy.* New York, London: Harper & Brothers.

Goldfield, Michael. 1989a. *The Decline of Organized Labor in the United States.* Chicago: University of Chicago Press.

Goldfield, Michael. 1989b. "Worker Insurgency, Radical Organization, and New Deal Labor Legislation." *American Political Science Review* 83(4):1257–1282.

Goldfield, Michael. 1990. "Class, Race, and Politics in the United States: White Supremacy as the Main Explanation for the Peculiarities of American Politics From Colonial Times to the Present." *Research in Political Economy* 12:83–127.

Goldfield, Michael. 1993. "Race and the CIO: The Possibilities for Racial Egalitarianism During the 1930s and 1940s." *International Labor and Working-Class History* 44(Fall):1–32.

Goldfield, Michael. 1994. "The Failure of Operation Dixie: A Critical Turning Point in American Political Development?," pp. 166–189 in *Race, Class, and Community in Southern Labor History,* edited by G.M. Fink and M.E. Reed. Tuscaloosa: University of Alabama Press.

Goldfield, Michael. 1997. *The Color of Politics: Race and the Mainsprings of American Politics.* New York: New Press, distributed by W.W. Norton & Co.

Goldstein, Donna M., and Kira Hall. 2017. "Postelection Surrealism and Nostalgic Racism in the Hands of Donald Trump." *HAU: Journal of Ethnographic Theory* 7(1):397–406.

Goluboff, Risa L. 2007. *The Lost Promise of Civil Rights.* Cambridge: Harvard University Press.

Gonick, Cy. 1965. "Students and Peace." *Canadian Dimension* 2(2):12.

Goodling, Judson. 1970. "Blue-Collar Blues on the Assembly Line." *Fortune,* July, 69–72.

Gordon, Todd. 2010. *Imperialist Canada.* Winnipeg: Arbeiter Ring Publishing.

Gosse, Van. 2005. *Rethinking the New Left: An Interpretative History.* New York: Palgrave Macmillan.

Gottschalk, Marie. 2000. *The Shadow Welfare State: Labor, Business, and the Politics of Health Care in the United States.* Ithaca: Cornell ILR Press.

Gould-Wartofsky, Michael A. 2015. *The Occupiers: The Making of the 99 Percent Movement.* Oxford: Oxford University Press.

Gourevitch, Alex. 2014. *From Slavery to the Cooperative Commonwealth.* Cambridge: Cambridge University Press.

Goutor, David. 2007. *Guarding the Gates: The Canadian Labour Movement and Immigration, 1872–1934.* Vancouver: UBC Press.

Gramsci, Antonio. 1978. "Some Aspects of the Southern Question," pp. 441–462 in *Selections from Political Writings (1921–1926),* edited by Q. Hoare. London: Lawrence and Wishart.

Granatstein, J.L. 1967. "The York South by-Election of February 9, 1942: A Turning Point in Canadian Politics." *Canadian Historical Review* 48(2):142–158.

Gray, Stanley. 1965. "The New Democratic Youth Convention." *Canadian Dimension* 2(6):23.

Green, William. 1934a. "There Is Incorporated in Every Industrial Code ...." *George Meany Memorial Archives* RG1-015 Office of the President, William Green Papers, 1888, 1909–1952, Series 2 Speeches and Addresses, 1925–1934 and undated, Box–Folder 2–33 Speeches n.d.

Green, William. 1934b. "A Labor Day Appraisement of National Planning and Economic Experimentation." *George Meany Memorial Archives RG1-015 Office of the President, William Green Papers,* 1888, 1909–1952, Series 2 Speeches and Addresses, 1925–1934 and undated, Box–Folder 2–33 Speeches n.d.

Green, William. 1945. "Speech to Labor-Management Conference, November 5–6, 1945." *National Archives* RG174 General Records of the Department of Labor Office of the Secretary Subject File of Secretary Lewis B Schwellenbach 1945–48, Box 12 Labor Management Conference-Conference of State Labor Commissioners to Consider the Norton Bill, Folder Labor–Management Conference Miscellaneous Speeches 1945.

Greenberg, Miriam and Penny W. Lewis, eds. 2017. *The City Is the Factory: New Solidarities and Spatial Strategies in an Urban Age.* Ithaca: Cornell University Press.

Greene, Julie. 1998. *Pure and Simple Politics: The American Federation of Labor and Political Activism, 1881–1917.* Cambridge: Cambridge University Press.

Greenhouse, Steven. 2010. "Most U.S. Union Members Are Working for the Government, New Data Shows." *New York Times*, January 1, B1.
Greenhouse, Steven. 2014. "Volkswagen Vote Is Defeat for Labor in South." *New York Times*, February 15, B1, http://nyti.ms/1jjPz2J.
Greenstone, J. David. 1969. *Labor in American Politics*. New York: Knopf.
Griffith, Barbara S. 1988. *The Crisis of American Labor: Operation Dixie and the Defeat of the CIO*. Philadelphia: Temple University Press.
Grondin, Gilles. 2015. "Marcel Pepin, l'homme du contre-pouvoir." Ph.D. dissertation, Department of Industrial Relations, Université de Montréal.
Gross, James A. 1981. *The Making of the National Labor Relations Board: 1933–1937*. Albany: State University of New York Press.
Gross, James A. 1995. *Broken Promise: The Subversion of U.S. Labor Relations Policy, 1947–1994*. Philadelphia: Temple University Press.
Gross, Jared S. 2004. "Yet Another Reappraisal of the Taft-Hartley Act Emergency Injunctions." *University of Pennsylvania Journal of Labor and Employment Law* 7(2):305–339.
Grubbs, Donald H. 1971. *Cry From the Cotton: The Southern Tenant Farmers' Union and the New Deal*. Chapel Hill: University of North Carolina Press.
Hacker, Jacob S. 2002. *The Divided Welfare State: The Battle Over Public and Private Social Benefits in the United States*. New York: Cambridge University Press.
Hannah, Mary. 2016. "The Fight for 15: Can the Organizing Model That Helped Pass Seattle's $15 Minimum Wage Legislation Fill the Gap Left by the Decline in Unions." *Washington University Journal of Law & Policy* 51:257–278.
Hansen, John Mark. 1991. *Gaining Access: Congress and the Farm Lobby, 1919–1981*. Chicago: University of Chicago Press.
Hardin, Charles M. 1952. *The Politics of Agriculture: Soil Conservation and the Struggle for Power in Rural America*. Glencoe: Free Press.
Harrell, Donovan. 2016. "$15 Minimum Wage Movement to Vote on Organizing Mass Fast-Food Worker Strike." *POLITICO*, http://politi.co/2bdpIMk.
Harrington, Michael. 1972. *Socialism*. New York: Saturday Review Press.
Harris, Howell J. 1982. *The Right to Manage: Industrial Relations Policies of American Business in the 1940s*. Madison: University of Wisconsin Press.
Hartz, Louis. 1955. *The Liberal Tradition in America: An Interpretation of American Political Thought Since the Revolution*. New York: Harcourt.
Hartz, Louis. 1964. *The Founding of New Societies: Studies in the History of the United States, Latin America, South Africa, Canada, and Australia*. New York: Harcourt.
Harvard-Harris Poll. 2017. August 2017: National Poll. Cambridge http://harvardharrispoll.com/wp-content/uploads/2017/08/HHP-August-Wave_Toplinee-Memo_Total-Only_Registered-Voters.pdf.
Hattam, Victoria C. 1993. *Labor Visions and State Power: The Origins of Business Unionism in the United States*. Princeton: Princeton University Press.
Haverty-Stacke, Donna. 2016. *Trotskyists on Trial: Free Speech and Political Persecution Since the Age of FDR*. New York: NYU Press.
Hawley, Ellis W. 1978. "The Discovery and Study of a 'Corporate Liberalism'." *The Business History Review* 52(3):309–320.

Haynes, John E. 1984. *Dubious Alliance: The Making of Minnesota's DFL Party.* Minneapolis: University of Minnesota Press.

Haynes, John E. 1986. "The New History of the Communist Party in State Politics: The Implications for Mainstream Political History." *Labor History* 27(4):549–563.

Heideman, Paul. 2016. "It's Their Party." *Jacobin* 20:23–39.

Helleiner, Eric. 2005. "A Fixation with Floating: The Politics of Canada's Exchange Rate Regime." *Canadian Journal of Political Science* 38(01):23–44.

Helleiner, Eric. 2006. *Towards North American Monetary Union? The Politics and History of Canada's Exchange Rate Regime.* Montreal: McGill Queens University Press.

Heron, Craig. 1984. "Labourism and the Canadian Working Class." *Labour/Le Travail* 13(Spring):45–75.

Heron, Craig. 1996. *The Canadian Labour Movement: A Brief History.* 2nd ed. Toronto: James Lorimer & Co.

Heron, Craig. 1998. *The Workers' Revolt in Canada, 1917–1925.* Toronto: University of Toronto Press.

Herrick, Elinore M. 1946. "The National Labor Relations Act." *The Annals of the American Academy of Political and Social Science* 248(November):82–90.

HEW Task Force. 1972. *Work in America: Report of a Special Task Force to the Secretary of Health, Education, and Welfare.* Cambridge: MIT Press.

Hewitt, Steven R. 1995. "'We Cannot Shoo These Men to Another Place': The On to Ottawa Trek in Toronto and Ottawa." *Past Imperfect* 4:3–30.

Hibbs, Douglas A., Jr. 1987. *The Political Economy of Industrial Democracies.* Cambridge: Harvard University Press.

Hicks, Ian. 2017. "West Virginia Right to Work Injunction Opposed by Attorney General Patrick Morrisey." *Wheeling News-Register*, March 8, www.theintelligencer.net/news/top-headlines/2017/03/west-virginia-right-to-work-injunction-opposed-by-attorney-general-patrick-morrisey/.

Hicks, John D. 1933. "The Third Party Tradition in American Politics." *The Mississippi Valley Historical Review* 20(1):3–28.

High, Steven. 1996. "Native Wage Labour and Independent Production During the 'Era of Irrelevance'." *Labour/Le Travail* 37(Spring):243–264.

Hild, Matthew. 2007. *Greenbackers, Knights of Labor, and Populists: Farmer-Labor Insurgency in the Late-Nineteenth Century South.* Athens: University of Georgia Press.

Hildebrand, George H. 1979. *American Unionism: An Historical and Analytical Survey.* Reading: Addison-Wesley Publishing Company.

Hill, Herbert. 1996. "The Problem of Race in American Labor History." *Reviews in American History* 24(2):189–208.

Hillman, Sidney. 1936a. "Hillman to Local 4, April 9, 1936, on Labor's Non-Partisan League." *Kheel Archives, Catherwood Library, Cornell University*, Collection 5619 Amalgamated Clothing Workers of America Records 1914–1980, Series XI: Speeches and Writings, Sub-series A Sidney Hillman, 1914–1946, Box-Folder 170-3.

Hillman, Sidney. 1936b. "Hillman's Address on Political Policy at the General Executive Board Meeting, Atlantic City." *Kheel Archives, Catherwood Library,*

Cornell University, Collection 5619 Amalgamated Clothing Workers of America Records 1914–1980, Series XI: Speeches and Writings; Sub-series A: Sidney Hillman, 1914–1946, Box–Folder170–3.

Hirano, Shigeo, and James M. Snyder. 2007. "The Decline of Third-Party Voting in the United States." *The Journal of Politics* 69(1):1–16.

Hirsch, Barry T., and David A. Macpherson. 2011. "Union Membership and Coverage Database from the CPS," www.unionstats.com.

Hochschild, Jennifer L. 1995. *Facing Up to the American Dream: Race, Class, and the Soul of the Nation*. Princeton: Princeton University Press.

Hoffman, von, Nicholas. 1971. "In Classless America, Blue-Collar Blues." *Washington Post*, March 15, B1.

Hogler, Raymond, Steven Shulman, and Stephan Weiler. 2004. "Right-to-Work Legislation, Social Capital, and Variations in State Union Density." *Review of Regional Studies* 34(1):95–111.

Hones, Kenneth W. 1938. "The New Party Movement." *Farmers Equity Union News*, May 1, 2.

Honey, Michael. 1992. "Operation Dixie: Labor and Civil Rights in the Postwar South." *Mississippi Quarterly* 45(4):439+.

Honey, Michael. 2000. "Anti-Racism, Black Workers, and Southern Labor Organizing: Historical Notes on a Continuing Struggle." *Labor Studies Journal* 25(1):10–26.

Honey, Michael K. 2007. *Going Down Jericho Road: The Memphis Strike, Martin Luther King's Last Campaign*. New York: W. W. Norton & Company.

Horn, Michiel. 1980. *The League for Social Reconstruction: Intellectual Origins of the Democratic Left in Canada, 1930–1942*. Toronto: University of Toronto Press.

Horn, Michiel. 1984. *The Great Depression of the 1930s in Canada*. Ottawa: Canadian Historical Association.

Horowitz, Gad. 1968. *Canadian Labour in Politics*. Toronto: University of Toronto Press.

Horowitz, Roger. 1997. *Negro and White, Unite and Fight! A Social History of Industrial Unionism in Meatpacking, 1930–90*. Urbana: University of Illinois Press.

Hout, Michael. 2003. "Money and Morale: What Growing Inequality Is Doing to Americans' Views of Themselves and Others." Survey Research Center Working Paper. University of California, Berkeley.

HRSDC. 2009. *Trade Union Application for Certification: General Private Sector Collective Bargaining Legislation*. Ottawa: Labour Program, Human Resources and Skills Development Canada. (www.hrsdc.gc.ca/eng/labour/labour_law/ind_rel/certif.pdf).

Huber, Evelyne, and John D. Stephens. 2001. *Development and Crisis of the Welfare State: Parties and Policies in Global Markets*. Chicago: The University of Chicago Press.

Hunt, Gerald, and David Rayside. 2000. "Labor Union Response to Diversity in Canada and the United States." *Industrial Relations: A Journal of Economy and Society* 39(3):401–444.

Huntington, Samuel P. 1950. "The Election Tactics of the Nonpartisan League." *The Mississippi Valley Historical Review* 36(4):613–632.

Hyman, Richard. 2016. "The Very Idea of Democracy at Work." *Transfer: European Review of Labour and Research* 22(1):11–24.

Ikenberry, G. John, and Theda Skocpol. 1987. "Expanding Social Benefits: The Role of Social Security." *Political Science Quarterly* 102(3):389–416.

Imai, Shin. 1981. "Deportation in the Depression." *Queen's Law Journal* 7:66–94.

Isaac, Larry, and Lars Christiansen. 2002. "How the Civil Rights Movement Revitalized Labor Militancy." *American Sociological Review* 67(5):722–746.

Isitt, Benjamin. 2011. *Militant Minority: British Columbia Workers and the Rise of a New Left, 1948–1972*. Toronto: University of Toronto Press.

Isserman, Maurice. 1993. *If I Had a Hammer...: The Death of the Old Left and the Birth of the New Left*. Urbana: University of Illinois Press.

Iton, Richard. 2000. *Solidarity Blues: Race, Culture, and the American Left*. Chapel Hill: University of North Carolina Press.

Jackson, Andrew. 2006. "Rowing Against the Tide: The Struggle to Raise Union Density in a Hostile Environment," pp. 61–78 in *Paths to Union Renewal: Canadian Experiences*, edited by P. Kumar and C.R. Schenk. Toronto: Broadview Press

Jacobs, Ron. 1997. *The Way the Wind Blew: A History of the Weather Underground*. New York and London: Verso.

Jacoby, Sanford M. 1985. *Employing Bureaucracy: Managers, Unions, and the Transformation of Work in American Industry*. New York: Columbia University Press.

Jacoby, Sanford M. 1991. "American Exceptionalism Revisited: The Importance of Management," pp. 173–200 in *Masters to Managers: Historical and Comparative Perspectives on American Employers*, edited by S.M. Jacoby. New York: Columbia University Press.

Jamieson, Stuart M. 1968. *Times of Trouble: Labour Unrest and Industrial Conflict in Canada, 1900–66*. Ottawa: Task Force on Labour Relations.

Jaumotte, Florence, and Carolina Osorio Buitron. 2015. *Inequality and Labor Market Institutions*. Washington, DC: International Monetary Fund Staff Discussion Note. (www.imf.org/en/News/Articles/2015/09/28/04/53/sointo71015a).

Jezer, Marty. 1982. *The Dark Ages: Life in the United States 1945–1960*. Boston: South End Press.

Johnson, J.R. 1993. "The Impact of the FTA on the Auto Pact," pp. 254–284 in *Driving Continentally: National Policies and the North American Auto Industry*, edited by M.A. Molot. Montreal: McGill Queens University Press.

Johnson, Susan. 2002. "Card Check or Mandatory Representation Votes? How the Choice of Union Recognition Procedure Affects Union Certification Success." *The Economic Journal* 112(479):344–361.

Johnson, Susan. 2004. "The Impact of Mandatory Votes on the Canada-US Union Density Gap: A Note." *Industrial Relations: A Journal of Economy and Society* 43(2):356–363.

Johnson, Susan. 2010. "First Contract Arbitration: Effects on Bargaining and Work Stoppages." *Industrial and Labor Relations Review* 63(4):585–719.

Jones, Ethel B. 1992. "Private Sector Union Decline and Structural Employment Change, 1970–1988." *Journal of Labor Research* 13(3):257–272.

Jones, William P. 2013. *The March on Washington: Jobs, Freedom, and the Forgotten History of Civil Rights*. New York: W. W. Norton & Company.

Juris, Hervey A., and Myron Roomkin. 1980. *The Shrinking Perimeter: Unionism and Labor Relations in the Manufacturing Sector*. Lexington: Lexington Books.

Kalleberg, Arne L. 2011. *Good Jobs, Bad Jobs*: the Rise of Polarized and Precarious Employment Systems in the United States, 1970s–2000s. New York: Russell Sage Foundation.

Katsiaficas, George. 1999. *The Imagination of the New Left: A Global Analysis of 1968*. Boston: South End Press.

Katz, Daniel. 2011. *All Together Different: Yiddish Socialists, Garment Workers, and the Labor Roots of Multiculturalism*. New York: New York University Press.

Katznelson, Ira. 1981. *City Trenches: Urban Politics and the Patterning of Class in the United States*. Chicago: University of Chicago Press.

Katznelson, Ira. 2013. *Fear Itself: The New Deal and the Origins of Our Time*. New York: W. W. Norton & Company.

Katznelson, Ira, Kim Geiger, and Daniel Kryder. 1993. "Limiting Liberalism: The Southern Veto in Congress, 1933–1950." *Political Science Quarterly* 108 (2):283–306.

Kaufman, Jason. 2009. *The Origins of Canadian and American Political Differences*. Cambridge: Harvard University Press.

Kazin, Michael. 1986. "The Great Exception Revisited: Organized Labor and Politics in San Francisco and Los Angeles, 1870–1940." *The Pacific Historical Review* 55(3):371–402.

Kazin, Michael. 1988. *Barons of Labor: The San Francisco Building Trades and Union Power in the Progressive Era*. Urbana: University of Illinois Press.

Kealey, Gregory S. 1981. "Labour and Working-Class History in Canada: Prospects in the 1980s." *Labour/Le Travail* 7(Spring):67–94.

Kealey, Gregory S. 1992. "State Repression of Labour and the Left in Canada, 1914–20: The Impact of the First World War." *Canadian Historical Review* 73 (3):281–314.

Kealey, Gregory S., and Bryan D. Palmer. 1982. *Dreaming of What Might Be the Knights of Labor in Ontario, 1880–1900*. Cambridge and New York: Cambridge University Press.

Kealey, Gregory S., and Bryan D. Palmer. 1986. "The Bonds of Unity: The Knights of Labor in Ontario, 1880–1900," pp. 37–65 in *The Character of Class Struggle: Essays in Canadian Working-Class History, 1850–1985*, edited by B.D. Palmer. Toronto: McClelland and Stewart.

Kealey, Gregory S. and Peter Warrian. 1976. *Essays in Canadian Working Class History*. Toronto: McClelland and Stewart.

Keenan, Greg. 2013. "CAW, CEP Union Merger Suggests Greater Power in Numbers." *The Globe and Mail*, August 8, www.theglobeandmail.com/news/national/unions-political-calculus-with-numbers-come-power/article13678660/.

Kelley, Robin D. G. 1990. *Hammer and Hoe: Alabama Communists During the Great Depression*. Chapel Hill: University of North Carolina Press.

Kellogg, Paul. 2015. *Escape From the Staple Trap: Canadian Political Economy After Left Nationalism*. Toronto: University of Toronto Press.

Kennedy, David M. 1999. *Freedom From Fear: The American People in Depression and War, 1929–1945*. Oxford: Oxford University Press.

Kerr, Clark. 1960. *Industrialism and Industrial Man: The Problems of Labor and Management in Economic Growth*. Cambridge: Harvard University Press.

Kersten, Andrew E. 2006. *Labor's Home Front: The American Federation of Labor During World War II*. New York: New York University Press.

Kettler, David, James Struthers, and Christopher Huxley. 1990. "Unionization and Labour Regimes in Canada and the United States: Considerations for Comparative Research." *Labour/Le Travail* 25(Spring):161–187.

Key, V. O. 1955. "A Theory of Critical Elections." *The Journal of Politics* 17(1):2–18.

Kimeldorf, Howard. 1988. *Reds or Rackets? The Making of Radical and Conservative Unions on the Waterfront*. Berkeley: University of California Press.

King, William Lyon Mackenzie. 1918. *Industry and Humanity: A Study in the Principles Underlying Industrial Reconstruction*. Boston: Houghton Mifflin Company.

King, William Lyon Mackenzie. 1930. "Diary Entry, September 22, 1930." Library and Archives Canada MG26-J13:236–237.

King, William Lyon Mackenzie. 1937. "Diary Entry, June 4, 1937." Library and Archives Canada MG26-J13:344–345.

King, William Lyon Mackenzie. 1943a. "Diary Entry, August 4, 1943." Library and Archives Canada MG26-J13:597–599.

King, William Lyon Mackenzie. 1943b. "Diary Entry, August 9, 1943." Library and Archives Canada MG26-J13:622–23.

Kingdon, John W. 1984. *Agendas, Alternatives, and Public Policies*. Boston: Little, Brown.

Kirbyson, Geoff. 2015. "Portage Avenue Tim Hortons Becomes Unionized." *Winnipeg Free Press*, June 11, www.winnipegfreepress.com/local/Portage-Avenue-Tim-Hortons-becomes-unionized-307064541.html.

Klare, Karl E. 1977. "Judicial Deradicalization of the Wagner Act and the Origins of Modern Legal Consciousness, 1937–1941." *Minnesota Law Review* 62:265–339.

Kleiner, Morris M. 2001. "Intensity of Management Resistance: Understanding the Decline of Unionization in the Private Sector." *Journal of Labor Research* 22(3):519–540.

Kohn, Stephen M. 1994. *American Political Prisoners: Prosecutions Under the Espionage and Sedition Acts*. Westport: Praeger.

Korstad, Robert and Nelson Lichtenstein. 1988. "Opportunities Found and Lost: Labor, Radicals, and the Early Civil Rights Movement." *The Journal of American History* 75(3):786–811.

Kostash, Myrna. 1980. *Long Way From Home: The Story of the Sixties Generation in Canada*. Toronto: James Lorimer & Co.

Kostuch Media. 2016. "Employees of Winnipeg KFC/Taco Bell Receive Union Certification." *Foodservice and Hospitality*, September 15, www.foodserviceandhospitality.com/employees-winnipeg-kfctaco-bell-receive-union-certification/.

Kostuch Media. 2017. "Second Winnipeg Tim Hortons Unionizes." *Foodservice and Hospitality*, July 27, www.foodserviceandhospitality.com/second-winnipeg-tim-hortons-unionizes/.

Krock, Arthur. 1932. "Republicans Hail Signs of Smith Rift – They Hope That Thrust at Gov. Roosevelt Will Develop Into a Fight in Convention." *New York Times*, April 4, 1, 10.

Kuitenbrouwer, Peter. 2017. "From New York to Seattle to Alberta: Ontario Not the Only One Targeting $15 an Hour Minimum Wage." *Financial Post*, June 1, http://business.financialpost.com/news/economy/does-a-minimum-wage-hike-hurt-or-stimulate-the-economy.

Kumar, Pradeep. 1993. *From Uniformity to Divergence: Industrial Relations in Canada and the United States*. Kingston: IRC Press Queen's University.

Kumar, Pradeep, and Chris R. Schenk, eds. 2006. *Paths to Union Renewal: Canadian Experiences*. Toronto: University of Toronto Press.

Kurjata, Andrew. 2017. "John Horgan Disappoints Both Site C Opponents and Supporters in Northeast B.C." *CBC News*, December 11, www.cbc.ca/news/canada/british-columbia/fort-st-john-site-c-dam-reaction-1.4443238.

KY3. 2017. "Missourians to Decide 'Right-to-Work' in November 2018." ky3.com. www.ky3.com/content/news/Missouri-laborers-celebrate-Right-to-Work-460325363.html.

Labor-Management Public Advisory Committee. 1953. "Summary of Minutes, Meeting No. 2, Thursday and Friday, March 5–6, 1953." *National Archives* RG174 General Records of the Department of Labor Office of the Secretary, Subject File of Secretary James P. Mitchell 1953–60, Box 18 1953 Organization Subject Files Committees Labor Department, Folder 1953 Labor Management Public Advisory Committee.

Labour Canada. 1977. "Strikes and Lockouts in Canada." *Historical Statistics of Canada*.

Labour Canada. 1980. *Directory of Labour Organizations in Canada*. Ottawa: Labour Canada, Labour Data Branch.

LaFollette, Philip. 1938. "Text of LaFollette's Speech Outlining the Proposed Program for New Party." *New York Times*, April 4, 12.

LaLonde, Robert J. and Bernard D. Meltzer. 1991. "Hard Times for Unions: Another Look at the Significance of Employer Illegalities." *The University of Chicago Law Review* 58(3):953–1014.

Lansing, Michael J. 2015. *Insurgent Democracy: The Nonpartisan League in North American Politics*. Chicago: University of Chicago Press.

Laslett, John H.M. 1967. "Socialism and the American Labor Movement: Some New Reflections." *Labor History* 8(2):136–155.

Laslett, John H.M., and Seymour M. Lipset. 1974. *Failure of a Dream? Essays in the History of American Socialism*. 1st ed. Garden City: Anchor Press.

Laycock, David, and Lynda Erickson, eds. 2015. *Reviving Social Democracy: The Near Death and Surprising Rise of the Federal NDP*. Vancouver: UBC Press.

Laycock, David H. 1990. *Populism and Democratic Thought in the Canadian Prairies, 1910 to 1945*. Toronto: University of Toronto Press.

Leab, Daniel J. 1967. "'United We Eat': The Creation and Organization of the Unemployed Councils in 1930." *Labor History* 8(3):300–315.

Leacy, F.H., M.C. Urquhart, and K.A.H. Buckley. 1983. *Historical Statistics of Canada*. Ottawa: Statistics Canada.

League for Social Reconstruction Research Committee. 1935. *Social Planning for Canada*. Toronto: T. Nelson & Sons Limited.
League for Social Reconstruction Research Committee. 1938. *Democracy Needs Socialism*. Toronto, New York: T. Nelson & Sons limited.
Leiserson, William M. 1940. "Letter of Dr. Wm. M. Leiserson to Dr. John R. Commons, Professor Emeritus of Economics, University of Wisconsin." National Archives RG174 General Records of the Department of Labor Secretary Frances Perkins, Box 153 Office of the Secretary Secy Frances Perkins General Subject File 1940–1945 National Labor Relations Board to Navy Department, Folder National Labor Relations Board 1940.
Lester, Richard A. 1958. *As Unions Mature: An Analysis of the Evolution of American Unionism*. Princeton: Princeton University Press.
Leuchtenburg, William E. 1963. *Franklin D. Roosevelt and the New Deal, 1932–1940*. New York: Harper & Row.
Levi, Margaret, David Olson, Jon Agnone, and Devin Kelly. 2009. "Union Democracy Reexamined." *Politics and Society* 37(2):203–228.
Levine, Rhonda F. 1988. *Class Struggle and the New Deal: Industrial Labor, Industrial Capital, and the State*. Lawrence: University Press of Kansas.
Levison, Andrew. 2013. *The White Working Class Today: Who They Are, How They Think and How Progressives Can Regain Their Support*. Washington, DC: Democratic Strategist Press.
Levitt, Cyril. 1984. *Children of Privilege: Student Revolt in the Sixties: A Study of Student Movements in Canada, the United States, and West Germany*. Toronto: University of Toronto Press.
Levitt, Kari. 1970. *Silent Surrender: The Multinational Corporation in Canada*. Montreal and Kingston: McGill-Queens University Press.
Levy, Peter B. 1994. *The New Left and Labor in the 1960s*. Urbana: University of Illinois Press.
Lewin, David and Shirley B. Goldenberg. 1980. "Public Sector Unionism in the US and Canada." *Industrial Relations: A Journal of Economy and Society* 19 (3):239–256.
Lewis, David. 1943. "Socialism Across the Border: Canada's CCF." *The Antioch Review* 3(4):470–482.
Lewis, John L. 1937. "Text of John L. Lewis's Radio Talk on CIO." *New York Times*, September 9, 6.
Lewis, Penny W. 2013. *Hardhats, Hippies, and Hawks: The Vietnam Antiwar Movement as Myth and Memory*. Ithaca: Cornell University Press.
Lévesque, Lia. 2016. "Front commun: le dernier des cinq syndicats approuve l'entente avec Québec." *La Presse*, March 31, www.lapresse.ca/actualites/201 603/31/01-4966257-front-commun-le-dernier-des-cinq-syndicats-approuve-lentente-avec-quebec.php.
Lichtenstein, Nelson. 1982. *Labor's War at Home: The CIO in World War II*. Cambridge: Cambridge University Press.
Lichtenstein, Nelson. 1989. "From Corporatism to Collective Bargaining: Organized Labor and the Eclipse of Social Democracy in the Postwar Era," pp. 122–152 in *The Rise and Fall of the New Deal Order, 1930–1980*, edited by S. Fraser and G. Gerstle. Princeton: Princeton University Press.

Lichtenstein, Nelson. 1995. *The Most Dangerous Man in Detroit: Walter Reuther and the Fate of American Labor*. New York: Basic Books.
Lichtenstein, Nelson. 2010. "Despite EFCA's Limitations, Its Demise Is a Profound Defeat for US Labor." *Labor: Studies in Working-Class History of the Americas* 7(3):29–32.
Lijphart, Arend. 1999. *Patterns of Democracy: Government Forms and Performance in Thirty-Six Countries*. New Haven: Yale University Press.
Lipset, Seymour M. 1950. *Agrarian Socialism: The Coöperative Commonwealth Federation in Saskatchewan, a Study in Political Sociology*. Berkeley: University of California Press.
Lipset, Seymour M. 1963. *The First New Nation: The United States in Historical and Comparative Perspective*. New York: Basic Books.
Lipset, Seymour M. 1989. *Continental Divide: The Values and Institutions of the United States and Canada*. Toronto: Canadian-American Committee.
Lipset, Seymour M. 1996. *American Exceptionalism: A Double-Edged Sword*. New York: W.W. Norton.
Lipset, Seymour M., and Gary W. Marks. 2000. *It Didn't Happen Here: Why Socialism Failed in the United States*. New York: W.W. Norton & Co.
Lipset, Seymour M., and Noah M. Meltz. 2004. *The Paradox of American Unionism: Why Americans Like Unions More Than Canadians Do, but Join Much Less*. Ithaca: Cornell ILR Press.
Lipset, Seymour M., Martin A. Trow, and James S. Coleman. 1956. *Union Democracy: The Internal Politics of the International Typographical Union*. New York: Anchor Books.
Lipsig-Mumme, Carla. 1989. "Canadian and American Unions Respond to Economic Crisis." *Journal of Industrial Relations* 31(2):229–256.
Lithwick, Dahlia. 2016. "Public Sector Unions Just Dodged a Major Bullet at the Supreme Court." *Slate*, www.slate.com/blogs/the_slatest/2016/03/29/public_sectors_unions_dodge_a_bullet_at_the_supreme_court.html.
Lofaso, Anne M. 2011. "Promises, Promises: Assessing the Obama Administration's Record on Labor Reform." *New Labor Forum* 20(2):64–72.
Logan, Harold A. 1948. *Trade Unions in Canada: Their Development and Functioning*. Toronto: Macmillan Co. of Canada.
Logan, John. 2002. "How 'Anti-Union' Laws Saved Canadian Labour: Certification and Striker Replacements in Post-War Industrial Relations." *Relations Industrielles/Industrial Relations* 57(1):129–158.
Logan, John. 2006. "The Union Avoidance Industry in the United States." *British Journal of Industrial Relations* 44(4):651–675.
Lopez, Steven H. 2004. *Reorganizing the Rust Belt: An Inside Study of the American Labor Movement*. Berkeley: University of California Press.
Lovin, Hugh T. 1971. "The Fall of Farmer-Labor Parties, 1936–1938." *The Pacific Northwest Quarterly* 62(1):16–26.
Lovin, Hugh T. 1975. "Toward a Farmer-Labor Party in Oregon, 1933–38." *Oregon Historical Quarterly* 76(2):135–151.
Lowi, Theodore J. 1984. "Why Is There No Socialism in the United States? A Federal Analysis." *International Political Science Review/Revue internationale de science politique* 5(4):369–380.

Lowitt, Richard, and Maurice Beasley. 1981. *One Third of a Nation: Lorena Hickok Reports on the Great Depression*. Urbana: University of Illinois Press.

Lubell, Samuel. 1941. "Post Mortem: Who Elected Roosevelt?" *Saturday Evening Post*, January 1, 9–11, 91–94, 96.

Luce, Stephanie. 2015. "$15 Per Hour or Bust: An Appraisal of the Higher Wages Movement." *New Labor Forum* 24(2):72–79.

Luxton, Meg. 2001. "Feminism as a Class Act: Working-Class Feminism and the Women's Movement in Canada." *Labour/Le Travail* 48(Fall):63–88.

MacDowell, Laurel S. 1978. "The Formation of the Canadian Industrial Relations System During World War Two." *Labour/Le Travail* 3:175–196.

MacGillis, Alec. 2016. "The Referendum That Might Have Headed Off Flint's Water Crisis." *ProPublica*, www.propublica.org/article/the-referendum-that-might-have-headed-off-flints-water-crisis.

Madland, David. 2015. *Hollowed Out: Why the Economy Doesn't Work Without a Strong Middle Class*. Berkeley: University of California Press.

Madsen, Deborah L. 1998. *American Exceptionalism*. Edinburgh: Edinburgh University Press.

Maioni, Antonia. 1998. *Parting at the Crossroads: The Emergence of Health Insurance in the United States and Canada*. Princeton: Princeton University Press.

Maki, Dennis R. 1982. "Political Parties and Trade Union Growth in Canada." *Relations Industrielles/Industrial Relations* 37(4):876–886.

Manley, John. 1998. "'Starve, Be Damned!' Communists and Canada's Urban Unemployed, 1929–39." *Canadian Historical Review* 79(3):466–491.

Manly, Chesly. 1937. "President Flayed by Lewis – CIO Boss Hits Democrat Aids as 'Traitors' – Threatens 3d Party Movement." *Chicago Daily Tribune*, September 9, 1.

Manza, Jeff. 2000. "Political Sociological Models of the US New Deal." *Annual Review of Sociology* 26(1):297–322.

Marable, Manning. 2007. *Race, Reform, and Rebellion: The Second Reconstruction and Beyond in Black America, 1945–2006*. 3rd ed. Jackson: University Press of Mississippi.

Marchak, Patricia. 1985. "Canadian Political Economy." *Canadian Review of Sociology/Revue canadienne de sociologie* 22(5):673–709.

Marshall, T.H. 1992. *Citizenship and Social Class*. London: Pluto Press.

Martinello, Felice. 1996. *Certification and Decertification Activity in Canadian Jurisdictions*. Kingston, Ontario: IRC Press/Industrial Relations Centre, Queen's University.

Martinello, Felice. 2000. "Mr. Harris, Mr. Rae and Union Activity in Ontario." *Canadian Public Policy/Analyse de Politiques* 26(1):17–33.

Marvit, Moshe. 2015. "The Supreme Court Case That Could Decimate American Public Sector Unionism." *These Times*, http://inthesetimes.com/working/entry/17595/friedrichs_v_california_teachers_association.

Marvit, Moshe. 2017. "Labor Opponents Already Have the Next 'Friedrichs' SCOTUS Case Ready to Go Under Trump." *These Times*, http://inthesetimes.com/working/entry/19776/will_trumps_supreme_court_reverse_fair_share_fees_unions_foes_hope_so.

Masters, Marick F., and John T. Delaney. 2005. "Organized Labor's Political Scorecard." *Journal of Labor Research* 26(3):365–392.

Masters, Marick F., Ray Gibney, and Tom Zagenczyk. 2006. "The AFL-CIO v. CTW: The Competing Visions, Strategies, and Structures." *Journal of Labor Research* 27(4):473–504.

Mathieu, Sarah-Jane. 2010. *North of the Color Line: Migration and Black Resistance in Canada, 1870–1955*. Chapel Hill: University of North Carolina Press.

Mauss, Armand L. 1971. "The Lost Promise of Reconciliation: New Left vs. Old Left." *Journal of Social Issues* 27(1):1–20.

Mayer, Gerald. 2007. "Labor Union Recognition Procedures: Use of Secret Ballots and Card Checks." *Federal Publications* (Paper 561):1–24.

Mayhew, David R. 1974. *Congress: The Electoral Connection*. New Haven: Yale University Press.

McAdam, Doug, Sidney G. Tarrow, and Charles Tilly. 2001. *Dynamics of Contention*. New York: Cambridge University Press.

McAlevey, Jane F. 2016. *No Shortcuts: Organizing for Power in the New Gilded Age*. Oxford: Oxford University Press.

McCammon, Holly J. 1990. "Legal Limits on Labor Militancy: U.S. Labor Law and the Right to Strike Since the New Deal." *Social Problems* 37(2):206–229.

McCammon, Holly J. 1994. "Disorganizing and Reorganizing Conflict: Outcomes of the State's Legal Regulation of the Strike Since the Wagner Act." *Social Forces* 72(4):1011–1049.

McCarthy, Michael A. 2017. *Dismantling Solidarity: Capitalist Politics and American Pensions Since the New Deal*. Ithaca: Cornell University Press.

McCartin, Joseph A. 2006. "Bringing the State's Workers in: Time to Rectify an Imbalanced U.S. Labor Historiography."*Labor History* 47(1):73–94.

McConnell, Grant. 1953. *The Decline of Agrarian Democracy*. Berkeley: University of California Press.

McCormack, A.R. 1977. *Reformers, Rebels, and Revolutionaries: The Western Canadian Radical Movement, 1899–1919*. Toronto: University of Toronto Press.

McCoy, Donald R. 1957. "The National Progressives of America, 1938." *The Mississippi Valley Historical Review* 44(1):75–93.

McHenry, Dean E. 1950. *The Third Force in Canada: The Cooperative Commonwealth Federation, 1932–1948*. Berkeley: University of California Press.

McInnis, Peter. 2011. "'Hothead Troubles': 1960s-Era Wildcat Strikes in Canada," pp. 256–290 in *Debating Dissent: Canada and the 1960s*, edited by L. Campbell, D. Clément, and G. Kealey. Toronto: University of Toronto Press.

McInnis, Peter S. 2002. *Harnessing Labour Confrontation: Shaping the Postwar Settlement in Canada, 1943–1950*. Toronto: University of Toronto Press.

McKay, Ian. 2005. *Rebels, Reds, Radicals: Rethinking Canada's Left History*. Toronto: Between the Lines.

McLarty, Norman. 1941. "McClarty Memo to M.J. Coldwell, December 4, 1941." *Library and Archives Canada* WLMK Correspondence Primary Series C-4866:1–7.

McMath, Robert C. J. 1995. "Populism in Two Countries: Agrarian Protest in the Great Plains and Prairie Provinces." *Agricultural History* 69(4):516–546.

McMillian, John C., and Paul Buhle. 2003. *The New Left Revisited*. Philadelphia: Temple University Press.

McNay, John T. 2013. *Collective Bargaining and the Battle of Ohio*. New York: Palgrave Macmillan.

McPhillips, David C. 1982. "Employer Free Speech and the Right of Trade-Union Organization." *Osgoode Hall Law Journal* 20:138–154.

McQuarrie, Michael. 2017. "The Revolt of the Rust Belt: Place and Politics in the Age of Anger." *The British Journal of Sociology* 68(S1):S120–S152.

McRae, Kenneth. 1964. "The Structure of Canadian History," pp. 219–262 in *The Founding of New Societies: Studies in the History of the United States, Latin America, South Africa, Canada, and Australia*, edited by L. Hartz. New York: Harcourt.

Meany, George. 1955. "Address to National Association of Manufacturers, December 9, 1955." *George Meany Memorial Archives* RG1-027 Office of the President, George Meany 1952–1960, Series 10: Speeches and Statements, 1952–1959, Box–Folder 59–76 NAM speech–1955 Dec9.

Meissner, Dirk. 2017. "NDP Asked to Form Government in B.C. After Liberals Defeated in Non-Confidence Vote." *Toronto Star*, June 29, www.thestar.com/news/canada/2017/06/29/bc-liberals-lose-confidence-vote-setting-stage-for-ndp-government-or-election.html.

Merelman, Richard M. 1991. *Partial Visions: Culture and Politics in Britain, Canada, and the United States*. Madison: University of Wisconsin Press.

MetroNews Staff. 2017. "State Supreme Court to Hear Arguments on Right-to-Work Law in September." *MetroNews*, May 22, wvmetronews.com/2017/05/22/state-supreme-court-to-hear-arguments-on-right-to-work-law-in-september/.

Michels, Robert. 1915. *Political Parties: A Sociological Study of the Oligarchical Tendencies of Modern Democracy*. New York: Hearst's International Library.

Milkman, Ruth. 1998. "The New Labor Movement: Possibilities and Limits." *Contemporary Sociology* 27(2):125–129.

Milkman, Ruth. 2006a. "Divided We Stand." *New Labor Forum* 15(1):38–46.

Milkman, Ruth. 2006b. *L.A. Story: Immigrant Workers and the Future of the U.S. Labor Movement*. New York: Russell Sage Foundation.

Milkman, Ruth, Stephanie Luce, and Penny W. Lewis. 2013. *Changing the Subject: A Bottom-Up Account of Occupy Wall Street in New York City*. New York: Russell Sage Foundation. (www.russellsage.org/research/reports/occupy-wall-street-movement).

Milkman, Ruth and Ed Ott, eds. 2014. *New Labor in New York: Precarious Workers and the Future of the Labor Movement*. Ithaca: Cornell University Press.

Miller, Berkeley, and William Canak. 1988. "The Passage of Public Sector Collective Bargaining Laws." *Political Power and Social Theory* 7:249–292.

Miller, John E. 1982. *Governor Philip F. La Follette, the Wisconsin Progressives, and the New Deal*. Columbia: University of Missouri Press.

Milligan, Ian. 2014. *Rebel Youth: 1960s Labour Unrest, Young Workers, and New Leftists in English Canada*. Vancouver: UBC Press.

Mills, Sean. 2010. *The Empire Within: Postcolonial Thought and Political Activism in Sixties Montreal*. Montreal: McGill-Queen's University Press.

Milton, David. 1982. *The Politics of U.S. Labor: From the Great Depression to the New Deal*. New York: Monthly Review Press.

Minchin, Timothy J. 2017. "Showdown at Nissan: The 1989 Campaign to Organize Nissan in Smyrna, Tennessee, and the Rise of the Transplant Sector." *Labor History* 58(3):396–422.

Mitchell, Greg. 1992. *The Campaign of the Century: Upton Sinclair's Race for Governor of California and the Birth of Media Politics*. New York: Random House.

Mizruchi, Mark S. 2013. *The Fracturing of the American Corporate Elite*. Cambridge: Harvard University Press.

Moe, Terry M. 1980. *The Organization of Interests: Incentives and the Internal Dynamics of Political Interest Groups*. Chicago: University of Chicago Press.

Moe, Terry M. and Michael Caldwell. 1994. "The Institutional Foundations of Democratic Government: A Comparison of Presidential and Parliamentary Systems." *Journal of Institutional and Theoretical Economics* 150(1):171–195.

Moley, Raymond. 1932. "Memo From Moley to Roosevelt, May 19, 1932." *Hoover Institution Library and Archives* Raymond Moley Papers, 1902–1971, Box 282, Folders 3–4: Memorandum outlining national program for recovery–written by Moley and others for Roosevelt–including draft of page in which first occurred the phrase "a New Deal" – May 19–1932.

Montgomery, David. 1979. *Workers' Control in America*. Cambridge: Cambridge University Press.

Montgomery, David. 1980. "Labor and the Republic in Industrial America: 1860–1920." *Le mouvement social* 111(April-June):201–215.

Moody, Kim. 1985. "Stumbling in the Dark: American Labor's Failed Response." *The Year Left: An American Socialist Yearbook* 1:87–108.

Moody, Kim. 1988. *An Injury to All: The Decline of American Unionism*. London and New York: Verso.

Moody, Kim. 2007. *US Labor in Trouble and Transition: The Failure of Reform From Above, the Promise of Revival From Below*. New York: Verso.

Moody, Kim. 2017. *On New Terrain: How Capital Is Reshaping the Battleground of Class War*. Chicago: Haymarket Books.

Moore, William J. 1998. "The Determinants and Effects of Right-to-Work Laws: A Review of the Recent Literature." *Journal of Labor Research* 19(3):445–469.

Moore, William J., and Robert J. Newman. 1984. "The Effects of Right-to-Work Laws: A Review of the Literature." *Industrial and Labor Relations Review* 38(4):571–585. (www.jstor.org/stable/2523992).

Moore, William J., and Robert J. Newman. 1988. "A Cross-Section Analysis of the Postwar Decline in American Trade Union Membership." *Journal of Labor Research* 9(2):111–125.

Morlan, Robert L. 1955. *Political Prairie Fire: The Nonpartisan League, 1915–1922*. Minneapolis: University of Minnesota Press.

Morris, Allie. 2017. "Right to Work Fails in NH House, 200–177." *Concord Monitor*, February 16, www.concordmonitor.com/Right-to-work-updates-on-house-vote-day-8137054.

Morris, Charles J. 2005. *The Blue Eagle at Work: Reclaiming Democratic Rights in the American Workplace.* Ithaca: Cornell ILR Press.

Morrow, Adrian. 2015. "Ontario Elementary Teachers Get Raise, Vigilance on Class Sizes." *The Globe and Mail*, November 8, www.theglobeandmail.com/news/national/ontario-elementary-teachers-get-raise-vigilance-on-class-sizes/article27171352/.

Morse, Wayne. 1942. "Speech by NWLB Public Member Wayne Morse to American Bar Association." *National Archives* RG174 General Records of the Department of Labor Secretary Frances Perkins, Box 119: Office of the Secretary Secy Frances Perkins General Subject File 1940–1945 Boards, Folder National War Labor Board 1942.

Morton, Desmond. 1986. *The New Democrats, 1961–1986: The Politics of Change.* Toronto: Copp Clark Pitman.

Morton, W.L. 1950. *The Progressive Party in Canada.* Toronto: University of Toronto Press.

Mosher, Ira. 1945. "Address by Ira Mosher, President, NAM." *National Archives* RG174 General Records of the Department of Labor Office of the Secretary Subject File of Secretary Lewis B Schwellenbach 1945–48, Box 41: Rules Committee-Press Conferences, Folder Plenary Sessions Verbatim Transcripts.

Moyers, Bill. 2012. "Is Labor a Lost Cause? Moyers & Company." *billmoyers.com*, July 6.

Murphy, Erin. 2017. "Iowa's Public-Sector Unions Brace for Impact of New Collective Bargaining Law." *The Gazette*, February 20, www.thegazette.com/subject/news/iowas-public-sector-unions-brace-for-impact-of-new-collective-bargaining-law-20170220.

Murray, Gregor. 2004. "Union Myths, Enigmas, and Other Tales: Five Challenges for Union Renewal." *Studies in Political Economy* 74(Autumn):157–169.

Muthuchidambaram, S. 1980. "Settlement of First Collective Agreement: An Examination of the Canada Labour Code Amendment." *Relations Industrielles/Industrial Relations* 35(3):387–409.

Najita, Joyce M. and James L. Stern, eds. 2001. *Collective Bargaining in the Public Sector: The Experience of Eight States.* New York: M. E. Sharpe.

NAM NIIC. 1945. "Public Relations Policy Committee Memo, 5/11/45." *Hagley Library* National Association of Manufacturers, Accession 1411, Series III-National Industrial Information Committee Records, Box 842 Folder Public Relations Policy Committee May–June 1945.

National Association of Manufacturers. 1938a. "NAM Documents Related to NLRA Amendment, 1937–1939." *Hagley Library* National Association of Manufacturers, Accession 1411, Series VII-Industrial Relations Department Records, Box137.

National Association of Manufacturers. 1938b. "NAM Legal Experts Analyze Industry's Stand for Wagner Act Amendments." *Hagley Library* National Association of Manufacturers, Accession 1411, Series VII-Industrial Relations Department Records, Box137–Folder Empl Rel–NLRA 1938.

National Association of Manufacturers. 1953. "Memo to William J. Grede, March 31, 1953." *Hagley Library* National Association of Manufacturers,

Accession 1411, Series VII-Industrial Relations Department Records, Box127–Folder Employee Relations Div–General–Apr–Dec 1953.

National Conference of State Legislatures. 2011. "2011 State and Legislative Partisan Composition." *ncsl.org*, www.ncsl.org/research/elections-and-campaigns/statevote-2010.aspx.

National Labor Relations Board. 1934. "Functions of the National Labor Relations Board and the Regional Labor Boards and Their Relations to Other Boards and Agencies of Government." *National Archives* RG174 General Records of the Department of Labor Secretary Frances Perkins, Box 86: Office of the Secretary Secy Frances Perkins, General Subject File 1933–1941, National Labor Relations Board to National Recovery Admin, Folder National Labor Relations Board October 1934.

National Labor Relations Board. 1985. *Legislative History of the National Labor Relations Act, 1935.* Washington, DC: U.S. Government Printing Office.

National Labor Relations Board. 2014. "NLRB Representation Case-Procedures Fact Sheet." *nlrb.gov*, www.nlrb.gov/news-outreach/fact-sheets/nlrb-representation-case-procedures-fact-sheet.

National Right to Work Committee. 2017. "Right to Work States – Timeline." *nrtwc.org*, https://nrtwc.org/facts-issues/state-right-to-work-timeline-2016/.

Naylor, James. 1993. "Politics and Class: The Character of 1930s Socialism in Canada." *Canadian Historical Association Meeting Presentation* (June):1–38.

Naylor, James. 2006. "Canadian Labour Politics and the British Model, 1920–50," pp. 288–308 in *Canada and the British World Culture, Migration, and Identity*, edited by P. Buckner, P.A. Buckner, R.D. Francis, and R.D. Francis. Vancouver: UBC Press.

Naylor, James. 2016. *The Fate of Labour Socialism: The Co-operative Commonwealth Federation and the Dream of a Working-Class Future.* Toronto: University of Toronto Press.

NDP Waffle. 1969. *The Waffle Manifesto: For an Independent Socialist Canada.* Toronto: Movement for an Independent Socialist Canada. (www.connexions.org/CxLibrary/Docs/CX5372-WaffleManifesto.htm).

Neatby, H. Blair. 1972. *The Politics of Chaos: Canada in the Thirties.* Toronto: Macmillan.

Neckerman, Kathryn M. and Florencia Torche. 2007. "Inequality: Causes and Consequences." *Annual Review of Sociology* 33: 335–357.

Nesbitt, Doug. 2015. "Roll Up the Boss to Win." *rankandfile.ca*, March 19, http://rankandfile.ca/2015/03/19/roll-up-the-boss-to-win/.

New York Times. 1932a. "Aggressive Address of Ex-Gov. Smith Features Meeting of Nation's Democrats." *New York Times*, April 4, 6, 7.

New York Times. 1932b. "Roosevelt Charges Neglect of 'Little Fellow'." *New York Times*, April 4, 1.

New York Times. 1936. "Tobin, Labor Leader, Praises Roosevelt – in Accepting Campaign Post, He Stresses New Deal Record in 'Humanitarian' Field." *New York Times*, July 7, 5.

New York Times. 1937. "Lewis Warns President to Support CIO or Face Bolt." *New York Times*, September 9, 1.

New York Times. 1970. "Blue-Collar Blues ... " *New York Times*, July 4, 20.

New York Times. 2008. "EDITORIAL: A Hopeful Year for Unions." *New York Times*, February 7, www.nytimes.com/2008/02/07/opinion/07thu3.html.

Nissen, Bruce. 1990. "A Post-World War II 'Social Accord'?," pp. 173–208 in *US Labor Relations, 1945–1989: Accommodation and Conflict*, edited by B. Nissen. New York; London: Garland Publishing, Inc.

OECD. 2017. "Trade Union Density, 1960–2014." *stats.oecd.org*, http://stats.oecd.org/Index.aspx?QueryId=20167.

Oestreicher, Richard. 1988. "Urban Working-Class Political Behavior and Theories of American Electoral Politics, 1870–1940." *The Journal of American History* 74(4):1257–1286.

Offe, Claus, and Helmut Wiesenthal. 1980. "Two Logics of Collective Action: Theoretical Notes on Social Class and Organizational Form." *Political Power and Social Theory* 1(1):67–115.

Olafsdottir, Sigrun. 2007. "Fundamental Causes of Health Disparities: Stratification, the Welfare State, and Health in the United States and Iceland." *Journal of Health and Social Behavior* 48(3):239–253.

Olson, Mancur. 1965. *The Logic of Collective Action: Public Goods and the Theory of Groups*. Cambridge: Harvard University Press.

Omi, Michael, and Howard Winant. 1986. *Racial Formation in the United States*. New York: Routledge.

Orloff, Ann S. 1993. *The Politics of Pensions: A Comparative Analysis of Britain, Canada, and the United States, 1880–1940*. Madison: University of Wisconsin Press.

Ornstein, Allan. 2007. *Class Counts: Education, Inequality, and the Shrinking Middle Class*. Lanham: Rowman & Littlefield Publishers.

Our Revolution. 2017. "Our Revolution Turns One." *OurRevolution.com*, August 24. https://ourrevolution.com/year-one/.

Owram, Doug. 1986. *The Government Generation: Canadian Intellectuals and the State, 1900–1945*. Toronto: University of Toronto Press.

Page, Benjamin I., and Lawrence R. Jacobs. 2009. *Class War? What Americans Really Think About Economic Inequality*. Chicago: University of Chicago Press.

Palmer, Bryan D. 1983. *Working-Class Experience: The Rise and Reconstitution of Canadian Labour, 1800–1980*. Toronto: Butterworth.

Palmer, Bryan D. 2009. *Canada's 1960s: The Ironies of Identity in a Rebellious Era*. Toronto: University of Toronto Press.

Panitch, Leo. 1992. "The NDP in Power: Illusion and Reality." *Studies in Political Economy* 37(Spring):173–188.

Panitch, Leo and Donald Swartz. 1984. "Towards Permanent Exceptionalism: Coercion and Consent in Canadian Industrial Relations." *Labour/Le Travail* 13 (Spring):133–157.

Panitch, Leo and Donald Swartz. 2003. *From Consent to Coercion: The Assault on Trade Union Freedoms*, 3rd ed. Toronto: University of Toronto Press.

Panitch, Leo and Donald Swartz. 2006. "Neo-Liberalism, Labour, and the Canadian State," pp. 347–378 in *Working in a Global Era: Canadian Perspectives*, edited by V. Shalla. Toronto: Canadian Scholars Press.

Pappas, Gregory, Susan Queen, Wilbur Hadden, and Gail Fisher. 1993. "The Increasing Disparity in Mortality Between Socioeconomic Groups in the United States, 1960 and 1986." *New England Journal of Medicine* 329 (2):103–109.

Pare, Mike. 2014. "Anti-UAW Group Hits Neutrality Pact at VW Chattanooga Plant." *Times Free Press*, February 10, www.timesfreepress.com/news/local/sto ry/2014/feb/10/anti-uaw-group-hits-neutrality-pact-vw-chattanooga/131353/.

Parker, Mike, and Jane Slaughter. 1994. *Working Smart: A Union Guide to Participation Programs and Reengineering*. Detroit: Labor Education & Research Project.

Parliament of Canada. n.d. "Federal Back to Work Legislation." *Parliament of Canada*, www.parl.gc.ca/Parlinfo/compilations/HouseOfCommons/Legislation /LegislationBackToWork.aspx.

Parmet, Robert D. 2005. *The Master of Seventh Avenue: David Dubinsky and the American Labor Movement*. New York: NYU Press.

Patterson, Samuel C., and Gregory A. Caldeira. 1988. "Party Voting in the United States Congress." *British Journal of Political Science* 18(1):111–131.

Pearson, Lester B. 1966. "Draft Letter From Pearson to Allmand Re: Bill C-170, May 9, 1966." *Library and Archives Canada* Lester B. Pearson Papers MG26 N4, Vol. 140, File 351.9 Federal Government Administration – The Civil Service of Canada – Collective Bargaining pt.1.

Penn, Ben. 2016. "Trump's Wage and Hour Division Likely to Reverse Course." *Bloomberg BNA*, www.bna.com/trumps-wage-hour-n57982082671/.

Penner, Norman. 1977. *The Canadian Left: A Critical Analysis*. Scarborough: Prentice-Hall of Canada.

Pentland, H. Clare. 1968. *A Study of the Changing Social, Economic, and Political Background of the Canadian System of Industrial Relations*. Ottawa: Task Force on Labour Relations, Privy Council Office.

Perkins, Frances. 1939. "Memo From Perkins to Thomas Re: S. 1264, 'a Bill to Amend the National Labor Relations Act'." *National Archives*, RG174 General Records of the Department of Labor Secretary Frances Perkins, Box 84 Office of the Secretary Secy Frances Perkins, General Subject File 1933–1941 National Labor Relations Board, Folder National Labor Relations Board Personnel.

Perlstein, Rick. 2010. *Nixonland: The Rise of a President and the Fracturing of America*. New York: Simon and Schuster.

Pethokoukis, James. 2016. "How the GOP Blew It on the Minimum Wage." *The Week*, March 31, http://theweek.com/articles/615602/how-gop-blew-mini mum-wage.

Petryshyn, J. 1982. "Class Conflict and Civil Liberties: The Origins and Activities of the Canadian Labour Defense League, 1925–1940." *Labour/Le Travail* 10 (Autumn):39–63.

Pepin, Marcel. 1968. *Le deuxième front*. Montréal: CSN.

Phillips-Fein, Kim. 2009. *Invisible Hands: The Businessmen's Crusade Against the New Deal*. New York: W.W. Norton & Co.

Pilon, Dennis, Stephanie Ross, and Larry Savage. 2011. "Solidarity Revisited: Organized Labour and the New Democratic Party." *Canadian Political Science Review* 5(1):20–37.

Pischel, Emma. 1909. "Socialist Party Membership Data: A Survey Circulated in 1908." *Socialist Party Official Bulletin* 5(8):2–3.

Piven, Frances F. and Richard A. Cloward. 1977. *Poor People's Movements: Why They Succeed, How They Fail*. New York: Vintage books.

POLITICO. 2016. "Full Text: Donald Trump 2016 RNC Draft Speech Transcript." *POLITICO*, http://politi.co/2a3oO4N.

Pope, James G. 2008. "How American Workers Lost the Right to Strike, and Other Tales." *Michigan Law Review* 103(3):518–553.

Porter, John. 1965. *The Vertical Mosaic: An Analysis of Social Power and Class in Canada*. Toronto: University of Toronto Press.

Post, Charlie. 1996. "The Popular Front: Rethinking CPUSA History" *Against the Current* 63(July-August):1–22. https://www.solidarity-us.org/node/2363

Postel, Charles. 2007. *The Populist Vision*. Oxford: Oxford University Press.

President's Advisory Committee on Labor-Management Policy. 1962. "Collective Bargaining: A Report by the President's Advisory Committee on Labor-Management Policy." *National Archives*, RG174 General Records of the Department of Labor Office of the Secretary of Labor, Records of Secretary of Labor Arthur J Goldberg 1961–1962, Box 155: President's Advisory Committee on Labor and Management Policy-President's Committee on Equal Employment Opportunities, Folder 1962–President's Advisory Committee on Labor and Management Policy (April–May).

Preston, William. 1994. *Aliens and Dissenters: Federal Suppression of Radicals, 1903–1933*. Urbana: University of Illinois Press.

Przeworski, Adam. 1985a. "Party Strategy, Class Organization, and Individual Voting," pp. 99–132 in *Capitalism and Social Democracy*. Cambridge and Paris: Cambridge University Press/Éditions de la maison des sciences de l'homme.

Przeworski, Adam. 1985b. "Social Democracy as a Historical Phenomenon," pp. 7–46 in *Capitalism and Social Democracy*. Cambridge and Paris: Cambridge University Press/Éditions de la maison des sciences de l'homme.

Rebick, Judy. 2012. *Occupy This*. Toronto: Penguin Canada.

Reburn, E.G. 1953. "Reburn to Campbell, November 12, 1953." *Library and Archives Canada* CMA papers, MG28 I230, Vol. 116, Folder Industrial Relations Labour Union Demands 1953.

Reeve, Elspeth. 2012. "In DC, Blue Collar Doesn't Mean What You Think It Means." *The Atlantic*, September 7, www.theatlanticwire.com/politics/2012/o 9/dc-blue-collar-doesnt-mean-what-you-think-it-means/56636/.

Reich, Robert B. 2015. *Saving Capitalism: For the Many, Not the Few*. New York: Alfred A. Knopf.

Renteria, Amanda and Dan Schwerin. 2015. "Re: Union Leaders, Members on SCOTUS Grant of Cert in Friedrichs v. CTA." *Wikileaks*, https://wikileaks.org /podesta-emails/emailid/16847.

Rhomberg, Chris. 2012. *The Broken Table: The Detroit Newspaper Strike and the State of American Labor*. New York: Russell Sage Foundation.

Richardson, Tyrone and Hassan A. Kanu. 2017. "Reverse Labor Board's Measures, Employer Advocates Tell Panel." *Bloomberg BNA*, www.bna.com /reverse-labor-boards-n73014453341/.

Riddell, W. Craig. 1993. "Unionization in Canada and the United States: A Tale of Two Countries," pp. 109–148 in *Small Differences That Matter: Labor Markets and Income Maintenance in Canada and the United States*, edited by D.E. Card and R.B. Freeman. Chicago: University of Chicago Press.

Riddell, Chris. 2004. "Union Certification Success Under Voting Versus Card Check Procedures: Evidence From British Columbia, 1978–1998." *Industrial and Labor Relations Review* 57(4):493–517.

Riddell, Chris. 2010. "The Causal Effect of Election Delay on Union Win Rates: Instrumental Variable Estimates From Two Natural Experiments." *Industrial Relations: A Journal of Economy and Society* 49(3):371–386.

Roberts, Barbara. 1986. "Shovelling Out the 'Mutinous': Political Deportation From Canada Before 1936." *Labour/Le Travail* 18(Fall):77–110.

Robinson, Archie. 1981. *George Meany and His Times: A Biography*. New York: Simon and Schuster.

Robinson, Ian. 1990. "Organizing Labour: Explaining Canada-US Union Density Divergence in the Post-War Period." PhD Dissertation, Department of Political Science, Yale University.

Robinson, Ian. 1993. "Economistic Unionism in Crisis: The Origins, Consequences, and Prospects of Canada-U.S. Labour Movement Character Divergence," pp. 19–47 in *The Challenge of Restructuring: North American Labor Movements Respond*, edited by J. Jenson and R. Mahon. Philadelphia: Temple University Press.

Roediger, David R. 1991. *The Wages of Whiteness: Race and the Making of the American Working Class*. New York: Verso.

Rogers, Joel. 1990. "Divide and Conquer: Further Reflections on the Distinctive Character of American Labor Laws." *Wisconsin Law Review* 1990(1):1–148.

Roomkin, Myron, and Richard N. Block. 1981. "Case Processing Time and the Outcome of Representation Elections: Some Empirical Evidence." *University of Illinois Law Review* 75:75–97.

Roosevelt, Franklin D. 1934. "Speech Regarding Executive Order 6763." *National Archives* RG74 General Records of the Department of Labor Secretary Frances Perkins, Box 86: Office of the Secretary Secy Frances Perkins, General Subject File 1933–1941, National Labor Relations Board to National Recovery Admin, Folder National Labor Relations Board June1934.

Rose, Joseph B. 1984. "Growth Patterns of Public Sector Unions," pp. 87–119 in *Conflict or Compromise: the Future of Public Sector Industrial Relations*, edited by M. Thompson and G. Swimmer. Montreal: Institute for Research on Public Policy.

Rose, Joseph B. and Gary N. Chaison. 1996. "Linking Union Density and Union Effectiveness: The North American Experience." *Industrial Relations* 35(1):78–105.

Rosenblum, Jonathan. 2017. *Beyond $15: Immigrant Workers, Faith Activists, and the Revival of the Labor Movement*. Boston: Beacon Press.

Rosenfeld, Herman. 2009. "The North American Auto Industry in Crisis." *Monthly Review* 61(2):18–36.

Rosenfeld, Jake. 2006. "Desperate Measures: Strikes and Wages in Post-Accord America." *Social Forces* 85(1):235–265.

Rosenfeld, Jake. 2014. *What Unions No Longer Do.* Cambridge: Harvard University Press.
Rosenfeld, Jake. 2016a. "French Lessons: Why Labor and Laborism Need One Another." *OnLabor,* https://onlabor.org/2016/07/07/french-lessons-why-labor-and-laborism-need-one-another/.
Rosenfeld, Jake. 2016b. "Labor and Politics: Learning the Right Lessons From 2016." *OnLabor,* https://onlabor.org/2016/11/23/labor-and-politics-learning-the-right-lessons-from-2016/.
Rosenof, Theodore. 1974. "The Political Education of an American Radical: Thomas R. Amlie in the 1930s." *The Wisconsin Magazine of History* 58(1):19–30.
Rosow, Jerome M. 1970. *The Problem of the Blue-Collar Worker.* Washington, DC: U.S. Department of Labor, http://eric.ed.gov/ERICWebPortal/recordDetail?accno=ED045810.
Ross, Stephanie, and Larry Savage, eds. 2012. *Rethinking the Politics of Labour in Canada.* Winnipeg: Fernwood Publishing Co.
Ross, Stephanie, and Larry Savage, eds. 2013. *Public Sector Unions in the Age of Austerity.* Winnipeg: Fernwood Publishing.
Rouillard, Jacques. 1981. *Histoire de la CSN: 1921–1981.* Montreal: Boréal Express.
Rouillard, Jacques. 1989. *Histoire du syndicalisme au québec: des origines à nos jours.* Montréal: Éditions du Boréal.
Rouillard, Jacques. 2004. *Le syndicalisme québécois: deux siècles d'histoire.* Montreal: Boréal.
Rubin, Beth A., Larry J. Griffin, and Michael E. Wallace. 1983. "'Provided Only That Their Voice Was Strong': Insurgency and Organization of American Labor From NRA to Taft-Hartley." *Work and Occupations* 10(3):325–347.
Rueschemeyer, Dietrich, Evelyne H. Stephens, and John D. Stephens. 1992. *Capitalist Development and Democracy.* Chicago: University of Chicago Press.
Salmond, John A. 1995. *Gastonia, 1929: The Story of the Loray Mill Strike.* Chapel Hill: University of North Carolina Press.
Saloutos, Theodore. 1969. "The New Deal and Farm Policy in the Great Plains." *Agricultural History* 43(3):345–356.
Saloutos, Theodore. 1974. "New Deal Agricultural Policy: An Evaluation." *The Journal of American History* 61(2):394–416.
Salvatore, Nick. 1982. *Eugene v. Debs: Citizen and Socialist.* Urbana-Champaign: University of Illinois Press.
Salvatore, Nick. 2012. "A Brief Ascendency: American Labor After 1945." *The Forum* 10(1):1–24.
Sanders, Bernie. 2016. *Our Revolution: A Future to Believe In.* New York: Thomas Dunne Books.
Sanders, M. Elizabeth. 1999. *Roots of Reform: Farmers, Workers, and the American State, 1877–1917.* Chicago: University of Chicago Press.
Sangster, Joan. 2010. "Radical Ruptures: Feminism, Labor, and the Left in the Long Sixties in Canada." *American Review of Canadian Studies* 40(1):1–21.
Saporta, Ishak and Bryan Lincoln. 1995. "Managers' and Workers' Attitudes Toward Unions in the U.S. and Canada." *Relations Industrielles/Industrial Relations* 50(3):550–566.

Savage, Larry. 2010. "Contemporary Party-Union Relations in Canada." *Labor Studies Journal* 35(1):8–26.

Savage, Larry. 2012. "Organized Labour and the Politics of Strategic Voting," pp. 75–87 in *Rethinking the Politics of Labour in Canada*, edited by S. Ross and L. Savage. Winnipeg: Fernwood Publishing Co.

Scheiber, Noam. 2017. "Trump Moves to Dismantle Obama-Era Labor Policies." *New York Times*, June 21, A13.

Schenk, Chris R. and Elaine Bernard. 1992. "Social Unionism: Labor as a Political Force." *Social Policy* 23(Summer):38–46.

Schlesinger, Arthur M. 1957. *The Crisis of the Old Order, 1919–1933*. Boston: Houghton Mifflin.

Schmidt, Regin. 2000. *Red Scare: FBI and the Origins of Anticommunism in the United States, 1919–1943*. Copenhagen: Museum Tusculanum Press.

Schrecker, Ellen. 1998. *Many Are the Crimes: McCarthyism in America*. Princeton: Princeton University Press.

Schrecker, Ellen. 1999. "McCarthyism's Ghosts: Anticommunism and American Labor." *New Labor Forum* 4(Summer):6–17.

Schwartz, Michael. 2011. Personal Communication, October 12.

Scipes, Kim. 2010. *AFL-CIO's Secret War Against Developing Country Workers: Solidarity or Sabotage?* Lanham: Lexington Books.

Scott, Jack. 1978. *Canadian Workers, American Unions*. Vancouver: New Star Books.

SDS. 2015. "The Port Huron Statement," pp. 239–284 in *The Port Huron Statement: Sources and Legacies of the New Left's Founding Manifesto*, edited by R. Flacks and N. Lichtenstein. Philadelphia: University of Pennsylvania Press.

Secunda, Paul M. 2012. "The Future of NLRB Doctrine on Captive Audience Speeches." *Indiana Law Journal* 87:123–146.

Seeber, Ronald L. and William N. Cooke. 1983. "The Decline in Union Success in NLRB Representation Elections." *Industrial Relations: A Journal of Economy and Society* 22(1):34–44.

Segrave, Kerry. 2009. *Film Actors Organize: Union Formation Efforts in America, 1912–1937*. Jefferson, NC: McFarland.

Shalev, Michael. 1980. "Trade Unionism and Economic Analysis: The Case of Industrial Conflict." *Journal of Labor Research* 1(1):133–173.

Shannon, David A. 1967. *The Socialist Party of America: A History*. Chicago: Quadrangle Books.

Shefter, Martin. 1986. "Trade Unions and Political Machines: The Organization and Disorganization of the American Working Class in the Late Nineteenth Century," pp. 197–276 in *Working-class formation: Nineteenth-Century patterns in Western Europe and the United States*, edited by I. Katznelson and A.R. Zolberg. Princeton: Princeton University Press.

Sheingate, Adam D. 2000. "Institutions and Interest Group Power: Agricultural Policy in the United States, France, and Japan." *Studies in American Political Development* 14:184–211.

Shover, John L. 1965. "The Farmers' Holiday Association Strike, August 1932." *Agricultural History* 39(4):196–203.

Silver, Nate. 2011. "The Effects of Union Membership on Democratic Voting." *New York Times FiveThirtyEight Blog*, February 26, https://fivethirtyeight.blogs.nytimes.com/2011/02/26/the-effects-of-union-membership-on-democratic-voting/

Silverstein, Eileen. 1993. "Collective Action Property Rights and Law Reform: The Story of the Labor Injunction." *Hofstra Labor Law Journal* 11:97–140.

Silvia, Stephen J. 2016. "Organizing German Automobile Plants in the USA: An Assessment of the United Auto Workers' Efforts to Organize German-Owned Automobile Plants." Düsseldorf: Hans-Böckler-Stiftung Study #349.

Singh, Sonia. 2015. "Back to School with Work to Rule in Ontario." *Labor Notes*, August 20, www.labornotes.org/2015/08/back-school-work-rule-ontario.

Sinyai, Clayton. 2006. *Schools of Democracy: A Political History of the American Labor Movement*. Ithaca: Cornell University Press.

Skocpol, Theda, and Kenneth Finegold. 1990. "Explaining New Deal Labor Policy." *The American Political Science Review* 84(4):1297–1315.

Slaughter, Jane. 1983. *Concessions and How to Beat Them*. Detroit: Labor Education & Research Project.

Slinn, Sara. 2004. "An Empirical Analysis of the Effects of the Change From Card-Check to Mandatory Vote Certification." *Canadian Labour and Employment Law Journal* 11:259–301.

Slinn, Sara, and Richard W. Hurd. 2011. "First Contract Arbitration and the Employee Free Choice Act: Multi-Jurisdictional Evidence From Canada." *Advances in Industrial & Labor Relations* 18:41–86.

Smith, Ashley. 2016. "Bullet No. 1247: What Did Quebec Public-Sector Unions Achieve?" *socialistproject.ca*, http://socialistproject.ca/bullet/1247.php.

Smith, David E. 1975. *Prairie Liberalism: The Liberal Party in Saskatchewan, 1905–71*. Toronto: University of Toronto Press.

Smith, Edwin S. 1937. "How the National Labor Relations Board Administers the Wagner Act." *National Archives* RG174 General Records of the Department of Labor Secretary Frances Perkins, Box 85: Office of the Secretary Secy Frances Perkins, General Subject File 1933–1941 National Labor Relations Board, Folder National Labor Relations Board 1937.

Snyder, David. 1977. "Early North American Strikes: A Reinterpretation." *Industrial and Labor Relations Review* 30(3):325–341.

Solberg, Carl E. 1987. *The Prairies and the Pampas: Agrarian Policy in Canada and Argentina, 1880–1930*. Stanford: Stanford University Press.

Sombart, Werner. 1976. *Why Is There No Socialism in the United States?* London: Macmillan.

Southworth, Caleb. 2002. "Aid to Sharecroppers: How Agrarian Class Structure and Tenant-Farmer Politics Influenced Federal Relief in the South, 1933–1935." *Social Science History* 26(1):33–70.

Stark, Louis. 1936. "Labor Chiefs Give Roosevelt Pledge; Berry and Lewis Tell Him That 30,000 Union Officials Back New Nonpartisan League; 4,000 Speakers Lined Up; Callers Say Manufacturers Association and Liberty League Drives Will Be 'Unmasked'." *New York Times*, May 12, 2.

Starobin, Joseph R. 1972. *American Communism in Crisis, 1943–1957*. Cambridge: Harvard University Press.

Statistics Canada. 2016. "Labour Force Survey." CANSIM table 282-0223.

Stein, Jason, and Meg Kissinger. 2015. "Scott Walker Signs Right-to-Work Bill." *Milwaukee Journal Sentinel*, March 9, www.jsonline.com/news/statepolitics/scott-walker-signs-right-to-work-bill-b99457819z1-295609181.html.

Stein, Jason, and Patrick Marley. 2013. *More Than They Bargained for: Scott Walker, Unions, and the Fight for Wisconsin*. Madison: University of Wisconsin Press.

Stepan-Norris, Judith, and Maurice Zeitlin. 2003. *Left Out: Reds and America's Industrial Unions*. New York: Cambridge University Press.

Stewart, J.C., and Hugh Dalton. 1948. "Letter From Stewart and Dalton to BC Labour Minister Wisner, Re: Bill 39 (Industrial Conciliation and Arbitration Act), March 22 1948." *Library and Archives Canada* CMA papers, MG 28 I230, Vol. 118, Folder IRDIA (#5) #2 1948.

Summers, Clyde W. 1979. "Industrial Democracy: America's Unfulfilled Promise." *Cleveland State Law Review* 28(1):29–49.

Sundquist, James L. 1983. *Dynamics of the Party System: Alignment and Realignment of Political Parties in the United States*. Washington, DC: Brookings Institution.

Swenson, Peter A. 2004. "Varieties of Capitalist Interests: Power, Institutions, and the Regulatory Welfare State in the United States and Sweden." *Studies in American Political Development* 18(01):1–29.

Taft, Philip. 1959. *The A. F. of L. From the Death of Gompers to the Merger*. New York: Harper & Brothers.

Taras, Daphne and Allen Ponak. 2001a. "Mandatory Agency Shop Laws as an Explanation of Canada-U.S. Union Density Divergence." *Journal of Labor Research* 22(3):541–568.

Taras, Daphne G. 1997. "Collective Bargaining Regulation in Canada and the United States: Divergent Cultures, Divergent Outcomes," pp. 295–342 in *Government Regulation of the Employment Relationship – IRRA 50th Anniversary Volume*, edited by B.E. Kaufman. Champaign: Industrial Relations Research Association.

Taras, Daphne G. and Allen Ponak. 2001b. "Union Security in Canada," pp. 229–248 in *The Internal Governance and Organizational Effectiveness Labor Unions: Essays in Honor of George Brooks*, edited by S. Estreicher, H.C. Katz, and B.E. Kaufman. New York: Kluwer Law International.

Tavernise, Sabrina. 2016. "'Both of Them Were Terrible': No Vote, No Regrets in Milwaukee." *The New York Times*, November 21, A11.

Temin, Peter. 2017. *The Vanishing Middle Class: Prejudice and Power in a Dual Economy*. Cambridge: MIT Press.

The Economist. 2015. "Why Trade Unions Are Declining." *The Economist*, September 28, 1–4, www.economist.com/blogs/economist-explains/2015/09/economist-explains-19.

Theoharis, Athan. 2002. *Chasing Spies: How the FBI Failed in Counter-Intelligence but Promoted the Politics of McCarthyism in the Cold War Years*. Chicago: Ivan R. Dee.

Thomas, Ken. 2011. "Bob King: If UAW Can't Organize Foreign Plants, 'I Don't Think There's a Long-Term Future' for Union." *Crain's Detroit Business*, January 18, www.crainsdetroit.com/article/20110118/FREE/110119848/bob-king-if-uaw-cant-organize-foreign-plants-i-dont-think-theres-a.

Thomason, Terry. 1994. "The Effect of Accelerated Certification Procedure on Union Organizing Success in Ontario." *Industrial and Labor Relations Review* 47(2):207–226.

Thomason, Terry and Silvana Pozzebon. 1998. "Managerial Opposition to Union Certification in Quebec and Ontario." *Relations Industrielles/Industrial Relations* 53(4):750–771.

Thompson, John H. and Allen Seager. 1986. *Canada 1922–1939: Decades of Discord*. Toronto: McClelland and Stewart.

Thompson, Mark. 1995. "The Management of Industrial Relations," pp. 105–130 in *Union-Management Relations in Canada*, edited by M. Gunderson and A. Ponak. Toronto: Addison Wesley.

Thwaites, James D., ed. 2007. *Travail et syndicalisme: origines, évolution et défis d'une action sociale*. 3rd ed. Québec: Les Presses de l'université Laval.

Tocqueville, Alexis de. 2004. *Democracy in America*. New York: Library of America.

Tomlins, Christopher L. 1979. "AFL Unions in the 1930s: Their Performance in Historical Perspective." *The Journal of American History* 65(4):1021–1042.

Trottman, Melanie. 2016. "New NLRB Election Rules Haven't Helped Unions Grow as Expected." *Wall Street Journal*, April 20, 1–2, www.wsj.com/articles/new-nlrb-election-rules-havent-helped-unions-grow-as-expected-1461190043.

Troy, Leo. 1990. "Is the U.S. Unique in the Decline of Private Sector Unionism?" *Journal of Labor Research* 11(2):111–143.

Troy, Leo. 1992. "Convergence in International Unionism, Etc.: the Case of Canada and the USA." *British Journal of Industrial Relations* 30(1):1–43.

Troy, Leo. 2000. "U.S. and Canadian Industrial Relations: Convergent or Divergent?" *Industrial Relations: A Journal of Economy and Society* 39(4):695–713.

Troy, Leo and Neil Sheflin. 1985. *US Union Sourcebook: Membership, Finances, Structure, Directory*. West Orange: Industrial Relations Data and Information Services.

Truman, Harry S. 1945. "Letter from Truman to Perkins, May 23, 1945." *National Archives* RG174 General Records of the Department of Labor Office of the Secretary Subject File of Secretary Lewis B Schwellenbach 1945–48, Box 25: War Assets Admin-White House Social, Folder White House General 1945.

Tucker, Eric. 2008. "The Constitutional Right to Bargain Collectively: The Ironies of Labour History in the Supreme Court of Canada." *Labour/Le Travail* 61 (Spring):151–180.

Turner, Julius, and Edward V. Schneier. 1970. *Party and Constituency: Pressures on Congress*. Baltimore: Johns Hopkins Press.

Turner, Ronald. 2005. "Ideological Voting on the National Labor Relations Board." *University of Pennsylvania Journal of Labor and Employment Law* 8:707–764.

Uetricht, Micah. 2014. *Strike for America: Chicago Teachers Against Austerity*. New York: Verso Books.

US Department of Labor. 1934a. "Analysis of the Revised Wagner Labor Bill Compared with Secretary Perkins' Suggestions." *National Archives* RG174 General Records of the Department of Labor Secretary Frances Perkins, Box

84: Office of the Secretary Secy Frances Perkins General Subject File 1933–1941 National Labor Relations Board, Folder National Labor Relations Board 1938.

US Department of Labor. 1934b. "Notes on 'National Labor Relations Board Tentative Draft of Policy – Second Draft – July 21, 1934'." *National Archives* RG174 General Records of the Department of Labor Secretary Frances Perkins, Box 86: Office of the Secretary Secy Frances Perkins, General Subject File 1933–1941 National Labor Relations Board to National Recovery Admin, Folder National Labor Relations Board August 1934.

US Department of Labor. 1935. "Memorandum for the President's Use in Conversation with New Members of the National Labor Relations Board." *National Archives* RG174 General Records of the Department of Labor Secretary Frances Perkins, Box 85: Office of the Secretary Secy Frances Perkins, General Subject File 1933–1941 National Labor Relations Board, Folder National Labor Relations Board August 1935.

US Department of Labor. 1968. "The New Campaign to Abolish the NLRB and Rewrite the Labor Act." *National Archives* RG174 General Records of the Department of Labor, Office of the Secretary of Labor, Records of Secretary of Labor W. Willard Wirtz 1962–1969, Box 579: Miscellaneous Board-Regional Preparedness Board, Folder 1968–Board–National Labor Relations The New Campaign to Abolish the NLRB & Rewrite the Labor Act 8-28-68.

US News and World Report. 1972. "U.S. Needs '30,000 New Jobs a Week to Break Even': Interview with George Meany, President, AFL-CIO." *US News and World Report*, February 21, 27–35.

Vachon, Todd E., Michael Wallace, and Allen Hyde. 2016. "Union Decline in a Neoliberal Age: Globalization, Financialization, European Integration, and Union Density in 18 Affluent Democracies." *Socius* 2:1–22.

Valelly, Richard M. 1989. *Radicalism in the States: the Minnesota Farmer-Labor Party and the American Political Economy*. Chicago: University of Chicago Press.

Vickers, Jill, and Annette Isaac. 2012. *The Politics of Race: Canada, the United States, and Australia*. 2nd ed. Toronto: University of Toronto Press.

Visser, Jelle. 2006. "Union Membership Statistics in 24 Countries." *Monthly Labor Review* 129(January):38–49.

Voss, Kim. 1993. *The Making of American Exceptionalism: The Knights of Labor and Class Formation in the Nineteenth Century*. Ithaca: Cornell University Press.

Voss, Kim. 2015. "Same as It Ever Was? New Labor, the CIO Organizing Model, and the Future of American Unions." *Politics and Society* 43(3):453–457.

Voss, Kim and Irene Bloemraad, eds. 2011. *Rallying for Immigrant Rights: The Fight for Inclusion in 21st Century America*. Berkeley: University of California Press.

Voss, Kim, and Pablo Gaston. 2016. "Been Down So Long, It Looks Like Up to Me: Shifting Targets, Changing Repertoires, and Internal Democracy in the U.S. Labor Movement." Unpublished working paper.

Voss, Kim, and Rachel Sherman. 2000. "Breaking the Iron Law of Oligarchy: Union Revitalization in the American Labor Movement." *American Journal of Sociology* 106(2):303–349.

Vössing, Konstantin. 2012. "Predictably Exceptional: The Failure of Social Democracy and the Formation of American Labour Politics in Comparative Perspective." *Party Politics* 20(5):767–777.

Walker, Jack L. 1974. "Performance Gaps, Policy Research, and Political Entrepreneurs: Toward a Theory of Agenda Setting." *Policy Studies Journal* 3(1):112–116.

Wallace-Wells, Benjamin. 2016. "How the Minimum-Wage Movement Entered the Mainstream." *The New Yorker*, March 31, www.newyorker.com /news/benjamin-wallace-wells/how-the-minimum-wage-movement-entered-the-mainstream.

Warskett, Rosemary. 1997. "Learning to Be 'Uncivil': Class Formation and Feminisation in the Public Service Alliance of Canada, 1966–1996." PhD Dissertation, Department of Sociology and Anthropology, Carleton University.

Washington Post. 1936. "Miners Offer Votes, Funds to Roosevelt." *Washington Post*, February 2, 1–2.

Watkins, Mel. 1968. *Foreign Ownership and the Structure of Canadian Industry: Report of the Task Force on the Structure of Canadian Industry*. Ottawa: Queen's Printer.

Webber, Patrick. 2009. "Entryism in Theory, in Practice, and in Crisis: The Trotskyist Experience in New Brunswick, 1969–1973." *Left History* 14(1):33–57.

Weil, David. 2014. *The Fissured Workplace: Why Work Became So Bad for So Many and What Can Be Done to Improve It*. Cambridge, MA: Harvard University Press.

Weiler, Paul C. 1980. *Reconcilable Differences: New Directions in Canadian Labour Law*. Toronto: Carswell Legal Publications.

Weiler, Paul C. 1983. "Promises to Keep: Securing Workers' Rights to Self-Organization Under the NLRA." *Harvard Law Review* 96(8):1769–1827.

Weiler, Paul C. 1984. "Striking a New Balance: Freedom of Contract and the Prospects for Union Representation." *Harvard Law Review* 98(2):351–420.

Wells, Don M. 1995a. "Origins of Canada's Wagner Model of Industrial Relations: The United Auto Workers in Canada and the Suppression of 'Rank and File' Unionism, 1936–1953." *The Canadian Journal of Sociology / Cahiers canadiens de sociologie* 20(2):193–225.

Wells, Don M. 1995b. "The Impact of the Postwar Compromise on Canadian Unionism: The Formation of an Auto Worker Local in the 1950s." *Labour/Le Travail* 36:147–173.

Western, Bruce. 1995. "A Comparative Study of Working-Class Disorganization: Union Decline in Eighteen Advanced Capitalist Countries." *American Sociological Review* 60(2):179–201.

Western, Bruce and Jake Rosenfeld. 2011. "Unions, Norms, and the Rise in U.S. Wage Inequality." *American Sociological Review* 76(4):513–537.

Wherry, Aaron. 2017. "Jagmeet Singh Brings Something New to the NDP." CBC News, October 2, www.cbc.ca/news/politics/jagmeet-singh-ndp-leader-analysis-aaron-wherry-1.4315882.

Whitaker, Reg. 1984. "Fighting the Cold War on the Home Front: America, Britain, Australia and Canada." *Socialist Register* 21:23–67.

Whitaker, Reg and Gary Marcuse. 1994. *Cold War Canada: The Making of a National Insecurity State, 1945–1957*. Cambridge: Cambridge University Press.
Whitaker, Reginald. 1977a. *The Government Party: Organizing and Financing the Liberal Party of Canada, 1930–58*. Toronto and Buffalo: University of Toronto Press.
Whitaker, Reginald. 1977b. "The Liberal Corporatist Ideas of Mackenzie King." *Labour/Le Travail* 2:137–169.
Whitaker, Reginald. 1986. "Official Repression of Communism During World War II." *Labour/Le Travail* 17(Spring):135–166.
Wiener, Jonathan M. 1979. "Class Structure and Economic Development in the American South, 1865–1955." *The American Historical Review* 84(4):970–992.
Wilkinson, Richard, and Kate Pickett. 2009. *The Spirit Level: Why Greater Equality Makes Societies Stronger*. New York: Bloomsbury Press.
Williams, Phil. 2014. "Corker, Aides Plan to Ignore 'Baseless' UAW Subpoenas." News Channel 5, April 16, www.newschannel5.com/news/newschannel-5-investigates/tennessees-secret-deals/corker-aides-plan-to-ignore-baseless-uaw-subpoenas.
Winders, Bill. 2005. "Maintaining the Coalition: Class Coalitions and Policy Trajectories." *Politics and Society* 33(3):387–423.
Winter, Ralph K. Jr. 1968. "Judicial Review of Agency Decisions: The Labor Board and the Court." *The Supreme Court Review* 53–76.
Wiseman, Nelson, and Benjamin Isitt. 2007. "Social Democracy in Twentieth Century Canada: An Interpretive Framework." *Canadian Journal of Political Science* 40(3):567–589.
Wiseman, Nelson, and Benjamin Isitt. 2013. "Early Socialism in Canada: International and Regional Impulses." *American Review of Canadian Studies* 43(4):512–528.
Woodall, Bernie. 2014. "Loss at Volkswagen Plant Upends Union's Plan for U.S. South." *Reuters*, February 14, www.reuters.com/article/us-autos-vw-election-idUSBREA1D1DP20140215.
Woods, H.D. 1962. "United States and Canadian Experience: A Comparison," pp. 212–240 in *Public Policy and Collective Bargaining*, edited by J. Shister, B. Aaron, and C. Summers. New York: Harper & Row.
Woods, H.D. 1973. *Labour Policy in Canada*. 2nd ed. edited by H.D. Woods, S. Ostry, and M.A. Zaidi. Toronto: Macmillan of Canada.
Workers United Canada Council. 2015. "Winnipeg Tim Hortons Restaurant to Be Represented by Workers United." *newswire.ca* press release, June 11, www.newswire.ca/news-releases/winnipeg-tim-hortons-restaurant-to-be-represented-by-workers-united-517925231.html.
Worster, Robert M., III. 2003. "If It's Hardly Worth Doing, It's Hardly Worth Doing Right: How the NLRA's Goals Are Defeated Through Inadequate Remedies." *University of Richmond Law Review* 38:1073–1095.
Worton, David A. 1969. "The Service Industries in Canada, 1946–66," pp. 237–286 in *Production and Productivity in the Service Industries*, edited by V.R. Fuchs. Ann Arbor: UMI.
Wright, Erik O. 1990. "Comparative Project on Class Structure and Class Consciousness: Core and Country-Specific Files [MRDF]. Madison: University of Wisconsin." Institute for Research on Poverty [producer]. Ann Arbor, MI: Inter-University Consortium for Political and Social Research [distributor].

Wright, Erik O., and Rachel E. Dwyer. 2003. "The Patterns of Job Expansions in the USA: A Comparison of the 1960s and 1990s." *Socio-Economic Review* 1(3):289–325.
Yarmie, Andrew. 2003. "Employers and Exceptionalism: A Cross-Border Comparison of Washington State and British Columbia, 1890–1935." *Pacific Historical Review* 72(4):561–615.
Yates, Charlotte A.B. 1993. *From Plant to Politics: The Autoworkers Union in Postwar Canada*. Philadelphia: Temple University Press.
Yates, Michael, ed. 2012. *Wisconsin Uprising: Labor Fights Back*. New York: NYU Press.
Yeselson, Rich. 2016. "How Labor Advocates Pushed the Democratic Party Left." *Dissent*, February 11, www.dissentmagazine.org/blog/how-labor-advocates-pushed-democratic-party-left-democratic-socialism-bernie-sanders-hillary-clinton.
YG Network. 2014. *Room to Grow: Conservative Reforms for a Limited Government and a Thriving Middle Class*. Washington, DC: Conservative Reform Network.
Young, James T. 1993. "The Origins of New Deal Agricultural Policy: Interest Groups' Role in Policy Formation." *Policy Studies Journal* 21(2):190–209.
Young, Walter D. 1976. "Ideology, Personality and the Origin of the CCF in British Columbia." *B.C. Studies* 32(Winter):139–162.
Zeitlin, Maurice and L. Frank Weyher. 2001. "'Black and White, Unite and Fight': Interracial Working-Class Solidarity and Racial Employment Equality." *American Journal of Sociology* 107(2):430–467.
Zieger, Robert H. 1995. *The CIO, 1935–1955*. Chapel Hill: University of North Carolina Press.
Zieger, Robert H. 2007. *For Jobs and Freedom: Race and Labor in America since 1865*. Lexington: University Press of Kentucky.
Zolberg, Aristide R. 1986. "How Many Exceptionalisms?," pp. 397–455 in *Working-Class Formation: Nineteenth-Century Patterns in Western Europe and the United States*, edited by I. Katznelson and A.R. Zolberg. Princeton: Princeton University Press.
Zook, Gary. 1978. "Letter From Zook to Carter Re: Labor Law Reform Bill, May 16, 1978." *National Archives* RG174, General Records of the Department of Labor, Office of the Secretary of Labor, Records of Secretary of Labor Ray Marshall 1978, Box 96: Public Information PI-11, Folder 1978 PI-11 Public Reaction Re Labor Law Reform Proposal In Behalf of the President June 1–10.
Zuberi, Dan. 2006. *Differences That Matter: Social Policy and the Working Poor in the United States and Canada*. Ithaca: Cornell ILR Press.
Zuberi, Dan. 2007. "Organizing for Better Working Conditions and Wages: The UNITE HERE! Hotel Workers Rising Campaign." *Just Labour: A Canadian Journal of Work and Society* 10(Spring):60–73.
Zuckerman, Jake. 2017. "WV House Joins Senate, Votes to Override Right-to-Work Veto." *Charleston Gazette-Mail*, April 7, www.wvgazettemail.com/news-politics/20170407/wv-house-joins-senate-votes-to-override-right-to-work-veto.
Zweig, Michael. 2017. "White Working-Class Voters and the Future of Progressive Politics." *New Labor Forum* 26(2):1–8.

Index

AAA. *See* Agricultural Adjustment Act
ABA. *See* American Bar Association
Abood v. Detroit Board of Education, 51–52
ACCL. *See* All-Canadian Congress of Labour
ACF. *See* American Commonwealth Federation
Act 10 (Wisconsin), 259–260
adjudication, conciliation and, 236–238
advanced industrialized countries, 23
AES. *See* Agricultural Extension Service
AFBF. *See* American Farm Bureau Federation
AFL. *See* American Federation of Labor
AFL-CIO. *See* American Federation of Labor-Congress of Industrial Organizations
AFSCME. *See* American Federation of State, County, and Municipal Employees
agency fee, 51. *See also* fair share fees
agency shop, 84
agrarian liberalism, 169–179
agrarian populism, 174
agrarian protest, 166
Agricultural Adjustment Act (AAA), 178
   core of, 178
   exclusion by, 179
Agricultural Extension Service (AES), 178
Alabama Sharecroppers' Union (ASU), 169, 179
alienation, 13
   in Canada, 252

   class issues in the United States as individual alienation, 250–254
Alito, Samuel, 52
All-Canadian Congress of Labour (ACCL), 172, 174, 185, 186
alt-labor, 261
American Bar Association (ABA), 131
American Commonwealth Federation (ACF), 182
American Dream, 19
American Exceptionalism, 21, 22–23, 25, 116, 197
American Farm Bureau Federation (AFBF), 178
American Federation of Labor (AFL), 126, 128, 129, 143, 144–147, 150, 154, 168, 181, 183, 186, 187, 191, 225, 230, 234
   no-strike pledge of, 234
American Federation of Labor-Congress of Industrial Organizations (AFL-CIO), 126, 129, 151, 191, 193, 215, 219, 258–259, 263, 266
   budget cuts at, 263
   contested election for leadership of, 258
   New Voice slate, 258
American Federation of State, County, and Municipal Employees (AFSCME), 150–151, 215
American Plan, 138
American Revolution, 25
Amlie, Thomas R., 182
Anaconda Brass Company, 235

Index

Angus Reid Strategies Group, 44
anti-colonial struggles, 210, 211, 212
anti-Communism, 216, 218
anti-Communists, 12–13, 192, 196–197, 204, 218
  crusades of, 197
  Liberal Party as, 204–205
anti-fascist struggles in 1970s (Portugal, Spain, Greece), 217
anti-immigrant policies, 147, 200
anti-union workers, 2
articulation model of parties, 161, 166–167
As Unions Mature (Lester), 127
ASU. *See* Alabama Sharecroppers' Union
auto assembly plant, 1
auto industry, 59–60
Auto Pact. *See* Canada-United States Automotive Products Trade Agreement

back-to-work legislation, 97
Bain, George Sayers, 81
bargaining units, 62
  certification of, 66
Barrett, Tom, 259–260
Bell, Daniel, 129
Bennett, Richard B., 138, 173
Bentham, Karen J., 81
Bernard, Elaine, 109
Biden, Joe, 20
Bill 7 (Ontario), 71–72
Bill 40 (Ontario), 71–72
Black Power movement, 150–151, 212
Block, Richard N., 111–112
blue collar blues, 251, 252
Bluestone, Barry, 128
Bonwit Teller, Inc., 96 N.L.R.B. 608 (1951), 242
boycotts, 96
Boys Market, Inc. v. Retail Clerks, 94
"Brains Trust" (CCF), 175–177
"Brains Trust" (Roosevelt administration), 176–177
British Columbia, 49, 80, 81, 99
  CCF electoral strength in, 184
  NDP government in, 264
Bronfenbrenner, Kate, 78–79
Brotherhood of Sleeping Car Porters (BSCP), 145
Brown v. Board of Education, 151
Bruce, Peter G., 107

BSCP. *See* Brotherhood of Sleeping Car Porters
Buhle, Paul, 198
building trades unions, 150, 214, 215
business cycle, 55

CAA. *See* Christian American Association
Canada. *See also* unions, Canada
  alienation in, 252
  class issues in, 248–250
  class issues in the United States compared to, 255
  class struggle in, 157
  Cold War and, 201–202
  collective bargaining in public sector of, 246–248
  collectivism in, 137
  first contract arbitration in, 80
  foreign trade and, 57
  government resistance to Wagner Act-style reforms in, 254
  historical trajectory of labor relations in, 49
  hostile attitudes of Canadian employers, 77
  indigenous peoples in, 148
  industrial peace and labor regime of, 243
  labor as class representative in, 222, 254, 265
  labor crisis in, 263–264
  labor laws in, 53
  labor regime formation process in, 232–240
  national values of, 118, 137–142
  nationalism in, 216–218
  New Left in, 208
  partisan conflict in, 171–174
  political system of, 159
  public sector unionism in, 213–214
  Red scares in, 202
  service sector employment in, 33
  state hostility to labor, 264–265
  strike regulation in, 92–98
  strikes in the United States vs., 100–105
  war cabinet in, 139, 187, 233
Canada Industrial Relations Board (CIRB), 99, 237
Canada Labour Code, 250
Canada-United States Automotive Products Trade Agreement (Auto Pact), 55, 59–60

Index

union density and, 61
Canadian Association of University Teachers (CAUT), 44
Canadian Auto Workers (CAW), 218
Canadian Brotherhood of Railway Employees (CBRE), 174
Canadian Catholic Confederation of Labour (CTCC), 172, 192
Canadian Charter of Rights and Freedoms, 52–53, 96
   Section 2(d), 96–97
Canadian Congress of Labour (CCL), 143, 144, 186, 187–188, 201, 205, 206, 207, 235
Canadian dollar, 57
Canadian Federation of Labour (CFL), 214
Canadian Industrial Relations: The Report of the Task Force on Labour Relations (Woods Report), 141, 249, 250, 252
Canadian Labour Congress (CLC), 152, 214
Canadian Manufacturers' Association (CMA), 140
Canadian New Left, 208
Canadian service sector, 5
Cannery and Agricultural Workers Industrial Union (CAWIU), 179
capitalism, 200
   coordination costs for working class vs. capitalist class under, 15
   global, 212, 268
   Great Depression challenging legitimacy of, 175–176
capitalist democracies, 132–133
captive audience meetings, 3
Card, David, 8, 221
card-check recognition, 63–64
Carey, James B., 230–231
Carter, Jimmy, 253
CAUT. *See* Canadian Association of University Teachers
CAW. *See* Canadian Auto Workers
CAWIU. *See* Cannery and Agricultural Workers Industrial Union
CBRE. *See* Canadian Brotherhood of Railway Employees
CCF. *See* Cooperative Commonwealth Federation
CCL. *See* Canadian Congress of Labour
Center for Individual Rights (CIR), 51

Center for Union Facts, 31
Center for Worker Freedom, 2
CFL. *See* Canadian Federation of Labour
Change to Win Federation (CtW), 259
Chartrand, Michel, 217
Chicago police riot (1968), 209
Chicago Teachers Union (CTU), 269–270
Chicopee Manufacturing Co., 107 N.L.R.B. 106 (1953), 242
Christian American Association (CAA), 82
Chrysler Corporation, 258
CIO. *See* Congress of Industrial Organizations
CIR. *See* Center for Individual Rights
CIRB. *See* Canada Industrial Relations Board
civil rights, 197–198
Civil Rights Act, 209
civil rights law, 151, 152
civil rights movement, 150–151, 214
   de-radicalization of, 215
Civil Service Commission (Canada), 246
CIW. *See* Coalition of Immokalee Workers
class, 19–21, 175–176, 208–212, 248–250, 257–258
class conflict, 188, 226–227
   government sensitivity to, 243
   in institutional channels, 240
   politicizing, 238
class divisions, 10
   intra-working-class divisions, 11
   in U.S., 19
class idea, 11, 26, 190, 194, 195, 222
   under attack, 257, 265
   as elusive in U.S., 263
   erasure of, 252, 254
   and organization of interests, 14–18
   political articulation and, 157–158
   rebuilding, 266
class identity, 147, 168, 258, 263
class interests
   institutionalization of, 239
   organization of, 14, 15
class issues
   in Canada, 248–250
   in the United States as individual alienation, 250–254
   in the United States as partisan "special interests," 10, 240, 243, 260, 263–264
   in the United States as rights questions, 240, 248, 250, 254–255

class issues (cont.)
    in the United States compared to Canada, 255
class mobility, intergenerational, 19
class representation, 17, 18, 222, 239–240, 254, 265
class struggle, 158
    in Canada, 157
    in U.S., 179
class warfare, 20–21
    one-sided, 130, 213, 258
class-consciousness, 168, 238
classless society, myth of, 19–22
Claxton, Brooke, 173
CLC. See Canadian Labour Congress
Clinton, Hillary, 261–262
closed shop, 84
CMA. See Canadian Manufacturers' Association
Coalition of Immokalee Workers (CIW), 261
Cold War, 13, 193–194
    anti-Communist hysteria in, 196–197
    Canada and, 201–202
    United States and, 193–194, 197, 199, 202, 211, 212, 216
collective action, 16
collective bargaining, 6, 18, 81
    bargaining unit certification, 66
    bona fide efforts to engage in, 115
    Canadian Charter of Rights and Freedoms on, 52–53
    collective bargaining agreement, 55–56, 63, 85, 90, 92–93, 94
    compulsory, 239
    coverage rates, 90–91
    democracy and, 249–250
    employers and, 249
    enforcing rights of, 233
    NAM recalcitrant approach to, 137
    negotiation and implementation of first collective bargaining agreement, 55–56
    policies promoting, 66–67
    for public sector, 260
    in public sector of Canada, 246–248
    in public sector of U.S., 245–246
    in war industries, 233
    wartime, 187
collective identities, 16
collective labor rights, 113

collectivism, 116–117
    in Canada, 137
    collectivist social policy, 132–133
    collectivist values, 125, 137, 154
    in New Deal era, 125–126
colonization, industrial (left political tactic), 209–210
Common Front (Quebec) 1972, 193, 194, 270
    2015 round of negotiations, 270
    general strike of 1972, 193, 217, 270
Communications Workers of America (CWA), 270
Communism, 164, 197, 203, 204–205
Communist Party, USA (CPUSA), 169, 203
    membership composition of, 196, 197
    Popular Front strategy of, 12–13, 196, 203
    unions led by members of, 169, 204
    working class base of, 203
Communist Party of Canada (CPC), 187
    Criminal Code, Section 98 banning of, 173
    declared illegal, 200–201
    Popular Front strategy of, 205–206
    unions led by members of, 187
community of interest (for collective bargaining), 62
community support campaigns, 2
Comparative Project on Class Structure and Class Consciousness, 47–48
concession bargaining, 258
conciliation
    adjudication and, 236–238
    compulsory, 115
    "cooling off" period and, 237
    tripartism and, 236–239
Conciliation Service, United States (USCS), 236–237
Confederation of National Trade Unions (CSN), 192
    idea of "second front," 192–193, 217, 266
conformity, 207
Congress of Industrial Organizations (CIO), 126, 129, 143, 144, 145, 149–150, 154, 155, 168, 179, 181, 183, 186, 187, 188, 191, 198, 199, 201, 204, 218, 230–231, 234, 266, 267
    no-strike pledge of, 234
Congress of Quebec Unions (CSQ), 217
Conroy, Pat, 235
Conservative party (Canada), 11–12

failures of addressing 1930s economic crisis by, 173
contract concessions, 258
contract law, 113
contract rights, 239
Cooperative Commonwealth Federation (CCF), 11–12, 106, 107–108, 146, 186–189
  beginnings of, 173–174
  composition of, 185
  declared "political arm of labour," 188
  electoral strength in British Columbia, 184
  farmer–labor politics and, 171–172, 185–186
  ideology of, 165
  Liberal Party and, 164
  as loyal Left, 205
  as Official Opposition, 184
  Regina Manifesto, 176
Corker, Bob, 1, 4–5
corporate consolidation, 267–268
corporate liberalism, 133–134, 138, 140
corporate liberals, 133, 138
cost-benefit analysis of collective action, 16
Couillard, Philippe, 270
CPUSA. *See* Communist Party, USA
CPC. *See* Communist Party of Canada
craft unionism, 49, 150
Criminal Code, Section 98, 173
critical realignment theory, 165
CSN. *See* Confederation of National Trade Unions
CSN Montreal Central Council, 217
CSQ. *See* Congress of Quebec Unions
CTCC. *See* Canadian Catholic Confederation of Labour
CTU. *See* Chicago Teachers Union
CtW. *See* Change to Win Federation
CWA. *See* Communications Workers of America

Daniels, Mitch, 260
Debs, Eugene, V., 169
decommodification of labor, 8
Dellums, C. L., 145
democracy
  basic rights of, 9–10
  collective bargaining and, 249–250
  working class and, 15
  workplace and, 10

Democracy Needs Socialism (League for Social Reconstruction), 176
Democratic National Committee, 170
Democratic Party, 11, 13, 109, 161, 183, 240
  allegiances to, 168
  distancing from labor, 253
  fractures in, 170
  labor influence in, 213
  labor-Democratic Party alliance, 109–110
  New Left and, 207–208
  1964 Democratic Convention, 208
  1968 Democratic Convention, 209
  Southern Democrats, 109–110
  working class and, 168
Department of Labor, United States (DOL), 227–228
  Wage and Hour Division, 261
Department of Labour, Canada, 138
Department of Munitions and Supply (DMS), 235
deregulation, 253–254, 257–258
Detroit, Michigan, 128–129, 144, 259, 262
Detroit Newspaper strike, 259
Diefenbaker, John, 246
dignity, workers' need for, 9
DMS. *See* Department of Munitions and Supply
DOL. *See* Department of Labor, United States
Drew, George, 205
Dubinsky, David, 145
due process, 111
dues checkoff, 84, 140–141, 246
Dunlop, John T., 126
Dunlop Commission, 80
Duplessis, Maurice, 163
Durkin, Martin P., 135
Duverger, Maurice, 163

economic development, 50
economic policy, 50, 153–154
Economic Policy Institute, 262
"economic squeeze" of blue-collar workers, 251
The Economist (magazine), 31
economistic unionism, 142, 144, 145
economy
  government intervention in, 172–173
Edwards, Richard, 127

EFCA. *See* Employee Free Choice Act
effects of political exclusion, 232–236
Eisenhower, Dwight D., 135, 231, 242
Electoral College, 262
electoral institutions, 159–160, 161, 189
electoral politics
  CCF electoral strength in British
    Columbia, 184
  Clinton 2016 campaign, 261–262
  critical elections, 165
  New Left and, 207–208
  1932 presidential campaign (U.S.), 165,
    170
  1934 California gubernatorial campaign
    (U.S.), 182
  1936 presidential campaign (U.S.), 180
  1942 York South by-election (Canada),
    188
  1943 Ontario provincial election
    (Canada), 188
  1960 presidential campaign (U.S.), 246
  2010 midterm elections (U.S.), 259–260
  US 2016 election in, 54.170
electoral systems, 162, 163
Emmanuel, Rahm, 269–270
Employee Free Choice Act (EFCA), 259
employee participation, 258
employees
  eligible to vote in NLRB representation
    elections, 68
  eligible to vote in OLRB certification
    applications, winning cases, 72
  involved in strikes as percentage of total
    non-farm employment, 100
  voting intentions of union and non-union,
    45–47
employer opposition to unions, 4, 47–50,
    257–258
  campaign to abolish NLRB by, 136
  card-check regulation and, 64
  to representation elections, 65
  tactics of, 64
employer resistance
  certification and, 74–78
  to NLRA, 225
  stalling tactics of, 79–80
employers
  collective bargaining and, 249
  employer free speech, 241
  hostile attitudes of Canadian employers, 77
  individual attitudes of, 48–49

property rights of, 112, 113
public sector, 38
social benefits from, 6
unfair labor practices filed against, 74
after World War II, 132
employment
  growth, 41
  shifts in, 39
employment discrimination regulations, 151
End Poverty in California (EPIC)
  movement, 182
endogeneity, 87
equality, 119–120
exchange rates, 57–59
  union density and, 58
Executive Order 10988 (Kennedy), 245
exports, 58

Fair Labor Standards Act (FLSA), 183
fair share fees, 51, 84. *See also* agency fees
  Republicans abolishing, 259–260
Farber, Henry S., 43, 88
Farm Equipment Workers (FE), 204
farm foreclosure moratorium, 179
farmer–labor parties, 182, 185, 188–189
Farmer–Labor Party (Minnesota), 178
Farmer–Labor Political Federation (FLPF),
    182
farmer–labor politics, 167, 169, 179, 181
  CCF and, 171–172, 185–186
farmers
  need for coalition with labor, 174–175
  New Deal coalition and, 167
  unrest during Great Depression and
    World War II, 10
Farmers' Holiday Association (FHA), 169
farmworkers, 179
FBI. *See* Federal Bureau of Investigation
FCA. *See* first contract arbitration
FE. *See* Farm Equipment Workers
Federal Bureau of Investigation (FBI), 200
Federal Emergency Relief Agency (FERA),
    179
Federal jurisdiction (Canada), 63, 66, 81,
    112
Federal Mediation and Conciliation Service
    (FMCS), 79, 237
Federbush Co., 121 F.2d 954, 957 (1941),
    242
feminism, 213–214
FERA. *See* Federal Emergency Relief Agency

Ferguson, John-Paul, 79–80
feudalism, 177
FHA. *See* Farmers' Holiday Association
Fight for $ 15, 261, 266–267
   unions and, 261
financialization, 267–268
Fine, Janice, 269
First Amendment, 52, 94
first contract arbitration (FCA), 78
   in Canada, 80
   legislation on, 81–82
first contracts, 78–80
   historical perspective on negotiation of, 80–82
   successful US private sector first contract negotiations, 79
Flint, Michigan, 93
FLPF. *See* Farmer–Labor Political Federation
FLSA. *See* Fair Labor Standards Act
FMCS. *See* Federal Mediation and Conciliation Service
Ford, Henry, 169
Ford Hunger March, 169
Ford Motor Company, 84, 243–244
Ford Service Department, 169
Ford Strike of 1945 (Windsor, Ontario), 84
foreign ownership of Canadian companies, 211–212
foreign policy of US, 219
foreign trade, Canada and, 57
"forgotten man," 161, 168, 170, 171, 173, 178
"fragment societies" (Hartzian concept), 23–24
Fraser, Douglas, 213, 258
free rider problem, 51, 56
free trade, 55, 60, 129, 262
freedom, 119–120
freedom of speech, 9–10, 53, 94, 223
   employer free speech, 241
Freeman, Richard, 45–46, 221
Friedrichs v. California Teachers Association, 51–52
Frymer, Paul, 151
FTA. *See* U.S.-Canada Free Trade Agreement
FTQ. *See* Quebec Federation of Labour

Gallup organization, 44

GDP. *See* gross domestic product
General Motors (GM), 128–129
geographic distribution of employment, 39–43, 87
George, Willis, 140–141
Ginger Group (in Canadian Parliament), 174, 175
Golden, Clinton, 126
Gompers, Samuel, 168
Gouzenko, Igor, 201
government
   class conflict sensitivity of, 243
   inequality addressed by, 121
   role of in labor relations, 120
Great Depression, 4
   agrarian protest sparked by, 166
   capitalism legitimacy challenged by, 175–176
   inequalities exacerbated by, 164
   national values shift resulting from, 125
   New Deal coalition and, 168
   union density in years prior to, 123
   worker and farmer unrest during, 10
   working class upsurge during, 254
Great Society programs, 110
Green, William, 128, 144–145, 225
gross domestic product (GDP), 58

Hand, Learned, 242
Harrington, Michael, 198
Harris, Mike, 71
Harris v. Quinn, 52
Harrison, Bennett, 128
Hartz, Louis, 23–24
Harvard Trade Union Program, 127
Haslam, Bill, 1
Health, Education, and Welfare, US Department of (HEW), 252
health care workers, 245
Health Services and Support v. B.C. (Health Services and Support – Facilities Subsector Bargaining Assn. v. British Columbia), 96
Hepburn, Mitchell, 188
Hersees of Woodstock Ltd. v. Goldstein, 96
HEW. *See* Health, Education, and Welfare, US Department of
High Court of Ontario, 237–238
Hillman, Sidney, 180, 181, 226
hiring halls, 150

Hoover, Herbert, 170
Hoover, J. Edgar, 205
Hopkins, Harry, 179
Horowitz, Gad, 163, 169
"Hot cargo" agreements, 93
House Un-American Activities Committee, 201–202
Hudgens v. NLRB, 94

IBT. *See* International Brotherhood of Teamsters
ideology, 50
IDIA. *See* Industrial Disputes Investigation Act
IFLWU. *See* International Fur and Leather Workers Union
ILGWU. *See* International Ladies Garment Workers Union
Illinois, 52, 246, 260
ILTP. *See* independent left third parties
ILWU. *See* International Longshore and Warehouse Union
imperialism, 212
imports, 58
income, top one percent share of, 7
independent contractors, 261
Independent Labour Parties (Canada), 174, 175
independent left third parties (ILTP), 160
 collapse of, 161–162, 183
 different levels of support for, 162
 divergence in, 163–164
 labor support for, 182
 New Deal coalition co-opting, 164
 organizing in 1930s, 169
 support for, 160, 166
 vote shares of, 162
independent political mobilization, 142–143
Indiana, 260
indigenous peoples, 148
individual rights, 18
individualism, 116–117, 132, 136
 class issues in the United States as individual alienation, 250–254
 conservative, 195
 laissez-faire values, 14, 22, 122–123
Industrial Disputes Investigation Act (IDIA), 139, 232–233
industrial legality, 232, 234
industrial peace, 14, 95, 139, 222–223, 232, 233–234, 237, 239
 Canadian labor regime and, 243
industrial pluralism, 13
industrial relations, 252
Industrial Relations and Disputes Investigation Act (IRDIA), 95, 235, 244
industrial unionism, 145
industrial unrest
 government intervention in, 13–14
Industrial Workers of the World, 266
Industry and Humanity (King, W.L.M.), 139
inequality
 economic, 8
 government intervention to address, 121
 Great Depression and, 164
 unions as tool against, 256
 institutional strength and legitimacy of labor regimes and/or labor unions, 102
interest groups, 17, 222, 254, 263
 labor as, 11, 14, 241
interest organization, 15, 108–111
interests
 business interests as public, 239
International Brotherhood of Teamsters (IBT), 209–210, 259
International Fur and Leather Workers Union (IFLWU), 204
international labor unions, 216
International Ladies Garment Workers Union (ILGWU), 145
International Longshore and Warehouse Union (ILWU), 204
International Monetary Fund, 8
Iowa
 House File 291, 263
IRDIA. *See* Industrial Relations and Disputes Investigation Act
"Iron heel of ruthlessness," 138
Isserman, Maurice, 199

Jackson, C.S., 187
Jamieson, Stuart M., 49, 50
Janus v. AFSCME, 56
JIC. *See* Joint Industrial Council
Jim Crow laws
 Jim Crow-era voting restrictions, 179
Johnson, Susan, 79
Johnston, Eric, 134
Joint Industrial Council (JIC), 138
judges, 228–229, 238

judicial review
  supremacy of, 113
Justice for Janitors, 266

Kasich, John, 260
Kellock-Taschereau Commission, 201
Kennedy, John F., 131, 245
Kennedy, Robert F. presidential campaign, 209, 246
Kentucky, 82, 169, 262–263
Kettler, David, 222
King, Bob, 1, 2
King, Martin Luther, Jr., 150–151
King, William Lyon Mackenzie, 138, 139, 234
  resistance to compulsory collective bargaining of, 233
  wartime labor policy of, 187
Knights of Labor, 266

labor, 223
  alt-labor, 261
  in Canada as class representative, 222, 254, 265
  Canada labor crisis, 263–264
  Canadian state hostility to, 264–265
  Democratic Party alliance with, 109–110
  Democratic Party distancing from, 253
  embedded in class idea, 10, 190
  embedded in pluralist idea, 17
  gap between New Left and, 209
  independent left third parties (ILTPs) and, 182
  influence within Democratic Party, 213
  leaders' legitimacy derived from New Deal coalition, 236
  Left postwar relations with
    Canadian, 213
    U.S., 315.10
  NDP and, 213
  Roosevelt pro-labor proposals, 226
  strengthening ties between New Left and labor in Canada, 210
  in the United States as interest group, 254, 263
  US foreign policy supported by, 324.30
  workplace and, 268
Labor boards
  involvement in labor disputes, 115–116
  Union and employer access to, 112
Labor Division of the National Democratic Campaign Committee, 181
labor injunction, 94, 249
Labor Law Reform Act 1977, 81, 253
  failure of, 253
labor laws, 4–5, 53, 113, 226, 254
  differences in, 256
  as impediment to organizing, 50
  regimes of, 61–62
  union density and, 54–57
  violations of, 3
labor market, 36
labor militancy, 95, 104, 183–184
  controlling, 237
labor movement, 9, 37–38, 142–144, 147, 151–152, 154–157, 213–215, 256–257, 266, 267
labor party
  as explanation for union density divergence, 25, 109–111, 189
labor regimes, 222, 254–255
  divergence of, 105
  erosion in the United States vs. stability in Canada, 240
  formation process of, 224–226
  industrial peace and, 243
  of New Deal coalition, 231–232
  organizing logics of, 256–257
  postwar development of, 223–224
  structure of, 226–227
    quasi-judicial, 227–229
    tripartite representational structure, 102, 230–232, 238–240
  US formation process of, 12, 224
labor relations
  Canada historical trajectory of, 49
  NDP and, 109
  political institutions and, 105
  post-World War II, 49
  U.S historical trajectory of, 67–68, 137
labor republicanism, 169, 266
labor republicans, 169
labor rights, 4, 60, 113, 137, 140, 145, 151, 224–226, 235–236, 245–248, 265
labor unions. *See* unions
labor–capital relations, 13
labor-management accord (post-World War II), 125–126, 127, 130
Labor-Management Group, 130
labor-management partnership, 258, 263–264
Labor-Management Public Advisory Committee, 135
labor-management relations, 134–135

Labor's Non-Partisan League (LNPL), 180
Labour Court model for labor regime, 238
Labour Gazette, 138
Labour Trilogy (Canadian Supreme Court decisions), 52–53, 96
LaFollette, Philip, 178, 182
LaFollette, Robert M., 181–182
LaFollette, Robert M., Jr., 182
laissez-faire values, 14, 22, 122–123
Landrum-Griffin Act (Labor-Management Reporting and Disclosure Act of 1959), 93, 99, 136
Langer, William, 178
Latin America, anti-colonial struggles in, 24
Laval University, 192
Laxer, James, 211
League for Social Reconstruction (LSR), 175–177
Leap Manifesto, 264
Lechmere, Inc. v. NLRB, 115
the Left, 193, 195. *See also* New Left; Old Left
  CCF as "loyal Left," 196, 205
  generational divide in, 198–199
  labor postwar relations with, 212
  repression of, 195, 200–201
Left Caucus (in NDP), 210
legal proceduralism, 223
Lehman Corporation, 177
Leiserson, William, 229
Lesage, Jean, 246
Lester, Richard, 127
Levitt, Kari, 211–212
Levy, Peter, 199
Lewis, David, 176, 211
Lewis, John L., 135, 168
Liberal Party (Canada), 11–12
  anti-Communist crusade of, 204–205
  CCF and, 164
liberalism. *See also* neoliberalism
  corporate liberalism, 133–134, 138, 140
  hegemony of, 219–220
  Lockean, 24, 163
  social welfare liberalism, 171
  "Tory-tinged" liberalism, 24, 138
Lincoln, Bryan, 47–48
Lipset, Seymour Martin, 22, 25, 46, 116–117
Little Steel Strike, 182
Livingston Shirt Corp., 107 N.L.R.B. 400 (1953), 242

LNPL. *See* Labor's Non-Partisan League
Local 174, Teamsters v. Lucas Flour Co., 94
local labor councils, 183, 186
Locke, John, 24
lockout, 91, 98, 259
logics of collective action, 14
loyal Left, 196
  CCF as, 205
LSR. *See* League for Social Reconstruction
Lubell, Samuel, 168
Ludlow Massacre, 138

mainstream media, 129
maintenance of membership (union security agreement), 84
management, 231, 239
  of business and industry, 119
  by stress, 258
  workers' rights and, 241–243
management's rights clause, 241
managers
  organizing opposed to by, 48
  survey questions for, 47–48
Manitoba, 3, 81, 173–174, 185, 264
Manitoba Federation of Labour, 3
Manitoba Labour Relations Board, 3
manufacturing sector
  union density and, 41–43
  World War II and, 43
March on Washington for Jobs and Freedom 1963, 215
Marcuse, Gary, 201–202
market forces, 36
Marshall, Ray, 132
Marxism, 169
mass mobilization, 224, 266
McCarthyism, 193–200, 202, 219–220. *See also* Red scares
  New Left and, 206–207
  purges of unions and union leadership resulting from, 216
McClellan Committee, 135–136
McGill University, 175–176, 221
McGovern, George, 192
McLarty, Norman, 139
McMillian, John, 198
McNeill, George E., 169
Meany, George, 129, 191–192, 215
Meighen, Arthur, 188
Meltz, Noah, 46
Memphis sanitation strike 1968, 214

Meredith v. Canada (A.G.), 52, 97
meritocracy, 19–20
MFDP. *See* Mississippi Freedom Democratic Party
Michigan, 82, 169, 260, 262. *See also* Detroit, Michigan; Flint, Michigan
middle class, 19, 263
"middle class" rhetoric, 19–20, 263
militant minority, 206, 207
Millard, Charles, 187
Milwaukee, Wisconsin, 260, 262
Mine, Mill, and Smelter Workers (UMMSWA), 204
mine safety, 262
minimum wage, 261, 266–267
Mississippi Freedom Democratic Party (MFDP), 208
Missouri, 82, 262–263
Mix, Mark, 1
Moley, Raymond, 170
moral economy, 142
Morse, Wayne, 131, 133
Mosher, Aaron, 174
Mosher, Ira, 134
Mounted Police Association of Ontario v. Canada (A.G.), 52, 97
Movement for an Independent Socialist Canada. *See* the Waffle
municipal workers, 245
Muse, Vance, 82

NAFTA. *See* North American Free Trade Agreement
National Association of Manufacturers (NAM), 129, 132–134, 225
collective bargaining, recalcitrant approach of, 137
lack of representativeness, 135
refusal to serve in representative capacity, 135
national characteristics hypothesis, 116–126, 154
National Domestic Workers Alliance (NDWA), 261
National Farmers Union (NFU), 169, 179
National Industrial Recovery Act, U.S., 1933 (NIRA), 144–145, 178, 180, 181, 224
declared unconstitutional, 180
efforts to implement, 227
Section 7(a) of, 180, 227

National Labor Board (NLB), 227
National Labor Relations Act, U.S., 1935 (Wagner Act) (NLRA), 62, 180, 204
bargaining unit certification and, 66
Charges of being "biased" and "one-sided,"225, 230
decades prior to, 125
Demands for Canadian version of, 184
early days of, 69
Efforts to undermine, 225
employer resistance to, 225
initial basis for, 224
judicial de-radicalization of, 115
Perceptions of Wagner Act, 180
racism and, 150
Section 7(a), 180
Section 8(d), 92–93
Section 13, 98
Section 14(b), 82
strikes and, 92, 98, 103–104
National Labor Relations Board (NLRB), 2, 62–63, 65, 183, 227. *See also* NLRB General Counsel (NLRB-GC)
case intake, 111–112
employer campaign to abolish, 136
members of, 226–227
under Obama administration, 261
political appointment to, 231
politicization of, 243
representation elections by
number of employees eligible to vote in, 68
union wins in, 68, 69
structure of, 113–114
non-partisan, 230–231
quasi-judicial, 228
unfair labor practices (ULPs) filed with, 74, 75
National Policy (Canada), 172, 184
National Progressives of America (NPA), 182
National Right to Work Foundation (NRTWF), 1, 51
National Right to Work Committee, 136
national values
of Canada, 118, 137–142
differences in, 122
Great Depression causing shift in, 125
postwar period shift in, 136
of U.S., 118
National War Labor Board (NWLB), 131
nationalism, 211, 212, 213, 220

nationalism (cont.)
  Anglophone Canada vs. Quebec
    nationalism, 211
  in Canada, 216–218
  diverging between the United States and
    Canada, 216
  in U.S., 218–219
NATO. See North Atlantic Treaty
  Organization
NDP. See New Democratic Party
NDWA. See National Domestic Workers
  Alliance
neoliberalism, 257
Nevada, 87
New Canadian Political Economy, 211
New Deal (failed effort in Canada), 11–12,
  164, 173
New Deal (United States)
  agricultural policy during, 167, 177
  labor policy during, 181
  "Second New Deal" reforms, 180
New Deal coalition, 11, 12–13, 110
  conservative agrarian bloc within, 178
  farmers and, 167
  Great Depression and, 168
  ILTPs co-opted by, 164
  labor leaders' legitimacy derived from, 236
  labor regime created by, 231–232
  workers and, 167
New Deal era, 122
  before, 123–125
  collectivism in, 125–126
  as "exception to the exception," 125
New Democratic Party (NDP), 8–9, 13, 25,
  106, 107–108, 194
  British Columbia government of, 264
  CCF becoming, 207
  internal conflict in, 264
  labor and, 213
  labor relations and, 109
  recent faltering of, 264
  working class and, 210
New Democratic Youth, 210
  Left Caucus within, 210
New Labour Trilogy (Canada Supreme
  Court decisions), 52–53, 97
New Left, 13, 158, 194, 195–196, 198
  antiwar, 194
  Canadian, 208
  cross-border pollination of, 207
  Democratic Party and, 207–208
  electoral politics and, 207–208
  entryism in Canadian, 210
  gap between labor and, 209
  McCarthyism and, 206–207
  Old Leftists and, 199
  radicalization, 212
  strengthening ties between labor and, 210
  turning to working class, 209
  Vietnam War and, 209
New York Taxi Workers Alliance
  (NYTWA), 261
Newfoundland and Labrador, 81
NFU. See National Farmers Union
NIRA. See National Industrial Recovery Act
Nixon, Richard, M., 251
NLB. See National Labor Board
NLRA. See National Labor Relations Act,
  U.S., 1935
NLRB. See National Labor Relations Board
NLRB General Counsel (NLRB-GC),
  111–112
NLRB v. Fansteel Metallurgical Corp, 93
NLRB v. Mackay Radio and Telegraph Co.,
  98
NLRB v. Sands Manufacturing Co., 94
NLRB-GC. See NLRB General Counsel
non-agricultural workers, 5, 100
  change in non-farm employment
    1922–1935, 124
Nonpartisan League (NPL), 178
non-partisanship, 230–231
non-union competition, 62
non-union jobs, 56
non-union workplaces, 10
non-unionized workers, 46–47
non-unionized workers in favor of unions,
  45–47
Norquist, Grover, 2
Norris-LaGuardia Act (Federal Anti-
  Injunction Act of 1932), 94
North American Free Trade Agreement
  (NAFTA), 55, 59
  lack of union protections in, 60
North Atlantic Treaty Organization
  (NATO), 210
North Dakota, 178
Noseworthy, Joseph W., 188
NPA. See National Progressives of America
NPL. See Nonpartisan League
NRTWF. See National Right to Work
  Foundation

nuclear holocaust, 207
NYTWA. *See* New York Taxi Workers Alliance

Obama, Barack, 259
  NLRB of administration of, 261
Occupy movement, 266–267
Ohio, 260
Old Left, 199, 207
OLRB. *See* Ontario Labour Relations Board
"On to Ottawa Trek," 173
One Big Union, 266
Ontario, 73–74
  certification applications in, 71
  representation applications in, 71–72
Ontario Court of Appeals, 96
Ontario Labour Court, 237
Ontario Labour Relations Board (OLRB), 70
  certification applications filed and granted, 70
  certification union win rate 1949–2009, 73
  employees eligible to vote in OLRB certification applications, winning cases, 72
  ULPs and certification application ratio, 76
Ontario teachers' unions, 270
open shop, 84
  campaigns for, 49
  mandates for, 84
  Taft-Hartley Act, 1947 and, 244
Operation Dixie, 149–150, 218
Order-in-Council PC 1003, 95, 139–140
Order-in-Council PC 2685, 139
Oregon Commonwealth Federation, 182
organizing
  constant need for, 55
  by CPUSA, 169
  falling activity and effectiveness of, 73–74
  ideas, 16–17
  by ILTPs in 1930s, 169
  interracial organizing, 149–150
  possibility of, 270
  shop floor, 267
  workplace organization, 269
organizing, opposition to, 4
  labor laws used for, 50
  by managers, 48

organizing logics of US and Canadian labor regimes, 17, 222, 256–257
orthodox Marxism, 169
Ottawa, Ontario, 140
Our Revolution, 266–267
OUR Walmart, 261

Palmer Raids, 200
Panitch, Leo, 97
parliamentary supremacy, doctrine of, 113
parliamentary systems, 107–108, 163
partisan conflict
  in Canada, 171–174
  structure of, 167
  in U.S., 167–171
PATCO. *See* Professional Air Traffic Controllers Organization
Patrons of Industry, 200
Pattern bargaining agreements, 258
PC 1003, 235, 237, 243–244
Pearl Harbor, 234
Pearson, Lester B., 246, 247
Peerless Plywood Co., 107 N.L.R.B. 427 (1953), 242
pensions, 8–9
Pentland, H. Clare, 49
Pepin, Marcel, 191, 192–193, 217
  idea of "second front," 192–193, 217, 266
Perkins, Frances, 131, 224–225, 230
permanent exceptionalism, 97
picketing, 92–93, 94, 96, 140, 188
pluralist idea, 10–11, 17–18, 222, 231–232, 254
Podgursky, Michael, 127
police
  Chicago police riot (1968), 209
  police brutality, 138, 184
  surveillance by, 200
policy, political use of, 167, 177
policy decisions, public sector and, 36–37
political articulation, 10, 16–17
political establishment, 1
political incorporation, 11, 166–167
political institutions, 10
  as explanation for U.S.-Canada union density divergence, 106–107, 154, 249
  labor relations and, 105
  working class power and, 106–107, 154
political parties
  critical realignment theory, 165

political parties (cont.)
  labor movement relation to, 9
  reflection and articulation models of, 161, 166
  role in organizing interests, 15, 108–109
political party discipline, 107–108, 114
political party systems, 110–111, 159, 163, 164, 165, 189, 208, 210
political power, 9
political representation, 9, 190
Ponak, Allen, 90–91
populism, 262
Port Huron Statement, 207, 215
postal workers, 246
  strikes by, 247, 248
post-industrial society, 199
Pozzebon, Silvana, 77
Preparatory Committee on Collective Bargaining in the Public Service, 246
presidential systems, 108, 114
President's Advisory Committee on Labor-Management Policy, 131
President's Labor-Management Advisory Committee, 134
prevailing wage, 260
private sector, 33–34, 35
  successful US first contract negotiations in, 79
  union density in 1961–2016, 60
  workplace injuries in, 262
private sector unions, 37–38
  legal environments of, 38
Privy Council (Canada), 200–201, 205
"The Problem of the Blue-Collar Worker" (Rosow), 251
Professional Air Traffic Controllers Organization (PATCO), 38–39, 253–254
Progressive Party (Canada), 181–182
  rise and fall of, 174
Progressive Party (Wisconsin), 181–182
Prohibition, 170
property rights, 112, 113, 140, 223, 239
protectionist trade agreements, 55
pro-union, 48, 66, 113
PSAC v. Canada, 52, 96
PSSRA. *See* Public Service Staff Relations Act
PSSRB. *See* Public Service Staff Relations Board
public sector
  collective bargaining in Canada, 246–248

collective bargaining in Indiana, 260
collective bargaining in U.S., 245–246
employers, 38
employment, as percentage of total employment, 37
growth of unionism in, 43
Ian Robinson on unionism in, 146
laws and legal cases dealing financial blows to unions in, 51–52
policy decisions and, 36–37
weak unions in, 143
public sector unionism
  in Canada, 213–214
  in U.S., 214–215
public sector unions, 37–38
  financial blow to, 51–52
  legal environments of, 38
Public Service Staff Relations Act (PSSRA), 247
Public Service Staff Relations Board (PSSRB), 247
public works programs, 232

quality of work life programs, 258
Quebec, 212, 217–218
  colonial status of, 212
  relation to US Black Power movement, 212
Quebec Common Front, 270
  2015 round of negotiations, 270
  1972 general strike, 193, 217, 270
Quebec Federation of Labour (FTQ), 217
Quiet Revolution (Quebec), 212

racial divisions, 155
  in Canada, 147, 148, 151–152
  as explanation for U.S.-Canada union density divergence, 10, 106, 147, 148, 152, 155
  "flattening" of white ethnic identities, 148, 166
  in national imagination, 148
  solidarity undermined by, 147
  in U.S., 148
racial justice, 145
racism, 147, 192
  NLRA and, 150
  Taft-Hartley Act and, 150
Rae, Bob, 71
railroads, 145
Rand, Ivan, 84

Index

Rand Formula, 84, 95, 243–244
  near-universal adoption of, 140–141
Randolph, A. Philip, 145
Raskob, John, 170
Rauner, Bruce, 260
RCMP. *See* Royal Canadian Mounted Police
Reagan, Ronald
  Reagan revolution, 253–254
Red scares, 12–13, 193, 194
  in Canada, 202
  divergent effects of, 202–206
  post-World War I, 200
  post-World War II, 12–13, 193–197
  purge of Left-led unions in Canada, 193–194, 196, 201, 207
  purge of Left-led unions in U.S., 196, 201, 216
redistributive policies, 20–21
Reference re Public Service Employee Relations Act (Alta.), 52, 96
reflection model of parties, 161
  central problem of, 166
Regina Manifesto (of CCF), 176
relief subsidies for US farmers during the Great Depression, 179
Renteria, Amanda, 261–262
replacement workers ("scabs" or "strikebreakers"), 98, 99
representation applications, 71–72
representation elections
  campaigns for, 63–64, 65
  employer opposition to, 65
  mandatory, 73
  by NLRB
    number of employees eligible to vote in, 68
    union wins in, 68, 69
  Unfair Labor Practices (ULPs) and, 75
Republic Aviation v. NLRB, 115
Republican Party, 259–260
Restaurant Opportunities Center (ROC), 261
Reuther, Walter, 129, 215
"right to manage," 13, 49, 126, 136, 240, 241
"right to scab," 93
right to work (RTW) laws, 51–52, 260, 262–263
  right-to-work zones, 260

union density divergence and, 85, 87, 89, 90–91
union density in RTW states vs. non-RTW states, 88, 89
union security and, 56, 82–90
Robinson, Ian, 102, 142, 144
  on public sector unionism, 146
ROC. *See* Restaurant Opportunities Center
Rockefeller, John D., 138
Rogers, Joel, 45–46
Roosevelt, Franklin D., 11, 161, 170–171
  pro-labor proposals from, 226
  re-election of, 180–181
  Roosevelt Recession, 182
Rose, Fred, 201
Rosow, Jerome M., 251–252
Royal Canadian Mounted Police (RCMP), 173
RTW. *See* right to work
Rueschemeyer, Dietrich, 15
Russian Revolution, 164
Rust Belt, 90
Ruttenberg, Harold, 126
RWDSU v. Pepsi (Retail, Wholesale and Department Store Union, Local 558 v. Pepsi-Cola Canada Beverages (West) Ltd.), 96
RWDSU v. Saskatchewan, 52, 96

Sachs, Alexander, 177
Sanders, Bernie, 266–267
  as outsider, 21
  working class and, 20
Saporta, Ishak, 47–48
Saskatchewan, 174, 81, 173, 174, 185, 264
Saskatchewan Federation of Labour v. Saskatchewan, 52, 97
Saskatchewan Grain Growers' Association (SGGA), 174
scabs ("replacement workers" or "strikebreakers"), 98, 99
Scalia, Antonin, 51
Schrecker, Ellen, 197
Schultz, George, 251
Schwartz, Michael, 198–199, 207
Schwerin, Dan, 261–262
scope of activity, 56
Scott, Francis, 176
SDS. *See* Students for a Democratic Society
Seattle General Strike, 200

secondary boycotts, 96
secret ballot representation elections, 62, 64
SEIU. *See* Service Employees International Union
Senate Bill 5 (Ohio), 260
seniority system, 150
Service Employees International Union (SEIU), 258–259
  budget cuts at, 263
  Justice for Janitors, 266
service sector, 43
  shift in employment toward, 32
SGGA. *See* Saskatchewan Grain Growers' Association
sharecroppers
  dependency on landlords, 179
shop floor organization, 267
Silent Surrender: The Multinational Corporation in Canada (Levitt), 211–212
Sinclair, Upton, 182
Singh, Kamta Roy, 3
slavery, 148, 155
Slichter, Sumner, 127
Smith, Al, 170–171
Smith, Edwin, 229
Smith Act (1940), 200–201
Snyder, Rick, 260
social benefits, 6
social citizenship, 9
social housing, 193
social movements, 9, 13, 110, 152, 155, 193, 215, 216
Social Planning for Canada (League for Social Reconstruction), 176
social policy, 8–9, 10, 21, 132–133
"social squeeze" of blue-collar workers, 251
social unionism, 142, 144, 145, 154–155
social welfare liberalism, 171
socialism, 125
  of Debs, 169
Socialist Party (US), 198
solidarity, 147
South (of United States), 1, 4, 39, 41, 43, 47–48, 87, 88–90, 140, 149, 151–152
South Carolina, 90
Southern bloc, 12–13
Southern Democrats, 109–110
Southern Tenant Farmers Union (STFU), 179
Soviet spies, 201

St. Laurent, Louis, 206
state labor regimes, 102
Steel Workers Organizing Committee (SWOC), 126, 187
Steelworkers Trilogy, 94
STFU. *See* Southern Tenant Farmers Union
strategic voting, 264
Strike waves
  In 1960s-70s, 104
  As "safety valve," 235
strikebreakers ("replacement workers" or "scabs"), 98–99
strikes, 48, 267. *See also* Common Front (Quebec), 1972
  AFL no-strike pledge, 234
  "Anti-scab" legislation, 99, 104–105
  Canadian Charter of Rights and Freedoms on, 52–53
  by Chicago Teachers Union, 269–270
  CIO no-strike pledge, 234
  coal, 169
  by CWA, 269–270
  Detroit Newspaper strike, 259
  employees involved in strikes as percentage of total non-farm employment, 100
  government workers on, 247
  "Hot cargo" agreements, 93
  Memphis sanitation strike 1968, 214
  Mid-contract strikes, 94, 95
  1964 Canadian postal strike, 247
  NLRA and, 92, 98, 103–104
  by PATCO, 253–254
  person-days idle as a result of, 101
  policy, 91–92
  by postal workers, 247, 248
  postwar strike wave, 235, 241
  rates of, 139–140
  regulation of, 92–98
  Right to strike, 52–53, 92–95, 96–100, 143, 246–248
  rules on scope of activity around, 56
  Seattle General Strike, 200
  secondary boycotts, 92–93, 96
  state troops used to break, 181
  strike rates, 104
Sympathy strikes, 95
Taft-Hartley Act, 1947 and, 92–93, 95, 97
textile, 169

union density and, 103
  in the United States vs. Canada, 100–105
Wildcat strikes, 94, 95, 121, 251
Winnipeg General Strike, 200
Students for a Democratic Society (SDS), 198–199
  Port Huron Statement of, 207, 215
Supreme Court, US, 52–53
Supreme Court of Canada, 52–53
surveillance, 200
Swartz, Donald, 97
Sweeney, John, 258–259
SWOC. *See* Steel Workers Organizing Committee
symbolic power, 38–39

Taft-Hartley Act (Labor-Management Relations Act of 1947), 12–13, 66, 82, 196–197, 241
  anti-Communist affidavit and, 241
  employer free speech and, 244
  open shop and, 244
  racism and, 150
  right-to-work and, 82
  Section 8(c) of, 242
  Section 208 of, 92–93
  Section 301 of, 92–93, 94
  Section 303 of, 92–93
  Section 305 of, 92–93
  strikes and, 92–93, 95, 97
Taras, Daphne, 90–91
tariffs, 50, 184
Task Force on Foreign Ownership and the Structure of Canadian Investment, 211
Task Force on Labour Relations (Woods Task Force), 141, 249–250
TDU. *See* Teamsters for a Democratic Union
teachers, 245
Teamsters for a Democratic Union (TDU), 209–210
tenant farmers, 179
Tennessee, 1
Textile Workers of America v. Lincoln Mills of Alabama, 94
"Third Way" politics, 264
Third World, anti-colonial struggles in, 210, 211
Thomason, Terry, 77
Tim Hortons, 3
  as mostly non-union, 5

Time (magazine), 215
TLC. *See* Trades and Labour Congress of Canada
Tobin, Daniel J., 181
de Tocqueville, Alexis, 23
Toryism and tory values, 22, 24, 116, 138, 159–160, 163, 188
trade agreements, 55, 59–60
trade policy, 55, 59–61
Trades and Labour Congress of Canada (TLC), 143, 144, 147, 172, 186, 201, 205, 207
Treaty of Detroit, 128–129, 144
tripartism, 113–114, 230, 238–239
  conciliation and, 236–239
Trotskyists, 200–201
Truman, Harry S, 131, 150, 183, 231, 242
Trump, Donald, 20, 21, 269
  faux populism of, 262

UAW. *See* United Auto Workers
UE. *See* United Electrical Workers
UFC. *See* United Farmers of Canada
UFC(SS). *See* United Farmers of Canada (Saskatchewan Section)
UFCW. *See* United Food and Commercial Workers
ULPs. *See* unfair labor practices
UMMSWA. *See* Mine, Mill, and Smelter Workers
UMWA. *See* United Mine Workers of America
Un-American, 18–19, 21
Underhill, Frank, 176
Unemployed Councils, 169
unemployment insurance, 8–9
unfair labor practices (ULPs), 63
  charges of, 3
  filed against employers, 74
  filed with NLRB, 74, 75
  OLRB, ULPs and certification application ratio, 76
  per certification attempt, 76–77
  representation elections and, 75
Unifor (Canada), 218, 264
union avoidance industry, 65
union certification, 55, 62–65, 104, 238
  annual union recertification votes, 263
  of bargaining units, 66
  "card-check" certification, 63–64
  changes in, 66

union certification (cont.)
  elections for, 66–67
  employees eligible to vote in OLRB certification applications, winning cases, 72
  employer resistance and, 74–78
  NLRB Representation Elections, Number Held and Number Won by Unions 1936–2016, 68
  NLRB Representation Elections, Number of Employees Eligible to Vote 1936–2009, 68
  OLRB, ULPs and certification application ratio, 76
  OLRB certification union win rate 1949–2009, 73
  Ontario applications for, 71
  ULPs per certification attempt, 76–77
union culture, 270
union density, 6, 7, 225, 256
  absolute change in number employed from 1939 to 2016 and, 40
  Auto Pact and, 61
  in Canada private sector, 35
  in Canada public sector, 34
  convergence hypothesis, 31–32, 36, 153
  decline, reasons for, 41
  divergence, explanations of, 105, 153, 155, 189–190, 256
  exchange rates and, 58
  geographic distribution of employment and, 43
  labor laws and, 54–57
  manufacturing sector and, 41–43
  policies effecting trajectories of, 55–56
  in pre-Depression years, 123
  in private sector 1961–2016, 60
  in public and private sectors, 33–34
  in public sector, 34
  rates, 6, 10–14, 32
  RTW laws and divergence in, 85, 87, 89, 90–91
  RTW states vs. non-RTW states, 88, 89
  in South Carolina, 90
  strikes and, 103
  union membership change 1922–1935, 124
  in US private sector, 34
  in US public sector, 35
  wage-setting and, 8
  World Values Survey (WVS) and, 122
union house visits, 2
union membership criteria, 150
Union nationale (Quebec), 205
union renewal, 259
union security, 85, 90–91, 93
  provisions, 90
  RTW and, 56, 82–90
union shop, 84
union stability, 256–257
unionization, 4, 8, 33–34, 36, 43, 61, 241, 242, 248, 253
unionization preferences, 44–47
unions
  attacks on, 257, 259–260
  attitudes toward, 119
  decentralized system of, 62
  Fight for $15 and, 261
  government intervention in, 50
  growth of, 36, 71–72, 137–138, 143, 153, 261
  internal union characteristics, 142–147, 154–155
  leverage of, 268
  membership of, 11, 38, 41–43, 44, 55–56, 90–92, 104, 123–125, 142, 172, 180, 249
  need for, 6–10
  non-unionized workers in favor of, 46–47
  public approval of, 44, 45
  public sector, financial blow to, 51–52
  scope of activity of, 56, 61, 91–92
  as "special interest," 253
  state neglect of, 167, 177, 183–184, 188–189, 232
  state repression of, 184, 187, 197, 232
  strength of, 8
  as tool against inequality, 256
  wins in NLRB representation elections, 68, 69
  in *Work in America* (HEW Task Force), 252
unions, Canada, 4
  Cold War and, 13, 193–194
  declaring independence from US parent unions, 194, 217–218
  decline of, 104, 153, 253–254
  "minimum Canadian standards" for, 217
  public sector unionism, 213–214
  union density in private sector of, 35
  union density in public sector of, 34

Index

union density rates in the United
    States and, 6, 10–14, 32
unions, US
    Cold War and, 193–194
    in crisis, 4
    decline of, 31, 153, 253–254
    Obama and, 259
    since mid-late 1970s, 257–258
    union density in private sector of, 35
    union density in public sector of, 34
    union density rates in Canada and, 6, 10–14, 32
United Auto Workers (UAW), 1–3, 128–129, 209–210
    Chrysler Corporation contract with, 258
    failure of, 4
United Electrical Workers (UE), 187, 204
United Farmers of Canada (Saskatchewan Section) (UFC(SS)), 174
United Farmers parties (Canada), 173–174, 185
United Food and Commercial Workers (UFCW), 259
United Food and Commercial Workers (UFCW) Local 503 v. Wal-Mart Canada, 53
United Mine Workers of America (UMWA), 209–210
United States (US), 125–137. *See also* unions, US
    class divisions in, 19
    class issues in Canada compared to, 255
    class issues in the United States as individual alienation, 250–254
    collective bargaining in public sector of, 245–246
    cultural DNA of, 22
    employer hostility to working-class power in, 165
    foreign policy of, 219
    House of Representatives, 259–260, 263
    as imperial hegemon, 211
    labor as interest group in, 254, 263
    labor laws in, 53
    labor long-term decline in, 11
    labor regime of, 12
    laissez-faire values in, 14, 22
    myth of classlessness in, 19–20
    national values of, 118
    nationalism in, 218–219
    partisan conflict in, 167–171
    political system of, 159
    public sector employment as percentage of total employment in, 37
    public sector unionism in, 214–215
    racial divisions in, 148
    Senate, 111, 113–114, 132, 181–182, 231, 253, 259, 260
    service sector employment in, 33
    strike regulation in, 92–98
    strikes in Canada vs., 100–105
    successful private sector first contract negotiations in, 79
    2016 election in, 18–19
    union density in private sector of, 35
    union density in public sector of, 34
    working class in politics of, 20
US regions
    Midwest, 31, 39, 41, 87, 90, 169, 178
    Northeast, 31, 39, 41, 43, 87, 90
    South, 1, 4, 39, 41, 43, 47–48, 87, 88–90, 140, 149, 151–152
    Southwest, 31, 39, 41, 90
University of Montreal, 192
University of Toronto, 174, 175–176, 211
University of Winnipeg Students' Association, 3
unpredictable scheduling, 261
US *See* United States
US Chamber of Commerce (USCC), 200.10
US dollar, 101.70, 104.190, 105.80
US–Canada Free Trade Agreement (FTA), 101.70, 106.90
    lack of union protections in, 60
USCC. *See* US Chamber of Commerce
USCS. *See* Conciliation Service, United States

Verizon, 269–270
Vietnam War, 209, 211
Volkswagen, 1
voluntarism, 138, 140
von Hoffman, Nicholas, 251

the Waffle (Movement for an Independent Socialist Canada), 194, 210–211
    Manifesto of, 211–212
wage controls, 234
wage theft, 261
wage-setting, 8
Wagner Act. *See* National Labor Relations Act, U.S., 1935

Walker, Scott, 259–260
  2012 recall election campaign, 260
Wallace, Henry A., 183
Walmart, 53
war industries, 233
War Measures Act (Canada), 187, 200–201
wartime labor policy, 187
  collective bargaining in war industries, 233
Washington, D.C., 2, 192, 215
Washington Commonwealth Federation, 182
Watkins, Mel, 211
Watkins Report, 211
WCL. See World Confederation of Labour
Weatherman, 209
Weil, David, 261
Weiler, Paul C., 80
welfare state, 23
West Virginia, 82, 260, 263
Western Conference of Labour Political Parties, 175
wheat prices, 172
Whitaker, Reg, 201–202
white supremacy, 150
Williams, G. H., 175
Wilson, J. Justin, 31
Wilson, W. Elliott, 244
Windsor, Ontario, 84, 244
Winnipeg General Strike, 200
Winnipeg Labour Council, 3
Wisconsin, 259–260
  Act 10 in, 259–260, 263
  protest against Act 10 in, 260
  Right to Work in, 260
  2016 election in, 262
women's rights, 193
Woods, H. D. "Buzz," 66, 141, 221, 249
Woods Report (Canadian Industrial Relations: The Report of the Task Force on Labour Relations), 141, 249–250, 252
Woodsworth, J. S., 175
Work in America (HEW Task Force), 252
  unions mentioned in, 252
Worker Representation and Participation Survey (WRPS), 45–46
workers. *See also* postal workers
  anti-union workers, 2
  of color, 262
  government workers on strike, 247
  health care workers, 245
  New Deal coalition and, 167
  unrest during Great Depression and World War II, 10
  workers' rights, 241–243
Workers United (WU), 3
Workers' Unity League (WUL), 172
worker-student divide, 209–210
workforce, 68
working class, 198
  base of CPUSA, 203
  Bernie Sanders and, 20
  democracy and, 15
  Democratic Party and, 168
  exclusion of, 263
  future of, 270–271
  NDP and, 210
  New Left turn to, 209
  political incorporation of, 256
  rebuilding idea of, 265–266
  universal social benefits and protections for, 109–110
  upsurge, during Great Depression and World War II, 254
  upsurge, state responses to, 248
  in US politics, 20
working class power
  political and institutional environment shaping, 125, 154
  political institutions and, 106–107, 154
  US employer hostility toward, 244.80
workplace injuries, 262
workplace organization, 269
workplace safety violations, 262
World Confederation of Labour (WCL), 192
World Values Survey (WVS), 117–119, 122
World War I, 164
World War II
  employers' plans after, 132
  labor relations after, 49
  manufacturing sector and, 43
  worker and farmer unrest during, 10
  workforce size since, 68
  working class upsurge during, 254
WRPS. See Worker Representation and Participation Survey
WU. See Workers United
WUL. See Workers' Unity League
Wurf, Jerry, 215
WVS. See World Values Survey
Wynne, Kathleen, 270

Books in the Series (continued from p. ii)

Christian Davenport, *How Social Movements Die: Repression and Demobilization of the Republic of New Africa*
Christian Davenport, *Media Bias, Perspective, and State Repression*
Gerald F. Davis, Doug McAdam, W. Richard Scott, and Mayer N. Zald, *Social Movements and Organization Theory*
Donatella della Porta, *Clandestine Political Violence*
Donatella della Porta, *Where Did the Revolution Go?: Contentious Politics and the Quality of Democracy*
Mario Diani, *The Cement of Civil Society: Studying Networks in Localities*
Nicole Doerr, *Political Translation: How Social Movement Democracies Survive*
Todd A. Eisenstadt, *Politics, Identity, and Mexico's Indigenous Rights Movements*
Diana Fu, *Mobilizing Without the Masses: Control and Contention in China*
Daniel Q. Gillion, *The Political Power of Protest: Minority Activism and Shifts in Public Policy*
Jack A. Goldstone, editor, *States, Parties, and Social Movements*
Jennifer Hadden, *Networks in Contention: The Divisive Politics of Climate Change*
Michael T. Heaney and Fabio Rojas, *Party in the Street: The Antiwar Movement and the Democratic Party after 9/11*
Tamara Kay, *NAFTA and the Politics of Labor Transnationalism*
Neil Ketchley, *Egypt in a Time of Revolution: Contentious Politics and the Arab Spring*
Joseph Luders, *The Civil Rights Movement and the Logic of Social Change*
Doug McAdam and Hilary Boudet, *Putting Social Movements in Their Place: Explaining Opposition to Energy Projects in the United States, 2000–2005*
Doug McAdam, Sidney Tarrow, and Charles Tilly, *Dynamics of Contention*
Holly J. McCammon, *The U.S. Women's Jury Movements and Strategic Adaptation: A More Just Verdict*
Olena Nikolayenko, *Youth Movements and Elections in Eastern Europe*
Sharon Nepstad, *Religion and War Resistance and the Plowshares Movement*
Kevin J. O'Brien and Lianjiang Li, *Rightful Resistance in Rural China*
Silvia Pedraza, *Political Disaffection in Cuba's Revolution and Exodus*
Héctor Perla Jr., *Sandinista Nicaragua's Resistance to US Coercion*
Federico M. Rossi, *The Poor's Struggle for Political Incorporation: The Piquetero Movement in Argentina*
Eduardo Silva, *Challenging Neoliberalism in Latin America*
Erica S. Simmons, *Meaningful Resistance: Market Reforms and the Roots of Social Protest in Latin America*
Sarah Soule, *Contention and Corporate Social Responsibility*
Sherrill Stroschein, *Ethnic Struggle, Coexistence, and Democratization in Eastern Europe*
Yang Su, *Collective Killings in Rural China during the Cultural Revolution*
Sidney Tarrow, *The Language of Contention: Revolutions in Words, 1688–2012*

Sidney Tarrow, *The New Transnational Activism*
Wayne P. Te Brake, *Religious War and Religious Peace in Early Modern Europe*
Ralph A. Thaxton Jr., *Catastrophe and Contention in Rural China: Mao's Great Leap Forward Famine and the Origins of Righteous Resistance in Da Fo Village*
Ralph A. Thaxton Jr., *Force and Contention in Contemporary China: Memory and Resistance in the Long Shadow of the Catastrophic Past*
Charles Tilly, *Contention and Democracy in Europe, 1650–2000*
Charles Tilly, *Contentious Performances*
Charles Tilly, *The Politics of Collective Violence*
Marisa von Bülow, *Building Transnational Networks: Civil Society and the Politics of Trade in the Americas*
Lesley J. Wood, *Direct Action, Deliberation, and Diffusion: Collective Action after the WTO Protests in Seattle*
Stuart A. Wright, *Patriots, Politics, and the Oklahoma City Bombing*
Deborah Yashar, *Contesting Citizenship in Latin America: The Rise of Indigenous Movements and the Postliberal Challenge*
Andrew Yeo, *Activists, Alliances, and Anti-U.S. Base Protests*